RENAISSANCE AND REFORM
IN TUDOR ENGLAND

OXFORD HISTORICAL MONOGRAPHS

Renaissance and Reform in Tudor England

The Careers of Sir Richard Morison
c.1513–1556

TRACEY A. SOWERBY

OXFORD
UNIVERSITY PRESS

OXFORD
UNIVERSITY PRESS

Great Clarendon Street, Oxford OX2 6DP

Oxford University Press is a department of the University of Oxford.
It furthers the University's objective of excellence in research, scholarship,
and education by publishing worldwide in

Oxford New York

Auckland Cape Town Dar es Salaam Hong Kong Karachi
Kuala Lumpur Madrid Melbourne Mexico City Nairobi
New Delhi Shanghai Taipei Toronto

With offices in

Argentina Austria Brazil Chile Czech Republic France Greece
Guatemala Hungary Italy Japan Poland Portugal Singapore
South Korea Switzerland Thailand Turkey Ukraine Vietnam

Oxford is a registered trade mark of Oxford University Press
in the UK and in certain other countries

Published in the United States
by Oxford University Press Inc., New York

© Tracey A. Sowerby 2010

The moral rights of the author have been asserted
Database right Oxford University Press (maker)

First published 2010

British Library Cataloguing in Publication Data
Data available

Library of Congress Cataloging in Publication Data
Data available

Typeset by Laserwords Private Limited, Chennai, India
Printed in Great Britain
on acid-free paper by the
MPG Books Group, Bodmin and King's Lynn

ISBN 978-0-19-958463-5

1 3 5 7 9 10 8 6 4 2

Acknowledgements

This book could not have been completed without the help of many people and institutions. My undergraduate tutors helped shape my interest in humanism, religion and politics, and without Anne Everett and Bill Stuart I might not have studied history at university at all. My greatest debt is to Steve Gunn, who was my tutor and supervisor. Steve suggested Morison to me and has read numerous drafts of my work at various stages. Throughout he has provided invaluable guidance and encouragement; I have profited enormously from his acuity and wisdom. Stephen Alford and Susan Brigden examined the D.Phil. from which this book stems; they generously provided shrewd criticisms and helpful suggestions for which I am very grateful. The early modern history community at Oxford has provided a welcoming and stimulating environment in which to work. My research on Morison has profited from discussions in and outside Oxford with Ian Archer, Andy Boyle, Andrew Cambers, James Carley, Paul Cavill, Barry Collett, Cliff Davies, David Grummitt, Felicity Heal, Andrew Hope, Anne Overell, Michael Riordan and James Shaw. I also benefited considerably from conversations over drinks and after seminars with Anna Bayman, Alex Gajda, Katherine Halliday, George Southcombe and Megan Wheeler. David and Judith Loades have provided enthusiastic support. Alastair Blanshard has been more than generous with his classical expertise, and Jack Lynch performed an extraordinary act of kindness for a relative stranger.

Without the generous support of the Arts and Humanities Research Council I would not have been able to undertake the postgraduate research from which this book stems; Merton College also kindly provided financial assistance in my final postgraduate year. My manuscript was completed while a British Academy Post-Doctoral Fellow and I am grateful to the British Academy for allowing me to do so. I started work on this book while a lecturer and Junior Research Fellow at Pembroke College, Oxford. I found a convivial and productive working environment there; my thanks go to everyone at Pembroke for being so welcoming and encouraging for so long. Working there has been fun, in large part due to Adrian Gregory and Stephen Tuck, who have taught me much more than they realize. Writing the book would have been much less enjoyable had I not also been lucky enough to find interested and dedicated students at Pembroke, though they must share some responsibility for how long it has taken me to finish it. Paul Cavill, Tiffany Stern, Joseph Manning and Jonathan Harris all read sections of the text; I am grateful to them for their wise suggestions. Any errors are, of course, my own.

Over the years Tiffany Stern, Tam Cohen, Samuel Kessler, Marcin Walecki and Gareth Mann have all provided incalculable personal support and much-needed diversions for which I will be forever grateful. Numerous other friends have put up with me (and, to a lesser extent, Morison) over the years and have been there throughout. I am indebted to them all, but my special thanks go to Rachel Bateson, Alastair Blanshard, Emma Britton, Chris Clarke, Liz Elliott, Ros Greener, David Harris, Michael Heasman, Max Lieberman, Helen Mitchell, Carolina Moura-Alves, Rebecca Parker and Nick Sample, who have endured more than most. My parents only just saw me start the project and had no idea where it would take me. I hope they would have liked it. I would like to express my deep gratitude to my former neighbours in Sedgefield, particularly Sarah and Fred Britton, and to Jon Turner for all their help during and after my parents' illnesses.

Last, but by no means least, I am greatly obliged to the staff of all the libraries and archives I have used for their patience and assistance; without their hard work, mine would have been impossible. My particular thanks go to the staff at the Bodleian Library, the British Library, and the Public Record Office, on whose time I have been most demanding.

March 2009

Contents

Abbreviations

AM	G. Townsend and S. R. Cattley (eds.), *The Acts and Monuments of John Foxe* (London, 1837–41)
APC	J. R. Dasent (ed.), *Acts of the Privy Council of England* (London, 1890–1907)
Apomaxis	R. Morison, *Apomaxis Calumniarum, convitiorumque, quibus Ioannes Cocleus . . . Henrii octavi, famam impetere . . . studuit* (London, 1537)
ARG	*Archiv für Reformationsgeschichte*
Ascham Letters	*The Letters of Roger Ascham*, trans M. Hatch and A. Vos (New York, 1989)
Berkowitz	D. S. Berkowitz, *Humanist Scholarship and the Public Order: Two Tracts against the Pilgrimage of Grace* (London, 1984)
BIHR	*Bulletin of the Institute of Historical Research*
BL	British Library
Booklist	BL Additional 40676, fos. 110^r–117^v
Bullingers Korrespondenz	T. Schiess (ed.), *Bullingers Korrespondenz* (Basel, 1904–6), vol. i. References are to document number.
C	Chancery, PRO
Cal. Pat.	*Calendar of Patent Rolls*
CCC	Corpus Christi College, Cambridge
Cecil Papers	*Calendar of the MSS of the . . . Marquis of Salisbury . . . preserved at Hatfield House*, Historical MSS Commission (London, 1883–1976), vol. ix. References are to document numbers.
CH	*Church History*
CPR	*Calendar of Patent Rolls*
CRP	*Correspondence of Reginald Pole*, ed. T. F. Mayer (Aldershot, 2002–4)
CS	Camden Society

CSPDE	*Calendar of State Papers, Domestic Series, of the Reign of Edward VI*, ed. C. S. Knighton (London, 1992). References are to document by number.
CSPDM	*Calendar of State Papers, Domestic Series, of the Reign of Mary I*, ed. C. S. Knighton (London, 1998). References are to document by number.
CSPFE	*Calendar of State Papers, Foreign Series, of the Reign of Edward VI*, ed. W. B. Turnbull (London, 1861). References are to document by number.
CSPFM	*Calendar of State Papers, Foreign Series, of the Reign of Mary I*, ed. W. B. Turnbull (London, 1861). References are to document by number.
CSPS	*Calendar of letters, dispatches, and state papers, relating to the negotiations between Spain and England, ed. P. de Gayangos (London, 1862–1954)*
CUL	Cambridge University Library
Discourse	BL Harley 353, fos. 130^r–8^v: 'A Discourse written by Sir Richard Morison the Kinge's ambassador with the Emperor. Observing the godly and vertuous Resolution of Kinge Edward VI upon the Emperor's Demound to have the Lady Mary the Kinge's sister to be allowed libertie of her Conscience in England'
DKR	Deputy Keeper's Reports, PRO
E	Exchequer, PRO
EcHR	*Economic History Review*
EHD	*English Historical Documents*
EHR	*English Historical Review*
Epistle	*An epistle of the moste myghty [and] redouted Prince Henry the viii . . . to all Christen princes, and to all those that trewly and syncerely professe Christes religion* (London, 1538)
Exhortation	R. Morison, *An Exhortation to styrre all Englyshe men to the defence of theyr countreye* (Berthelet, 1539). All references are to the English Experience facsimile edition (Amsterdam, 1972).

Formularies	J. Lloyd (ed.), *Formularies of Faith* (London, 1856)
HALS	Hertfordshire Archives and Local Studies
HJ	*Historical Journal*
HLQ	*Huntington Library Quarterly*
HMC	Historical Manuscripts Commission
HoP	History of Parliament, *History of the Commons*
HR	*Historical Research*
Invective	R. Morison, *An Invective ayenste the great and detestable, vice, treason* (London, 1539). All references are to the English Experience facsimile (Amsterdam, 1972).
JBS	*Journal of British Studies*
JHI	*Journal of the History of Ideas*
JMH	*Journal of Modern History*
JMRS	*Journal of Medieval and Renaissance Studies*
KB	King's Bench, PRO
Lamentation	R. Morison, *A Lamentation wherin is shown what ruin cometh of sedition* (London, 1536)
LP	J. S. Brewer (ed.), *Letters and Papers Foreign and Domestic of the Reign of Henry VIII* (London, 1862–1932)
Luther's Works	J. Pelikan (ed.), *Luther's Works* (St Louis, 1955–86)
Nuntiaturberichte	G. Kupke (ed.), *Nuntiaturberichte aus Deutschland*, i: *1550–52* (Berlin, 1901)
OL	H. Robinson (ed.), *Original Letters Relative to the English Reformation* (Cambridge, 1846–7). References are to document number.
OUA	Oxford University Archive
Parliamentary Speech	BL Cotton Titus BI, fos. 109^r–16^v: Morison's 1540 speech to Parliament.
Persuasion	BL Cotton Faustina CII, fos. 5^r–22^v: 'A perswasion that the Laws should be in Laten'
PLRE	R. J. Fehrenbach and E. S. Leedham-Green (eds.), *Private Libraries in Renaissance England* (Marlborough, 1992–)
PMLA	*Publications of the Modern Language Society of America*

PP	*Past and Present*
PRO	The National Archives: Public Record Office
PROB	Records of the Prerogative court of Canterbury, PRO
Protestation	*A Protestation made for the most mighty and moste redoubted kynge of Englande . . . wherin is declared, that neyther his hyghenes, nor his prelates, neyther any other prynce, or prelate, is bounde to come or sende, to the pretended councell* (London, 1537)
Remedy	R. Morison, *A Remedy for Sedition* (London, 1536)
RQ	*Renaissance Quarterly*
RR	*Renaissance and Reformation*
Sacraments	SP6/8, fos. 137^r–50^v: 'Treatise on the Seven Sacraments'
SBTRO	Shakespeare Birthplace Trust Records Office
SCJ	*Sixteenth Century Journal*
SP	State Papers, PRO
STC	A. W. Pollard and G. R. Redgrave, *A Short Title Catalogue of Books Printed in England, Scotland and Ireland and of English Books Printed Abroad, 1475–1640*, rev. K. Pantzer (London, 1976–91)
TRHS	*Transactions of the Royal Historical Society*
TRP	P. L. Hughes and J. F. Larkin (eds.), *Tudor Royal Proclamations*, i: *The Early Tudors (1485–1553)* (New Haven, 1964)
Var. Coll.	Historical Manuscripts Commission, *Various Collections* (London, 1914), vol. vii
VCH	*Victoria County History*
WARD	Court of Wards and Liveries: Inquisitions Post Mortem, PRO
Whole Works	J. A. Giles (ed.), *The Whole Works of Roger Ascham* (London, 1865)
WRO	Worcester Record Office
WSRO	Wiltshire and Swindon Record Office, Trowbridge
Zurich ZB	Zurich Zentralbibliothèque

Introduction

Richard Morison (*c.*1513–56) is a familiar, if shadowy, figure to most early modern historians. Chiefly known as Henry VIII's most prolific propagandist, Morison is frequently depicted as a mercenary hack. A paid government pen, he condemned more principled figures such as Thomas More, John Fisher and Reginald Pole for their opposition to Henry's policies, and he did so in panegyrics aimed at instilling obedience to the overbearing king. Yet this image of Morison does not bear close scrutiny. Equally importantly, it is rather different from the perception of Morison held by many of his contemporaries: a committed evangelical and talented humanist.

Morison was born into obscurity; so much so that Essex, Oxfordshire, Hertfordshire and Yorkshire have all been suggested for his county of birth.[1] It seems most likely that he or his family came from the North-East as he used colloquial terms such as 'crackers', 'nygher' and 'keeling'.[2] His scholarship to study at Thomas Wolsey's new Oxford foundation, Cardinal College, and his later links to the cardinal may also point to a northern connection. It was, perhaps, from his northern archdiocese that the cardinal drew scholars to fill his newly established college in Oxford. After an education at Oxford and Padua, Morison returned to England in 1536 to begin a long career serving the crown in a variety of capacities. Over the next four years, he produced propaganda tracts for the government, wrote theological determinations, performed diplomatic duties and pursued an active political career. For most of this time he was a member of Cromwell's household or an attendant

---

[1] T. Tanner, *Biblioteca Britannica-Hibernica* (London, 1748), 532; A. Wood, *Athenae Oxonienses, 1500–1714* (Oxford, 1813–20), i. 239; J. A. Venn, *Alumni Cantabrigienses* (Cambridge, 1924), I. iii. 216; J. Berkenhout, *Biographia literaria* (London, 1777), i. 467–8.

[2] *Berkowitz*, 123, 124, 140. This may do no more than support the information gathered in the 1634 visitation of Hertfordshire, which identified Morison's father as Thomas Morison, formerly of Chardwell, Yorkshire. W. C. Metcalfe (ed.), *Visitation of Hertfordshire 1572 & 1634* (London, 1886), 116.

at court. In 1539 he was elected as an MP for the first time and was appointed to serve in the King's Privy Chamber. Little trace of Morison survives for much of the early 1540s, but it is clear that he built up his landed base and attached himself to a godly circle encompassing many key figures. In Edward VI's reign he served on three religious committees, attended Parliament and represented his king at the court of the Holy Roman Emperor, Charles V. He ended his life a religious exile in Strasbourg. An accomplished scholar, diplomat, theologian and politician, Morison was linked to the leading political and religious figures of the time: Thomas Cromwell, Catherine Parr, the Dukes of Somerset and Northumberland, John Calvin, Heinrich Bullinger and Peter Martyr Vermigli—to name but a few.

A problem facing any biographer of Morison is the unevenness of the extant sources. There is relatively little surviving evidence relating to Morison's activities before 1536, between 1541 and 1547 and after 1553. Every reasonable effort has been expended to seek Morison out in the archives, but for these years he has left little trace in the records of central government, and his own papers do not survive. We probably only have as many papers as we do relating to Morison in the 1530s thanks to the seizure of Cromwell's goods in 1540. A relative lack for the 1540s is not surprising as Johnston has shown that the majority of state papers for the 1540s derive from war and diplomacy.[3] While it is not always possible to be sure what Morison was doing in these years, it is clear that there are some areas where we can be pretty certain he was not active: it seems highly unlikely, for instance, that he was employed in the secretariat. The wealth of material for Morison between 1550 and 1553 can be attributed to Morison's ambassadorial role, which meant that many of his dispatches were preserved by the government. Sadly very few of Morison's own papers have survived outside the state archive.[4] A consequence of these lacunae is that the book that follows is not a straightforward, chronological biography. Instead, it adopts a thematic approach, with each theme treated in a roughly chronological manner. Morison is contextualized within each of the careers he followed: he is considered as a scholar, propagandist, politician, reformer, diplomat and dissident exile.

Two themes dominate this study: Morison's humanism and his evangelicalism. Morison was a celebrated 'man of letters' who operated

---

[3] A. Johnston, 'William Paget and the Late Henrician Polity', Ph.D. thesis (St Andrews, 2004), ch. 1.

[4] There are a small number of documents relating to Morison's estates in HALS.

within academic groups at Oxford, Cambridge and Padua. Even after he decided to engage in the active life of politics, he continued to pursue intellectual interests, corresponding, as we shall see, with scholars as diverse as John Beckinsau, Damiano a Gois, John Caius and Johann Sturm. He was an established figure in Tudor intellectual life to whom many other scholars turned for patronage, including his friend and brother-in-law Christopher Hales, who was himself a friend of Heinrich Bullinger.[5] Hence a study of Morison has much to contribute to our understanding of Tudor humanism. It cannot solve the 'problem' of English humanism identified by Fox, that so few English humanists shared the same social, economic or political values,[6] because this 'problem' was endemic to humanism itself. But Morison can help to elucidate just how varied and vibrant early Tudor intellectual culture was, and some of the influences that made it so.

Ever since the publication of McConica's seminal study of English humanists the historiography of Tudor intellectual culture has been dominated by assessing the influence of Erasmus' ideas in England. McConica saw the moral philosophy of Erasmus as the guiding force of English intellectual culture until the reign of Edward VI;[7] although Fox questioned the significance of Erasmian thought, Wooding and Bernard have reasserted that Erasmianism was key not just to intellectual life, but also to the religious culture of Henry VIII's England.[8] Meanwhile Bradshaw has characterized Erasmian philosophy as fundamental not just to English humanism, but to transalpine humanism more generally at least until the deaths of More and Erasmus.[9] Despite this historiographical trend, focused studies have shown that many English humanists, like More and Tunstall, who were devotees of Erasmus were not always happy to see his ideas applied in the English context.[10] Even though Richard Pace's 'Christian humanism' was influenced by

---

[5] *LP* Addenda I ii 1484.

[6] A. Fox, 'Facts and Fallacies: Interpreting English Humanism', in *idem* and J. Guy, *Reassessing the Henrician Age* (Oxford, 1986), 9–34.

[7] J. K. McConica, *English Humanists and Reformation Politics under Henry VIII and Edward VI* (Oxford, 1965).

[8] A. Fox, 'English Humanism and the Body Politic', in Fox and Guy, *Reassessing the Henrician Age*, 34–51; L. Wooding, *Rethinking Catholicism in Reformation England* (Oxford, 2000); G. W. Bernard, *The King's Reformation* (New Haven, 2005).

[9] B. Bradshaw, 'Transalpine Humanism', in J. H. Burns and M. Goldie (eds.), *Cambridge History of Political Thought 1450–1700* (Cambridge, 1994), 85–131.

[10] A. Stewart, 'The Trouble with English Humanism: Tyndale, More and Darling Erasmus', in J. Woolfson (ed.), *Reassessing Tudor Humanism* (Basingstoke, 2002), 78–88.

Erasmus it also owed much to Italian trends.[11] The influence of Italian ideas was more pervasive still, with the works of figures such as Battista Mantuan having a substantial impact on Tudor education, while broader Italian intellectual trends became influential in later Tudor England.[12] Study in Italy, especially at Padua, had a significant impact: Zeeveld outlined how a group of scholars, Morison included, who studied at Padua, were later recruited by the crown; Woolfson illustrated how the influence of Padua University extended beyond government administration.[13] By studying individual engagement with the ideas scholars encountered on the Italian peninsula, we can explore the Italian connection in more depth, as Mayer's work on Thomas Starkey has demonstrated.[14] Here Morison can prove informative. Throughout his life, he turned to the works of Italian humanists such as Marc Antonio Sabellico and Niccolò Machiavelli. His recognized position as a scholar of some note, and the considerable library he amassed, mark Morison out as a figure of some importance in our understanding of Tudor humanism.

McConica's study had a further legacy: it depicted English humanism before Edward VI's reign as separate from Protestant thought. In his scheme it was 'the Erasmian gospel, undogmatic yet definite and discernible [that] provides the continuous thread' through Henrician intellectual culture.[15] A more secular vision of English humanism was put forward by Caspari, who described an English humanism marked by an educational philosophy that was predominantly secular and aristocratic; there was little room for evangelical doctrine.[16] Fox believed that 'from 1530 onwards, humanism and religion tended to be pursued as contiguous, though separate, interests in different spheres of human life'.[17] Morison's humanism was never purely secular nor was it Erasmian. Even when contemplating how the laws of England might be codified, he had godly purposes in mind. Morison may be one of the

[11] C. Curtis, 'Richard Pace's *De fructu* and Early Tudor Pedagogy', in Woolfson, *Reassessing Tudor Humanism*, 43–77.

[12] L. Piepho, *Holofernes' Mantuan: Italian Humanism in Early Modern England* (Oxford, 2001); M. Wyatt, *The Italian Encounter with Tudor England: A Cultural Politics of Translation* (Cambridge, 2005).

[13] G. Zeeveld, *Foundations of Tudor Policy* (London, 1948); J. Woolfson, *Padua and the Tudors* (Cambridge, 1998).

[14] T. F. Mayer, *Thomas Starkey and the Common Weal* (Cambridge, 1989).

[15] McConica, *English Humanists*, 12.

[16] F. Caspari, *Humanism and the Social Order* (New York, 1968).

[17] Fox, 'Facts and Fallacies', 30.

many 'civic' humanists that Rex espies,[18] but his sense of patriotism and service to the commonweal was never divorced from his commitment to the gospel. In this he was not alone, as his friend and colleague Richard Taverner also brought evangelical beliefs to the humanist table.[19] Many of the patronage networks Dowling traced were demonstrably evangelical.[20] Here too, the influence of Italian experiences and writers should not be underestimated, as Overell has suggested.[21]

Morison's political career can help us assess how English humanists engaged in the *vita activa*. Those who chose to engage in politics used Cicero to defend their decision and to build their notions of how counsel should be undertaken and received.[22] Like many of his contemporaries, Morison was a 'civic' humanist who believed that he should put his talents and education to the service of the commonwealth. He wrote panegyric poetry and polemical tracts, and his scholarship continued to be an important factor in his career progression, not least for his perceived suitability to sit in the 1539 Parliament. Historians as diverse as Wooding, Starkey and Dowling have all pointed to Henry VIII's wish for a cultivated, learned court.[23] Morison would have fitted into such a political culture well; indeed the sheer variety of his activities illuminates the political utility attached to humanistic training by Henry and his government. Elton outlined the activities of many of the scholars drawn to Thomas Cromwell's patronage and household who were concerned with reforming the economic, social and legal problems of the realm.[24] A more concerted analysis of Morison's career than that provided by Elton offers further insights into the household and activities of the king's chief minister.

The politics of Henry VIII's reign has long been dominated by the notion of faction. Whether Henry was a weak king, easily influenced

---

[18] R. Rex, 'The Role of English Humanists in the Reformation up to 1559', in N. S. Amos, A. Pettegree and H. van Nierop (eds.), *Education of a Christian Society: Humanism and the Reformation in Britain and the Netherlands* (Aldershot, 1999), 28–40.

[19] J. K. Yost, 'German Protestant Humanism and the Early English Reformation', *Bibliothèque d'humanisme et Renaissance*, 32 (1970), 613–25.

[20] M. Dowling, *Humanism in the Age of Henry VIII* (London, 1986).

[21] M. A. Overell, *Italian Reform and English Reformations, c.1535–c.1585* (Aldershot, 2008).

[22] J. Guy, 'The Rhetoric of Counsel in Early Modern England', in *idem, Politics, Law and Counsel in Tudor and Early Stuart England* (Aldershot, 2000).

[23] Dowling, *Humanism*, ch. 1; D. R. Starkey, *The Reign of Henry VIII: Personalities and Politics* (London, 1985); L. Wooding, *Henry VIII* (Abingdon, 2008).

[24] G. R. Elton, *Reform and Renewal: Thomas Cromwell and the Commonweal* (Cambridge, 1973).

by those around him, or a strong king who manipulated factions to his will, Henry's court looms large in the historiography of his politics.[25] Morison's career can help to cut through the paradigm of factional politics. It provides a case study for why an individual political actor was advanced, what duties he undertook, and what degree of specialization was apparent. As Gunn suggested, by looking at individual careers and not just at flashpoint events we can profitably move beyond an interpretative scheme that is overly dependent upon faction.[26] Walker's work on Anne Boleyn has demonstrated that even this most contested of factional events can be productively explained without recourse to laying the blame on factional struggles or an overbearing king. And by taking such an approach a more complex, sophisticated picture of Tudor political culture emerges.[27]

Bernard has advocated an alternative vision of Henrician politics in which the king descended into tyranny in the 1530s. For Bernard, a tyrant was 'a ruler whose aims and methods deliberately, systematically and damagingly break the conventions of the society over which he or she rules'.[28] While there is no denying that Henry broke many societal conventions when he broke with Rome, it is less clear that he deserves the label tyrant. Henry's contemporaries largely viewed tyranny in terms of the failure of the monarch to adopt virtuous counsel and work for the good of the commonweal.[29] According to Erasmus it was the pursuit of his own interests over those of his subjects that made a tyrant: 'if someone rules to suit himself and assesses everything by how it affects his own convenience, then it does not matter which title he bears: in practice he is certainly a tyrant, not a prince.'[30]

Walker has also conceptualized Henry's later reign as a tyranny where the king put his own interests before those of his subjects, leaving English humanists in need of new literary strategies to counsel their king and restrain his tyrannical impulses. Asking the question 'how did well informed individuals react to the growing realization that they were living through something previously unthinkable: the slide into an

---

[25] See for instance Starkey, *Personalities and Politics*; E. W. Ives, *Anne Boleyn* (Oxford, 1986); J. S. Block, *Factional Politics and the English Reformation 1520–1540* (London, 1993).

[26] S. J. Gunn, 'The Structures of Politics in Early Tudor England', *TRHS*, 6th ser. 5 (1995), 71.

[27] G. Walker, 'Rethinking the Fall of Anne Boleyn', *HJ*, 45 (2002), 1–29.

[28] G. W. Bernard, 'The Tyranny of Henry VIII', in Bernard and Gunn, *Authority and Consent*, 113.

[29] Guy, 'Counsel'.

[30] D. Erasmus, *Education of a Christian Prince*, ed. L. Jardine (Cambridge, 1997), 25.

English tyranny?' Walker identifies a shift from the *speculum principis* tradition towards a more internal satirical and stoic literary culture.[31] This begs the question: was Morison writing his propaganda tracts 'under tyranny'? And if so, could he too invoke literary strategies in order to get the king and the broader political community to listen to his own views? Or would his tracts, written for the king, merely reflect the king's will?

While some of Henry's subjects certainly believed that he had descended into tyranny in the 1530s, many others did not. The king was keen to emphasize that his policies stemmed from what he believed to be in the best interests of his realm. Wooding has recently steered a *via media* arguing for a strong, principled king who controlled factions, yet who was not a tyrant in any straightforward sense.[32] One hallmark of a tyrant was that he did not receive good counsel and here, too, there is evidence to question the label of tyranny: even in the 1540s Henry VIII was demonstrably consulting his council on a regular basis.[33] As will become apparent this study of Morison does not support the notion of a tyrannical Henry, not least due to the polemical strategies Morison employed. He did not view the king as a tyrant in the 1530s, though it seems likely that he believed that Henry had fallen into the trap of listening to flatterers in the 1540s. For many of Morison's contemporary humanists, such as Thomas Elyot, the defence against tyranny lay in a strong and educated nobility;[34] for Morison it lay in adherence to scripture by all levels of society, though he did think that nobles and gentlemen should lead the way. Morison's political career suggests that Henry did not tyrannically impose his own views on his courtiers, nor was he manipulated by court factions or influential favourites. Both the tyrannical and the factional interpretations of Henry's reign hinge on the assumption that 'the England of Henry VIII . . . experienced the politics of manipulation in an acute form',[35] even if they disagree on who was being manipulated. But Tudor politics was not simply concerned with manipulation: persuasion was important, but so too were compromise, accommodation, consultation and ability.

Any study of Henry VIII's most prolific propagandist must dwell at some length on the tracts he produced. In the period 1536–9,

---

[31] G. Walker, *Writing Under Tyranny* (Oxford, 2005), 2.   [32] Wooding, *Henry VIII*.
[33] Johnston, 'William Paget', ch. 3.   [34] Guy, 'Counsel', 296–7.
[35] D. Starkey, 'Intimacy and Innovation: The Rise of the Privy Chamber, 1485–1547', in D. Starkey (ed.), *The English Court from the Wars of the Roses to the Civil War* (London, 1987), 101.

propaganda from Morison's pen dominated official literature. Although Morison's printed works have received a fair degree of scholarly attention, the fundamental assumption that they constitute uncomplicated obedience literature has left much scope for further analysis.[36] Some readers may object to the term propaganda. In the 1530s Henry and his government systematically tried to persuade his people of the rectitude of his cause through a variety of media: sermons, prayers, pageants, imagery and print. Despite the negative connotations associated with the term, propaganda in its educative and persuasive sense seems an appropriate way of designating tracts such as the *Remedy for sedition*. The study that follows goes beyond the assumption that polemical tracts were mere obedience literature and examines the tracts on their own terms and in their own context. It provides the first comprehensive examination of Morison's polemical tracts as a coherent canon.

A fuller contextual examination of Morison's tracts has much to offer us. At one level they tell us about the government's message in the crucial years after the Break with Rome as a new conception of church and kingship was articulated in these works. Aspects of this theory of kingship have been articulated by historians such as Baumer, Zeeveld, Elton and King, but significant elements have been overlooked.[37] In particular, one key propaganda tract, Morison's *Comfortable Consolation* (1537), has not received any prior analysis. Morison's tracts were a significant means by which Henry's subjects were informed of his policies and the developing governmental rhetoric. Contrary to the prevailing historiography, Morison was no mere sycophant. He pursued his own agenda and tried to influence the direction of Henry VIII's religious policy; he did so using ideas and imagery that are more commonly associated with evangelical exiles, or the more mainstream Protestant authors of Edward VI's and Elizabeth I's reigns. In Morison's hands government rhetoric was unambiguously evangelical: rooted in the authority of scripture, it also encouraged its readers to understand Henry's religious policies in providential terms. Underwood has demonstrated Cromwell's patronage of openly evangelical works by William

---

[36] For a rare exception, see S. Mottram, *Empire and Nation in Early English Renaissance Literature* (Cambridge, 2008).

[37] F. le van Baumer, *The Early Tudor Theory of Kingship* (1940); Zeeveld, *Foundations*, ch. 4; G. R. Elton, *Policy and Police: The Enforcement of the Reformation in the Age of Thomas Cromwell* (Cambridge, 1972), ch. 4; J. N. King, *Tudor Royal Iconography: Literature and Art in an Age of Religious Crisis* (Princeton, 1989).

Marshall.[38] Cromwell's sponsorship of Morison is an even more clear-cut case. Indeed, the rhetoric of government polemic, and of Morison's tracts in particular, helps to explain some of the apparent ambiguities of the English Reformation, such as why the Act of Six Articles of 1539 was not, as Ryrie has convincingly demonstrated, universally considered a bar to further reform by English evangelicals.[39] Consequently Morison's tracts, like his social contacts in the 1540s, offer us a potential bridge between early English evangelicals and Edwardian developments.

Government propaganda also offers insights into the major issues of the day, including foreign policy. In the late 1530s there was a real possibility that England might face invasion, a fact of which Henry VIII's government were all too aware. Consequently some polemical tracts were composed at moments of heightened tension in international relations, yet others tried to influence foreign powers. Even domestic propaganda could have an international context. England was not, as Elton insisted, becoming more isolated from the continent at this point;[40] rather Henry's government had a keen eye on the international situation and used propaganda tracts (including Morison's) to persuade continental rulers of the justice of his cause and to gain allies, as well as suggesting to his English subjects that England had supporters on the continent. By 1536, the government conceived of polemical tracts as diplomatic tools both to relay information to Henry's ambassadors abroad and to provide them with ideas and facts for use in diplomatic negotiations. Thus Morison's tracts are important for understanding not only how Henry VIII represented himself to his subjects, but also how he wished foreign dignitaries and scholars to view him. Henrician polemics and the uses to which they were put were often more sophisticated than previous studies have suggested.

There are two assumptions about propaganda that this study seeks, at least in part, to test: that it was deliberately falsified and that it was unpopular. Perhaps surprisingly, Morison was concerned with the accuracy of his tracts; there seems to have been both a conscious effort in government propaganda not to put into print anything that could not be defended and a sense that a consistent message should be articulated. The assumption of unpopularity is more difficult to counter. Where reactions

---

[38] W. Underwood, 'Thomas Cromwell and William Marshall's Protestant Books', *HJ*, 47 (2004), 517–36.

[39] A. Ryrie, *The Gospel and Henry VIII: Evangelicals in the Early English Reformation* (Cambridge, 2003).

[40] Elton, *Policy and Police*, ch. 4.

to print survive, it is often because someone reacted negatively to it and someone else reported them for it. Recent scholarship has emphasized the political awareness of a wider section of sixteenth- and seventeenth-century society than historians had previously thought.[41] Much of this work has focused on the importance of orality and rumour, which have also been increasingly prioritized in studies of news transmission and propaganda,[42] but this should not obscure the importance of printed propaganda. Orality and literacy were not distinct activities; reading could be, and frequently was, an oral activity, which had the promise to broaden the potential audience for government tracts.[43] Most of Morison's tracts survive in multiple editions, suggesting they enjoyed a not insubstantial readership. Shagan's insistence that the English Reformation was a negotiated process[44] makes the messages being articulated and disseminated by the government even more crucial: if we do not understand them, how are we to know what people in the parishes thought they were negotiating? As the predominant voice of the Henrician government, it is important to know what Morison said and to suggest what effect this might have had.

Morison played a much larger role in the English Reformation than has hitherto been appreciated: an adapted version of one of his compositions was even used (as was Morison himself) during English theological discussions with representatives of the Lutheran Schmalkaldic League in 1538. A respected theologian, during the years 1536–9 he helped to draft official doctrinal statements, translated works by leading reformers into English and composed theological treatises, most of which were drafted under the aegis of Thomas Cromwell. Significantly he was also asked to produce statements of doctrine in the run-up to the *Bishops' Book* even though he was not entitled to a seat in convocation. Morison's theological opinion mattered and was often invoked by other scholars looking for patronage from the vicegerent. This study reinforces McEntegart's depiction of the period

---

[41] E. Shagan, *Popular Politics and the English Reformation* (Cambridge, 2003); T. Harris (ed.), *The Politics of the Excluded* (Basingstoke, 2001); M. J. Braddick and J. Walter (eds.), *Negotiating Power in Early Modern Society* (Cambridge, 2001).

[42] For example E. Shagan, 'Print, Orality and Communications in the Maid of Kent Affair', *JEH*, 52 (2001), 21–34; A. Fox, 'Rumour, News and Popular Political Opinion in Elizabethan and Early Stuart England', *HJ*, 40 (1997), 597–620.

[43] A. Fox, *Oral and Literate Culture in England 1500–1700* (Oxford, 2000); T. Watt, *Cheap Print and Popular Piety 1550–1640* (Cambridge, 1991).

[44] Shagan, *Popular Politics*.

to 1539 as one marked by religious debate and curiosity, where the lines only slowly hardened in the conservatives' favour.[45]

Three decades ago Bonini claimed to have proven that Morison held Lutheran beliefs in the 1530s, largely relying on what she believed to be Morison's commonplace book. Unfortunately her main evidence, a translation of Luther's *Sermon on Psalm 127* that is now in the National Archives, has no association with Morison.[46] However, a concerted study of Morison's surviving theological writings will reveal his attachment to Lutheran theology in the 1530s. Morison was open about his evangelical beliefs and freely promoted them; this may be one of the reasons why his theological activities fade from the records after the Act of Six Articles was passed. After Cromwell's fall, Morison did not leave the court in disgrace. Rather, he was part of a powerful evangelical clique that also comprised Anthony Denny and the Duchess of Suffolk. From the very start of Edward VI's reign Morison was actively involved in the Reformation once more. He served on important commissions that removed the vestiges of the old church and established the new, emerging as an important supporter of reform in the Edwardian regime. Like Cranmer and many other English evangelicals, Morison's religious views seem to have shifted towards a Swiss position on the Eucharist by 1549.[47] Despite this, he maintained friendships with reformers along quite a wide theological spectrum.

Evangelical concerns were also central to Morison's diplomatic activities. He consistently pursued amicable relations with the Protestant princes and numerous evangelical scholars and reformers. Consequently, Morison's diplomatic career not only offers insights into the foreign policy goals of Northumberland's regime, but also tells us much about how England wanted to be perceived religiously. Diplomacy was about more than fact-finding and negotiation, it was also about creating impressions and developing links. It was a commonplace in contemporary

[45] R. McEntegart, *Henry VIII, the League of Schmalkalden, and the English Reformation* (Woodbridge, 2002).
[46] C. R. Bonini, 'Lutheran Influences in the English Reformation: Richard Morison Re-examined', *ARG*, 64 (1973), 206–23; *idem*, 'Richard Morison, Humanist and Reformer under Henry VIII', Ph.D. thesis (Stanford, 1974), 141–54. Mistakenly believing all of SP6/4 to be Morison's commonplace book, Bonini argued that Morison was a Lutheran using a tract (SP6/4, fos. 1ʳ–48ʳ) that had no association with him. The article is inaccurate in a number of places.
[47] See, for example, D. MacCulloch, *Thomas Cranmer, A Life* (London, 1996); Ryrie, *Gospel*.

diplomatic theory that 'the prince is knowen by the Ambassador'.[48] Morison cultivated scholars and reformers within the Strasbourg–St Gall axis that MacCulloch sees as crucial to the course of the English Reformation[49] particularly in Strasbourg and Zurich. This was, in part, due to personal interests, but it also served to create closer links between England and the major reformers, and to create the impression that England was more reformed than proved to be the case. Morison's embassy, then, firmly places the English Reformation in its European context.

Morison permits a study of the training and career progression of an English diplomat in the formative years of resident diplomacy. His diplomatic career both highlights the need for more studies of English diplomatic methodology and casts doubt on some of the existing literature. Bell suggested that the English diplomatic corps only exhibited signs of professionalism in Elizabeth I's reign.[50] Yet Morison was well-prepared for his first major embassy as he had over a decade of diplomatic service under his belt. His career suggests that a more complex notion of professionalism is needed when conceptualizing the English diplomatic corps. It also underlines the readjustments that English diplomacy, as well as English foreign policy, needed to make to incorporate England's new Protestant identity. Morison's embassy to the court of the Holy Roman Emperor, Charles V in 1550–3 occurred during a transitional period in English diplomatic practice that had repercussions for later generations of diplomats. Protestant diplomats, representing Protestant powers at Catholic courts, had to learn the boundaries within which they could defend their religion. Morison's Protestantism both undermined his political effectiveness and determined the recommendations he made on English foreign policy. During his embassy, Morison continued to pursue his academic interests. This led him to devise innovative practical solutions to some of the problems associated with ambassadorial service and act as patron to foreign evangelicals.

With the accession of Mary I, Morison's long service to the crown came to an end. Once the restitution of Catholicism became a certainty,

---

[48] O. Landi, *Delectable demaundes, and pleasant questions* (London, 1566), fo. 69.

[49] D. MacCulloch, *Tudor Church Militant: Edward VI and the Protestant Reformation* (London, 1999), 57–63; *idem, Thomas Cranmer*, 173–9, 356–8.

[50] G. Bell, 'Elizabethan Diplomacy: The Subtle Revolution', in M. R. Thorp and A. J. Slavin (eds.), *Politics, Religion and Diplomacy in Early Modern Europe* (Kirksville, MO, 1994), 267–89.

Morison left England for a safe haven abroad. Despite his position as one of the most senior politicians to flee abroad in Mary's reign, his activities in exile have attracted little scholarly interest. As someone with considerable overseas experience Morison provides an important case study of how the process of exile was planned and experienced, as well as offering insights into the coherence and organization of the exile community more broadly. Diplomatic service had brought him into contact with a range of continental scholars and reformers and these contacts were to prove crucial to his personal choices in exile. Morison was also the most experienced propagandist to choose exile, a fact that has not been appreciated by historians in the past. Establishing Morison's role in the Marian exiles' polemic is a difficult task, but it seems highly unlikely that he was not involved at some level. He certainly continued to write and was closely associated with other polemicists. Sharpe and Zwicker have called for historians 'to situate early modern lives beyond national boundaries'.[51] In Morison's case, it is simply not possible to understand his life or the impact his actions had unless he is considered in an international context.

[51] K. Sharpe and S. Zwicker, *Writing Lives: Biography and Textuality, Identity and Representation in Early Modern England* (Oxford, 2008), 3.

1

The Scholar

OXFORD UNIVERSITY

Morison arrived at Cardinal College to study the Arts during Michaelmas Term 1525.[1] His previous education cannot be traced. John Bale's claims that Morison attended one of the country's leading schools cannot be verified, nor does there seem to be any basis to the traditional association between Morison and Eton. Instead, Morison was probably educated in a northern grammar school.[2] An impoverished scholar, Morison was awarded a petty canonry. This entitled him to a stipend, and paid his college and university fees.

Cardinal College was an impressive foundation: Wolsey had endowed it with £2,000 in land, which was to support a dean, sixty senior canons, forty petty canons, twenty pensioners, thirteen chaplains, twelve lay clerks, sixteen choristers, a music teacher, twenty-three servants and four legal officials.[3] Wolsey's pedagogical provisions were equally impressive. He attempted to bring the most recent scholarship to a predominantly inward-looking Oxford, so Morison was set to receive the most advanced education available in England, from some of the leading scholars of his day. Four college readers were to cover logic, dialectic, philosophy and humanity; six chairs provided public lectures in theology, canon law, philosophy, civil law, medicine and the humanities. Daily theology lectures were provided on the New Testament, Old Testament and the *Quaestiones* of Duns Scotus. Hence the exposition of the Bible, which was more in line with humanist principles, was given equal weight to scholastic authors. By the time Morison received his BA

---

[1] OUA, Register H, fo. 185ʳ.

[2] J. Bale, *Illustrium Maioris Britanniae scriptorum* (Wesel, 1548), NNiiʳ; T. Harwood, *Alumni Etonienses* (Birmingham, 1797). There were over twenty grammar schools in Yorkshire in the period 1510–25. J. A. H. Moran, *The Growth of English Schooling 1340–1548* (Guildford, 1985), Appendix.

[3] Dowling, *Humanism*, 77–8.

in 1529 the theology chair was held by Nicholas de Burgo, who was involved in Henry VIII's campaign to annul his marriage to Catherine of Aragon. Humanities students could hear two public lectures a day: in the morning an exposition of a renowned rhetorician such as Cicero, Quintilian or Trapezuntius; in the afternoon either rudimentary Greek or, for advanced students, more difficult Greek authors such as Isocrates, Philostratus, Aristophanes and Hesiod. In addition, Plautus and Terence were central to the college syllabus. Lectures in canon law were to be based around the *Decretals* and the letters of Gregory and Boniface, using the best commentaries available. These took place at the same time as the civil law lectures, which were to focus on the *Pandects* or the *Codex*. Also scheduled to speak at 7 a.m., the philosophy professor was required to cover the natural, moral and metaphysical thought of Aristotle and to lecture occasionally on Plato. In the afternoon, the professor of medicine primarily expounded the texts of Hippocrates, Avicenna and other famous medical authors.[4] The sum of Wolsey's efforts then, was to add a vast array of classical literature to the predominantly scholastic texts of the main university curriculum.

Wolsey's efforts to fill his college with the leading scholars of the day were no less ambitious, although he largely had to settle for native talent. He persuaded the leading Spanish humanist Juan Luis Vives, the respected English scholar Thomas Lupset, and the noted Greek Matteus Calphurnius to teach there for a time and tried to recruit Romolo Amasei for the oratory chair. Wolsey's ambition for a trilingual college remained unrealized, as no Hebrew lecturer was appointed before his fall from grace in November 1529.[5] Considerable effort also went into assembling the new college's library. Wolsey commissioned transcripts of the Greek manuscripts that the notable Greek scholars Cardinal Basil Bessarion and Domenico Grimani had donated to Venice, and also tried to acquire copies of the Vatican's Greek manuscripts.[6] Morison, then, was given access to scholars of both national and international standing and would have followed a broad, modern curriculum. He would also have been able to attend the public lectures at Bishop

---

[4] G. D. Duncan, 'Public Lectures and Professorial Chairs', in J. K. McConica (ed.), *The History of the University of Oxford*, iii: *The Collegiate University* (Oxford, 1986), 339–42; Dowling, *Humanism*, 78–9; V. Murphy, 'Nicholas de Burgo', *ODNB*, 8.803–4.

[5] Zeeveld, *Foundations*, 25; Duncan, 'Public Lectures', 341; S. L. Greenslade, 'The Faculty of Theology', in McConica, *Collegiate University*, 316. Morison, however, clearly learnt Hebrew at some point. See below p. 60.

[6] P. Gwyn, *The King's Cardinal* (London, 1990), 343; Dowling, *Humanism*, 78–9.

Fox's recent foundation, Corpus Christi. These covered a wide range of classical authors from Cicero to Pliny as well as fifteenth-century Italian humanists such as Lorenzo Valla and Angelo Poliziano. So he could have chosen to hear a wide range of lectures on topics outside the requirements for the BA.[7] Given the later evidence for his breadth of studies, it seems likely that he did.

In lectures Morison received a blend of traditional education and more recent humanist pedagogy, but the arts syllabus of the university was still dominated by the commentaries of medieval Oxford scholars. In order to satisfy the requirements for the BA degree, Morison had to study certain prescribed authors. The basic texts that Morison should have studied for logic were Porphyry's *Isagogue*, the *Liber sex principiorum*, Aristotle's *Predicamenta* and *Sophistici elenchi*, and either his *Topics* or *Prior Analytics* or Boethius' *Topics* (i–iii). Grammar required Morison to have heard lectures on Priscian's *Institutiones grammaticae* and Donatus' *Barbarisms*; Arithmetic the *Algorismus*, *De sphaera*, *Comptus ecclesiasticus*, and Boethius' *Arithmetica* and *Theoretica planetarum*. For rhetoric, the standard texts were Aristotle's *Rhetorica* and either Boethius' *Topics* (Book iv), the pseudo-Ciceronian *Rhetorica ad herennium*, Ovid's *Metamorphoses* or Virgil's poetry. Most subjects, such as geometry, astronomy and music, remained focused on the same authors (Euclid, Aristotle, Ptolemy and Boethius) and medieval commentaries, as they traditionally had.[8] Despite Morison's good later knowledge of philosophical texts, it is unlikely that he received any official tuition in philosophy in his first few years, as this was usually part of the MA.

The increased interest in Greek evident in both Fisher's and Wolsey's foundations was also present in Oxford's humanities and theology faculties. Morison became a skilled Grecian and pursued theological studies in the 1530s. He may have attended theology lectures at Oxford, where he would have encountered a largely conservative faculty.[9] Little provision was made for patristic studies; if Morison did study the church fathers during his time in Oxford, it was self-motivated. Much better arrangements were made for the scholars' pastoral religious education.

---

[7] For further details see J. K. McConica, 'The Rise of the Undergraduate College', in McConica, *Collegiate University*, 21–5.

[8] J. M. Fletcher, 'The Faculty of Arts', in McConica, *Collegiate University*, 174, 161–2; J. M. Fletcher, 'Developments in the Faculty of Arts, 1370–1520', in J. Catto (ed.), *The History of the University of Oxford*, ii: *Late Medieval Oxford* (Oxford, 1992), 315–45.

[9] Ibid., 314–15.

Morison could have attended up to forty sermons a year as a result of Wolsey's benefaction, while a section of the Bible was read and expounded daily over dinner.[10]

Morison was influenced by the fellows and scholars of Cardinal College and maintained friendships with many of them well beyond the 1520s. The College warden, Nicholas Lental, made a sufficiently strong impression for Morison to transfer a pension to him in 1539.[11] Wolsey staffed his college with a large number of Cambridge scholars, including John Clerk, Richard Cox, John Friar and John Frith. Edward Foxe, later bishop of Hereford, a leading reformer, and a colleague of Morison's, probably helped Wolsey to pick out the scholars.[12] Many of the Cantabrigians were suspected of belonging to an evangelical group in Cambridge who had narrowly escaped prosecution for religious heterodoxy in 1525. Among the other scholars who received positions at the college were Morison's friends Richard Taverner and Gervase Tyndale, who were also evangelicals.[13]

Shortly after the arrival of the Cantabrigians, plague broke out in Oxford. Morison and his fellow scholars continued their studies a safe distance away at Poughley monastery.[14] Whilst there, they were exposed to the ideas of several continental humanists and reformers. The evangelical John Clerk delivered lectures in his chambers on Paul's Epistles 'to yonge men and siche as wer of ii iii or iiii yers contynuans in the university'. This might not have later come to worry the authorities had Luther's commentaries on Paul's Epistles not been uncovered among his books. The evangelical lessons and reading continued even after their return to Oxford, with John Friar playing a prominent role. In early 1528, the evangelicals came to the notice of the University officials. Thomas Garrett, who had moved to Oxford from London in order to sell heretical books, was arrested and many of his customers exposed. He had been soliciting Greek tuition from scholars and using the lessons to introduce them to the ideas of a range of continental reformers. As well as copies of Tyndale's New Testament, Morison's

---

[10] Greenslade, 'Faculty of Theology', 321; Gwyn, *King's Cardinal*, 350.

[11] *LP* XIII ii 1255.

[12] *LP* IV ii 3536; A. Wood, *History and Antiquities of the Colleges and Halls in the University of Oxford* (Oxford, 1790), ii. 25–6; Zeeveld, *Foundations*, 26–9.

[13] Ibid., 28–9; C. H. Cooper, *Annals of Cambridge* (Cambridge, 1862), i. 311; W. A. Clebsch, *England's Earliest Protestants* (London, 1964), 46, 78–80; Dowling, *Humanism*, 82–3.

[14] The former religious house of Poughley was part of the college endowment. Wood, *History*, ii. 26; *LP* IV i 1137.10, iii 5285, App. 103.

contemporaries also had access to works by Michael van Hoochstraten, John Hus, John Wycliffe, Philip Melanchthon, Martin Luther, Ulrich von Hutten, Jacobus Latomus, Johannes Oecolampadius, Johannes Pomeranus, Martin Cellarius, Johannes Brent, Martin Bucer, Germanus Brixman and Ulrich Zwingli.[15] At least six different Lutheran titles had been on sale in Oxford as early as 1520.[16] Yet Henry VIII had made his dislike for Lutheran doctrine apparent with the publication of his *Assertio septem sacramentorum*, the burning of Lutheran books in Oxford in 1521 and the subsequent campaign he waged against Luther.[17]

The evangelical network extended beyond Cardinal College, encompassing Gloucester Hall, St Albans, Corpus Christi and Magdalen. It sufficiently worried the university authorities that they arranged to have all of the halls and colleges searched for illicit books simultaneously. Garrett refused to reveal the names of his customers, but did confess to criticizing the adoration of saints and to supplying Lutheran books to Oxbridge scholars.[18] A number of scholars including Anthony Dalaber, John Frith, Richard Taverner, Robert Ferrar, Nicholas Udall and Henry Cole were definitely involved, as were numerous unnamed junior scholars.[19] The university commissary determined that the majority were not obstinate heretics. Ultimately the most senior were forced to do public penance and spent a few months in unpleasant Oxford prisons, but the majority recanted and did not receive any lengthy punishment. As 'most part of them be nott by name condemyd by the churche' we do not know who these junior scholars were.[20] This policy of treating the majority of the Lutheran scholars through quiet and charitable persuasion fits with Wolsey's broader policy of dealing with heretics after 1526.[21] More Lutherans remained in the city. At Easter, Dr Rowham preached a sermon in defence of Luther and the scholars who supported

[15] SP1/47, fos. 16ᵛ, 65ʳ⁻ᵛ, 11ʳ; E36/120, fo. 11ᵛ; *LP* IV ii 3968, 4017, 3962. Dowling, *Humanism*, 82–3. Garrett was the rector of Thomas Forman, who had warned the Cambridge evangelicals of a book search, suggesting a link between the Oxford and Cambridge evangelical groups.

[16] F. Madan (ed.), 'The Day Book of John Dorne', *Oxford Historical Society, Collectanea*, vol. 1 (Oxford, 1885), 71–177.

[17] The best account of this campaign is R. Rex, 'The English Campaign against Luther in the 1520s', *TRHS*, 5th ser. 38 (1989), 85–106.

[18] E36/120, fo. 11ʳ; London Guildhall 9531/10, fo. 122ʳ⁻ᵛ.

[19] Wood, *History*, ii. 29–31; Zeeveld, *Foundations*, 85.

[20] W. T. Mitchell (ed.), *Epistolae academiae 1508–1596*, Oxford Historical Society, New ser. 26 (Oxford, 1980), nos. 157, 160; E36/120, fo. 11ᵛ.

[21] See C. D'Alton, 'The Suppression of Lutheran Heretics in England, 1526–1529', *JEH*, 54 (2003), 228–53.

him, while as late as June the underground Lutherans were still active in Oxford, posting 'famous lybelles and billes' on 'chirche doores' at night.[22] Morison's role in this evangelical group is difficult to trace. He was certainly at Poughley and was later closely associated with many of those accused of heresy: Friar and Cole were close friends in Padua, Udall an associate at court. Although he clearly held Lutheran views by the time he left Oxford, his name does not occur in the few remaining records of the affair.[23] Morison, then, was probably one of the unnamed junior scholars who soon recanted, or he managed to avoid punishment and detection.

On 19 January 1528 Morison supplicated for admission to the bachelor's degree. While it was common in the 1520s for the university to permit supplication for the degree after three years, Morison petitioned two terms earlier than this. He was given leave to lecture in the arts, was admitted to the BA and determined in Lent of the following year.[24] In 1530 his name was still appearing on the college accounts, but by this time he had taken up service in Wolsey's household.[25] His experience there later prompted Morison to praise the cardinal for the pastoral devotion shown in his northern diocese: on holy days Wolsey would visit the parishes and 'there cause one or other of his doctors to make a sermon unto the people . . . He saw why churches were made. He began to restore them to their right and proper use.'[26] It may have been at this point that Wolsey granted Morison, 'scoler', a lifelong pension of 53s. 4d., which later allowed Morison to travel first to Cambridge and then to Paris and Padua.[27]

After leaving Wolsey's service, Morison headed for Cambridge, apparently to visit Hugh Latimer, who was a keen promoter of Lutheranism in the university in the late 1520s.[28] Morison left Cambridge an ardent supporter of Latimer's religious views. He later commented to Thomas Cranmer that the establishment of true religion in England could only be expected from the archbishop and Latimer, and in 1537 he praised Latimer for preaching the gospel 'sincerely, purely and honestly'. While

---

[22] SP1/47, fo. 149ᵛ; 1/48, fo. 206ᵛ [*LP* IV ii 4125, 4418].

[23] Most historians date Morison's evangelical conversion to his years in Italy. See for example J. Woolfson, 'Sir Richard Morison', *ODNB*, 39.188.

[24] Fletcher, 'Faculty of Arts', 165; OUA Register H, fos. 185ʳ, 196ᵛ, 206ʳ.

[25] E36/104, fo. 7ᵛ.   [26] *Berkowitz*, 134–5.

[27] J. Caley and J. Hunter (eds.), *Valor Ecclesiasticus temp. Henr. VIII* (London, 1810–34), v. 175.

[28] *LP* VI 1582; A. G. Chester, *Hugh Latimer* (New York, 1978), chs. 3–4.

in Cambridge, Morison also associated with the evangelical scholar
William Gonnell, who had tutored Thomas More's children in the
1520s and had advised on the education of Henry VIII's illegitimate
son. Gonnell introduced Morison to Cranmer on several occasions; they
dined together at least once.[29] At this stage Morison does not appear
to have established any lasting links with the archbishop. No evidence
has survived to link Morison to any particular college, although the
frequency of his contact with King's scholars in the 1530s might point
to an earlier link to that hall.

OVERSEAS STUDIES AT PADUA UNIVERSITY

Morison's next position was as a scholar-companion to Wolsey's illegitimate son, Thomas Winter. In the late 1520s Winter studied on
the continent under the direction of distinguished scholars such as
Thomas Lupset. His other accomplished scholar-companions included
John Bekinsau, a sometime reader of Greek in Paris, and the future
diplomat Richard Pate. Despite the money lavished on his education,
Winter was not the most promising scholar. After Wolsey's fall from
grace, Winter lost most of the benefices his father had bestowed upon
him. Only a pension as a king's scholar, secured by Thomas Cromwell,
kept him afloat. In January 1532, Winter was given licence to leave
the country with three servants, William Belson, George Lawson and
George Hampton, two of whom had been in Winter's household in
the 1520s.[30] Morison also accompanied Winter. Their first port of
call was Paris University. In February, Winter spent four days with
Reginald Pole and Thomas Starkey there before continuing his journey
southward to Italy. By July, Winter was in Venice; by October he was
settled in nearby Padua. Along the way, Morison occasionally acted as
Winter's secretary.[31]

At Padua, Morison joined the university and settled into a diverse
range of studies. Zeeveld and Woolfson have between them established
the importance of Padua University for the development of Tudor
intellectual culture.[32] Morison was one of the Paduan scholars recruited

[29] *LP* VI 1582; *Apomaxis*, Viv[r]; S. F. Ryle, 'William Gonnell', *ODNB*, 22.723.
[30] Ibid., 766.12; A. A. Chibi, 'John Beckinsau', *ODNB*, 4.869; J. Lock, 'Thomas Winter',
ODNB, 60.700; Zeeveld, *Foundations*, 62–4.
[31] Ibid., 79; *LP* V 338, 1210, 1453; SP1/73, fo. 166[r] [*LP* V Add. 24].
[32] Zeeveld, *Foundations*, *passim*; Woolfson, *Padua*, *passim*.

by Cromwell to serve the crown. His time in the Veneto not only equipped him for a career in royal service, but also established him as an eclectic scholar in contact with some of the leading academics in Europe.

While in Padua, Morison associated with numerous other Englishmen, many of whom became close friends, including Michael Throckmorton, Richard Shelley, John Mason and Thomas Starkey. Morison's friendship with these figures also had its more light-hearted side: he encouraged Shelley to pass his leisure time 'with a little music . . . wislier than I did then understand'.[33] Although Mayer was undoubtedly right to argue that Morison and Starkey were less friendly and their ideas not as similar as Berkowitz believed, he goes too far with his corrective.[34] Morison wrote at least eleven letters to Starkey from Italy, in which he, at least, assumed a close friendship. Moreover Edmund Harvel, the English agent in Venice, worried that Starkey was writing to him principally because Morison was staying with him. In 1536 he asked Starkey to 'cesse not to write now' that Morison had departed.[35]

Morison was a registered member of the law faculty, which throughout the 1530s attracted Europe's leading legal scholars, including Johannes Fichardus, Johannes Muslerus and, towards the end of the decade, Ulrich Zasius and Modestius Pistores. In 1531–3 Viglius Zuichemus, the first editor of the Greek paraphrases ascribed to Teofilo (1534) and author of commentaries on the *Institution*, was a professor of law at Padua. Paduan legal studies continued to be dominated by the Bartolist school of thought in the sixteenth century. Thus the Paduan approach to the *Corpus Juris Civilis* was based largely on centuries of glosses and explications, in contrast to the more humanist approach of scholars such as Angelo Poliziano and Guillaume Budé, who stripped the *Corpus* of the additions of the glossators and attempted to establish the original meaning of the *Codex*, *Digest* and *Pandects* through a combination of historical and philological methods. One Paduan tutor who bridged the Bartolist and humanist approaches to the law was Marco Mantova Benavides. Morison's compatriots Thomas Starkey and Henry Cole were both inspired by Mantova's conciliarism.[36] Morison would also have heard the evangelically inclined Mantova's law lectures, and may have

[33] *LP* XIII ii 827.   [34] Mayer, *Starkey*, 5.
[35] BL Cotton Nero BVII, fo. 124ᵛ [*LP* X 970].
[36] B. Brugi, *L'Università dei Giuristi in Padova nel cinquecento* (Venice, 1922), 33–4; Woolfson, *Padua*, 45–6; T. F. Mayer, *Cardinal Pole in European Context* (Aldershot, 2000), 385–408.

been directly influenced, as he was later to deploy conciliar arguments on Henry VIII's behalf.

In August 1534, after several years studying at the university, Morison was elected *conciliarus* of the English nation (members) of the law faculty. As such he represented the nation to the university; collectively the *conciliari* made up the university's executive council under the rector. Morison's contemporaries therefore placed a large amount of trust in him. He had to be registered to study law to be eligible to stand for the position. Other members of the law faculty rooted out those who were not law students and would undoubtedly have attacked Morison on this charge had they had the chance. Politicking within the faculty by the jurist Jean Coras surrounded Morison's election: Coras challenged three other Englishmen's right to vote. The larger issue at stake was the election of the university rector. Within weeks of being elected *conciliarus* Morison was removed from office for attending a conventicle intended to prevent a Frenchman being chosen as rector. This may have had a religious motivation.[37] Morison's evangelical beliefs certainly remained strong throughout his time abroad. In a begging letter to Cranmer, Morison expressed the optimistic belief that the English nobility supported true religion and church reform.[38]

Morison's study of civil law suggests that he was contemplating a career in church or government administration. Civil law was a useful tool for any Tudor civil servant; many of Henry's bishops, bureaucrats and ambassadors possessed civilian training. The civil law played a prominent role in the justifications of Henry's Royal Supremacy and Morison later used his working knowledge of the civil law in several of his polemical tracts.[39] His legal interests extended to suggesting that English law might be codified along the lines of the *Corpus Juris Civilis*; he even produced a demonstration volume to show how this might be achieved. Morison's efforts may well have been inspired by the attempts of Andrea Gritti to introduce the principles of the *Corpus Juris Civilis* to Venice. The issue of law reform was being discussed in 1530s Venice and Morison may well have heard of the fate of the *correzione Gritti* of 1537 from Harvel. Gritti's proposals were rejected, at least in part, due to the desire of the patricians to retain customary privileges and

---

[37] Woolfson, *Padua*, 34–5.   [38] *LP* VI 1582.

[39] Morison alluded to the civil law in the *Apomaxis*, *Remedy*, *Protestation*, *Epistle* and his *Persuasion*.

Morison was aware that a defence of custom might be one barrier to the implementation of his (less radical) scheme in England.[40]

Morison's studies at Padua reveal that he was interested in pursuing a broader range of studies than just civil law. By his own admission, he wanted to return to England skilled in Greek philosophy and theology. Though there is little direct evidence of his theological studies, Morison's later writings indicate that he was well versed in the ideas of contemporary theologians and patristic authors and had a working understanding of medieval theologians. He certainly kept an eye on theological publications in the Veneto, noting the large number of Erasmus' *Paraphrases* on Paul's letters to the Romans available.[41] The lectures he attended reflected his interest in Greek, including those of Sebastiano Fausto da Longiano.[42] Fausto was a dedicated Lutheran and may have introduced Morison to the works of Francesco Petrarch; his commentary on this author, which treated Petrarch as a proto-Protestant, was published at Venice in 1532[43] and such ideas would have appealed to the young scholar. Morison was seemingly also a tutor of Greek himself: George Lily, able to read numerous classical texts, attributed his skills to the instruction he had received from Morison, with whom he had read Euripides and Aristophanes.[44]

Aristotle dominated Paduan philosophy, a point not lost on the English students there. During his time in the Veneto Morison bought both the works of Aristotle himself, which he boasted he would read in their entirety, as well as numerous commentaries on the Greek philosopher.[45] He later owned a substantial collection of Greek texts, which included a large number of works by and commentaries on Aristotle.[46] He studied with Giuseppe Polonus, the pupil of the celebrated Aristotelian philosopher Marcantonio Passeri de Genova, and at the very least attended de Genova's lectures as philosophy chair. Although de Genova took a largely scholastic approach and defended Averroes' Latin translations of his favourite authors (Theophrastus, Themistius and Simplicius), he blended this with more recent humanist philology. When de Genova employed political analogies, he turned not

---

[40] J. Shaw, *The Justice of Venice* (Oxford, 2006), 13–15; *Persuasion*, fos. 20^r–1^r.
[41] BL Cotton Nero BVI, fos. 160^r, 149^r [*LP* X 320, IX 687].   [42] *LP* IX 1034.
[43] W. J. Kennedy, *Authorizing Petrarch* (London, 1994), 67–72.
[44] BL Cotton Nero BVI, fos. 167^r, 156^r [*LP* IX 1034, X 321]; *LP* VIII 581.
[45] P. F. Grendler, *Universities of the Italian Renaissance* (London, 2002), 403; *LP* VI 314, IX 102, 103.
[46] A discussion of Morison's Greek books can be found in Chapter 8.

to Aristotle, but to Plato, a tactic that Morison was frequently to adopt after his return to England.[47]

In addition Morison attended the humanities lectures of Giovan Battista Egnazio, a close friend of Gasparo Contarini. Egnazio had collaborated with the Aldine press on several Latin histories before taking up the Latin chair at Padua in 1520. A dedicated Ciceronian, he was also vociferously opposed to both clerical and secular tyranny.[48] In 1533, Winter, and presumably also Morison, heard the lectures of the professor of literature and accomplished Ciceronian Lazarro Bonamico. Bonamico tutored students regardless of their religious views and had connections to the English community in the Veneto, lodging with Reginald Pole in Padua in the following year.[49]

Morison kept a keen eye on Italian literary trends. On at least one occasion, he sent Starkey a copy of verses by a contemporary author 'Blosius' celebrating the emperor's exploits against the Turks.[50] He was also familiar with recently printed books, including Paulo Giovio's *Commentario de la cose de Turchi* (1532).[51] Morison became acquainted with the works of two authors that he was to employ extensively in his own literary endeavours: Marc Antonio Sabellico and Niccolò Machiavelli. The Italian humanist Sabellico's world history was gaining popularity among reformers as it offered several strands of thought that reinforced an anti-papal message. Sabellico dated the institution of the papacy to the pontificate of Boniface III, following the *Historia Vitis Pontificum* of Bartholomaeus Sacchi de Platina, a former papal librarian with unimpeachable credentials and motivations. Once Nicholas of Cusa and Lorenzo Valla had demonstrated that the *Donation of Constantine* was a forgery, it lost its potency as a tool with which to censure the papacy, although other gifts accepted by the papacy could still be criticized. Hence Sabellico's emphasis on the emperor Phocas as the originator of the papacy had its uses. It allowed later authors, including Morison, to put a polemical spin on the origins of the papacy. Concurrently, Sabellico's emphasis on the equality of Venice and Rome

---

[47] Mayer, *Starkey*, 54–5, 194–5; J. B. Ross, 'Venetian Schools and Teachers, Fourteenth to early Sixteenth Centuries: A Survey and Study of Giovanni Battista Egnazio', *RQ*, 29 (1976), 536–56; *LP* IX 103.

[48] *LP* IX 1034, VIII 581.

[49] BL Cotton Nero BVI, fo. 122ʳ [*LP* VI 314]; Mayer, *Starkey*, 53.

[50] BL Cotton Nero BVI, fo. 161ʳ [*LP* X 320].

[51] *Berkowitz*, 100–1. Suggested by Morison's praise of the Turks in the *Lamentation* (Aiiiʳ). Giovio's *Commentary* was translated into English in 1546.

was attractive to those seeking to undermine the importance of the Holy See, as were his recurrent criticisms of the long-standing financial abuses of the papacy. Morison's admiration for Sabellico and historical application of his work was relatively unusual among Englishmen at this time—it was not until Elizabeth's reign that knowledge of the historian's works became more widespread.[52]

Morison was the first English author to refer to Machiavelli in print and he was still reading Machiavelli's works in the 1550s. He admired Machiavelli's mastery of the vernacular; one of his reasons for reading the Florentine's works was probably to improve his own written style.[53] Machiavelli was also a useful author from whom to draw pertinent anecdotes. By the time Morison left Italy, the *Discourses* and *Florentine History* had appeared in print. He may also have read *The Prince*, which was circulating in manuscript,[54] for though Morison did not cite *The Prince*, he did draw references from the *Discourses* on three occasions and once utilized the *Florentine History*.[55] Given the reliance of the *Discourses* on Livy, this may merely reflect Morison's preference for classical over more recent exempla.

Zeeveld suggested that Morison viewed Machiavelli as a master of practical doctrine.[56] Certainly, when Morison described his friend Nicholas Throckmorton as a 'Machiavelist' in 1551, it was in recognition of his political acumen.[57] Moreover, in Bishop Kennet's seventeenth-century collections of maxims, Morison is credited with a saying that implies a Machiavellian influence: 'Policy is not the learninge of some ruler, but the observation of circumstances, with a present mind in all junctures of affaires.'[58] Morison would have found support for some of Machiavelli's principles in Erasmus' *Enchiridion*, a text he certainly read.[59] Despite his apparent recognition of Machiavelli's superior ability

---

[52] R. A. Chavasse, 'The Reception of Humanist Historiography in Northern Europe: M. A. Sabellico and John Jewel', *Renaissance Studies*, 2 (1988), 327–38. By 1530 two Venetian editions of Sabellico's *Opera* had appeared, as well as several Venetian editions of his *Enneads* and *History of Venice*. For Morison's use of Sabellico see ch. 2.

[53] SP68/10, fos. 12^r–13^r [*Cal. For.*, 530].   [54] Zeeveld, *Foundations*, 77.

[55] *Apomaxis*, Xii^{r-v} (*Florentine History*, 1.3–4); *Remedy*, Bi^r (*Discourses*, 1.8; taken from Dante's *Convivio*, I. ii. 54, not from *De monarchia* as Machiavelli states); *Remedy*, Eii^v (*Discourses*, 1.54); *Invective*, aiv^v–v^r (*Discourses*, 3.6). Dante's depiction of papal monarchy as corrupt would have appealed to Morison and it is possible that he had also read Dante's works.

[56] Zeeveld, *Foundations*, 14.

[57] SP68/9, fo. 111^r [*Cal. For.*, 489]. This suggests that Morison had read *The Prince*.

[58] BL Sloane 1523, fo. 30^r.

[59] F. Raab, *The English Face of Machiavelli* (London, 1964), 10–11.

as a political commentator, Morison did not employ the Florentine's political doctrines in his own tracts. Machiavelli's notions of *virtù* and *nobilitas* are difficult to reconcile with Morison's own position on these topics. He may have openly praised Machiavelli, but his printed use of the Florentine was exclusively historical. Morison was not alone in citing Machiavelli's works with approval: William Thomas and Henry Parker, Lord Morley, also did so.[60] However, Morison never went as far as the author of the 'Machiavellian Treatise', who extensively used the political tenets of Machiavelli's *Prince* and *Discourses* in a treatise offering advice to Philip and Mary on topics including the succession.[61]

Padua had the leading medical school in Europe at this time. Many of Morison's English friends in Padua, including John Friar and Thomas Starkey, were either medical students or clearly interested in medical matters. Morison's letters from Italy reveal that he too had a keen interest in medicine and he was surprisingly well informed about occurrences within the faculty of medicine. He knew about the struggles for precedence between two tutors, Marcus Antonius and Vincenzio Maggio of Brescia; Henry Cole later expected Morison to be familiar with two other Paduan physicians. Morison's medical interests may have developed out of his fascination with Greek; scholars at Padua in the first half of the sixteenth century were attempting to reconstruct the Greek canons of Hippocrates and Galen, challenging the dominance of the Arabic tradition. In 1534, he may well have heard Matthew Curzio's exposition of Galen in Greek. If Morison received any medical tuition, it may have been at the hands of the tutors Marcus Antonius and Vittorio Benedicto Faventino, who had contacts with the English Paduans.[62] Morison's interest in medicine was enduring. John Caius, who also studied at Padua, believed that his edition of a Galenic text would appeal to Morison in 1544, and in the late 1540s Morison read some of Caius' medical manuscripts.[63] By the 1550s Morison owned a substantial collection of medical texts in Latin and Greek.

    [60] C. Morris, 'Machiavelli's Reputation in Tudor England', *Il Pensiero Politico*, 2 (1969), 417.
    [61] P. S. Donaldson (ed.), *A Machiavellian Treatise by Stephen Gardiner* (Cambridge, 1975), 16–19.
    [62] Woolfson, *Padua*, ch. 3; *LP* VII 900ii; IX 917, 648; BL Cotton Nero BVI, fos. 144[r], 150[r] [*LP* IX 687, XI 513].
    [63] J. Caius, *Pergameni nobilissimi medici libri aliquot Graeci . . .* (Basel, 1544), Aa2[v]; *idem*, *A boke or counseill against the disease commonly called the sweate, or sweatyng sicknesse* (London, 1552), Avi[r–v].

Non-medics owning several medical texts was not unusual, but the extent of Morison's collection was.[64]

Morison cultivated friendships with many of the other students at Padua. He claimed to have known Cosimo Gheri de Fano, a keen Aristotelian, 'wonderfull well'. Gheri was, in Morison's opinion, 'as well lerned a yonge man as fewe were in Italy', who was accomplished in 'elegante and eloquent' literature.[65] Gheri was also connected to Starkey, Pole and several other members of the English community in the Veneto.[66] While it is tempting to extrapolate from Morison's association with Gheri that he also associated with Gheri's wider academic clique and many prominent reform-minded Catholics, there is no concrete evidence to support this.[67] Morison corresponded with some of his Paduan associates after his return to England, including Portugal's foremost humanist, Damiano a Gois. This friendship later splintered as a result of their divergent political and religious allegiances: in October 1540 a Gois sent a sycophantic letter to Reginald Pole which denounced Morison as an ingrate.[68] Yet just one year earlier when a Gois was assisting Beatus Rhenanus with an improved edition of Tertullian, he called upon Morison's help procuring a variant manuscript of Tertullian from the Royal Library, which contained passages that were not in the Froben edition of March 1539. Morison dutifully petitioned his friend John Leland, the Royal Librarian, who granted his request. Although Morison sent the manuscript to a Gois, Leland had to reassure Rhenanus in June that it was on its way to Sélestat. Leland strongly implied that a Gois was being disingenuous, providing useful context for a Gois' letter to Pole.[69]

INFORMAL STUDIES IN VENICE

Winter proved to be an unreliable patron. He soon complained of the shame of his poverty. Cromwell was concerned and gave Winter

[64] P. M. Jones, 'Science and Medicine', in L. Hellinga and J. B. Trapp (eds.), *Cambridge History of the Book in Britain*, iii: *1400–1557* (Cambridge, 2000), 446–7. For Morison's library, see ch. 8.

[65] *Exhortation*, Cvii[r].   [66] Mayer, *Starkey*, 194.

[67] A. Overell, 'An English Friendship and Italian Reform: Richard Morison and Michael Throckmorton, 1532–38', *JEH*, 57 (2006), 485–8, explores the possibilities.

[68] M. Bataillon, *Études sur le Portugal au temps de l'humanisme* (Coimbra, 1952), 141–5; *LP* XVI 154.

[69] http://www.tertullian.org/articles/petitmengin_malmesbury_eng.htm.

40s., but Winter's servants did not get paid—George Lawson, for one, quickly found himself destitute. After a brief absence, Winter was back in Padua by April 1533, but was less welcome; unable to secure lodging with a respectable family, he had to rent a house.[70] Morison was also left financially compromised. He was driven to write begging letters home to England to Cranmer, Cromwell and (after 1534) Starkey. Necessity forced Morison to borrow money from his friends, many of whom were not much better off: in February 1536 he owed them over 37 crowns. One friend, John Friar, wrote to Starkey singling out Morison's extreme poverty for special mention. Soon afterwards Morison abandoned all hope of further aid from Winter, who had consistently failed to send him a loan or help him sell his pension, despite his many requests. Fortunately Starkey sent money, without which Morison claimed he would not have survived. At one point Morison was so poor that he could not even afford to clothe himself, joking to Starkey that he must be Michael Throckmorton's servant, as he was dressed in his livery (clothes). On 4 May 1536, confident of a position in England, Morison promised Starkey that he would soon thank him in person.[71]

In the summer of 1535 Morison's penury forced him to abandon his official studies. He moved to Venice where he resided in the households of Reginald Pole and Edmund Harvel, an English agent. Pole's household was a locus for many English and continental scholars.[72] Harvel's quasi-ambassadorial household also offered a potential refuge for English scholars. Barrington has argued that Harvel, not Pole, was the most important point of contact for Englishmen in Italy in the late 1530s and 1540s. He pointed out that Pole's household was much more international than Schenck, Zeeveld and other earlier commentators were prepared to admit and that Pole and his household were peripatetic, which necessarily limited Pole's ability to act as a focus for the English diaspora. Morison's case shows that both Pole and Harvel were important potential patrons for English scholars in the Veneto.[73] At a key moment Pole provided vital financial aid (Morison later punned that Pole had saved him from (Thomas) Winter's cold), but Pole's itinerancy limited his utility as a patron: when Pole left Venice

---

[70] *LP* V 1210, 1285 (iii, v, vi), 1452, 1670; BL Cotton Nero BVI, fo. 122[r] [*LP* VI 314].

[71] Ibid., fo. 148[r], SP1/103, fos. 122[r], 229[r] [*LP* IX 1011, X 661, 801]; *LP* VII 1311, 1318, IX 101–3, 198, 687, X 320–1, 417–19, 565, 660.

[72] Mayer, *Prince and Prophet*, 50–4; idem, *Starkey*, ch. 6.

[73] Caius, *Pergameni nobilissimi medici*, Aa2[r]; R. Barrington, 'Two Houses Both Alike in Dignity: Reginald Pole and Edmund Harvel', *HJ*, 39 (1996), 895–913.

the financial aid he had given Morison ended.[74] Morison's numerous letters to England asking for financial assistance suggest that the help he received from Pole was either intermittent, or insufficient, or both. Furthermore, Mayer has demonstrated the precariousness of Pole's own finances, which severely limited his ability to act as a traditional patron.[75] For a destitute evangelical scholar such as Morison, the 'spiritual patronage' that Pole offered would not have been sufficient in financial or spiritual terms.

In September 1535 Pole stayed with Harvel, before moving to a house on the Grand Canal. By 14 November he had moved again and was staying with Donato Gianotti, the reform-minded advocate of oligarchic republicanism. It is not clear whether Morison accompanied Pole or remained with Harvel, but he certainly remained in contact with Pole's household as in December 1535 George Lily described Morison as 'one of our flock'.[76] Pole's household attracted a range of Italian scholars, as Mayer has vividly shown. Morison's continued association with it will have brought him into contact with the philosophers Benedetto Lampridio and Lazarro Bonamico, who stayed there in October 1535.[77] Morison certainly knew and was probably on friendly terms with Gianotti, as one of Morison's friends assumed a familiarity existed between the two men.[78] Yet Barrington's observation that Pole and Morison's relationship was one of sometime patron to destitute scholar, rather than friendship, seems correct.[79] In Harvel's household, Morison may have made other important contacts and associated with Italian and German evangelicals. Certainly by the late 1530s and 1540s, Harvel knew a number of Protestants, including his physician and secretary.[80] Morison, like Harvel, may well have heard the renowned Italian preacher Pier Paulo Vergerio as in December 1535 both Morison and Vergerio were in Venice.[81]

In the summer of 1535 Morison was so destitute that he was forced to pawn some books. Pole brought relief in August, helping

---

[74] *LP* X 320; SP1/103, fo. 122ʳ [*LP* X 661].
[75] T. F. Mayer, 'When Maecenas was Broke: Cardinal Pole's "Spiritual" Patronage', *SCJ*, 27 (1996), 419–35.
[76] *LP* IX 819, 1034, X 565. The designation is ambiguous.
[77] Mayer, *Starkey*, 196–8.
[78] *LP* X 320; BL Cotton Vitellius BXIV, fo. 264ᵛ.
[79] Barrington, 'Two Houses', 902. Mayer erroneously attributes *LP* XI 74 to Morison (*CRP*, i.116). Pole's claims in *CRP*, i.233 appear to be overstated.
[80] J. Woolfson, 'Edmund Harvel', *ODNB*, 25.644–5.
[81] A. J. Schutte, *Pier Paul Vergerio* (Geneva, 1977), 96–7; *LP* IX 1029.

Morison to recover his Aristotle, though he still could not afford
the Greek commentaries he felt were essential to his studies.[82] Even
when in deepest penury, Morison paid attention to his library: 'I was
owght of al apparel, certayne bookes I coud not choose but by.'[83]
Morison's appeals to Cromwell for patronage eventually paid dividends,
perhaps helped by the petitions of his friends in England. By the
end of February 1536, he was assured that Cromwell's sponsorship
was on its way. Morison therefore offered to return to England if
Cromwell thought he could serve his country.[84] By the end of March
he was even more confident of Cromwell's favour and requested money
for 'the Greek authors, which you know, either cannot be bought
in England or are sold for the most unfair prices'.[85] Morison most
likely returned to England in possession of a notable collection of
Greek texts. He certainly told Starkey of his ambition to return to
England with a library full of books and was hopeful that Cromwell
would cover his expenses.[86] In the meantime Cole had kindly taken
a chamber in Padua for him; Morison planned to stay there, 'untyl
I be compellyd otherwise', though he was unsure how he would
afford it.[87]

Although he had kept enough terms at various universities to warrant one, there is no concrete evidence that Morison ever received
a higher degree than his BA. He was described as 'magister' on a
bishop's register in 1539, but there is no record that he received an
MA from Padua, which rarely awarded degrees lower than doctorates
in the sixteenth century.[88] Morison may simply have been following too broad a programme of study in these years to satisfy the
requirements of any specific degree. Another explanation may lie in
the fact that Paduan degrees were the most expensive to obtain in
Europe at this time. Morison, who was constantly borrowing money
from his friends, may not have been able to afford to supplicate.
Although there does not seem to be surviving evidence that he petitioned to be allowed to take his degree without paying the fees,
as Edward Wotton had successfully done in 1525, this remains a
possibility.[89]

---

[82] *LP* IX 102, 103.   [83] SP1/103, fo. 122ʳ [*LP* X 661].   [84] *LP* X 372, 224.
[85] SP1/103, fo. 32ʳ [*LP* X 565].
[86] BL Cotton Nero BVI, fo. 161ʳ [*LP* X 320]; *LP* X 417.
[87] SP1/103, fo. 122ʳ [*LP* X 661].
[88] WRO 716.093/2648/9/iii, fo. 2ʳ; Grendler, *Universities*, 172–3.
[89] Woolfson, *Padua*, 15.

THE *VITA ACTIVA*

Morison strongly believed that it was the scholar's duty to put his education to the service of his country. Intellectual ability and 'vertuos qualities' were gifts from God; anyone who possessed them should use his talents appropriately and should not 'take the fruytes and profettes' thereof 'to hys owne use'. Consequently Morison composed treatises in 'the houres whych I have had to use at myn own libertie', with the aim of aiding his king and commonweal.[90] In May 1536 Morison left Italy for a career in royal service. His journey back to England took him through Germany, where he paid keen attention to agricultural practices.[91] Within a few months of setting foot on English soil Morison was composing works of printed propaganda for the government. He penned two tracts against the Pilgrimage of Grace (*A Remedy for Sedition* and *A Lamentation*) in 1536; one tract to celebrate the birth of Prince Edward (*A Comfortable Consolation*); one treatise in defence of the Royal Supremacy and Divorce (*Apomaxis*); two tracts against the General Council called by Paul III (*A Protestation* and *An Epistle*) in 1537 and 1538; a tract on the Exeter Conspiracy (*An Invective against Treason*) in 1538–9; and *An exhortation to stirre all Englyshe men to the defence of theyr countreye* (1539). The arguments and implications of Morison's literary efforts will be discussed in later chapters. Here, a brief analysis of Morison's sources when writing will demonstrate how extensively he brought his learning to bear in the service of the state and how greatly deserved was his scholarly reputation.

In Berkowitz's judgement Morison's *Remedy* and *Lamentation* 'displayed an erudition that could not but have impressed the generality while it delighted the humanists'.[92] The judgement of Morison's contemporaries was certainly favourable. One humanist friend lauded him as one of England's 'ornaments of literature'.[93] Another considered Morison an outstanding rhetorician possessed of exceptional eloquence, who 'writes Greek and Latin skilfully'.[94] If all of Morison's tracts are analysed, it becomes apparent that Morison was an even more accomplished scholar than Berkowitz thought. It is not possible to trace all of the exact references upon which Morison drew, as a number of the

---

[90] *Persuasion*, fos. 7[r], 5[r].   [91] *Remedy*, Eiv[r].
[92] *Berkowitz*, 65. Much of the discussion that follows is indebted to Berkowitz's study.
[93] Caius, *Pergameni nobilissimi medici*, Aa2[v].   [94] Bale, *Scriptorum Britanniae*, NNii[r].

examples he cites could plausibly have been taken from more than one work. Moreover, there is no reason to believe that Morison had all of his sources to hand when composing his works. From the very start of his education, Morison would have been expected to learn passages from classical authors by heart.[95] He would have been able to reproduce sections of classical texts from memory, which perhaps explains why his precise source text can sometimes be difficult to trace.

Morison certainly drew upon an extensive range of sources in his surviving literary works. The *Remedy* contains a greater proportion of classical references than Morison's later tracts, although these are also saturated with ancient exemplars. In these later compositions, biblical examples become more prominent, which is unsurprising given that Morison's message was becoming increasingly evangelical.[96] The *Comfortable Consolation* even invoked Firmianus Lactantius on the praise men owed to God.[97] Morison relied heavily on historical works for exempla with which to illustrate his polemical tracts and treatises. His reliance on Greek histories, which were not as widely printed or read as Latin ones,[98] marks him out as unusual. Herodotus was used extensively, supplying Morison with many of the exempla for the *Remedy* and *Lamentation*.[99] Morison also drew extensively upon Plutarch's *Parallel Lives*, probably because it was considered a good source of moral philosophy.[100] He cited incidents from the *Lives* of Agis, Alexander, Demosthenes, Marcus Cato, Pyrrhus, Themistocles, Aemilius, Anthony and Brutus, and his reliance on Plutarchan sources also extended to the *Moralia* and the Pseudo-Plutarchan *Parallelae Minoria*. Indeed one of the drafts of the *Remedy* advocated that the reader peruse Plutarch, whose works were not yet widely available in English.[101] Two passages of the *Invective* were based on Pliny's *Natural History*, which Morison also referred to in a draft sermon.[102] Berkowitz has traced Morison's use of Diodorus Siculus and Diogenes Laertius in

---

[95] U. Potter, 'Performing Arts in the Tudor Classroom', in L. Kermode and J. Scott-Warren (eds.), *Tudor Drama Before Shakespeare* (Basingstoke, 2004), 145–7.

[96] See below, chs. 2–3.　　[97] *Comfortable Consolation*, Dii^v.

[98] P. Burke, 'A Survey of the Popularity of Ancient Historians, 1450–1700', *History and Theory*, 5 (1966), 135–8.

[99] *Berkowitz*, 266–7. Herodotus (ii.74) was also cited in the *Persuasion* (fo. 6^r).

[100] Burke, 'Ancient Historians', 142.

[101] Remedy, Ci^v–Cii^r, Fii^v, Gi^v, Eii^r; *Berkowitz*, 66, 97; *Invective*, Di^v, Bv^v, Aiv^v; *Persuasion*, fo. 18^v; *Exhortation*, Av^r, Av^v–Avi^r (Themistocles); *Comfortable Consolation*, Biii^r–iv^v; SP6/13, fo. 32^r.

[102] *Invective*, Bv^r, Bvi^{r-v}, SP1/123, fo. 168^v; Pliny, *Natural History*, 7.16, 8.40, 33.19.

his 1536 tracts.[103] Morison also invoked Roman historians, frequently using Livy, Herodian, Dio Cassius and, more unusually, Tacitus;[104] he quoted from Justin and Julius Caesar at least once.[105] And as his historical references were not limited to ancient texts, he also drew upon several more recent writers including Froissart, Paulo Giovo, Machiavelli and Sabellico.[106]

Morison's reliance upon Greek authors was even more extensive than Berkowitz noted and the range of authors used by Morison is more extensive still if one also considers his later works. In addition to the Greek historians, Berkowitz traced Morison's use of Julian, Lycurgus, Demosthenes, Plato, Aristotle and Achilles Tatius in his 1536 tracts,[107] and unpublished notes add the lives of Artaxerxes and Nicias. Morison called upon some of these authors again; certainly mentions of Demosthenes are made in later compositions.[108] He had read a number of Plato's Dialogues, quoting from the *Phaedo*, *Hipparchus*, *Charmides* and *Timaeus* in his letters and in his literary efforts.[109] He used anecdotes from Sophocles on at least one occasion[110] and even more unusually, Morison drew upon Greek poetry in the later works. An epigram by Ausonius featured in the *Exhortation*, as did one by the more obscure Statyllius Flacus.[111] Morison's extensive citation of Greek literature was unusual by the standards of his day.

Philosophical precepts from Plato and Aristotle also run through Morison's works, which is unsurprising given his exposure to their ideas in Padua. That said, the only direct citation from Aristotle that can be affirmed is from the *Nicomachean Ethics* and it is difficult to find much that is distinctive about Morison's Aristotelianism.[112] Plato featured prominently in the *Remedy*, but often Morison applied Plato to the English situation without direct quotation. Thus Morison summarized Plato's views on the inability of youth and the 'common people' to discuss matters of law: 'it is no part of the people's play to discuss

---

[103] *Berkowitz*, 66, 260, 263–8.

[104] *Invective*, aiii^r; Dio Cassius, *Roman History*, 77.1–4; *Berkowitz*, 66, 164, 243; *Invective*, av^{r-v}; Tacitus, *Annals*, xv.54–5.

[105] Justin, *Epitome of Trogus Pompeius*, 15.3; *Apomaxis*, Oii^v; *Berkowitz*, 91.

[106] See below chs. 2–3.   [107] *Berkowitz*, 66, 260, 263–8.

[108] SP6/4, fos. 51^r–68^r, Demosthenes, *Olynthiacs*; *Invective*, aiii^r, Dio Cassius, *Roman History*, 77.1–4.

[109] SP1/81, fo. 52^r; Plato, *Hipparchus*, 231d; *Berkowitz*, 127, 155; *Comfortable Consolation*, Bi^r; Plato, *Phaedo*, 60b–c.

[110] *Exhortation*, Av^v and possibly also *Invective*, Av^v.

[111] Ausonius, *Epigrams*, 10; *Exhortation*, Civ^r, Di^v.   [112] *Berkowitz*, 81–4.

acts made in the parliament'.[113] Equally Morison plundered Plato
for exempla.[114] Not rigidly attached to the ideas of one philosopher
over another, Morison blended their ideas with notions drawn from
other sources to produce a synthesis that fitted his overall argument.
Indeed Morison's overall schema, which increasingly worked towards a
Christian, godly commonwealth, in many ways more closely resembled
Augustine's *City of God* than Plato's *Republic*.

As Berkowitz noted, Morison seemingly found Latin authors less
useful when composing his propaganda tracts, though he did draw
anecdotes from Ovid, Seneca and Livy, as well as from Frontinus.[115]
Unpublished notes by Morison add Oppian and Ulpian to the list and
also include general references to Seneca and Cicero.[116] Ciceronianism
was strong in England,[117] and Morison, as one might expect, was well
versed in Ciceronian precepts. The absence of a direct citation of Cicero
that Berkowitz noted in the *Remedy* and *Lamentation* is certainly not
true of Morison's later compositions.[118] Here he drew directly upon
the *Orator*, the *Brutus* and the *Letters to Atticus*, as well as adopting
more general principles, such as that found in *De Legibus* that law
was the foundation of the welfare of the state.[119] Even if he did not
draw as many exempla from Cicero for his treatises and polemics
as one might expect, Morison often quoted Cicero in his personal
correspondence.[120]

Classical literature also influenced Morison's writings in less immediately obvious ways. In 1538–9, he published tracts that worked as
an Invective and an Encomium (the *Invective* and the *Exhortation*),
the two sides of the classical coin. He may have ignored Quintilian's
warnings (*De Oratore*, 12:9) on restraining invective, but he did adopt
the basic structure of the classical genre. In doing so he was following in

113 *Berkowitz*, 65, 66, 116, 118, 146, 150, 152, 155, 156, 279–80.
114 *Comfortable Consolation*, Bi^{r–v}; Plato's *Phaedo*, 60b–c.
115 *Berkowitz*, 66, 111, 140, 267–9; *Remedy*, Ciii^v, Seneca, *To the Emperor Nero on Mercy*,
I; *Remedy*, Aiii^r, Fiii^r; *Exhortation*, Cv; *Stratagems*, IV.7.vi; IV.3.iv; I.10.iv.
116 SP6/4, fos. 53^r–8^r.
117 H. Jones, *Master Tully: Cicero in Tudor England* (Nieuwkoop, 1998); J. Richards,
Rhetoric and Courtliness in Early Modern Literature (Cambridge, 2003); J. W. Binns, *Intellectual
Culture in Elizabethan and Jacobean England: The Latin Writings of the Age* (Leeds, 1990),
ch. 15.
118 *Berkowitz*, 66, 150, 261.
119 *Comfortable Consolation*, Dv^v, Cicero, *De Oratore* 2; Woolfson, *Padua*, 66–7, 167;
Persuasion, fo. 10^v, Cicero, *Brutus* 41; *Invective*, Bii^r, Cicero, *Letters to Atticus*; SP6/4,
fo. 67^{r–v}.
120 See for example SP1/112, fo. 181^r [*LP* XI 1481].

the footsteps not just of Cicero, but also of many Italian humanists.[121] Moreover, Morison's views on language were undoubtedly influenced by the revival of Quintilian's ideas as much as recent developments in philological methods.

A familiarity with a wide range of theological authors is apparent in Morison's works. His *Treatise on the Seven Sacraments* referenced fifteen patristic works, as well as medieval (Bede, Lombard, Aquinas, St Bernard, Rabanus Maurus) and modern authors (Erasmus and Melanchthon). Elsewhere he translated Johann Sturm and Martin Luther, and utilized the philological methods of Sante Pagnini.[122] In addition Morison was evidently interested in Tertullian's works.[123] His heavy reliance upon patristic authors reflects a trend among reformers, who were drawn to the potential of church history to reinforce their vision of the doctrine of their church and its ecclesiology. Unsurprisingly, given the importance he attached to it, Morison extensively quoted from scripture, the bulk of his references being from the Old Testament, with the exception of those in the *Treatise on the Seven Sacraments*. He did not use any of the available English texts and his method of translation makes it impossible to identify which of the Latin or Greek versions he was using, however.

Morison's surviving tracts indicate he was a much more accomplished scholar than even Berkowitz thought. In them, he conveyed a vast wealth of classical ideas whilst appropriating stories that were not otherwise easily available in English. This was, in part, undoubtedly Morison posturing for other English intellectuals. However, he probably also had a more altruistic motive: extensive citation from classical sources might not be as obvious a means of transmitting classical ideas as the translation of a complete text, but it was nonetheless significant. It was yet another way of improving the moral precepts available to Englishmen. In some respects, though on a smaller scale, it was reminiscent of the collections of ancient wisdom published by Morison's contemporaries Vives and Erasmus.

THE TRANSLATOR

Morison's humanist background and linguistic proficiency led him to engage in an activity that was fundamental to the humanist mindset:

---

[121] O. Kristeller, 'Humanism', in C. B. Schmitt and Q. Skinner (eds.), *The Cambridge History of Renaissance Philosophy* (Cambridge, 1988), 125.

[122] See below pp. 60, 74–6, 174–7.

[123] http://www.tertullian.org/articles/petitmengin_malmesbury_eng.htm.

translation. Rendering classical and Renaissance texts into the vernacular made ideas more widely available and thus improved the moral
and intellectual life of the state. This was an area where Morison's
scholarly interests could easily coincide with service to the crown. He
translated at least four discrete texts during his career: one classical
(Frontinus' *Stratagems*), one humanist (Vives' *Introduction to Wisdom*)
and two evangelical (Sturm's *Epistle* and Luther's *Freedom of a Christian
Man*).[124] Moreover he did not just undertake translations himself; he
also advocated that his friends translate. In 1548 Henry, first baron
Stafford rendered one of the seminal works of the Royal Supremacy,
Edward Foxe's *De vera differentia*, into English, encouraged by his
'frend Master Morrison', who had provided his source text.[125] Morison may have intended to help a conservative friend appear more
acceptable to Edward's government, or he may equally have hoped
that exposure to an early and effective work in defence of the Royal
Supremacy would help Stafford accommodate himself to the evangelical
regime.

Tudor humanists considered every aspect of the art of translation.
Laurence Humphrey's treatise *Interpretatio linguarum . . .* (1559) ranked
three possible methods of translation. First, purely literal translations
which were least acceptable: this form of translation, which frequently
resulted in nonsensical texts, had been a common practice in the medieval period. Secondly, there were overly loose translations: these too
were undesirable. Thirdly and ideally, Humphrey's translator would
adopt a *via media*, attaching equal importance to the words chosen
and the meaning of the passage under consideration.[126] An approach
that rejected an overly literal approach in favour of one more appre-
ciative of the sense of the text was in line with humanist sensibilities
and philological practice. The methodology Humphrey advocated was
employed by a number of Tudor translators. Thomas Wyatt sought
'rather the profite of the sentence then the nature of the wordes' in
translating Plutarch, while Thomas Twynne gave primacy to 'the intent

---

[124] Wood, Tanner and Berkenhout all believed Morison had translated Ludovicus Vives'
Satellitum sive symbola, but if he did, no trace remains (see for example Berkenhout, *Biographia
Literaria*, i. 468). Although the earliest English adaptation of the interlude *Calisto and Melebea*
has sometimes been attributed to Morison, John Rastell is a more likely candidate. G. Ungerer,
Anglo-Spanish Relations in Tudor Literature (Bern, 1956), 17–30.
[125] H. Stafford, *The true dyfferens betwen the regall power and the Ecclesiasticall power*
(London, 1548), Aii[v].
[126] Binns, *Intellectual Culture*, 210.

of the Authour'.[127] Morison also adopted this approach: his translations are fairly accurate, non-literal renderings of the original texts. He was, however, occasionally guilty of augmenting his references. Thus in the *Exhortation* he recounted and expanded a Greek epigram.[128]

As long as Morison rendered his source text without changing its meaning, he avoided being castigated by his contemporaries. Even with a theological work, the words did not have to be translated exactly, provided the theology was not altered. As Erasmus' New Testament had illustrated, the context and sense of a passage was paramount. Morison owned many philological texts including works by Alexander Alexandro, Guillaume Budé, Sante Pagnini, Angelo Poliziano and Lazare de Baif, which undoubtedly influenced his understanding of methods of translation.[129]

Morison's translations were certainly marked by an awareness of contemporary debates on language and translating practice. In the late fifteenth and early sixteenth centuries, humanists increasingly perceived the utility of their vernacular languages. In acting as a translator, Morison also recognized the benefits of the vernacular. Yet he still thought English an inferior language, apologizing to Starkey for writing in the 'rude' tongue (English).[130] In his *Perswasion that the law shold be in Laten*, Morison lamented the English language's lack of variety, deeming the legal terminology of English insufficient in comparison to the more expansive Latin vocabulary.[131] Many of Morison's contemporary scholars also considered the English language to be a necessary, but poor alternative to Latin, Greek and French. The predominant criticism of English remained its limited vocabulary. It was often derided as a 'vulgar language', a 'vulgare and naturall tongue', a 'grosse tongue . . . a rude and barren tong' which was full of 'barbarousnesse'.[132] Other humanists, however, were more generous: some, like John Caius,

---

[127] T. Wyatt, *Of the quyet of mynde* (London, 1528), Aii^v; T. Twynne, *Dionysius Periegetus, The surveye of the world* (London, 1572), *iv^{r–v}.

[128] *Exhortation*, Di^v. The epigram read: 'A man finding gold, left his halter; but the one who could not find the gold he had left, hanged himself with the halter he had found.' Morison probably found the epigram in the *Florilegium diversorum Epigrammatum in Septem Libros*. My thanks go to Alastair Blanshard for his help on this matter.

[129] BL Additional 40767, fos. 110^r–14^v.

[130] BL Cotton Nero BVI, fo. 113^r, SP1/103, fo. 229^r [*LP* X 661, 801].

[131] *Persuasion*, fo. 9^v.

[132] J. Bury, *A Godly Advertisement or good counsel of the famous orator Isocrates* (London, 1557), Aiii^v; T. Forrest, *A perfect looking glass for all estates* (London, 1580), Aiv^r; N. Howard, *A briefe chronicle . . . gathered first by Eutropius* (London, 1564), Bii^v; W. Barker, *The Bookes of Xenophon* (London, 1552), Avi^r.

believed the process of translation always robbed a work of some of its elegance.[133]

Despite his criticisms of the English language Morison believed in maintaining its purity and rejected the notion of appropriating terms from other languages. He warned that there 'shall arise doubts in a tonge that smelleth of the Latynyte but in deade barbarouse and far from it'.[134] Morison's concerns were probably sparked by classical texts, especially the works of Quintilian, who had condemned both the appropriation of foreign words into Latin and the adoption of neologisms, without regard for the ramifications of this for Latin grammar and style (*De Oratore* 1.5.5–8). Cicero, in contrast, advocated the use of neologisms, which would soon be softened by usage (*De natura deorum* 1.95). Morison's fellow humanists shared his concerns with the purity of their native language. Although Thomas Elyot in the *Boke named the Governour* had littered his text with Latin appropriations, later humanists such as Thomas Wilson, Roger Ascham and John Cheke were to disapprove of 'inkhorn' terms.[135] They asserted that foreign augmentations did not benefit the language, but instead diluted the purity of an adequate vernacular. Cheke believed that English should be written 'cleane and pure, unmixt and unmangeled with borrowing of other tunges'.[136] As Peter Burke has shown, this 'defensive purism' in the vernacular was also apparent across Europe and was advocated by the likes of Pietro Bembo and Henri Estienne. This paralleled a move by writers such as Leonardo Bruni, Christophe Longueil and Étienne Dolet to defend the purity of Latin.[137] Morison may not have created a systematic scheme like Anthony Gilby's new English orthography, but he clearly shared the same concerns over the purity of the English language that later inspired the efforts of Gilby and pervaded the writings of figures such as Thomas Smith.[138]

Morison put into practice the principles he had advocated in his *Perswasion*, paying attention to the etymology he considered so important.[139] Although he protested the inadequacy of his translation of

---

[133] Caius, *Counseill*, Avi[r–v].   [134] *Persuasion*, fos. 9[v]–10[r].

[135] T. Elyot, *The boke named the Governor* (London, 1531); J. M. Major, *Sir Thomas Elyot and Renaissance Humanism* (Lincoln, 1964), 17–20.

[136] Cheke's letter, printed in T. Hoby, *The courtier of Count Baldessar Castilio* (London, 1561), Zv[r]. See also J. Cheke, *The Gospel According to St Matthew*, ed. J. Goodwin (London, 1843), 15–16.

[137] P. Burke, *Languages and Communities in Early Modern Europe* (Cambridge, 2004), 142–6, 66–79.

[138] C. Shrank, *Writing the Nation in Reformation England* (Oxford, 2002).

[139] *Persuasion*, fo. 9[r].

Frontinus, contemporary opinion hailed its high quality. Peter Betham recommended it, praising Morison as a 'well learned' man of 'swete and eloquent spekynge' before moving on to a discussion of the use of pure English. Betham's opinion was shared by the only modern editor of Morison's works.[140] By using words considered to be truly English, Morison was one of the earliest English humanists to concern himself with the purity and limitations of the vernacular.

Morison was also keen to preserve the purity of his Latin. His letters from Padua and Venice in the 1530s, which remain the major indication of his attitude, are written primarily in Latin, with Italian and Greek asides. Morison did not mingle terms within the languages. He also appears to have been favourably inclined towards Cheke's proposals for a revised pronunciation of ancient Greek. At Cambridge in the early 1540s, Cheke and his fellow Greek scholar, Thomas Smith, argued that the corrupted contemporary practice of pronouncing Greek should be replaced with a pronunciation that more accurately reflected the pronunciation used by the ancients.[141] During Morison's embassy to the Imperial court, his secretary Roger Ascham promoted Cheke's pronunciation, starting a debate with the Heidelberg scholars Hubert Leodius, Nicholas Cisner and Jacobus Micyllus over whether the pronunciation of Greek used on the continent was correct, or if it was a corruption that had become tradition.[142] Morison certainly knew of Ascham's correspondence; he was following the debate and may have joined in himself.[143] Concurrently, Ascham compared Morison favourably to the 'Athenians' at Cambridge (Cheke, Smith, Wilson). Could he have done so, if Morison's views had not closely accorded with his own?

ASSESSMENT

Morison returned to England an eclectic, erudite scholar, well versed in civil law, philosophy and theology, interested in current debates

---

[140] P. Betham, *The precepts of warre, set forth by Iames the erle of Purlila* (London, 1544), Aiv[r]; *Berkowitz*, 65.

[141] On these debates see J. B. Mullinger, *The University of Cambridge* (Cambridge, 1911), 50–62; W. Hudson, *The Cambridge Connection and the Elizabethan Settlement of 1559* (Durham, NC, 1980), 43–6.

[142] L. V. Ryan, *Roger Ascham* (Stanford, CA, 1963), 141–2.

[143] *Whole Works*, I.ii.37.

on language, and familiar with the works of influential contemporary authors. He was a cosmopolitan scholar, well versed in humanist theories and methods, whose education and continued interests demonstrate the vibrancy of Tudor humanism and its eclecticism. To see early sixteenth-century English humanism as overwhelmingly Erasmian is to do it a disservice. Intellectual culture in this period was much more diverse, drawing on classical and modern continental ideas, particularly those current in Italy. Morison was well equipped for a career in government service and he could easily have entered English administration. However, a career as a government polemicist was marked out for him, and it was in this field that he primarily came to apply his considerable learning.

2

The Propagandist: Part 1

'THE BEST PROPAGANDIST PEN IN HENRICIAN ENGLAND'[1]

Morison was by far the most prolific of the propagandists working for Henry VIII in the 1530s. Over four years he produced at least nine tracts and may have been responsible for others. His works are best known for statements of seemingly unquestioning support for Henry such as 'Obey ye your kynge'.[2] Indeed, Morison's tame pen has almost become a historical commonplace. Baumer placed Morison firmly within the polemical tradition that established a 'cult of authority' under Henry VIII.[3] Zeeveld, Rex and Betteridge have all followed Baumer in making obedience the central theme of Morison's polemic.[4] Ryrie has located Morison among those evangelicals at court who were competing 'to make ever more extravagant claims of loyalty', while Sharpe has described Morison as an early modern 'spin doctor'.[5] Cooper went further still, following the Misses Dodds in suggesting that Morison deliberately misled his audience for the sake of a polemical point, such was his dedication to instilling conformity in Henry's subjects.[6] For Elton, Morison followed a different master and it was Cromwell, not Henry, who directed the course of the propaganda campaigns.[7] Yet the

---

[1] Elton, *Policy and Police*, 199.   [2] *Lamentation*, Ciii[v].

[3] Baumer, *Theory of Kingship*.

[4] Zeeveld, *Foundations*, ch. 4; R. Rex, 'The Crisis of Obedience: God's Word and Henry's Reformation', *HJ*, 39 (1996), 863–94; T. Betteridge, *Literature and Politics in the English Reformation* (Manchester, 2004), 44–6.

[5] Ryrie, *Gospel*, 60; K. M. Sharpe, *Reading Revolutions: The Politics of Reading in Early Modern England* (London, 2000), 31.

[6] J. P. D. Cooper, *Propaganda and the Tudor State: Political Culture in the West Country* (Oxford, 2003), ch. 6; M. H. and R. Dodds, *The Pilgrimage of Grace 1536–7 and the Exeter Conspiracy 1538* (Cambridge, 1915), vol. ii, chs. 22–3.

[7] Elton, *Policy and Police*, 185–6, 190–3, 199–207.

fundamental assumption that Morison was an unquestioning agent of
the government has largely gone unchallenged.

There is no denying that discussions of obedience and denunciations
of treason and rebellion are central to almost all of Morison's tracts.
However, Morison's works are more complex than this. They give us
insights into the ideology of the Henrician government and can shed
light on the direction of Henrician religious and foreign policy. They
also reveal that even the pens working for the government were not
unquestioning in their support for their king. Rather, they were yet
another group jostling to promote their own policy suggestions, and
their tracts were a very public means of doing just this.

THE LAMENTATION

Background

While Morison had been in Italy, events had moved quickly in England.
Henry VIII's rejection of Catherine of Aragon, his marriage to Anne
Boleyn and repudiation of papal authority in 1533–4 were to have
great consequences for Morison's own career. The English community
in the Veneto were aware of the developments in the English church,
although, as Morison noted, much of the news they heard was distorted.[8]
Partly due to the magnitude of events in England, and partly to their
misinterpretation on the continent, Henry's government sponsored a
vast array of printed propaganda aimed at justifying and defending
Henry's Royal Supremacy to domestic and international audiences. It
was in this arena that Morison was to start his career in England. He
was first asked to produce a defence of the annulment of Henry's first
marriage and the establishment of the Royal Supremacy in answer to a
continental propagandist, but the publication of this tract was delayed
as his pen was required to deal with more pressing events.

In 1536, when rebellion broke out in the north of England, printed
propaganda was used not just to dissuade Henry's rebellious subjects
from further insurrection, but also to persuade Henry's other subjects
not to join the Pilgrims. The government had to produce responsive
propaganda against the Lincolnshire Rising and the Pilgrimage of
Grace and did not have the time to plan pre-emptive works. Two

---

[8] *LP* IX 198.

printed tracts purportedly written by the king denounced rebellion and dealt with specific complaints of the rebels.[9] During the course of the rebellion, Morison and several other scholars such as Thomas Starkey were commissioned to write polemical tracts against the northern rebels. By no means all of these were printed, but they may all have circulated in manuscript. Certainly 'a letter sent to the commons that rebel' was intended for dissemination. Alongside the king's answers to the rebels, two works by Morison, a *Lamentation* and *Remedy for sedition* were ultimately chosen for publication and distribution. The *Lamentation* was probably written before 15 October, the *Remedy* sometime after 26 October.[10] Although they were issued anonymously, they were both undoubtedly from Morison's pen.[11] Morison informed his friend Henry Philips that he had written 'my lamentacion' 'in a after none and a nyght' and that he had 'made a reamedy of sedition'. His embarrassed claims that 'I am compelled to do thynges in such haste, that I am ashamed to thynke they be myn when I se them abrode' was probably mere posturing: many passages from the two tracts are almost identical to passages in his *Apomaxis*.[12] Baskerville has shown that several points were moderated before the *Remedy* appeared in print, but this was a question of emphasis not content.[13]

Several references in the *Remedy* and the *Lamentation* indicate that they were written with a London audience in mind. Thus Morison praised 'the noble and faythefull citie of London' for its loyalty, in contrast to the 'rude countreyes'. Appealing to the inhabitants of London could secure the support of key conservatives at court and encourage the loyalty of the capital. On a more general note, Morison took issue with divisive titles such as northern and southern, arguing that they were a cause of resentment. It would be far better if 'we were all called Englyshemen, of this countrey, or that, as of Yorke and London'.[14] Throughout his works, Morison consistently appealed to English identity and sought to bind Englishmen to their king and his policies. Indeed Morison had England itself appeal to the commons to be

---

[9] *Ansvvere made by the kynges hyghnes to the petitions of the rebelles in Yorkeshire* (London, 1536); *Ansvvere to the petitions of the traytours and rebelles in Lyncolneshyre* (London, 1536).

[10] SP1/113, fos. 250ʳ–5ᵛ; SP6/9, fos. 219ʳ–21ʳ; Zeeveld, *Foundations*, 175–7.

[11] C. R. Baskerville, 'Sir Richard Morison as the Author of Two Anonymous Tracts on Sedition', *Library*, 4th ser. 17 (1937), 83–7. Extant drafts of the tracts are at SP6/13, fos. 16ʳ–24ʳ, 25ʳ–33ʳ [*LP* XI 1409]; SP1/240, fos. 228ʳ–30ʳ.

[12] SP1/113, fo. 212ʳ [*LP* XI 1482].   [13] Baskerville, 'Richard Morison', 86–7.

[14] *Lamentation*, Ciiʳ; *Remedy*, Diiiᵛ, Eiʳ⁻ᵛ.

loyally unified behind Henry VIII.[15] The tracts were also undoubtedly among the books the king had sent to the northern rebels by 2 November. Henry himself claimed he would be content if the rebels would 'bestow some time in the reading of an honest remedy as of so many extreme and desperate mischiefs'.[16]

'Obey ye your kynge'

The main purpose of the *Lamentation*, the reason for its very composition, was to denounce sedition and instil true obedience, the 'badge of a trewe christen man', to the anointed king. Kings should be treated with reverence, and even slight infringements on their sovereignty should be feared. Thus Morison related David's contrition for cutting Saul's robe: even this act by one of God's elect was an affront to Saul's dignity. Englishmen were meant to be shamed further by Morison's account of the subservience of the Turks to their master. Disobedience and disrespect towards princes was against God's ordinance. Consequently, Morison's readers were exhorted to 'Obey thy prince' and 'gyve your prynce suche thynges, as perteyne unto hym'. If obedience was a Christian duty, then sedition was a sin. Morison directly equated disobedience to the king with betrayal of the country: 'Who is he that can thynke him selfe to have any veyne of an honeste man, that feareth not god, that loveth not his countrey, that obeyeth not his prince?' 'Traitor' was interchangeable with 'rebel'. Morison pointed out that honest men should 'deteste and abhorre sedicious traytours' and that nothing was more odious to God than treason. Indeed, disobedience would incur the full list of curses in Deuteronomy 28.[17]

As its title emphatically stated, the *Lamentation* was written to show *'what ruyne cometh of seditious rebellyon'*. One obvious consequence was the breakdown of order and the rule of law. The rebels were intent on 'spolynges, ravyshementes, burnynges, exilyng of all honest and quiete persones, and settynge up of theves, murderers, and manquellers'. Consequently, law-abiding citizens were facing financial difficulties: 'honeste howseholders shall be utterly undone . . . gentyll men for lacke of their rentes shalbe fayn to lay their landes to morgage'. The rebels were seeking quick gains to the detriment of the future prosperity of the realm.[18] Sedition not only threatened good governance, but also

---

[15] *Lamentation*, Aiv^{r-v}.   [16] Zeeveld, *Foundations*, 175.
[17] *Lamentation*, Aii^r–Aiii^v, Ciii^{r-v}.   [18] Ibid., Biv^v, Aii^v, Bi^v–ii^r.

increased the threat of invasion by a foreign power. If Lincolnshire
was prepared to take up arms against England, Morison asked, was it
any wonder that France and Scotland were also tempted? Internal strife
weakened England's defence against its vigilant enemies: 'dissention
dissention, hath bene the ruyne, the venome, the poyson of all great
estates'.[19] Morison related several classical exemplars to underline his
point. Julius Caesar had been unsuccessful invading England until
a rebellion divided the country, while sedition had also ruined the
Spartans.[20]

The *Lamentation* directly engaged with the rebels' complaints. One
of these was their objection to the terms of the fifteenth recently granted
by Parliament.[21] Morison argued that the taxes were due recompense
for the costs Henry had incurred suppressing the recent rebellion in
Ireland and the 'greate expenses' he had incurred fortifying Dover,
Calais and Berwick and protecting his subjects from foreign threats.
Morison accused the rebels of being willing to 'sette all Englande by
the eares' for 'a shyllyng in the pounde'. This was pure greed as only
those who were assessed at over ten shillings had to pay a 'lyttell money'
in tax.[22] The rebels also criticized Henry's councillors. In response,
the *Lamentation* described Henry as a 'prudent prince' who loved his
advisers for their 'vertues, qualities, fidelitie'. Traitors would naturally
oppose Henry's councillors, 'in whome vertue shyneth', as they resisted
what was best for the realm. In a reference to 'Captain Cobbler', one
of the leaders of the Lincolnshire rising, Morison argued that it was
inappropriate for 'Cobblers' to dictate or even discuss 'what lordes, what
byshops, what counsaylours, what actes statutes and lawes are mooste
mete for a common welthe' and how could they know whose opinions
to follow in matters concerning religion? The only valid arena in which
to voice concerns about policy and the law was Parliament, which was
actually responsible for passing precisely those measures now disputed
by the commons.[23] The absurdity of Henry ceding to the demands
of suitors 'that seke nothynge but dissention, shedyng of bloude, and
ruyne of the hole realme' was illustrated by reference to a Plutarchan
fable of a snake whose head had agreed to let the tail lead for a while.
As a result, the snake ran into stones, pricked himself with thorns, and

19 Ibid., Aiv[v].   20 Ibid., Bi[r]–Bii[r].
21 *Berkowitz*, 167, 170. The repeal of taxes also featured in the Pontefract Articles of
December 1536.
22 *Lamentation*, Ci[r–v], Aiii[r], Biv[v].
23 Ibid., Aiv[r], Biii[r]. Morison also noted that many MPs 'are among your rout'.

was frequently endangered.[24] A realm needed proper leadership by its rightful head.

'Abbeys Shulde Downe'[25]

One of the York articles of 1536 denounced the dissolution of the smaller monasteries as 'a great hurt to the commonwealth'.[26] In order to undermine support for the monastic cause, the *Lamentation* depicted monks as seditious and ungodly. Morison claimed the monks had been agitating for the recent sedition, preferring rather to destroy their country than 'not have for their harlottes'. They had forsaken their vows, taken up arms against their king and God's laws and had 'turned their coules in to iackes, their portesis and beadis into billes, bowes'. Their lack of integrity was further demonstrated in the contrast between their long deliberations over whether they could accept Henry as their Supreme Head and their willingness 'to have made a Cobbler their heed' in rebellion.[27]

Morison asked if the monks publicly practised as vile a sin as treason against their king and country, what private sins might they have committed 'in their cloisters, where they might do al mischiefe?' These religious men, he contended, passed their days in 'ydelnes' or in 'sowynge sede in other mens forowes'. Alluding to the recent visitations of the monasteries, he claimed 'these holy hooded religious have theym selfe confessed and confirmed' the true horror of their sinful lives.[28] Consequently, Morison was puzzled that 'the puttinge away of maynteyned lecherie, buggery, and hypocrisie, shuld be the cause of this rebellious insurrection'. Despite the punishment demanded by the law, Henry had been merciful and merely expelled the monks guilty of abuses from their houses. The civil law would have demanded that Henry 'putteth them to deth'.[29] Moreover only those monasteries and monks in which abuses had been rife faced dissolution. Morison sought to tap into what he claimed were traditional anti-monastic and anti-clerical sentiments, asking his audience: 'Howe longe have you cried, monkes, priestes have to moch? Howe long have we al praied, god sende the kynge such counsaile, that he maye see goodes that were yvell spente,

---

[24] *Lamentation*, Ci[v]–Cii[r]; Plutarch, *Life of Agis* 3.   [25] *Lamentation*, Biii[v].

[26] *Berkowitz*, 166.   [27] *Lamentation*, Bii[v], Cii[v].

[28] Ibid., Bii[r]–Biii[v]. This suggests Morison had seen the *Comperta compactata*.

[29] *Lamentation*, Biii[r]–iv[v]. Morison appears to be referring to both 25 Henry VIII, c. 6 and the *Institutes*, IV.xviii.4.

tourned into a better use?' To ensure this 'better use' Henry first had to
take the monasteries into his own hands. The policy of dissolution had
been supported by the King's Council and Parliament, and therefore
the realm. Indeed, it was a response to Parliament's petition that the
'abbeys shulde downe' and that the 'spiritualitie shoulde have lesse'. Here
Morison was presumably alluding to the *Supplication of the commons*,
as much as to the passing of 27 Henry VIII, c. 8 dissolving the smaller
monasteries. Parliamentary anti-clericalism was not Morison's invention
and his anti-monastic line was also taken in works by Wilfrid Holme
and Francis Bigod published in 1535–6.[30]

'To Redresse Thynges of Religyon'

Morison castigated the papists for their suppression of scripture. They
could 'not abyde scripture to com in place', as it would expose their
exploitation of Christendom.[31] A similar stance had been taken in the
anonymous *A treatise vvherin Christe and his techynges, are compared
with the pope and his doings* (1534), which asserted that the pope
sacrificed scripture in order to augment his own power. By the time
Morison started writing for Henry's government, the regime's anti-
papal polemic was well established. Thomas Swinnerton's *Little treatise
against the muttering of some papists in corners* (1534) had outlined the
anti-papal stance for a vernacular market: the pope had no claim to
authority in England and his interest was purely fiscal. Another tract by
Swinnerton outlined the errors of some popes and their penchant for
schism.[32] Morison's claims that popes stirred sedition therefore drew on
an established rhetoric.

Morison's *Lamentation* went further than earlier English polemics:
it defined the papacy not just as a rival source of authority in the
church, but also as the head of a distinct religion. Morison believed:
'nothynge to apperteyne more to a kynges office, then to redresse
thynges of religyon, to putte downe hypocrisye, and to restore honestie
to her place agayne'. Opposing the papacy, then, was Henry's duty as
king, but his obligations were more wide-ranging; he had to 'redresse
thynges of religion'. Thus right at the start of his writing career,
Morison placed conditions on Henry's kingship. It was contingent

---

[30] *Lamentation*, Biii[r–v]; S. E. Lehmberg, *The Reformation Parliament 1529–36* (Cambridge, 1970), 138–42; Hoyle, *Pilgrimage*, 51, 88.

[31] *Lamentation*, Bii[v].

[32] T. Swinnerton, *A muster of schismatic bishoppes* (London, 1534).

upon Henry and his subjects to destroy all enemies of God's word and true religion.[33]

Henry had already fulfilled some of his kingly duties purely by removing the pope's 'tyrannous decrees' and 'abomynable lawes, whiche I might calle lustis'. Indeed, Morison punned that sending 'popes bulles into their owne pastures' was one of the king's responsibilities. Henry, in contrast to the pope, was propagating the true faith: his 'people nowe be welle taughte whiche so longe hath ben deluded'. What had been achieved so far, however, was but a shadow of what was to come: Morison told his readers that Henry had taken great care to 'see religion restored' in England and he could not imagine anything 'more godly than the appositions which are now in hand'.[34] This was undoubtedly a reference to Cromwell's Injunctions of August 1536, which required the Creed, Ten Commandments and Lord's Prayer to be taught in English and that every parish church acquire a copy of the English New Testament.[35] Henry's rejection of the papacy and subsequent religious policies had created a special relationship between him and God: 'god shal fyght for the kinge in this behalfe: unto whom for the settynge out of his moste holy worde, I dare boldly saye, god is more bound, if god may be bound to man, than he is to al the priestes, monkes, friers, cardinals, and popes that have ben this fyve hundred yeres'. Moreover, Morison claimed 'god whan hym lusteth, canne make his ennemyes fyght for hym, whan they thynke mooste to fyght ayenste hym'.[36] Morison was beginning to develop a providentially tinged covenantal theory of kingship.

A REMEDY FOR SEDITION

Background

The *Lamentation* was not met with straightforward enthusiasm. Criticisms of the tract found their way back to Morison before he had finished the *Remedy* and so Morison attempted to answer them. If his efforts had not pleased all men 'the trowth is, it was not myn intent'. Morison's attack on monastic novices was particularly unpopular; he was told he 'shold have left [it] owght'. Commanded to speak the truth,

---

[33] *Lamentation*, Cii[r], Bii[v].   [34] Ibid., Cii[r–v].

[35] R. Rex, *Henry VIII and the English Reformation* (London, 1993), 119–20, 123.

[36] *Lamentation*, Bii[v], Cii[v].

Morison felt he could not omit it.[37] Whereas the *Lamentation* aimed to discourage further rebellion, the *Remedy* also sought to diagnose the ills of the body politic and offer solutions.

'True and Loyall Obeysance'[38]

In the *Remedy* Morison tried to shame his compatriots by demonstrating that even pagans had cared more for their kings and commonwealths. The Egyptians and Persians had highly reverenced their kings, while the Scythians' patriotism had made their country impenetrable.[39] Many even put the commonwealth before their own families: Damatria, a Spartan, killed her son for failing to defend his country; while both Brutus and Titus Manlius slew their sons when they realized the danger they posed to Rome.[40] However, in the *Remedy* Morison was primarily concerned with how England's problems could be rectified. He envisaged the English commonwealth as a Platonic body politic in which each section of the commonwealth had a specific role in the social hierarchy for which it was best suited; any attempt to take on the functions of another section would be disastrous. All people, of whatever rank, should content themselves with 'that whiche god shal send us, or with that, we by our owne industry shall laufully gette'.[41] Morison argued that mercy should be shown to the rebels: the rebellious, or diseased, parts of England's body should be treated with medicine, not amputated.[42] Here, as in the *Lamentation*, Morison was exploiting the political currency of merciful kingship.[43]

One of the root causes of poverty, and therefore sedition, in England was, Morison believed, the 'fertilite and welthynes' with which England was endowed. Blessed with abundance, the 'thirde parte of Englande' had become slothful. It did not help that England was overrun with alehouses. As a result, many people were poor and towns had decayed.

---

[37] SP6/13, fo. 27ᵛ [*LP* XI 1409].   [38] *Remedy*, Aiʳ.

[39] Ibid., Ciʳ–iiʳ (Herodotus, iv.71, 68, 83–143; Diodorus Siculus, *Bibliotheca Historia* iii.5.2).

[40] *Remedy*, Ciiᵛ–iiiᵛ (Herodotus, i.133, ii.177; Livy, *Decades* ii.3–5, viii.7). Morison later returned to the theme (Eiiʳ) citing the example of Themistocles (Plutarch, *Life of Themistocles* 31.3).

[41] *Remedy*, Biiiʳ.

[42] Ibid., Civᵛ–Diʳ. This followed a discussion (Ciiiᵛ) based on Seneca, *To the Emperor Nero on Mercy* I, of Caesar's merciful treatment of Cinna. The manuscript took a less generous attitude.

[43] For the importance of mercy to Tudor kingship, see K. J. Kesselring, *Mercy and Authority in the Tudor State* (Cambridge, 2003), esp. 3–22.

Morison contrasted his countrymen with industrious Germans, Italians
and French. Rural poverty was one of the reasons why the malicious
rumours circulating in the North that eating white bread, pigs, geese or
capons would have to be 'agreed before with the kynge', had caused such
a stir. If England cultivated more ground and invested greater efforts in
agriculture it could grow crops on the heaths and might even be able to
export grain to other countries.[44]

'The Saulfegarde of a Comune Welthe'[45]

Morison was faced with the task of condemning the social pretensions
of the rebels whilst simultaneously justifying the presence of base-born
men among Henry's most trusted advisers. In general, a 'comonwelthe
is then welthy and worthy his name when every one is content with his
degree'. However, in the *Remedy*, Morison also advocated that rewards
should be dispensed according to merit, regardless of a man's birth:
'trewe nobilitie is never but where vertue is . . . this onely to be the way
of promotion, and here nobilitie to consyste'. These virtues were 'gyftes
of the mynde', chiefly wisdom, justice and temperance.[46] Morison
adhered to this position throughout his life, commenting after Edward
VI's death that: 'The people must neades be happier when the nobility
do pass of honour as they should, the nobles must needs embrace vertue,
when they for nothing other counted with their sovereign but vertue,
but knowledge, but upright dealing, but truth and loyalty.'[47]

Morison's views on nobility were close to those of a contemporary
humanist, Juan Luis Vives, who may have influenced him during his
years in Oxford. In 1540 Morison translated Vives' *Introduction to
Wisdom*, which emphasized the correlation between nobility and virtue:
'True and perfect nobilitie, springeth of vertue.'[48] The *Remedy* echoed
Vives' belief that talented men should be given a chance to advance
themselves. Drawing upon Plato's *On Justice* Morison argued that
justice was essential to the social order as well as the law. He derided the
prevailing contemporary opinion that men 'must be tried by our birth
and not by our qualities'. Those who were endowed with mental acuity,
in particular, should be advanced.[49] He applied his meritocratic views to
all forms of office-holding. In a draft of the *Remedy* Morison advocated

---

[44] *Remedy*, Fi[r], Eiii[v]–iv[r]. A rumour of licences for certain foods appeared in the proclamation of 29 October (*TRP*, i.168).
[45] Ibid., Diii[r].   [46] Ibid., Aiv[v], Bii[v].   [47] *Discourse*, fo. 135[r].
[48] *Introduction to Wisdom*, Bvii[v].   [49] *Remedy*, Bi[v], Bii[r–v].

that officials should be made up exclusively of 'those that nature hath endewed with synguler virtues, and fortune without breache of lawe, sette in high dignitie'. By the time this was published, Morison had specified which virtues he thought important: 'they only ought to be officers, that are known to be discrete, politique, wyse.'[50]

Morison was not unfixing social rank.[51] Instead he was asserting that some men of great military or intellectual distinction were born outside their rank and should be allowed to take their true place. The sons of noblemen would not be deposed or lose their wealth, but they should only be given positions of responsibility within the realm if their natural acuity warranted it. Thus the welfare of a country was contingent upon the adequate education of its political elites. Morison praised the Jews' diligent education of their youth, which put Christians to shame. He perceived a division between the traditional ruling classes and the educated bureaucrats who were making their presence felt at court: 'it is almost thought disgraceful in England to be noble and learned'. Inadequate effort and expertise were put into educating the nobility and gentry, yet Morison considered precisely these groups to be key components in creating an adequately educated society, 'for as noble men be, so theyr servauntes are'. If the evil education of nobles could ruin a commonwealth, their appropriate education was its safeguard, particularly in religious matters. Uniformity of belief within the noble caste would ensure the conversion of all of society. Thus noblemen and most gentlemen should have appropriate tutors appointed.[52]

Morison recognized that not all English children could receive a school education. Consequently, he also advocated the encouragement of English industry and vocational training. Promoting 'honest craftes' and training the younger generations in 'honest occupations' was one way to reduce poverty and restore the nation's towns to their former wealth. As Morison surmised: 'no man is borne a craftis man, youth must be beter brought up, or ever the olde lyve welthely'.[53] For Morison, then, vocational training or a more scholarly education should be given where appropriate. These notions prefigured in miniature many of the ideas later found in Thomas Smith's *Discourse of the Commonweal* (1549).[54]

---

[50] SP6/13, fo. 16ʳ; *Remedy*, Aivᵛ. [51] Zeeveld thought otherwise (*Foundations*, 211).
[52] *Remedy*, Diiᵛ–Divʳ; *LP* X 660. [53] *Remedy*, Ciiiᵛ, Eivʳ, Diiᵛ, Fiiʳ⁻ᵛ.
[54] [T. Smith], *A Discourse of the Common Weal of this Realm of England*, ed. M. Dewar (Charlottesville, VA, 1969).

Morison had also demonstrated a concern for literacy and reading in the *Lamentation*. At several points in the tract, he directed the reader to several other texts for reference. Thus readers were advised to 'Loke [at] the histories' to learn how sedition had been an essential ingredient in the overthrow of regimes in the past. In particular they should 'Rede Paulus Orosius' on Caesar's attempts to invade England and 'Loke on Froissart' on Urban VI and Clement VII.[55] His later tracts, the *Comfortable Consolation* and *Invective*, also revealed his continuing concern with reading and education. In these tracts Morison recommended reading the 'histories of the ethnickes', 'old histories' and Froissart.[56] The majority of Morison's encouragements to his audience to pursue additional reading themselves, however, related to biblical examples.

'Knowlege of the Worde of God'[57]

In the *Remedy* Morison refuted the rebels' opinion that Henry's commands contravened those of God. Henry, as David before him, was rightly the spiritual leader of his people, not the pope, who was not even a true Christian. Religious uniformity under Henry's guidance was essential for the safety and quiet of the commonwealth. Religious education and the propagation of scripture was one of the keys to removing the threat of future sedition. Morison asked, 'Can they hear God's laws yea, though they be but easily preached, and not abhor sedition and rebellion?' Throughout the *Remedy* he consistently stressed the link between knowledge of scripture and obedience.[58] In doing so, he was using rhetoric reminiscent of earlier Henrician polemics.[59] However, he was not simply using Tyndalian obedience rhetoric rooted in scripture to reinforce the Royal Supremacy as Mottram has argued.[60] Rather, Morison was constructing a picture of godly rule over a godly commonwealth which was to have greater repercussions for monarchical theory.

Contrary to the opinion of many, Morison believed that the 'preachyng of the gospel is not the cause of sedition but rather lacke of preachyng it'. Indeed, Henry had 'wholly intended this many years' to

---

[55] *Lamentation*, Bi^{r-v}, Ci^r. Richard Pynson published Lord Berners' English translations of Froissart in 1523 and 1525. Orosius was available in German, French and Italian translations.

[56] *Comfortable Consolation*, Cvi^r, Cii^r; *Invective*, Aiv^r, aii^r.   [57] *Remedy*, Ei^v.

[58] Ibid., Diii^v–iv^r, Ei^v–Fi^v.   [59] Rex, 'Crisis of Obedience', 863–94.

[60] Mottram, *Empire and Nation*, 130–5.

'bring in the Word of God'. How could men know their obligations to God and the King, if they did not have access to scripture? The blame, in part, lay with the bishops: 'Religion toke a great falle, honestie was sore wounded, that daye that richesse entred into theyr hartes.' Now the prelates of the church should lead the way; the commons would follow. Consequently Morison recommended a sermon campaign to propagate the gospel, as even poor men could attend sermons.[61] Once again, Morison outlined that the king had a religious duty to his people. Henry was well aware of this: 'by his long experience and also by his knowledge in good letters, [Henry] wel perceyveth, that the chiefe honour, that a christen prince shulde seke, is the savynge of his people'. Morison later explicitly assured Henry's subjects that their king sought 'nothynge so ernestly as the savyng of their sowles'.[62] Rather than praise Henry at length himself, Morison quoted from a letter written by Erasmus and would have also cited Juan Luis Vives, but could not afford the space.[63] The effect was to create an image of Henry as a godly king, concerned for his subjects' spiritual welfare.

THE *APOMAXIS*

Background

Morison was also commissioned to write propaganda aimed primarily at foreign audiences. Henry VIII's government not only secured the publication on the continent of numerous pieces of polemic, but also, from 1530 onwards, deliberately oversaw the diplomatic distribution of key propaganda tracts to foreign scholars, rulers and courtiers.[64] Part of this persuasive effort involved suppressing critical tracts, and if that failed, responding to them. In August 1535 a book by John Dobneck, alias Cochlaeus, was brought to the attention of Henry's government. Cochlaeus' *De matrimonio* was a damning condemnation of Henry's Divorce and Royal Supremacy. Cochlaeus defended the legitimacy of Henry's first marriage and Julius II's power, as pope, to dispense against any potential impediments, giving full support to papal *plenitudo*

---

[61] *Remedy*, Eiii[r–v], Div[v].   [62] Ibid., Gii[r], Bi[v], Diii[r].

[63] Ibid., Fiii[r]–Fiv[v]. This was a letter from Erasmus to Henry dated 15 May 1519 which was printed in his *Epistolae . . . ad diversos* (Basel, 1521). Berkowitz suggests Henry himself brought the letter to Morison's attention.

[64] T. A. Sowerby, ' "All *our* books do be sent into other countreys and translated": Henrician Polemic in its International Context', *EHR*, 121 (2006), 1271–99.

potestatis. In his schema, Henry's evil councillors had convinced him to
usurp the pope's authority; those English scholars who supported an
interpretation of Leviticus favourable to Henry's case merely subverted
scripture for their own ends.[65] Cochlaeus' arguments seemed outdated:
he adhered to the medieval and canon law justifications of papal power
without any acknowledgement that they might have been challenged
by the reformers.[66] Cromwell complained to the Imperial ambassador
about the tract, asserting that it unfairly and maliciously slandered the
king. After being informed that Cochlaeus wrote under the protection of
George, Duke of Saxony, Henry made diplomatic requests to the duke
to have Cochlaeus' book suppressed and Cochlaeus himself punished.
If Henry was refused, the English ambassadors had books to publish
in the king's defence.[67] Thomas Cranmer and several other scholars
were asked to review Cochlaeus' work and determine if it warranted
an answer. They eventually determined it did not: the book contained
nothing new and the author was not respected.[68]

Ultimately Morison was recruited to refute Cochlaeus' tract. No
statement of the exact reasoning behind this has survived, but there
are three reasons which must have figured strongly. First, continental
condemnations of Henry's rejection of papal authority and his execution
of More and Fisher continued.[69] Secondly, Reginald Pole had been
pressured into giving the king his opinion on the Royal Supremacy.
Although Starkey and Tunstall were confident it would be favourable,
this was less than certain.[70] Thirdly, recent political events further
confused matters. Anne Boleyn was seen by many as the cause of the
Break with Rome. Her execution in May 1536 therefore held out the
prospect of rapprochement with the papacy. Thus a tract that restated
a defence of the Supremacy without alluding to the king's recent
embarrassments was desirable. There are several reasons why Morison
was recruited to write the *Apomaxis*. He was tapped into the continental
climate from his time in Padua and Venice and certainly recognized the
predominantly negative attitude to Henry's recent actions that prevailed

---

[65] J. Dobneck (Cochlaeus), *De matrimonio . . . Regis Engliae, Henrici Octavi, congratulatio disputatoria* (Leipzig, 1535).
[66] G. Wiederman, 'Cochlaeus as Polemicist', in P. N. Brooks (ed.), *Seven Headed Luther* (Oxford, 1983), 195–206.
[67] *LP* VIII 948, IX 825. These were probably early justifications of the Royal Supremacy such as Gardiner's *De vera obedientia* and Foxe's *De vera differentia*.
[68] *LP* VIII 1125, 1126.   [69] *LP* IX 330, 868, X 82, 458, XII ii 127.
[70] Mayer, *Starkey*, 210–12.

abroad. Morison had studied Greek, theology and civil law, and had a strong grounding in the arts and philology, all of which equipped him to rebut Cochlaeus' arguments. He must have started working on the tract either before he left Italy or shortly afterwards, as only three months after he departed Venice, Harvel was aware that he had been asked to write a book. Morison's 'witte and lerning', he was sure, would 'bring al things to good conclusion'.[71] By September, Cole also expected to see Morison's book shortly.[72]

Almost from its very inception, the tract was designed to work as a polemic not just against Cochlaeus' *De matrimonio*, but also against Pole should it prove necessary. Six days after Morison left Venice, his friend Michael Throckmorton also departed for the English court carrying the manuscript of Pole's long-awaited treatise on Henry's divorce and church order. *De unitate ecclesiae* was not the defence of his actions that Henry had sought and been led to expect by Pole's friends in England, Tunstall and Starkey. However, he may never have known the true extent of Pole's venom, as he deputed scholars at court to read the book for him and report back. Thomas Starkey asked that a committee of 'them wych bothe had lernyng to juge and wold wey the mater indyfferently' be appointed to examine Pole's book. On the eventual committee were Starkey, Tunstall, John Stokesley and Morison.[73] If we can infer more about its overall composition from the few known members, this committee was composed of conservatives and those who were friendly towards Pole. Such committees were employed by Henry to discuss texts produced on the continent that were critical of his newly established Supremacy, or his marital struggles.[74] While Tunstall and Stokesley wrote to Pole, urging him to reconsider, Morison produced an abstract of *De unitate*.[75] The title given to this manuscript, which described Pole as an 'evyll wylled man', was not an attempt by Morison to dissociate himself from Pole, but the addition of another hand. Indeed, Morison was generous to Pole in his English abbreviation of Pole's text. The most critical passage in Morison's paraphrase was a far cry from Pole's vitriol, abridged as 'he saith the greate Turke used not such crueltie, as the kinge doth. He at the taking of the Rhodes, compelled no man to professe thynges agenst ther conscience.'[76] Early

---

[71] SP1/106, fo. 26ʳ [*LP* XI 328].   [72] BL Nero BVI, fo. 150ʳ [*LP* XI 513].
[73] Mayer, *Starkey*, 231–2.   [74] See, for example, below pp. 78–9.
[75] Pole had wanted Tunstall to perform this task. Mayer, *Starkey*, 41.
[76] SP1/103, fos. 58ʳ–63ʳ [*LP* X 975ii]. First noted by T. F. Dunn, 'The Development of the Text of Pole's *De unitate ecclesiae*', *Papers of the Bibliographical Society of America*, 70

the next year, Morison and Cole both attested that when Pole had agreed to undertake the work, he had not held the view of papal authority that he eventually articulated in *De unitate*.[77] In the end, however, Pole could not be induced to change his mind. He did refrain from publishing his diatribe against Henry until 1539, making it difficult for the Henrician government to refute his tract without seeming to score an own goal. Morison, who told Cromwell he wished the *Apomaxis* was a refutation of Pole's tract, recognized the difficulty of attacking Pole unless 'Mr traitor poles booke' appeared in print first.[78] Before Morison's book was fully printed, rebellion broke out in Lincolnshire, and the edition had to be postponed. The tract was then revised on at least two occasions before it was finally printed.[79]

Historians have suggested dates ranging from 1536 to 1538 for the composition of the *Apomaxis*.[80] In 1537 Morison took up work on the *Apomaxis* once more, after Paul III had sent a papal sword to the King of Scots.[81] The deterioration of the woodcut border on the title page of the *Apomaxis* indicates that it was printed after the *Bishops' Book*, probably in late 1537 or early 1538. Johannes Cochlaeus had certainly read the tract by March 1538, when he chose to refute it.[82] However, it seems that the *Apomaxis* was not widely circulated until later that year, when it was probably reissued. In early June, Morison complained that were it not for the time and embarrassment that a rumour naming him a gentleman of the King's Privy Chamber had caused him, 'Cocleus had ben abroade'.[83] Morison's dedicatory letter to Cromwell is dated shortly afterwards and was probably added to a text already printed.

The *Apomaxis* was framed as a humanist work. Its title page was one of Berthelet's more decorative, and the printer's symbol, Lucrece, followed Morison's text. A poem in elegant syncopated Latin introduced the work, and an errata sheet concluded it. It is the latter that most clearly demarcates the *Apomaxis* as intended for overseas consumption. Humanists frequently attacked the worth of their fellow scholars' ideas

---

(1976), 457. For Pole's campaign against Henry VIII see T. F. Mayer, *Reginald Pole: Prince and Prophet* (Cambridge, 2000), ch. 2.

[77] SP1/106, fo. 129[v] [*LP* XI 402.3].   [78] SP1/112, fo. 181[r] [*LP* XI 1481].

[79] SP1/133, fos. 68[r]–155[v], 1/141, fo. 168[r–v], 6/13, fos. 62[r]–85[r].

[80] Zeeveld, *Foundations*, 164–5; Elton, *Policy and Police*, 191; McConica, *English Humanists*, 177.

[81] *Apomaxis*, Pii[v].

[82] J. Cochlaeus, *Scopa . . . in araneas Richardi Morysini Angli* (Leipzig, 1538).

[83] SP1/133, fo. 243[r] [*LP* XIII i 1296].

if their Latin was inaccurate. The inclusion of a simple errata sheet helped avoid such attacks.

The Royal Supremacy

A major theme of the *Apomaxis* was the defence of the Royal Supremacy and the refutation of papal authority. Morison also used the now standard Old Testament prototypes Saul and David to demonstrate that temporal powers should exercise control over the spiritual jurisdiction. Both Saul and David were anointed of God and enjoyed dominion over all areas of governance, including their people's spiritual well-being. Moses and Samuel had also exercised jurisdiction over the spiritual realm. Henry was, therefore, the indisputable head of the church of England, whether he, or other princes, had previously permitted the papal supremacy.[84] Morison refuted claims that papal *plenitudo potestatis* had biblical foundations. They stemmed from a misreading of John 21D, which should be taken as purely supervisory. The pope had deliberately exploited this, convincing the people that his *dominium* was divinely ordained.[85] Morison also drew upon historical evidence to demonstrate that papal primacy was not divinely instituted. Richard Sampson's *Oratio* had demonstrated just how effectively a historical approach could support the king's case.[86] Morison followed Bartolomaeus Sacchi de Platina's *Historia Vitis Pontificum*, dating the papal primacy to Boniface III's pontificate, arguing that it was the eastern emperor Phocas who had established the papacy over 600 years after the beginning of Christianity. His immediate sources, however, were the Anglo-Saxon historian Bede and the Italian humanist Marc Antonio Sabellico.[87] Phocas, instead of receiving God's favour, had been rewarded by the loss of a substantial part of his empire and the sack of Rome; he was captured, had his hands and feet amputated and was drowned. After this dubious start, Boniface forced himself and papal primacy on the administration of the Empire, by getting the church hierarchy to take positions in secular government. Once the Empire had capitulated, the rest of Christendom soon followed. It was

---

[84] *Apomaxis*, Iiii^r–Kii^r.   [85] Ibid., Hi^v–ii^v.

[86] A. Chibi, 'Richard Sampson, his "Oratio" and Henry VIII's Royal Supremacy', *Journal of Church and State*, 39 (1997), 543–60.

[87] *Apomaxis*, Diii^r–Eiii^r; Bede, *Ecclesiastical History of the English People*, ed. B. Colgrave and R. A. B. Mynors (Oxford, 1969), ii. 1–4; M. A. Sabellico, *M. Antonii Coccii Opera* (Basel, 1560), ii. 529–31.

no coincidence that at this time, the Saracens and Turks emerged.[88] Morison, then, went much further than earlier Henrician polemics, such as *De vera obedientia*, which had also used Phocas. He found the argument so useful that he included an abridged version in another tract, his *Comfortable Consolation*.[89] In relating the Phocas story, Morison was in good company. Continental reformers such as Luther and Bernardino Ochino also used it to show the fraudulent foundations of the papacy while English polemicists writing after Morison such as John Bale and John Foxe also exploited the Phocas story.[90]

Part of Morison's strategy in the *Apomaxis* was to defend the earlier Supremacy polemics and their authors. He did so mainly because Cochlaeus had accused these writers and Henry's leading councillors of corrupting the king. By defending such figures, Morison was also asserting the validity of the Supremacy. He asked if England had 'ever had anyone more learned' than Stephen Gardiner and Edward Foxe or anyone 'as equipped to defend the cause of truth or crush the audacity, the pride, the impiety of the most arrogant popes?' Cuthbert Tunstall, meanwhile, hardly needed Morison's praise: even Thomas More admitted he was 'one of the most learned, most prudent and honest men in the world today'.[91] Meanwhile, Morison castigated Cochlaeus for unfairly slandering the learned Sampson.[92] The *Apomaxis* included encomia to other senior Henrician figures including, understandably, Thomas Cranmer, Archbishop of Canterbury.[93] Morison's praise of Hugh Latimer, who 'preached the gospel more sincerely, purely and honestly' than other men, was probably aimed at those continental reformers who, like Bucer, regarded Latimer as a leader of the English evangelicals.[94] Of Henry's advisers, it was Cromwell who received the most fulsome praise. Morison dedicated the tract to the Vicegerent, whom he credited with helping to expel Roman tyranny and restore true religion in England despite the demands of diligently attending to the administration of England.[95] Henry was also eulogized throughout the tract. Here Morison called on independent witnesses, reproducing the same Erasmian passage he had included in the *Remedy*, and asserting that

---

[88] *Apomaxis*, Div^v–Eii^v.   [89] *Comfortable Consolation*, Cii^v–iii^r.

[90] *Luther's Works*, 41.90, 277, 292, 297–9; K. Benrath, *Bernardine Ochino of Siena* (London, 1876), 190, 218; King, *Tudor Royal Iconography*, 140; J. Bale, *The seconde part of the Image of both churches* (Antwerp, 1545), 123–5, 132–4.

[91] *Apomaxis*, Xi^r–v.   [92] Ibid., Oi^r.   [93] Ibid., Viii^r.

[94] Ibid., Viv^r; McEntegart, *League of Schmalkalden*, 93.   [95] *Apomaxis*, aii^r–iv^v.

Vives and Melanchthon had expressed equally favourable opinions.[96] Although the tracts justifying the Royal Supremacy were separate works, dealing with different aspects of the Supremacy and its consequences, their utilization of the *Collectanea satis copiosa* lent them an essential coherence. The argument of the *Apomaxis* and its praise of the Henrician polemicists underscored the consistency of Henry's polemics to date, aided, no doubt, by the second edition of *De vera differentia* in 1538.

Morison also attacked Cochlaeus' credentials to write on the Supremacy and Henry's marriage, claiming that Cochlaeus was an unexacting scholar, who misused scripture and tried to cover his academic inadequacies with vicious vitriol.[97] Even the title of the *Apomaxis* attacked Cochlaeus: he was 'a poor theologian and professor of the arts, [an] impudent buffoon'.[98] Indeed, Cochlaeus was such a bad theologian that he did not realize that Scotus, Bonaventure and Aquinas, on whom he based his arguments, had been discredited as theological authorities in favour of scripture.[99] In contrast, Morison based his arguments on scripture and patristics. Moreover, Morison claimed that Cochlaeus had misrepresented the scale of learned opposition to Henry: the only friar Henry had executed who was a doctor was Bocking; the others were all bachelors.[100] In order to discredit Cochlaeus further, Morison accused him of accepting a bribe in return for ceasing to write against Luther.[101]

Defending the King's Actions

The *Apomaxis* was also a defence of the major developments of the 1530s. One of the most important was Henry's annulment of his marriage to Catherine of Aragon. Morison could not understand how Cochlaeus, who had condemned Henry VIII for abandoning Catherine, could question the invalidity of Henry's first marriage, when Sampson and the universities of Paris and Padua had all found in the king's favour.[102] The marriage question was yet another area where the pope had exceeded his jurisdiction: only scripture had the authority to settle the matter. In granting Henry and Catherine a bull of dispensation, Julius II had acted outside the law and deserved to be punished as any

---

[96] Ibid., Ri^v–iii^r.   [97] Ibid., Qi^r–Rii^r, Liv^v.
[98] Ibid., ai^r.   [99] Ibid., Biii^v.
[100] R. Rex, 'The Execution of the Holy Maid of Kent', *HR*, 114 (1991), 219.
[101] *Apomaxis*, Nii^v.   [102] Ibid., Aiii^v.

secular magistrate would be.[103] Although the king had once defended
the papal cause as Cochlaeus had pointed out, he now recognized it as
erroneous.[104]

Morison, as Foxe, Tunstall and Stokesley had before him, outlined
the invalidity of Henry VIII's first marriage. He did so by examining the
biblical passages at the heart of the matter to show unequivocally that the
king was right. Cochlaeus' position on seemingly conflicting passages
of scripture was that the church, namely the pope, had the right to
adjudicate. Englishmen writing before Morison had given precedence to
the passage in Leviticus over Deuteronomy. Morison, however, believed
that scripture could not contradict itself. Using humanist philological
methods drawn from Sante Pagnini, Morison established that there
were many different meanings of the word 'brother' in the Bible, which
'the Hebrew noun easily proves'. Jerome himself had used the noun
in four different ways. Leviticus 20:21 referred to a real, or german
brother, which was not the case in Deuteronomy 25:5.[105] This gave
both biblical passages equal validity and left the authority of scripture
intact, while Henry VIII's case for an annulment was still proven.
Morison's stance, then, was different from that of Robert Wakefield,
who argued that the Deuteronomic exception only pertained to Jews,
not Christians.[106]

Morison's *Apomaxis* discredited Henry's high-profile traitorous subjects. Elizabeth Barton, the Nun of Kent, had attracted a large group
of supporters before her execution in 1534 with her prophecies that
had condemned the king, predicted his death if he did not amend, and
had also emphasized the importance of traditional forms of religion
such as the mass and pilgrimages.[107] Morison believed that the nun had
been the pawn of the devil, who wanted to stop Henry revoking papal
authority. He recounted her fits in lurid detail and accused her of sexual
promiscuity. However, despite the impressive visual display the nun put
on to fool impressionable Englishmen, she had herself confessed to being
a fraud.[108] In insisting that Barton faked her prophecies, Morison followed the official stance taken in the statute which condemned her and

[103] *Apomaxis*, Civ^v –Di^v.   [104] Ibid., Aiv^v. Cochlaeus, *De matrimonio*, Aiii^v.

[105] *Apomaxis*, Ziii^v –aiii^v, Cii^r –iv^r.

[106] V. Murphy, 'The Literature and Propaganda of Henry VIII's First Divorce', in
D. MacCulloch (ed.), *The Reign of Henry VIII* (Basingstoke, 1995), 140–1.

[107] Shagan, 'Print, Orality and Communications'; A. Neame, *The Holy Maid of Kent: The
Life of Elizabeth Barton, 1506–1534* (London, 1971), 140–8.

[108] *Apomaxis*, Ti^r –ii^v.

the sermon accompanying it.[109] Barton's prophecies were just another failed papal scheme designed to keep England under Roman control.

Morison also discussed one of Henry's most controversial actions since the Break with Rome: the executions of Cardinal John Fisher and Sir Thomas More for treason in June and July 1535, which had provoked widespread criticism of Henry abroad. Pope Paul III had issued two letters on 26 July to Francis I and Ferdinand, King of the Romans condemning the king for Fisher's execution and calling for his deprivation. Fisher was compared to Thomas Becket, while Henry was depicted as an adulterer, heretic and schismatic. Francis I sent a copy of the papal brief to England, where Stephen Gardiner drew up a response that depicted Fisher as a traitor rightly executed in accordance with the law. Manuscripts of Gardiner's 'Se sedes illa Romana' were distributed at foreign courts.[110] Thus when Morison wrote the *Apomaxis*, there was no printed defence of the executions, but foreign dignitaries had already heard the government's line. Morison took essentially the same stance as Gardiner: More and Fisher were traitors. A letter from Morison to Cromwell from 1535 shows that even before he was commissioned to write the *Apomaxis*, Morison was suggesting ways of portraying the executions in order to convince continental Europe of their justice. He argued that although in normal circumstances mercy and clemency should be used, this should not be the case if in showing mercy to one man, thousands more were brought into jeopardy.[111] In the *Apomaxis* Morison again asserted that More and Fisher were traitors guilty of putting the pope and his tyranny before the king; they therefore deserved to be punished as the law demanded. Henry had offered them mercy, but their obstinacy sealed their fate. Just as indefensible as their betrayal of the king, was More's and Fisher's placing of the pope before scripture. Fisher was the worst, a 'harmful enemy' of the gospel.[112]

Anti-Papal Polemic: 'Veritas Vincit'

In the *Apomaxis*, as in his other tracts, Morison deplored the financial corruption of the papacy. Since its very beginning, the popes had

---

[109] L. E. Whatmore, 'A Sermon against the Holy Maid of Kent', *EHR*, 58 (1943), 463–75. Neame deemed Morison's account of Barton's fits too bizarre to be invented (*Holy Maid*, 141–6).
[110] *LP* XIII 1095, 1116, 1117; P. Janelle, *Obedience in Church and State* (Cambridge, 1930), 12–19, xxvi–xxxii; *LP* IX 848.
[111] *LP* VI 198.   [112] *Apomaxis*, Xi^v, Vii^r–Yi^r, Yiv^v–Ziii^v.

consistently used their primacy for their own financial gain. This even
extended into spiritual matters, including the selling of indulgences,
which popes had used with other similar devices to keep Christendom
enslaved. Popes had encouraged men to seek their salvation in 'pardons,
stations, cowls and thousands of things he most perniciously invents
that attack complaints on the question of his imposture and robbery'.
However, this served to bring their souls into danger, as they were
diverted from their true duty to seek salvation in Christ.[113] Indeed,
popes had propagated belief in purgatory, as a means of scaring men
into obeisance. Yet this was a false doctrine which condemned innocent
children and imperilled men's souls.[114]

Morison asserted that Rome was so corrupt it was worse than Nin-
eveh, Babylon, Sodom and Gomorrah combined.[115] This was in contrast
to the apostolic foundations of the church, when the spiritual leaders
lived pure lives and forsook temporal goods and honours. Indeed, it
was the pursuit of riches and power that had taken the pope, who was
after all a bishop, away from the cure of souls. Only the removal of the
corrupt, usurping hierarchy would lead people to forsake all corruption
and allow the restoration of the true church. Any hope of a General
Council solving the problems of the church was now gone, so Henry
had taken his own church in hand.[116] This was largely because the pope
would stop at nothing to protect his power. Morison relayed a passage
from Machiavelli which showed an earlier pope's interference in temporal affairs: when the people of Rome defied him, he transferred their
power to elect emperors to the Germans. Popes would also set Christian
nations against each other, even when the Turk threatened, rather than
lose a small part of their domain. Indeed, now Henry had uncovered the
pope's deceit and denied him any influence in England, the pope was
urging foreign rulers to invade his realm. This was undoubtedly why he
had sent a sword to the King of Scots. Consequently Morison directed
the tract not just at Cochlaeus, but at the universal army of papists.[117]
Thus in the *Apomaxis*, as in his vernacular tracts, Morison defined the
papacy as a military as well as a spiritual enemy.

It was the king's duty to protect the spiritual welfare of his people:
God's law had been erected to enable princes to prevent their subjects
committing sin. Henry, Christ's true servant, had already gone a long

113 *Apomaxis*, aiii^r, Div^r–Eiii^v.   114 Ibid., Gi^v, Hi^v, Pii^r, Yiv^r.
115 Ibid., Liv^r.   116 Ibid., Ei^v–iv^r, Iiv^v, Mi^{r-v}.
117 Ibid., Xii^{r-v}, Pi^v–ii^v, Riii^r–Siii^r, Aiv^v.

way to achieve this by expelling papal idolatry. Morison's criticism of papal abuses and commentary on the Break with Rome was tinged with evangelicalism. His introductory poem on the subject 'truth conquers' (veritas vincit) set the scene for the rest of the tract. It heralded the restoration of the true religion of Christ and the extirpation of papal trickery. As England had been blessed, Morison stressed the need for appropriate godly celebration.[118] Moreover, the poem tied England's Reformation into a longer line of religious reform: 'veritas vincit' was a Hussite motto.[119]

The highest authority in Morison's *Apomaxis* was scripture. It was on scripture that Morison founded his reasoning, and on this that the king based his church. Morison explicitly referred to the recent re-establishment of Christ's faith. More significantly, he openly praised Luther, who in his opinion had been the clear victor in all his controversies with Cochlaeus. Luther had also unambiguously demonstrated how church ceremonies had been abused by the papists. While the king abhorred papalism, 'his men are introducing Lutheranism into the realm' in its place. Indeed, Morison claimed the king had no problem with Lutheranism, which was based on scripture, unlike Roman Catholicism.[120] Although this was a short passage it was a significant one. Morison was signalling to the outside world that Henry intended to embrace Lutheran doctrines.

Assessment

Although historians have previously plundered the *Apomaxis* for information on figures such as the Nun of Kent, it has received very little attention as a coherent tract.[121] Morison followed the conventions of an older debate on the relative jurisdictions of temporal and papal authorities, but he did so largely because Cochlaeus, whom he was refuting, held on so rigidly to outdated justifications of papal primacy.[122] However, Morison crucially extended these arguments and incorporated those of

---

[118] Ibid., Kii^{r-v}, Lii^r–Mi^r, Pi^r, Ai^v.

[119] T. Fudge, *The Magnificent Ride* (Basingstoke, 1998), 245–6.

[120] *Apomaxis*, Ciii^v, Iiii^r, Nii^v, Oiv^v.

[121] Neame, *Holy Maid*, 141–6; Shagan, *Popular Politics*, ch. 2.

[122] L. P. M. Nicod, 'The Political Thought of Richard Morison: A Study in the Use of Ancient and Medieval Sources in Renaissance England', Ph.D. thesis (London School of Economics, 1998), ch. 4, mistakenly attributed this to the (questionable) influence of Renaissance thinkers such as Roselli on Morison.

Gardiner, Sampson and Foxe on the Royal Supremacy. Consequently his work was rhetorically consistent with most of the earlier Henrician polemics. He also conceived of the English church in historical terms, which allowed him to argue against the papacy from a new angle. The *Apomaxis*, written primarily for a foreign audience, reproduced much of the same polemic that was finding its way into Morison's vernacular tracts, including a defence of Luther. From the very first, Morison was proud of the *Apomaxis*. He believed he had produced an effective anti-papal work, telling Cromwell that 'other men hath but tickled the pope, I truste I have so pricked hys power, that men shal say, I knowe the way, to anger popes'.[123] He was to go on to write several other tracts which proved even more troublesome for the papacy.

HENRY'S CAMPAIGN AGAINST GENERAL COUNCILS

Background

In 1535, Pope Paul III despatched papal legates to proclaim a forthcoming General Council. Over the next two years strenuous efforts were made to persuade the leaders of Europe to attend the Council, which was to be held at Mantua.[124] By 1537 he looked increasingly likely actually to hold, rather than just call, this Council, which was certain to condemn Henry VIII and his church. Early in his divorce proceedings Henry had appealed to the judgement of a General Council; he now had to produce an apologetic that condemned the papally summoned Council while still preserving the spirit of his earlier rhetoric.[125] Henry issued statements and supported a propaganda effort outlining, justifying and exhorting the English opposition to any Council summoned by papal authority. The full significance and reception of these tracts has been largely neglected, as has Morison's central role in the campaign. Briefly examined by le van Baumer in the context of the theory of the Royal Supremacy, it has largely been dismissed by subsequent commentators on Henrician polemics. Elton believed the tracts unimportant for

---

[123] SP1/112, fo. 181ʳ [*LP* XI 1481].

[124] H. Jedin, *History of the Council of Trent* (London, 1957), i. 290–312.

[125] P. A. Sawada, 'Das Imperium Heinrichs VIII und die erste Phase seiner Konzilspolitik', *Reformata Reformanda*, 1 (1965), 476–507.

domestic propaganda, McConica thought they had very little to do with the English humanist community.[126] Becker, Brockman, Sawada and Mayer have all examined aspects of English interest in General Councils in this period, but their analyses are far from comprehensive and for the most part shy away from discussing the government's main statements on the Council.[127] Yet the tracts show how General Councils were reconciled with the Henrician government's post-Supremacy conception of the English church. Moreover, they demonstrate just how seriously Henry and his advisers took the threat of the General Council in the late 1530s and illuminate the direction of English diplomacy in this fraught time.

Opinions on General Councils, particularly on the subject of the authority necessary to call one, had been canvassed even before the issue of a papal bull summoning a Council to Mantua required Henry to take a public stance. Indeed, included in a memoranda of 'thinges necessary as it seemeth, to be remembered before the brekyng up of the parliament' (c.1534) was the item 'also to be enquired of the lerned men of this realm who hathe power to call a General Council (secretly) for what cause it ought to be gathered and who ought to have voice therin'. This was followed by a short exposition in a different hand on precisely this topic, which claimed that it was Christian princes to whom 'yt apperteyneth to call by ther countrey agreement and none otherwise a generall counsayle'.[128] Richard Sampson and Edward Foxe were appointed to determine if a General Council or the bishop of Rome possessed the higher authority. The result was a foregone conclusion: the same set of instructions also asserted that the pope was 'not in auctoryte above the Generall Counsaile'.[129] Ecclesiastical authority, especially General Councils, also provided the subject for another text written for the king. In June 1536 the convocation of Canterbury pronounced on the more specific matter of the Council of Mantua, asserting that neither an individual prince, nor the bishop

---

[126] Baumer, *Theory of Kingship*, 49–56; Elton, *Policy and Police*, 171–2; McConica, *English Humanists*, 172–3.

[127] H.-J. Becker, *Appellation vom Papst an ein allgemeines Konzil* (Cologne, 1988), 264–9; T. Brockman, *Die Konzilsfrage in den Flug- und Streitschriften des deutschen Sprachraumes 1518–1563* (Göttingen, 1998), ch. 4; P. A. Sawada, 'Two Anonymous Tudor Treatises on the General Council', *JEH*, 12 (1961), 197–214; T. F. Mayer, 'Thomas Starkey: An Unknown Conciliarist at the Court of Henry VIII', *JHI*, 49 (1988), 207–27.

[128] BL Cotton Cleopatra EVI, fos. 330ʳ–1ᵛ.

[129] *State Papers Published under the Authority of his Majesty's Commission. King Henry the Eighth* (London, 1830), I.411–4.

of Rome could call a Council of his own accord without the consent of other sovereign princes.[130]

One of the main objectives of Henrician diplomacy with the Schmalkaldic League following the election of Alexander Farnese to the papacy in 1534 had been an agreement on the course to be taken against a papally summoned Council, as McEntegart has shown. Initially, it was hoped that they would be able to agree on a theological position to be taken at any Council. Even when theological consensus floundered, there had been continued hope of a common policy concerning General Councils, as neither side wished to be left isolated and vulnerable to military attack from its religious opponents. Thus it was determined by 1537 that neither party would attend a General Council without the other.[131] An important facet of the dialogue between Henry and the Schmalkaldic League was the exchange of tracts stating official policy. Morison translated the League's answer to the papal legate, Pier Paulo Vergerio. The League had sent Henry VIII a copy with an explanatory letter in 1536, which emphasized the pope's material motives for calling a Council. The princes maintained that they had expressed their desire for 'a Christen counsel, an honest and holy assemble a fre parliament, wher every man with owt feare may frankely utter that he hath in hys harte' for many years at the German Diets. Yet they believed that Vergerio was summoning them to a Council totally under papal control, rather than a genuinely General Council run by 'men best, and best lerned, not only princes, but also lay men'. Furthermore, the authority to call a Council did not rest solely in the hands of the pope or bishops 'but also emperors all have made great cownsels as Constantine and Theodosius'. Both the civil and spiritual powers were part of the church, so both should be represented and heard at any Council; only then, 'when good and lerned judges, be elected by the consentes of the parties', and the 'old church' restored, would the pronouncements of the Council have any moral weight.[132]

Morison's Involvement

Morison's main contribution to Henry VIII's campaign against the General Council was the composition of two tracts: *A protestation made*

[130] *LP* VI 1488–9; D. Wilkins (ed.), *Concilia Magnae Britanniae et Hiberniae* (London, 1737), iii. 809–10.

[131] McEntegart, *League of Schmalkalden*, 33–71.

[132] BL Cotton Cleopatra EVI, fos. 316r–17v.

for the most mighty and moste redoubted kynge of Englande (1537) and *An epistle of the moste myghty [and] redouted Prince Henry the viii* (1538). His earlier translation of the Germans' answer to Vergerio gave him knowledge of the general tenor of argument and the most contentious points as far as England's prospective allies were concerned. Indeed, the Henrician campaign appears to have interacted with a simultaneous wave of pamphlets produced in Germany.[133] When the *Protestation* came to the attention of the Schmalkaldic League they believed themselves to be the intended target audience. Their tract had been unceremoniously delivered to Henry several months late; they thought this had provoked Henry to commission his own pamphlet.[134] Although the *Protestation* was written before Henry received the Germans' tract, the League was probably correct to assume that it was predominantly directed at them.

On 20 July 1537 Bishop Foxe wrote to Cromwell informing him that he had 'sent unto master Morison' to bring him 'the protestation, in Laten'.[135] Foxe was heavily involved in overseeing governmental propaganda at this time; Morison was employed extensively in these efforts. When his friend John Leland discussed how deficient General Councils were in dealing with the current divisions within Christendom in his anti-papal tract, *Antiphilarchia*, he noted that 'many things which relate to this' were expounded, 'partly by corvine [Corvinus], partly by Richard Morysino'.[136] Morison was almost certainly the final author of the *Protestation*, but he composed it by drawing upon the responses and determinations of several high-ranking clergymen. The *Protestation* was many months in the making; during this time the opinions of several bishops and theologians were called for and assessed. Edmund Bonner's opinion on the 'books for the protestation' was requested in May. He strongly recommended publicizing the king's views on the General Council. Bonner, Dr Petre and Dr Gwent examined these books and provided a substantial response, in which they recommended the issue of two books—one for the king and another for the clergy.

---

[133] Sowerby, 'Henrician Polemic', 1283–7.

[134] McEntegart, *League of Schmalkalden*, 78–80.

[135] SP1/123, fo. 25ᵛ [*State Papers*, I.555; *LP* XII ii 289]. *Illustris. ac potentis. regis, senatus, populique Angliae, sententia, et de eo concilo, quod Paulus episcopus Roma Mantuae futurum simulauit, et de ea bulla* (London, 1537) was also known as the Latin Protestation: BL Arundel 97, fo. 14ʳ [*LP* XIII ii 1280].

[136] CUL, E.e.5.14, fo. 184ᵛ. Anthony Corvinus had published anti-Council literature in the Empire.

Although Bonner's views on the content of these tracts were apparently sidelined, his letter demonstrates the consultative process behind the *Protestation*.[137]

The argument for Morison's authorship of the *Protestation* is further strengthened by Cromwell's choice to rewrite the tract when the threat of a General Council became imminent once more. Morison was commissioned to render the tract suitable for republication in the new atmosphere and to 'se [it] printed'. Morison's critique indicates that one of the reasons for changing it was a concern for a closer alignment of the English position with the Schmalkaldic League's objections to the proposed Council: 'The Germaines have nothing in ther answere, but I am sure it is at the leste touched in ours. Many argumentes ar handled in thys, that they leave utterly utterly [*sic*] untouched. Again if we shold say thinges comply every as they say, we might then seame to repete thers, and not to wryght our own.' As the *Protestation* was popular and had been issued in the king's name Morison thought it could not be substantially altered without damaging the king's reputation and the perceived integrity of the English stance: 'If it shoulde cum oute, as I am bidden, the moste parte changed, many thynges lefte owte, whych be both trewly spoken, and cannot but do good . . . men of other nations, may reken, that either we be afrayde or ashamed to say as we have sayde. They may thinke thynges pass lyghtely here, that ar so litel whyle liked.' Morison suggested that rather than introducing any specific alterations, the text might be republished with a slight augmentation. He provided a draft passage that amended the section dealing with the establishment of papal authority over England by common consent. It argued that England had been deceived into granting its permission, and now would reclaim what rightfully belonged to it by re-establishing true religion. He also claimed to have a further two or three leaves that might be added to the tract before republication.[138]

Morison's proposed additions to the tract were only partially accepted. The extra paragraph he had proposed was compressed into a single sentence.[139] However, an introductory letter was added, which complemented the subject matter of the *Protestation*. It summarized many of the main points, which were dealt with at greater length in the earlier tract and situated the discussion firmly in the circumstances

---

137 *LP* XII i 1244, ii 7.
138 BL Cotton Cleopatra EVI, fos. 323^r–4^v, 283^r [*LP* XII i 1311, 745].
139 *Protestation*, Ciii^{r-v}.

of April 1538. England's consistency was preserved; Henry was not continuously issuing new protestations and breeding confusion, unlike his Roman rival.[140] That Morison also composed this introductory letter is suggested by an extant fragment of an early Latin draft in his hand; it may have grown from the two or three leaves of extra material he had sent to Cromwell earlier.[141] The final *Epistle* was a much-expanded version, which had been scrutinized by the king himself.[142]

The Anti-Conciliar Message

The *Protestation* and *Epistle* echoed many points made by earlier tracts on the validity of a General Council, and in doing so showed definitively that the Council of Mantua in no way resembled the English notion of a true Council. To do so, both tracts had to deal with an important issue: papal claims that Henry VIII was schismatic. They stressed Henry's avid desire for a General Council and emphasized that England had never broken unity with the true catholic church. As Defender of the Faith, Henry had long since undertaken to protect and preserve the 'olde honour and pristine dignitie' of scripture and used this claim to legitimate his church's departure from the Roman fold.[143] By emphasizing the restoration of scripture and criticizing the unquestioning acceptance of custom, the tracts reinforced justifications of the Supremacy and also stressed England's similarities to the Germans. Moreover, the Henrician stance on scriptural authority expressed in Morison's vernacular tracts was developed by specifically emphasizing the central place of scripture as an authority at any General Council. Henry's aspirations to protect scripture and the doctrine founded on it were again prominent in the *Epistle*.[144]

In line with earlier statements on General Councils, both tracts utterly refuted the power of the pope to call a General Council. Popes had no jurisdiction over the English in any instance and all power erroneously given to the papacy was now duly returned to the king in line with 'bothe

---

[140] *Epistle*, Aiii^r.

[141] BL Cotton Cleopatra EVI, fos. 322^{r-v}, 324^r. The relationship was first noted in *LP* XIII i 709. For a comparison of the two texts see T. A. Sowerby, ' "A brave knight and learned gentleman": The Careers of Sir Richard Morison c. 1513–1556', D.Phil. thesis (Oxford, 2006), 98–9.

[142] SP1/133, fo. 166^r [*LP* XIII i 840].   [143] *Protestation*, Avi^r, Aii^r.

[144] Ibid., Civ^v; BL Cotton Cleopatra EVI, fos. 316^r–17^v; *Ursachen so die Chür und Fürsten auch Stende und Stedte . . . darumb sie Babst Pauli des namens des dritten/ ausgeschrieben Concilium* (Schmalkalden, 1537), B^r–Biii^r; *Epistle*, Aiii^r, Avii^r.

the lawes cyvile and also the lawes of god'.[145] This right to call a General Council rightly rested with the emperor, kings and princes: if the pope claimed this power it was yet another unjustified usurpation.[146] Indeed the tracts echoed the assertions of earlier conciliarists such as Marsilius of Padua, that the right to call a Council was the prerogative of the human legislator. The English wished for a 'franke and free' Council, where every man could state his mind without fear of reprisals, called in peacetime by the Christian princes. The assembly proposed by the pope was in no way the Council 'free for all partes and universall' that the English desired.[147]

The tracts also questioned the practicalities of a Mantuan Council. Mantua was too small to host the full number of people summoned. Anywhere in Italy was too closely under the influence of the pope for any truly free Council to be convened there. Moreover, Paul III had not issued any notice of safe conduct for those who disagreed with him, which guaranteed a reduced turnout.[148] This was particularly problematic for England as the pope had condemned the English in advance and was continually 'provokyng al men, by al the meanes that he can, to endomage us and our countreye'. Thus any attempt by Henry to attend the Council would entail personal and national dangers. No one could expect him to contravene natural law and attend.[149]

Timing posed further practical problems: France and the Empire were at war and a Turkish assault on Christendom threatened. In such circumstances it was not safe for any prince to leave his country unattended, even for the sake of a General Council.[150] The wars also occasioned the undesirable precedent of the presence of an army at the Council, which was portrayed as yet another papal tool to control the Council's decisions: 'wordes can not contrevayle weapons, reson is not harde, where souldiours are hyred to rage'.[151] Paul III's call for a Council in such circumstances was presented as proof that he was insincere about church reform. Either he wished to obtain conciliar approval for the retention of his usurpation, or he did not want a General Council at all, as 'both the time that he indicted it, and also the place, where he appointed it to be, might assure hym of this'.[152] Indeed, the pope intended nothing more than the continuation of abuses and extortion

[145] *Protestation*, Aiii^v, Av^{r-v}, Civ^{r-v}. Restated in the *Epistle*, Av^r.
[146] *Protestation*, Aviii^r, Cv^r.   [147] Ibid., Avii^r, Bii^v; *Epistle*, Aiii^r.
[148] *Protestation*, Biii^{r-v}.   [149] *Protestation*, Bv^r–vi^v. Restated in the *Epistle*, Aiv^r–viii^r.
[150] *Protestation*, Bii^r–iii^v, Aiv^{r-v}; *Epistle*, Avi^r.   [151] *Protestation*, Cii^r; *Epistle*, Bi^v.
[152] *Protestation*, Avii^{r-v}, Aii^r–iii^r.

of material gains: 'Is it mervayle, if the bishop of Rome beinge iudge, no man repynynge, no man ayensayinge, the defenders of the papacy obteine, that popishe auctoritie, nowe quaylynge and almoste fallen, be sette up ayene?'[153] Those cardinals chosen to adjudicate at Mantua were the supposedly learned men raised to the cardinals' bench, men promoted by the pope 'as he thynketh most mete and most redy to defende frauds and untrouthes'. Thus any papally summoned Council would follow the same course as its predecessors, which had only been called to pursue profit and legitimize errors.[154]

Morison argued that the pope's disingenuousness insulted the dignity of princes. The abortive Council of Mantua had proved his lack of sincerity, while the tardiness of the bull of prorogation proved in how little regard he held the temporal powers.[155] The *Epistle* sketched this papal failure in comic terms. The pope's hospitality was so great that he invited the whole world to a Council in another man's city. However, it was the failure of the pope to procure Mantua that Henry most wanted emphasized. This was all the proof needed to show the world that his claims to universal authority over the church were without foundation—he could not even guarantee where his Council would be held.[156]

The *Protestation* paved the way for Henry to conduct autonomous consultations on religious matters at a local level until circumstances permitted the calling of a truly General Council, when it pronounced that 'we thinke it nowe be beste, that every prince call a councille provincial and every prince to redress his owne realme'.[157] Conveniently, this gave Henry carte blanche to determine theology without reference to any external bodies. So in refuting the Council of Mantua, Henry was also given a justification for the determinations that led to the publication of the *Bishops' Book* in October 1537. This notion of Henry holding a provincial assembly in lieu of a General Council was also current on the continent, where it was viewed unsympathetically by papalists. The bishop of Verona, for one, referred to the debates surrounding the *Bishops' Book* as a *conciliabulum*, although he scathingly suggested that Henry might surpass himself and try to excommunicate the pope.[158]

---

[153] Ibid., Aiv^r.
[154] Ibid., Aii^v, Aiv^r–v^r, B^r–ii^r. The *Epistle* claimed the Council would be 'abused to lucre and gains' (Aiii^r–v^r).
[155] *Protestation*, Bviii^r, Ci^r–v, Cii^v; *Epistle*, Aviii^v–Biii^r.
[156] Ibid., Aviii^v–Biii^r; SP1/131, fos. 31^r–2^v [*LP* XIII i 695].   [157] *Protestation*, Cv^v.
[158] *LP* XII i 1053.

Morison developed the notion of using an English provincial council to determine English doctrine, and it was present in many other official writings of this period. One tract which dealt with the issue of determining the meaning of scripture argued that it could be determined on a local level until it was possible to hold a General Council.[159] *A Treatise proving by the king's lawes* (1538) argued that if no true General Council was possible then Parliament might determine matters at the king's behest.[160] Here, the author was anticipating the process behind the Act of Six Articles of the following year.

THE DISSEMINATION OF THE TRACTS

The *Protestation* and *Epistle* were probably the most widely disseminated Henrician propaganda tracts. In England the *Protestation* ran to two English and three Latin editions, though it is likely that many of the Latin copies were intended for distribution abroad. Henry's agents ensured the *Protestation* was widely read abroad, even going so far as to give away free copies at the Frankfurt book fair.[161] Meanwhile, the *Protestation* was circulating in humanist channels and English scholars were passing copies on to continental reformers.[162] In the Holy Roman Empire, the *Protestation* was so heavily in demand that it was published twice in Latin and at least four times in German translation. Editions appeared in Augsburg, Nuremberg, Strasbourg and Wittenberg—all influential Imperial cities.[163] According to Giovanni Morone, bishop of Modena and papal nuncio at Venice, the *Protestation* was incredibly popular, 'everywhere read and read again'. Even more importantly, the bishop believed it was strongly influencing popular opinion, steadily turning it against the pope.[164] Henry's *Epistle* was

---

[159] SP6/1, fos. 238^r–9^r.

[160] *A Treatise Proving by the King's laws that the bishops of Rome had never right to any supremitie within this realm* (London, 1538), Di^r.

[161] Jedin, *Council of Trent*, i. 335. Reyner Wolffe and Christoff Froschauer conveyed English tracts to the Frankfurt book fair in the 1530s.

[162] *LP* XII ii 1116, 844, 845.

[163] Hans Lufft, who was based in Wittenberg, was responsible for the Latin imprints of 1537 and 1538. This was not the pseudonymical Hans Lufft who had printed English exile tracts. German editions were printed by: H. Steyner, Augsburg, 1537; H. Lufft, Wittenberg, 1537; J. Petri, Nuremberg, 1537 (possibly also a second edition); W. Rihel, Strasbourg, 1537.

[164] *LP* XII ii 1001.

published on 8 April 1538, and went through three Latin and four English print runs. At least five German editions appeared, based on the translation of Justas Jonas. Concurrently several Latin editions were imprinted in Wittenberg and Augsburg.[165] Berthelet printed a French edition of the *Epistle* and *Protestation* in 1539.[166] Once more Henry's government promoted the extensive circulation of the tract and ambassadors stationed in England sent back copies of the *Epistle* to their governments.[167]

Both tracts were envisaged as works of reference for English diplomats when discussing England's policy on General Councils. Copies were dispatched to English ambassadors at the French and Spanish courts.[168] Bonner and Heynes, ambassadors to Spain, were instructed to 'gather instruction by the discourses of the kinges majesties protestacion' and 'the epistle added upon the prorogacion'.[169] The *Protestation* was not always received positively. In November 1537, Thomas Wyatt was out of favour at the Spanish court partly for exceeding his instructions to discuss the General Council frankly with Charles and insulting the pope, and partly because he was allegedly encouraging other courtiers to study heretical pamphlets. Given Wyatt's brief on the General Council, the *Protestation* was probably one of these texts.[170]

Although the *Protestation* was independent of the League's latest declaration on the General Council, it resonated with all of the central issues articulated by the Germans. John Frederick, duke of Saxony, and several other members of the Schmalkaldic League contemplated one of several German editions of the *Protestation* with approval. They were further encouraged to learn that Henry had allowed the publication of an English translation of 'the League's Confession and Apology'.[171]

---

[165] *LP* XIII i 709n; P. Ullhart, Augsburg, 1538; P. Seitz, Wittenberg, 1538; J. Klug, Wittenberg, 1538, 1539 (possibly two editions). There was also another distinct 1538 edition which lacks any imprint information beyond the date. Ullhart and Seitz both produced Latin imprints in 1538 and 1539. Justas Jonas was a correspondent of Cromwell's by 1536, when he was promoting a religious agreement between England and Wittenberg, and a common policy on General Councils. It is possible that Cromwell asked him to translate the tract into German and have it printed.

[166] *L'Epistre du roy d'Angleterre, Aux princes & peuple Chrestien: touchant le Concile à venire . . . Auec vn liuret composé par maniere de Protestation.* I am grateful to Andrew Pettegree for bringing this to my attention.

[167] *LP* XIII i 781.   [168] *LP* XIII i 840, ii 1280.

[169] SP1/131, fo. 32ᵛ [*LP* XIII ii 695].   [170] *LP* XII ii 870, 1031.

[171] Ibid., 1088, 1089.

Furthermore, the League's reasons for refusing to recognize the Council were printed in English before the year was out.[172] Miles Coverdale's translation advertised that Henry was not alone, while also showing the Germans the resonance of their respective positions. Indeed the spread of the *Epistle* and *Protestation* was far from hindered by the similarity of their message to that contained in several German pamphlets issued in 1537–9, by authors such as Anthony Corvinus and Luther.[173] The continental success of the English propaganda was also due in part to the scarcity of Catholic counter-attacks. Antonio Massa and Albert Pighius both wrote detailed refutations of the English tracts; Massa's does not appear to have been published. Even when Cochlaeus did publish pro-Council tracts in 1537 and 1538 at his nephew's press, the lack of demand for them bankrupted his nephew. Other pro-papal tracts on the Council were publicly ridiculed, such as the *Epistle for the Council* of Bishop Fabri of Vienna, which Johan van Kampen punned was 'worthy of a blacksmith'.[174]

Henry was going to considerable lengths to persuade his fellow kings and princes of the invalidity of the Council of Mantua and its successor. The Germans were specifically targeted as they were seen to, and indeed did, have most in common with Henry's position. Henry, then, was serious about pursuing an alliance with the Schmalkaldeners. If they could not yet (and as it turned out never could) agree on the theological stance to be taken at a Council, then they could at least agree on what constituted a valid Council and be seen to take a united stance against an unjust one. The similarity of their printed polemics against the Council and the knowledge of their diplomatic negotiations may have been sufficient to create the impression (both at home and abroad) that they had a much more solid alliance than was in fact the case.

THE CONTINUING CAMPAIGN

The impression of a strong alliance with the Schmalkaldic League was also cultivated by domestic propaganda. Here again Morison was

---

[172] M. Coverdale, *The causes why the Germans wyll not go, nor consente unto that council, which Paul iii . . . hath called to be kepte at Mantua* (London, 1537). This was a translation of *Ursachen . . . . des dritten ausgeschrieben Concilium.*

[173] For an overview of much of the German anti-Council literature see Brockmann, *Die Konzilsfrage*, ch. 4.

[174] Jedin, *Council of Trent*, i. 335–6.

involved: his translation of the *Epistle that Johan Sturmius ... sent to the cardynalles and prelates* (1538) demonstrated that continental Protestants were equally dissatisfied with the pope's attempts to reform the church and that his proposed General Council was not an adequate response to the problem. In 1537 a commission, appointed by Paul III to investigate the abuses in the church, reported its findings and recommendations for reform. The commission consisted of twelve cardinals well known for their reforming zeal, including Contarini, Sadoleto, Cortese, Pole and Giberti. They recommended far-reaching reforms in the granting of dispensations and absolutions; the issuing of indulgences; residency requirements; the supervision and accountability of confessors, pastors, universities and printing presses, regardless of any exemptions previously purchased. Moreover, they asserted that such reforms could only be achieved via the reform of the curial administration and (in an appendix) recommended the reform of Rome itself.[175] Sturm's *Epistle* was a response to this commission; he prefaced his *Epistle* with a pirated text of the report.[176]

In his *Epistle*, Sturm integrated conciliar rhetoric with more traditional Lutheran censures of the papacy. Thus Morison's translation of the tract helped to locate Henry's conciliar propaganda within the overarching anti-papal campaign, deriding papal authority and practices. It can also be seen as part of a concerted effort to align England with the League's position and a continuation of the policy of publicizing important German Protestant tracts in English. In a short section, Morison (rather imaginatively) translated Sturm's praise for England's religious position as 'aloone perelesse, wonderfullye amended: England maye be a mirrour, a guyde, a teacher, an example to all the reste'.[177]

Sturm's *Epistle* censured the commission and its recommendations. His main criticisms lay in their apparent unwillingness to tackle problems in Rome, the absence of any consideration of doctrinal matters, and that the commission itself seemed to be merely an attempt by the pope 'under the colour of correctinge of a fewe thinges, [to] go aboute to recover your usurped auctoritie'.[178] Structural and evangelical considerations permeated the work, which denounced the practices and doctrines of

---

[175] Ibid., i. 423–8; D. Fenlon, *Heresy and Obedience in Tridentine Italy: Cardinal Pole and the Counter Reformation* (Cambridge, 1972), 42–3.

[176] J. Sturmius, *De eadem re, ad Cardinalis caeterosquae viros ad eam consultationem delectos* (Strasbourg, 1537); *Concilium delectorum cardinalem ac aliorum Praelatorum de emendanda* (Strasbourg, 1538). The latter was not reproduced in the English version.

[177] Sturmius, *Epistle*, Eii[v]–iii[r].   [178] Ibid., B[r–v], Bviii[r]–Ciii[v], D[r].

the Roman church as corrupt. Morison retained passages that were unambiguous in their support of Luther, for example: 'Ye can never make the name of Luther so hated, but that whan your falshod is knowen, the trouth woll appere.'[179] This demonstrated sympathy with the theological position of the Schmalkaldic League, though it is unclear whether Morison preserved such passages out of personal optimism or governmental attempts to woo the League. By retaining them, Morison was associating the government with support for Lutheran sentiments.

Explicit references to General Councils abounded in Sturm's *Epistle*. Sections of the tract made an appeal for a true and free General Council along similar lines to those envisaged by the German princes and the English authorities, 'let there be appoynted a councille, where frely, and without feare of punyssshemente, men maye saye theyr myndes, in all mattiers'.[180] The papacy and its adherents could not be exclusive judges at such a Council, as they were 'moost accused', a position also taken in Henry's *Epistle* and *Protestation*.[181] Sturm lamented that previous popes' exploitation of General Councils for their own purposes had eroded the estimation in which Councils were held, and expressed his hope that this could be restored by a free Council.[182] Sturm feared that no German bishop would be heard at a General Council and that the coming Council would follow the Council of Constance and destroy the true promoters of the faith. The cardinals were also accused of being so full of preconceptions that they had condemned the Germans without hearing them or reading their books.[183]

Several further tracts were printed that were complementary to Henry's campaign against a tyrannical Council called by a corrupt papacy. Like Sturm's *Epistle* they placed the *Protestation* and *Epistle* in a line of English polemic differentiating papal Councils from true Councils. *A treatise concernynge generall councilles, the byshoppes of Rome and the clergy* (1538) used scriptural evidence to articulate in an accessible manner the theological argument against a General Council convened and managed by the papacy.[184] In 1539 John Gough printed *An abbreviation of all general councils*, a translation and expansion of Jean Le Maire des Belges' *Traicté de la difference des schismes et des conciles*

---

[179] Sturmius, *Epistle*, Dv[v], Eiii[v]–iv[r], Fiv[r–v].   [180] Ibid., Eii[r]–iv[v], Fvii[r]–viii[r].

[181] Ibid., Cvii[r].   [182] Ibid., Av[r–v], Fvi[v]–Fvii[r].   [183] Ibid., Ciii[v], E[v], Bvi[v]–vii[r].

[184] Sawada, 'Two Anonymous Tudor Treatises', 197–214. Sawada mistakenly attributed the surviving manuscript copy (Hatfield House, 46) to Alesius, but it is not in his handwriting and Alesius' tract was probably written in Latin. [C. St German], *Treatise concernynge generall councils, the byshoppes of Rome and the clergy* (London, 1538).

de l'eglise (Paris, 1511). Le Maire's treatise argued that all the schisms suffered by the catholic church stemmed from the morally corrupt papacy while highlighting that temporal rulers could and had called General Councils. That the tract was written before the Break with Rome helped lend credence to the official Henrician polemics produced by Morison.[185]

The *Apomaxis* and the General Council tracts demonstrate the importance Henry VIII continued to attach to his international reputation. From the very first, Morison was envisaged as a polemicist whose works could be used on the continent. As well as issuing a tract in his own name he was responsible for both of Henry's statements on the General Council, the only major works to be issued in Henry's name aimed at a foreign audience in the later 1530s. Thus as well as being the main voice of the king in England, he was the main voice of the king abroad.

[185] J. Britnell, 'Anti-Papal Writing in the Reign of Louis XII: Propaganda and Self-promotion', in J. and R. Britnell (eds.), *Vernacular Literature and Current Affairs in the Early Sixteenth Century* (Aldershot, 2000), 49–52.

3

The Propagandist: Part 2

THE *COMFORTABLE CONSOLATION*

Background

On 12 October 1537 Henry VIII's long-awaited male heir was born. Edward's birth was the most fervently celebrated event of the reigns of the first four Tudors and was met with bonfires, bell-ringing, feasting and large-scale celebrations,[1] but Jane Seymour's death on 22 October interrupted the festivities and sent the court and country into mourning. Henry's government was eager to capitalize on Edward's birth and encourage compliance with the crown. To this end Morison composed a *Comfortable Consolation*. It was not a propaganda tract in the same sense as the *Remedy* or the *Lamentation* as it was not written to allay a specific threat, counter a particular criticism or justify a new policy. Instead, it was positive propaganda, designed to commend Henry, his actions and his family. The Royal Supremacy and evangelical progress were promoted and the country instructed on proper behaviour. That more copious propaganda in this positive vein may have existed than is now extant is suggested by the fragment appropriately dubbed a *Panegyric of Henry VIII as abolisher of papal abuses* (London, 1536–7), which also praised the king and Queen Jane.

The professed purpose of the *Comfortable Consolation* was to reassure England that it should celebrate Edward's birth rather than mourn Jane's death. Consequently, it juxtaposed the joy and sorrow caused by each event. Jane had been a good queen and England had had 'great cause to desire her long continuance with us'.[2] Yet Edward was the greatest blessing, meaning tragedy was to be feared. Therefore Morison

---

[1] S. J. Gunn, 'War, Dynasty and Public Opinion in Tudor England', in Bernard and Gunn, *Authority and Consent*, 139–41.

[2] *Comfortable Consolation*, Aiii^r, Aiv^v, Avii^r, Bviii^v.

told the story of Paulus Aemilius, whose fears that disaster would befall his 'commonwealthe' after a victorious military campaign were only alleviated when fortune visited him with personal, rather than public tragedy. Morison portrayed Jane's death as a similarly fortuitous event that guaranteed Edward's survival.[3]

As with most of the polemical works written in this period, the *Comfortable Consolation* actually worked on a number of levels and contained a number of discrete, but complementary, messages. On one level it was a eulogy for Jane Seymour. Jane's virtues, among which were honour, shamefastness and knowledge, were typographically highlighted. A more careful reading would have revealed a more extensive encomium to Jane's constancy, chastity and other praiseworthy qualities. Morison also acknowledged Jane's Seymour heritage, describing her as 'a fayre PHENIX'.[4] This use of the Seymour family crest was picked up by contemporary poets: 'Phoenix Jane dies, a Phoenix borne, we're sad | That no one age two Phoenixes e're had'.[5] Despite her numerous personal virtues, Jane's greatest accomplishment was giving birth to Edward. It was this for which she would be most remembered and honoured by posterity: 'All englysshe men may saye, Blessed was thy wombe, that hath brought forth so fayre fruite.'[6]

Morison ventriloquized the dead queen, providing seven pages which he claimed Jane would say 'if she coulde nowe speake to us'. He first used Jane to console the nation. Now in 'blysse', her life had exceeded her hopes and expectations. Thus the country should celebrate her good fortune rather than mourn her passing. She had died at the best possible time, when the country could not help but be happy; any excessive mourning was an unjustified 'disapprovynge of goddis ordynance'. Morison also had Jane advocate subservience to the king and stress its benefits: 'saving the pleasure that man taketh of honest actes, the highest pleasure that manne or woman fyndeth upon erthe, is to runne hardest in a princis favour'. She appealed to her supporters to 'serve your kynge, obey his highnes' for the love they bore her. This emphasis on obedience was in keeping with the dead queen's motto, 'bound to obey and serve'. Jane's dying wish linked deference to Henry with the hopes bound up

---

[3] Ibid., Biii[r]–iv[v]. Plutarch, *Life of Aemilius* 35–6.

[4] *Comfortable Consolation*, Avii[v], Div[v]–vi[r].

[5] Quoted in J. N. King, *English Reformation Literature* (Princeton, 1982), 165. Strikingly similar Latin verse also circulated: 'Phoenix Jana nato Phoenice, dolendum | Secula Phoenices nulla tulisse duas' (Foxe, *Actes and Monuments*, 5.148).

[6] *Comfortable Consolation*, Div[v].

with Edward's, and the dynasty's, future: she would consider the love the people felt for her 'imploied to the profytte of myn heyre, if you gyve it all to hys father'.[7] Loyalty to Henry, regardless of what one thought of his policies, was the only guarantee that his male and undisputedly legitimate heir reached maturity safely before he inherited the crown.

'the moste mighty and excellent kyng HENRY the VIII'

A substantial portion of the *Comfortable Consolation* was designed to extol Henry's kingly virtues. Kesselring has shown that conspicuous displays of mercy were important to the Tudor state.[8] Morison recognized the polemical utility of merciful kingship. Henry had pardoned thousands of his 'unkinde and unnatural subjectes', even though he could have legally executed all of the rebels of 1536. Henry, as he 'graciously consydereth the highest lawe in a realme, to be, the welth and saveguard of his subiectes' had offered the rebels a chance to rehabilitate themselves as useful members of the commonwealth.[9] Morison also emphasized that Henry was a 'lerned kinge' who exercised 'great wisdome and high knowledge'. Henry's learning was not confined to the arts, but also embraced 'divyne letters' or theology.[10] Moreover, Henry's long reign had furnished him with extensive practical knowledge of governance, which was of equal virtue to his learning. Henry was paralleled with Hannibal, who, when he had listened to the philosopher Phormio deliver a lecture on military tactics, had heard nothing that matched his own experience as a general. Morison also boldly asked, 'What can Aristotel say, perteynynge to the rule of a realme, that kynge Henry the viii hath not experience of it?'[11]

Morison continued a theme strong in the *Lamentation* and the *Remedy*, praising Henry's astute uncovering of the pope's deceits. Fearful that Henry's learning would lead him to discover the truth, the pope had tried to retain Henry's fidelity by granting one of his 'tycklynge tytles' and had named Henry *defensor fidei*. But the bribe had not worked: Henry had expelled the papacy from his realm and thwarted its plans, becoming the defender of the true faith: 'they ment gyle, but god had in dede chosen hym even soo'.[12] Morison again

---

[7] *Comfortable Consolation*, Aiv^r–vii^v.   [8] Kesselring, *Mercy*, 19–21.
[9] *Comfortable Consolation*, Ci^v. Morison drew upon Cicero, *De Legibus* III.3.8.
[10] *Comfortable Consolation*, Bi^r, Cv^r, Div^r.
[11] Ibid., Dvii^r–viii^v. Cicero, *De Oratore* II.75.   [12] *Comfortable Consolation*, Div^r.

accused popes of protecting their usurped power by deliberately sowing discord and 'civyle warres' in nations that challenged them such as the Bohemians and Germans. More recently, the papacy had turned against England, hoping to reverse Henry's rejection of its power. The pope and his followers had not just attempted to raise the commons of England, but had also tried 'to send in our enemies upon us'. He 'wold have us slaine' for rejecting his authority and was manifestly not the paternal influence he claimed.[13] This was not mere polemic on Morison's part—the government now knew of Reginald Pole's legation to find support for an invasion of England.

Consule Verbum Domini

In the *Comfortable Consolation* Morison promoted two distinctive evangelical tenets. The first was the authority of scripture and its necessity for salvation. Morison refined his earlier stipulation that kings should 'redresse thynges of religion', to include their duty to 'sette forthe the word and glorie of god'. Jehosophat was the Old Testament exemplar invoked as the ideal. Early in his reign, he had sent out members of his nobility with 'men well sene in the lawe of god' who taught his people the 'lawes of god'.[14] England had suffered spiritual bondage as popes had subverted the true faith, deliberately turned people from Christ and his word and had erroneously encouraged all levels of society to think 'nothing lesse . . . [to] appertayne unto them than the knowledge of scripture'. Morison drew a direct biblical parallel between England and the Israelites on this point:

It was to trewe in this oure realm, it is to trewe in other yet, that the prophet Elias sayeth in the person of god. My people (sayth he) was made captyve, was brought in to bondage, bycause they had no knowledge of me and my worde, the nobilitie dyed for hunger, the multitude dryed away for thurst. The texte meaneth, a famine of goddis worde, to have reigned longe amonges the people.[15]

It was the implications for salvation of scriptural understanding that underlay Morison's continued stress on access to the word of god. Thus the importance of scripture in the *Comfortable Consolation* went beyond the general concern with obedience apparent in most Henrician

---

[13] Ibid., Civ^v–v^v. German anti-papal polemic also consistently emphasized the divisive activities of the papacy.
[14] *Comfortable Consolation* Ev^v–vi^r.   [15] Ibid., Cii^{r-v}, Cvi^v.

propaganda of the 1530s. Unlike Gardiner and Sampson, Morison was
not appropriating a Tyndalian language of scripture-based obedience
to make a conservative vision of the English church more attractive to
Henry VIII.[16] Morison viewed scripture as the basis for the English
church, the standard by which doctrine should be measured and a means
to grace for the individual.

Despite papal machinations, Henry had recognized the importance of
scripture. Whereas in Morison's *Remedy*, Henry had 'wholly intended'
to 'bring in the word of god', he had now done more to promote
knowledge of the word and for 'the serchynge out of trouth' than any
of his predecessors. Morison depicted Henry's actions as a laudable
example that other princes should follow if they wished to worship god
effectively.[17] Moreover, he left Henry's subjects in no doubt that Henry
himself advocated a new religious programme founded on scripture:

His grace biddeth us to harken to the prophete Ezechiel, that saythe, walke
not in the preceptis of your fathers, kepe not their decrees, walke onely in my
precepts, kepe my decrees & lyve in them. Seke saith Christ & ye shall be
opened. Where shalte thou seke? In thy fathers lyfe? Thou runnest into the
darke. Thou shalt but wander, excepte thou take a candel with the. The candelle
is, as the Prophet sayeth, the word of god.

Thus Morison established scripture as Henry's professed basis for his
church. Once again, he linked scripture to the duties of kingship,
asserting that kings should take counsel from the word of God.[18] He
also implied that Henry would be unsympathetic to arguments that
long-standing custom validated ceremonies and rituals. Henry's actual
stance on 'unwritten verities' was, as Morison knew, more complicated
at this point.[19]

Henry had shown himself to be sympathetic to vernacular scripture as
early as the 1520s, while Cromwell's injunctions of 1536 had provided
that every church had to have an English Bible by August 1537 and
had required that congregations receive regular instruction on several
articles of the faith.[20] Concurrently, this emphasis on the centrality of
scripture to Henry's reforms was becoming increasingly important in
Henry's pictorial iconography. Joos van Cleve's portrait of Henry of
c.1535 depicted a king informed by scripture, an iconography more fully

---

[16] For the conservatives' use of Tyndale see Rex, 'Crisis of Obedience', 863–94.
[17] *Remedy*, Eiii[r]; *Comfortable Consolation*, Eiii[v].   [18] Ibid., Evi[r], Fi[r].
[19] See below, ch. 5.   [20] Rex, *Henry VIII*, 119–20, 123 and n. 25.

explicated by the title page of the great Bible in 1539.[21] Morison's tracts were developing this iconography and integrating it into discussions of obedience and English identity.

It is hardly surprising, then, to find that individual Bible reading was advocated in the *Comfortable Consolation*. Morison recommended his readership peruse Old Testament stories. These safe educational texts would prove his points and 'the sense of these texts maye well be sene without any expositour'. Morison also assumed throughout that his readers would have access to the New Testament. More specifically he advocated that all men should 'Take counsel at the word of God', that the whole temporality should know scripture and that it was the duty of kings to make the word of god available to the masses.[22] He implicitly anticipated official policy: he argued for individual reading, nearly a year before Cromwell's 1538 Injunctions gave it official sanction. Although, sensibly, he never explicitly promoted individual reading of the New Testament, this was clearly his intention. Morison was not alone in advocating Bible reading before it gained official sanction. Early defenders of Tyndale had argued strongly in favour of vernacular scripture, and several works printed in the 1530s outlined the moral and didactic benefits of studying the Bible.[23] However, there was one crucial difference: Morison's exhortations came in a pamphlet issued by the government.

'puttyng away idolatrie' (Ev^v)

A second area in which Morison angled for further reform was that of images. He approvingly discussed three Old Testament kings' suppression of idolatrous practices and thereby flatteringly located Henry within a tradition of godly, reforming kings responsible for centrally led iconophobic initiatives. Asa was praised for his godly campaign against idols and superstition and his dispassionate enforcement of religious decrees, even against his own mother. This was a pointed reference, probably aimed at gaining sympathy for Henry's treatment of Mary.[24] Henry was also positioned alongside Hezekiah, who had rejected the idolatry of his father and commanded his priests to 'make clene the hous of god', and Jehosophat, whose campaigns against idolatry were rewarded by divine

---

[21] King, *Tudor Royal Iconography*, ch. 2.

[22] *Comfortable Consolation*, Ei^r, Eiii^v, Evi^r, Evii^{r-v}, Eviii^r.

[23] J. F. McDiarmid, 'Humanism, Protestantism, and English Scripture, 1533–1540', *JMRS*, 14 (1984), 121–38.

[24] *Comfortable Consolation*, Eiii^v, Eiv^r.

protection from his enemies and widespread renown.[25] Asa, Hezekiah and Jehosophat were useful exempla on which to draw as they were among the Old Testament prototypes for Henry's Supremacy in earlier tracts such as Gardiner's *De vera obedientia* and Foxe's *De vera differentia*. Asa's iconoclasm even featured in the royal picture collection by 1542, where it was one of a small number of images that were radical in the English context.[26] Henry could thus have no objection to the use of such kings in his iconography. Yet Morison's use of Jehosophat in 1537 had a subversive edge: although he had been a notable maintainer of the laws and a godly king, he had allowed vestiges of idolatry to remain. Consequently Morison could praise Henry whilst pointing out that if future reform did not come then Henry's subjects, like Jehosophat's before them, would remain unreformed in their hearts. By invoking Jehosophat, Morison pointed out just how far Henry's church still had to go, as John Bale was later to do in his *Epistle exhortatory*.[27]

In 1536 the sixth of the Ten Articles, 'Of Images', had addressed the need to discourage adoration of images. Meanwhile, several local saint cults, such as those in Pilton in Devon, were suppressed as a consequence of the monastic dissolutions. Yet official instructions to remove images on a local level were first issued in Cromwell's Injunctions of October 1538.[28] The *Comfortable Consolation* expressed approval for Henry's existing iconophobic policies and promoted the further reform of images ahead of official policy. Again, Morison avoided overstepping the mark; he did not advocate violent iconoclasm.

There is also the possibility that Morison covertly advocated communion in both kinds. Morison lamented that 'men have not sought their salvation at Christe, at his blode, at his death' but had instead been fooled by indulgences and other papal inventions. Later in the tract, Morison asserted that the papacy had diverted the 'lyvely water that runneth to everlastynge lyfe', but Henry had ensured that they 'shall no more converte this hevenly liquor unto their lucre, ambition, pride, arrogancy'. Thanks to Henry, in England 'every man may nowe drinke his salvation, whiche before gulled in nothing but untrouthes'.[29] The

---

[25] *Comfortable Consolation*, Ev[v]–vii[v].

[26] W. A. Shaw (ed.), *Three Inventories of the Years 1542, 1547 and 1549–50* (London, 1937), 54; S. Foister, *Holbein and England* (London, 2004), 151.

[27] On Bale see C. Bradshaw, 'The Exile Literature of the Early Reformation: "Obedience to God and the King" ', in Amos, Pettegree and von Nierop, *Christian Society*, 118–19.

[28] M. Aston, *England's Iconoclasts* (Oxford, 1988), 224–37.

[29] *Comfortable Consolation*, Biv[v], Evi[v]–vii[r].

use of watery language when discussing salvation was not unusual, which makes it difficult to determine if these passages are merely rhetorical, or if they were advocating further reform. In his theological works Morison was clearly in favour of communion in both kinds. He may have been unable to resist a jibe that only the initiated would appreciate, but which would advertise his own reforming credentials.

'the singular providence and dryfte of god'

As well as advocating religious policies not yet in force, the *Comfortable Consolation* simultaneously developed a providential picture of Henry's reign, marking an important progression in Morison's ideological construction of Henry's kingship. In the *Lamentation* and the *Remedy*, providentialism was present, but it was not an essential feature of the tracts. Thus Morison could claim that the Lincolnshire rebels had merely served to strengthen ties between Henry and his nobles, and that England had been sent rain to 'to save us from our bloodshedding' (a reference to the flooding of the Don on 26 October 1536). He could also assert that God had chosen Henry rather than his elder brother Arthur to be king and ask if God had gone to such lengths to ensure Henry's kingship, who were the rebels to complain? Although Morison had pointed out in the *Lamentation* that God was bound to Henry 'for the settynge out of his moste holy worde', he had not yet articulated a fully fledged providential interpretation of Henry's reign.[30]

As Henry was God's elect king, 'chosen and sent us by the hand of god, and his clere election', all threats to his reign had ultimately worked out to his benefit.[31] The adversity and seditions he faced were a sign of God's favour, an opportunity to win fame and glory. The feats of rulers who were severely tested were immortalized by chroniclers so that posterity could appreciate their greatness. At the start of Henry's reign, God had signalled his favour by James IV's defeat at Flodden. More recently, the Nun of Kent's machinations had failed to harm Henry; instead his adept handling of her would earn him 'immortall fame, eternall praise in all countreys'. Similarly, that Henry had suppressed the 'sediciouse commotions' of the Pilgrimage of Grace without sustaining any damage testified to God's enduring favour: 'he woll our most gracious soveraigne lorde the kyng to be honoured of us and served, as one, whose welthe and savgarde he hathe taken upon hym'. Indeed every obstacle faced by

---

[30] *Remedy*, Biii[r], Cii[r]; *Lamentation*, Bii[v].   [31] *Comfortable Consolation*, Div[r], Ei[r].

Henry had 'brought hym at the last, high praise and great honour'; all his enemies had been overcome. By testing Henry, God was granting him literary immortality.[32]

More than other kings, Henry had been picked for a special purpose, to free his country from servitude to the papacy. He was 'a minister chosen, and even sente to bringe such thinges to passe as of a longe season have bene moche agayne thy commandment and pleasure kept downe. We se from how many ieopardies, from his present dangers, his highness onely by thy providence hath ben preserved.' Only Henry had triumphed where other princes had failed and removed the pope from his kingdom in reward for his evangelical efforts.[33]

The *Comfortable Consolation* situated Henry VIII within a providential dynasty. Henry VII had reigned with 'the speciall favour of god' and had consequently survived 'many sedicions' and the 'folysshe malyce' of 'fonde traytours'. Henry VIII himself had inherited 'the imperyall crowne of this realme, by the singular providence and dryfte of god'. Jane and Edward were further signs. God, 'by his moste hyghe providence and bountie' had removed Henry from 'unclene' marriages and 'provided his grace in pure and chaste matrimony an heire, a goodly prince, an assured token, that he intendeth his graces sede to reygne over us'. Morison explicitly linked Edward's fortuitous birth to the extirpation of the papacy: 'We se the pope is gone, our prince is comme, a devourer of our commen welthe is driven out, a staye of all our welfares is sente from heven.'[34] Edward's birth provided a clear succession within the country, removing any reliance on daughters of dubious legitimacy, who might marry outside the realm and allow 'strange blood' to rule England after Henry's death. Edward was the ultimate providential statement, the undeniable proof of God's favour and a sign of a new covenant between England and God: 'O fortunate countreymen, ar not we nowe newly bounde unto god, that hath sent us one whose brethe we ought more hartileye to have craved of god, than any yea, than all worldly treasures?'[35] Morison was, then, developing a theory of England as a covenanted nation over a decade before it became implicit in the works of Edwardian writers, or explicitly developed in the propaganda of the Marian exiles.[36]

---

[32] *Comfortable Consolation*, Diii^{r-v}, Cviii^{r-v}, Ci^r.   [33] Ibid., Biv^v–vii^r, Diii^v, Ci^r.
[34] Ibid., Di^v–ii^r, Cviii^r, Div^{r-v}.   [35] Ibid., Eii^r, Dvi^v, Bvi^r.
[36] J. Shakespeare, 'Plagues and Punishment', in P. Lake and M. Dowling (eds.), *Protestantism and the National Church* (London, 1987), 108–9.

Morison was unique in using such providential rhetoric in his pamphlets. Claims that England was a chosen nation dated back to the fourteenth century and assertions that Henry was God's chosen ruler may have been commonplace.[37] Morison drew upon this pre-existing tradition, but gave it a new direction by constructing a picture of Henry's kingship which was inescapably religious: Henry was gradually fulfilling his prophetical mission to reform the English church. Such an understanding of Henry's kingship is not present in the tracts which developed the rhetoric on which Henry's church was founded: the *Glasse of Truthe*, Gardiner's *De Vera Obedientia* or Foxe's *De Vera Differentia*. Nor is there any trace in the prefaces to the King's and Bishops' Books. This strand of thought was soon taken up by Morison's colleague, Richard Taverner, who likened Henry's rule to the providential reign of Hezekiah due to the 'wonderfull zeale he beareth to the auau*n*cement of godes true religion' in 1539.[38] However, it was not until the 1540s, and Edward's reign in particular, that providential interpretations of Henry's church reforms became a central component of English evangelical writing.[39] Morison should be appreciated as a potential bridge to such later developments.

'give tha*n*kes unto god'[40]

Morison's providential rhetoric had a further consequence: it highlighted the ongoing need for reform. The *Comfortable Consolation* recognized England's inadequacies and issued warnings to his countrymen. A new covenant required renewed religious commitment from the people of England: if they squandered God's gifts they would incur his wrath. Jane's death highlighted the mortality of princes and that God could take Edward away if he deemed England unworthy.[41] England had been remiss in worshipping God in the past and needed to reform. If God withdrew his favour now, then 'the faulte is ours'. Consequently, Morison repeatedly urged his readers to give reverence and thanks to God, to show they were worthy of such extraordinary fortune.[42] God wished for England's praise, not because he needed it, but 'because he

---

[37] J. W. McKenna, 'How God became an Englishman', in D. J. Guth and J. W. McKenna (eds.), *Tudor Rule and Revolution* (Cambridge, 1982), 25–43.

[38] R. Taverner, *A catechisme or institution of the christen religion* (London, 1539), Aiv^r.

[39] C. Davies, *A Religion of the Word: The Defence of the Edwardian Reformation* (Manchester, 2002), 178–83.

[40] *Comfortable Consolation*, Civ^v.   [41] Ibid., Avi^v.   [42] Ibid., Dii^v, Dviii^{r–v}.

coveyteth to doo us stylle good'. While ringing church bells, making bonfires and holding processions might show other men how the nation felt, God demanded true, internal worship and thanks. Morison therefore exhorted his readers to have 'bournynge myndes [and] inflamed hartes, where the sparkles of hotte charitie may flye from neighbour to neighbour, house to house. Towne to towne, countrey to countrey'.[43] Living a godly life was a more appropriate means of thanksgiving than the traditional celebrations that had met Edward's birth. Like their king, Englishmen should put their faith in God. Worship and faith were the two keys to continued providential favour.[44] Reformation had to come at a personal, as well as a doctrinal level.

In a manuscript tract ostensibly about legal reform, Morison also dealt with the theme of lay behaviour and its role in the commonwealth. His *Persuasion* asserted that England should celebrate and give thanks to God for its deliverance from the papal pharaoh. Englishmen celebrated the Battle of Agincourt and the defeat of the Danes at Hoptide, and similarly the Jews celebrated Passover. How much more apt would it be for Englishmen to 'make bonfires go in procession lauding god with our mouthes and all kynde of instruments' to celebrate Henry's victory over 'th'auncient enemie', the pope? England's triumph was even greater, as Henry had defeated the antichrist himself. However, unlike the Israelites, England needed to remain vigilant as its pharaoh still lived.[45] Ignoring the pope could prove counter-productive and might allow him a way back into English hearts once his evil deeds had been forgotten. This was necessary as popes had disseminated their doctrines using every means at their disposal, through schools, songs, books and plays. Popes had even recognized that Irish scholars' excellent recitations of canon law, despite their deficiencies in comprehension, engendered unwarranted respect for the papacy among the Irish.[46] It is unclear if Morison had any specific knowledge of religious affairs in Ireland, but it is significant that he was trying to explain why Ireland was so troublesome, given the rebellion of 1534 and the problems of the Irish Reformation Parliament.

Morison believed popery to be so ingrained that an aggressive campaign was needed to eradicate it completely. He was aware of the limitations of a print campaign: it could never satisfy everyone and considerable diligence was needed to ensure that any books produced

[43] *Comfortable Consolation*, Eii^v, Ei^{r-v}.   [44] Ibid., Avii^r, Ev^r, Biv^r.

[45] *Persuasion*, fos. 15^v, 17^{r-v}.   [46] Ibid., fos. 16^r, 14^r–15^r.

were free of errors and doubtful doctrines. Morison advocated a patient and strategic approach to those still attached to popery, who should be persuaded of the truth using those tools—'playes, songes and bokes'—previously employed by popes. Furthermore, a time of year should be appointed to teach the wickedness of the pope and his usurped power. Plays specifically were to be turned to Morison's purpose, an idea founded on his belief that 'in to the common people thynges soner enter by the eies thenn the eares'.[47] Plays were an integral part of most schools' curricula and Morison's appreciation of the utility of the dramatic arts probably developed at university.[48] He was not alone in viewing Robin Hood plays as a source of lewd behaviour and disrespect towards the officers of the law. A nationwide proclamation limited the performance of plays in 1544 for these reasons.[49] Yet the Robin Hood plays that Morison so ardently opposed were still an integral part of the religious life of many English parishes in the 1530s.[50] Morison recommended these plays 'be forbidden and deleted' and replaced by plays which 'set forthe and declare truely before the peoples eies the abomination and wickedness of the bishop of Rome, monkes, freres, Nonnes'.[51] Just as he did in his printed works, Morison was suggesting a programme for practical religious change that reached even the lowest levels of society.

Morison's suggestion had seemingly been taken on board by the summer of 1539, when the French ambassador, Marillac, reported that there was scarcely a feast or pastime anywhere in England that was not in some sense anti-papal. Ingram has suggested that the Prince's Players were used to spread the government's message from 1538, when they start to appear in provincial records on a regular basis. Cromwell also took John Bale into his service, where he wrote anti-papal plays such as *King Johan* and patronized a group of players in the later 1530s, although their activities are less well documented.[52] More of Morison's ideas may have found their way into the drama Cromwell sponsored: Cromwell's accounts for February 1539 include a payment

[47] Ibid., fos. 16ʳ–17ᵛ, 18ᵛ.   [48] Potter, 'Performing Arts', 145–50.
[49] The London authorities had taken action much earlier. *TRP*, i.240; R. W. Heinze, *Proclamations of the Tudor Kings* (Cambridge, 1976), 8.
[50] P. W. White, 'Holy Robin Hood! Carnival, Parish Guilds and the Outlaw Tradition', in Kermode and Scott-Warren, *Tudor Drama*, 67–89.
[51] *Persuasion*, fo. 18ʳ⁻ᵛ.
[52] *LP* XIV i 1137. W. Ingram, *The Business of Playing: The Beginnings of the Professional Theatre in Elizabethan London* (London, 1992), 77–81; W. R. Streitberger, *Court Revels, 1485–1559* (Toronto, 1994), 144; *LP* XIV i 1137.

for the costume of 'Divine Providence when she played before the King'.[53]

National Identity: 'all true englyshe hartes'[54]

In the *Comfortable Consolation* Morison appealed to patriotic sentiment even more than he had in the *Lamentation* and *Remedy*. In the *Lamentation* Morison adopted the authorial voice of England itself; in later works he encouraged his readers to identify themselves collectively as England. Vanhoutte was wrong to argue that Morison promoted a secular patriotic vision and that consequently his England 'demands obedience independently of issues of religion and royal rule'.[55] Equally Morison was not, as Mottram has suggested, using 'mother England' (a figure that nowhere appears in Morison's works) to take on 'the rhetoric of resistance'.[56] While Mottram and Vanhoutte are both correct to point out that Morison's England was not co-terminous with Henry VIII, his body politic rhetoric gave every member of the commonwealth a part to play in civil society, from the king to the lowliest commoner. Moreover, Morison constructed a notion of kingship that was explicitly linked to the English Reformation, as was his concept of the subject. Founded on scripture and pure doctrine, the English church was due protection from its head (the king) and support from its body (Henry's subjects). England itself was God's elect nation. These themes were to be developed even further in Morison's *Invective* and *Exhortation*.

THE *INVECTIVE*

Background

In mid-June 1538 Imperial and French ambassadors concluded a truce at Nice which secured a ten-year cessation of hostilities. Charles and Francis met at Aigues-Mortes in mid-July, where they agreed to defend Christendom and work to bring heretics back to the church. Further negotiations in December committed Francis to abandoning

---

[53] *LP* XIV ii 782.   [54] *Comfortable Consolation*, Ai[r].
[55] J. Vanhoutte, 'Engendering England: The Restructuring of Allegiance in the Writings of Richard Morison and John Bale', *Renaissance and Reformation*, 20 (1996), 55.
[56] Mottram, *Empire and Nation*, 107–16.

relations with England and joining a crusade.[57] An already hostile diplomatic environment was worsened when Paul III confirmed Henry's excommunication and by Cardinal Pole's mission to France and Spain to gather support against Henry. Henry thus lost the relative security and leverage he had enjoyed as a result of the two monarchs' rivalry and became even more concerned with the prospect of a joint campaign against him for religion.[58]

It is in the context of this increasing external threat that the government's reaction to a potential internal danger, the 'Exeter Conspiracy' in autumn 1538, should be viewed. The cardinal's brother, Geoffrey Pole, who had been arrested in August, was finally examined on 26 October. Geoffrey's interrogators were largely concerned with two factors: illicit contacts with the cardinal and extracting the names of as many other transgressors as possible.[59] The result was the arrest and eventual execution of large swathes of Pole's family and friends, some of whom had been in Henry's inner circle. The Misses Dodds' view that the Exeter conspiracy was a government construct has found widespread support among historians. Höllger has gone further still, seeing Henry's moves against the Poles as a means to both put pressure on, and exact his revenge against, the cardinal.[60] The conspirators were accused of uttering treasonous words, wishing Henry's death and the reinstatement of popery, and of burning the letters that would have incriminated them. There does not appear to have been any decisive plan to remove Henry, but rather a general dissatisfaction with his policies since his rejection of Catherine and a shared sympathy for Reginald Pole. Yet there was sufficient evidence for the government, and ultimately parliament, to conceive of the Exeter affinity as a real threat.

Henry's treatment of the conspirators provoked widespread criticism abroad. Foreign ambassadors to England doubted the conspiracy's existence and queried the evidence against the accused. Castillon even claimed the so-called conspiracy was created by Henry, as 'quite some time ago this king told me that he would exterminate the house of

[57] R. J. Knecht, *Francis I* (Cambridge, 1982), 291–4.
[58] Further details of Anglo-Spanish relations in this crucial period can be found in S. Brigden, ' "The shadow that you know": Sir Thomas Wyatt and Sir Francis Bryan at Court and in Embassy', *HJ*, 39 (1996), 13–18; J. J. Scarisbrick, *Henry VIII* (London, 1968), 360–1.
[59] C. Höllger, 'Reginald Pole and the Legations of 1537 and 1539: Diplomatic and Polemical Responses to the Break with Rome', D.Phil. thesis (Oxford, 1989), 86–8.
[60] Dodds and Dodds, *Pilgrimage*, ii. chs. 22–3; Elton, *Policy and Police*, ch. 4; Cooper, *Propaganda*, ch. 6; H. Pierce, *Margaret Pole, Countess of Salisbury 1473–1541* (Cardiff, 2003), chs. 5–6. Höllger, 'Reginald Pole', 98–100, 110–18.

Montagu, which still belongs to the White Rose and to the house of
Pole, of which the cardinal is'.[61] In France, many priests, including the
Bishop of Limoges, openly preached against Henry's religious policy
and labelled him a tyrant. Although Henry had some success insisting
that they be prosecuted in accordance with Anglo-French treaties,
Francis soon tired of Henry's seemingly petty concerns. The criticisms
continued in France and Scotland well after the Exeter conspiracy had
been suppressed, encouraged by Reginald Pole's legatine mission.[62]

A propaganda campaign was needed to influence foreign and domestic
opinion. In this atmosphere, Morison composed *An Invective ayenste
the great and detestable, vice, treason*, a government apologetic for the
executions. Three editions, all with a 1539 imprint, survive, suggesting
that it was widely disseminated. It was written and printed sometime
between the executions of Montagu and Exeter on 9 December 1538
and 16 January 1539, when Castillon had obtained a copy. Morison's
omission of Nicholas Carew's name either suggests that he had finished
composing the tract before Carew's arrest on 31 December, or indicates
a reluctance to condemn Carew in print before he had been convicted
in court.[63]

Evidence

By 1539, Morison was undisputedly Henry VIII's leading propagandist
and a natural choice to write against the conspiracy. There may have
been a further reason, though. Gervase Tyndale, a witness against
the countess of Salisbury, claimed to know 'Master Moryson' from
their days at Cardinal College. Tyndale offered to put Richard Ayer,
another potential informant, in touch with Cromwell through either
a kinsman, Gerome Lyn, or Morison. Tyndale probably did contact
Morison, as one notable element from his evidence appeared in the
Invective. He alleged that the Countess of Salisbury would not allow
any of her tenants to own 'the Newe Testament yn Englych or any
other new [books] w*hich* the Kyng Hynes hath pryvelyged'. One of
his informers had been persecuted for his evangelical efforts; Tyndale
himself was forced to leave Warblington after the countess discovered his
evangelical beliefs. Morison similarly reported the countess's hostility
to vernacular scripture, in particular that her family considered it 'a

---

[61] Quoted in Höllger, 'Reginald Pole', 84.   [62] *LP* XIV i 37, 92, 227, 371.1–2, 773.
[63] Ibid., 72.

cryme judged great enough for to put any theyr servants out of service
if they were spyed with a new testament in theyr hands'.[64] Morison
blamed this abhorrence of scripture on the countess's son, Reginald
Pole.

The official roots of the *Invective* can be discerned in close textual
similarities between the tract and the trial records. Morison recounted
the words of Henry Courtenay, marquis of Exeter: 'I truste to have a
fayre day over these knaves that rule aboute the kyng: I trust to se a
mery worlde one daye.'[65] This section of text is almost identical to the
accusation made against Exeter at his trial, that on 20 August 1538 he
had said 'I truste onse to have a fayre day upon thise knavys which rule
abowte the kynge and I trust to se a mery world one day.'[66] Morison
further asserted that Exeter had said, 'I truste to see a chaunge of this
worlde, knaves rule about the kynge: but I trust one day to gyve them a
buffet.' This was an agglomeration of two different statements, alleged
to have been made at different times. In the first statement, Exeter
expressed his approval of Cardinal Pole and disapproval of Henry's
actions. Morison did not need to quote this directly, as the *Invective*
blamed the Exeter affinity's treason on their collaboration with and
support for Pole. After professing support for Pole, Exeter had stated:
'I trust to se a chaynge of this worlde.' On a different occasion, he had
shaken his fist and exclaimed to Geoffrey that 'knaves rule aboute the
kynge; I trust to geve them a buffett one day'.[67] Although Morison
faithfully reproduced the words used to condemn Exeter, combining
two separate utterances sharpened the polemic. Morison also accused
Henry Pole, Lord Montagu of talking and dreaming of the king's death.
The legal evidence presented against Montagu included evidence that
he had 'dreamyd that the kynge is ded' in March 1537, had frequently
suggested that Henry would die of his leg injury, that 'yff he [Henry]
wyll serve us so we shall be happely rydd' and that the king's death
would be greeted with 'ioly styrryngs'.[68] Morison summed up numerous
treasonable outbursts by Montagu as 'lewde prophecies of the world to
come, of the tyme that shoulde make hym and his mery, if he might
tary it'. Again, the phraseology was suggested by an indictment against

[64] BL Cotton Appendix L, fo. 85ʳ [*LP* XIII ii 817]; *Invective*, Cviiᵛ. Pierce's suggestion (*Margaret Pole*, 118) that Tyndale was planted by Cromwell is unlikely, given Tyndale's comments.

[65] *Invective*, Civʳ⁻ᵛ.   [66] KB8/11/2, mm. 9ʳ, 18ʳ [*LP* XIII ii 979.17].

[67] *Invective*, Civʳ; KB8/11/2, mm. 8ᵛ, 9ʳ, 10ʳ, 18ʳ, 25ʳ [*LP* XIII ii 979.17, 15].

[68] *Invective*, Cviᵛ; KB8/11/2, mm. 4ʳ, 5ʳ⁻ᵛ, 26ʳ [*LP* XIII ii 979.7].

Montagu.[69] Other interrogatories can be firmly linked to the *Invective*. Hugh Holland confessed to conveying a message from Reginald Pole to Pole's mother, the countess of Salisbury: 'if I wist thatt she was of the opinion, that oth[ers] bee ther, mother as she is my*n* I wolde treade uppon h[er] w*ith* my feete'.[70] In a long passage designed to blacken Pole's name, Morison similarly reported Pole had sent his mother word that 'if he knew her to be of the same opinion, that the king is of, he wold treade her under his fete'.[71] When Morison made a statement of fact, rather than opinion, he backed it up with evidence which could be substantiated by the legal records.

The wide range of evidence catalogued against the conspirators established the authority of the *Invective*. Morison even claimed to have been present at the trials and executions, describing the conduct of the conspirators, which may well have been the case.[72] Thus Morison composed an officially sanctioned tract that accused the conspirators in some of the same terms and with the same evidence that was actually used to condemn them in court. His methodology when writing the *Invective* was picked up by contemporaries. Nicholas Bacon, Robert Cary and Thomas Denton suggested that the nation's most distinguished lawyers be employed in cases such as treason trials, enabling them to produce more accurate and appealing official accounts against the traitors: 'whereby they being so privy to the matter, [may] the more truly and lively in their chronicles set forth the same'.[73] The *Invective* may even have inspired their suggestion.

Identifying the Enemy

The *Invective*'s preface clearly set out Morison's main purpose in writing; he wished to demonstrate the unlikelihood of any traitor being able to harm Henry, who had God's special protection. Morison demonstrated how God had rewarded traitors against heathen regimes with abject failure, and simultaneously emphasized the threat that treason posed to the realm itself. He did so using a number of classical examples such as Perrenius, Plautianus and Sejanus.[74] Underlying the tract was the

---

[69] *Invective*, Cvii[r]. KB8/11/2, mm. 5[v]–6[r], 21[r]: 'A tyme wyll come. I feare me we shall not tary the tyme. Iff we may tary the tyme we shall do well inough.'

[70] SP1/138, fo. 161[r] [*LP* XIII ii 797.1].   [71] *Invective*, Cvii[v]–viii[r].

[72] Ibid., Evii[v], Fi[v].   [73] *EHD 1485–1558*, 572–3.

[74] *Invective*, aiii[r]–vi[v]. Although this passage was clearly inspired by Machiavelli, *Discourses*, III.6 (on conspiracies), Morison added details which are not found in Machiavelli's text.

message that God upheld the established social order, even in idolatrous or heathen regimes. Thus it was not for men to try to subvert society. In order to provide a contrast to the actions of prominent contemporaries Morison related tales of faithful servants and dogs who demonstrated the intense loyalty all subjects owed to their king.[75]

The *Invective* worked on another level as a vitriolic condemnation of Reginald Pole. Pole had actively tried to raise support for international military action against Henry VIII during the Pilgrimage of Grace and had promoted the General Council Henry was so desperate to avoid; by 1539 he was again trying to mobilize Charles V and Francis I to invade England.[76] Morison portrayed Pole as the central force behind the Exeter Conspiracy, 'the very pole, from whense is poured all this poison'; he was an 'archetraytour', an English Judas, hated by God and despised by all creatures. Pole's classical education should have taught him that his treason would not succeed. Yet he remained undeterred, lured away from loyalty to his king by papal bribes. He had also abused Henry's goodwill and commendations, falsely claiming to be Henry's nephew in order to establish himself in Italian society.[77] Morison's depiction of Pole as the instigator of the conspiracy was paralleled in English diplomatic argument at the time and endured in officially sponsored polemic even after Henry's death.[78] The attack on Pole has often been taken by historians to be the main purpose of the tract.[79] However, the *Invective*'s anti-Pole polemic represents just one theme in a tract which should more rightly be seen in a similar context to the *Remedy*, *Lamentation* and *Comfortable Consolation*.

Although Pole was Morison's arch-traitor, it was his family, the Poles and Courtenays, who had immediately threatened Henry by virtue of their prolonged close proximity to his person. Morison highlighted that both families had received manifold grants and prestigious appointments from Henry and his father. The Poles and Courtenays had returned Henry's favour and patronage with ingratitude and betrayal, by talking of the king's death and harbouring military ambitions. Morison included evidence of Exeter's military intentions against Henry. Exeter had

---

[75] *Invective*, Biv[v]–vi[v]. Based on Pliny's *Natural History* (8.40, 7.16) and Plutarch's *Life of Anthony* (76.4).

[76] Höllger, 'Reginald Pole', *passim*; Mayer, *Prince and Prophet*, ch. 2.

[77] *Invective*, Cviii[r], Bviii[r–v], Biii[r]–iv[r], Di[r].

[78] G. F. Nott, *The Works of Sir Thomas Wyatt the Elder* (London, 1815), ii. 508–11 [*LP* XIV i 280]; *Hall's Chronicle*, 826.

[79] See most recently Cooper, *Propaganda*, 159–61.

commanded his servant Kendall to 'make as many men in redynes as he coulde, whiche myght serve within an houres warning'.[80] This was a reference to the 1531 accusations against Exeter for illegal retaining, which had resulted in his banishment from court. Cooper has highlighted the polemical effect of omitting the date of the illegal retaining: Exeter's actions would take on a new perspective if Henry had a legitimate heir.[81] Morison may have conflated the old accusation with more recent ones, but the prospect of a military threat was not without foundation in the legal records he had to hand. The evidence presented against Montagu, Exeter and Geoffrey recorded their approval of Reginald Pole's recent actions. Pole had, with papal backing, been attempting to persuade foreign princes to invade England; the *Invective* ensured this became widely known.[82] Geoffrey had allegedly considered joining the Pilgrimage of Grace, while Montagu was accused of criticizing Lord Darcy, a prominent figure in the Pilgrimage, for attacking the Council instead of the 'hed' [Henry].[83] Furthermore, in September 1538, William FitzWilliam, earl of Southampton, had uncovered rumours that Geoffrey Pole planned to take an armed force to Reginald Pole at Easter 1539.[84] Morison linked the 'breakfast' that Exeter had wanted to give Henry's courtiers in 1531 with his actions in 1536–7 to show a continuous stream of treasonable intent. During the Pilgrimage of Grace, Geoffrey Pole had thought himself to 'be at the begynnyng of the breakefast, to the whiche the Marquis [of Exeter] was byddyng styl his gestes'. More specifically, this was tied to Hugh Holland's confession that he had relayed a message from Cardinal Pole that Geoffrey and Montagu 'shulde not sturre while he came'.[85] The Exeter affinity's actual ability to raise sufficient troops in 1538 is to some extent irrelevant. What mattered was their intentions and the strategic importance of their lands on the south-west coast.[86] Any hint that they might be conspiring with Pole's legation had to be taken seriously.

There were sufficient witnesses to make the marquis guilty by the terms of the 1534 Treason Act, that it was treason to 'malicyously wyshe

---

[80] *Invective*, Ei^v, Ciii^r–vii^r; KB8/11/2, mm. 5^v–6^r, 21^r.

[81] *LP* V 340, 416; Cooper, *Propaganda*, 154–5.

[82] Mayer, *Prince and Prophet*, ch. 2; *Invective*, Dii^v.   [83] KB8/11/1, mm. 5^r, 21^r.

[84] Dodds and Dodds, *Pilgrimage*, ii. 307–9; *LP* XIII ii 392, 393.

[85] SP1/140, fo. 3^v, 'the king shuld have a brekefast before michelmas daye' [*LP* XIII ii 961.1, 961.2]; SP1/138, fo. 179^r [*LP* XIII ii 804.2]; *Invective*, Dii^v–iii^r. Geoffrey's desire to be with Reginald on the continent is frequently found in KB8/11.

[86] Pierce, *Margaret Pole*, 157–62.

will or desire by wordes or writinge, or by crafte ymagen invent practise or attempte, any bodily harme to be done or comytted' against the king.[87] Yet official unease at almost exclusive reliance upon the Act in condemning the conspirators is implied by Morison's inclusion of more evidence against Exeter. At his trial Exeter had 'foyled and staggerde in suche sorte, that all menne might see his countenance, to avouch that, that his tonge could nat without moche foltring deny'.[88] As further proof of the conspiracy Morison noted that on the scaffold the traitors 'did all acknowlege their offences towarde the kinge'.[89] Scaffold confessions of guilt and repentance were common in the Tudor period as part of a set piece in which the audience were educated in the evil of sedition and the need to die reconciled to the state and God, with the repentant condemned setting themselves up as examples.[90] Thus it is significant that Morison felt it necessary to include such detail as evidence of guilt. Geoffrey Pole proved key to revealing the true extent of the conspiracy. When he had been arrested, the government had been unaware of any conspiracy; it had only come to light once Geoffrey confessed following a failed suicide attempt. Probably in response to contemporary rumours Morison emphasized that Geoffrey had freely confessed without fear of torture. For polemical purposes, Geoffrey's confession became more sudden and complete in the *Invective* than the piecemeal revelations suggested by the surviving documents.[91]

To Morison, it was hardly surprising that the Poles had turned to treason—they supported the wrong religion, so could not be trusted to have political integrity: 'if these men had not ben enemies to the gospel, haters of goddis worde, they coulde never have fallen in to suche an abhomynable sorte of treasons'. This link between sedition and wrong religion was more explicit in their obstructive actions—they had deliberately hindered the king's religious policies when the opportunity arose. Morison also warned his readers that anyone who doubted the king's supremacy was by definition a traitor.[92] Once again, Morison

---

[87] 26 Henry VIII c. 13.

[88] *Invective*, Fi[v]. Höllger, 'Reginald Pole', 96–7, suggests Exeter was prevented from speaking at his trial.

[89] *Invective*, Fii[r].

[90] L. B. Smith, 'English Treason Trials and Confessions in the Sixteenth Century', *JHI*, 15 (1954), 417–98.

[91] *Invective*, Eiii[r]–vi[v]. For a detailed account of the surviving evidence see Höllger, 'Reginald Pole', 93–105. Contemporary rumours are recorded in the *[Spanish] Chronicle of King Henry VIII*, ed. M. A. S. Hume (London, 1889), ch. 9.

[92] *Invective*, Cvii[r–v], Fiii[v].

was identifying papal supporters as religious enemies of the king and his subjects.

'Ah lord, thy providence is wonderful'[93]

The *Invective* developed several themes found in Morison's earlier tracts. In particular, his vision of Henry as God's elect king, chosen to bring his elect nation, the English, out of the yoke of idolatry and servitude to Rome and lead England to true religion, found full expression. Henry was 'his chosen king, a prynce that chyefelye above all thinges, hath soughte and seketh, to sette forthe his glorie, to restore his holy worde, to put downe hypocrysie, to banishe idolatry, and finally to bring this ones to passe, that all his people, may be as they ar called, that is trewe chrystians'.[94] To Morison God had chosen Henry to repel the papacy from England:

Ah lord, thy providence is wonderful, thou blyndest, thou gevest lyght, thou hardnest, thou dost entre where thy pleasure is. Some runne faste, and yet come shorte, bycause they lose the waye: some tary long, and yet be formest. Thou appoyntest a tyme to call in thyne electe, that wander, thou turneste theyr hartes to the, when thy pleasure is, that straied amonges them, whiche were and be ferdest frome the. Of all the miracles and wonders of our time, I take the change of our soveraygne lordes opinion in matters conceninge Religion, to be even the gretest.

Henry's extirpation of the papacy from England was doubly miraculous as he had once been its defender and had once seemed the least likely ruler to reject popery.[95]

Henry's deliverance from danger was also portrayed as providential, no doubt in part to counter accusations that Henry had fabricated the conspiracy. Exeter and Edward Neville had been in his trusted inner circle for over thirteen years and had had plenty of opportunities to harm him; it was a miracle that Henry had survived the danger. Similarly, Geoffrey's bungled suicide attempt had ultimately turned events to Henry's favour, and the full extent of the threat had been revealed.[96] Any future treachery against Henry was futile because God would protect him, just as he had protected him from the plans of the Poles, Courtenays and the Pilgrims.

[93] *Invective*, Div^r.   [94] Ibid., avi^r.   [95] Ibid., Div^{r–v}.   [96] Ibid., Ei^v–v^v.

In the iconography of the *Invective*, Henry was closely linked to David. Morison implied that like David, Henry had sinned, but had repented, reformed and received forgiveness. Henry, however, enjoyed even greater favour than David as he had not known of the danger surrounding him.[97] Morison thus drew upon an established iconography to depict Henry as a learned king, whom God would protect in adversity. At the same time he appealed to Henry's own notion of his kingship.[98] Henry's subjects had more cause to be grateful for Henry and his feats than Israel had for David; if they did not recognize the debt they owed to God now, they probably never would. To show their gratitude, they should imitate David and write 'himnes and dities of thankes' in his praise. The punishment for ingratitude, Morison warned, would be severe, as God 'ofte layeth sore to his chosen and elect people forgetfulnes of his benefitis toward them'.[99] This was set against the stark knowledge that England's arch-enemy the pope wanted foreign princes to invade England.

Usage

The *Invective* was deliberately used to ensure conformity in diplomatic apologetic. In audiences with foreign diplomats Henry emphasized that the executions had been justified and detailed the evidence against the conspirators. Meanwhile, Henry's own ambassadors were given the *Invective* to help them defend their king's actions. Henry sent Wyatt 'a pretty boke' to help him detail the Poles' and Courtenays' treason. Meanwhile, Wriothesley believed that 'thise thinges of the Merquis, Montacute, Nevel and Carrowe' would be 'translated and sent also in to other partys'.[100] Morison's *Invective* and the parallel English diplomatic efforts apparently had some effect on foreign opinion. Pole was told that Charles's cool attitude towards him stemmed from the English portrayal of him. Pole himself felt the need to refute Morison's *Invective* in his *Apologia ad Carolum Quintum*, which was intended as the preface to *De Unitate*.[101]

---

[97] Ibid., Aiv[r], Avii[r–v].
[98] King, *Tudor Royal Iconography*, 76–81; P. Tudor-Craig, 'Henry VIII and King David', in *Early Tudor England: Proceedings of the 1987 Harlaxton Symposium*, ed. D. Williams (Woodbridge, 1989), 183–206.
[99] *Invective*, Aiv[r]–v[r], Ai[v].
[100] BL Harley 282, fo. 47[r], SP1/143, fo. 15[r] [*LP* XIV i 280, 233]; *LP* XIV i 37, 72, 208.
[101] Mayer, *Reginald Pole*, 98; T. F. Mayer, *A Reluctant Author: Cardinal Pole and his Manuscripts* (Philadelphia, 1999), 52–3; *CRP*, i.243–4.

The diplomatic usage of the *Invective* reflected England's deteriorating international relationships. At the start of February, the French ambassador, Castillon, announced his recall. No replacement was named, and over the next few weeks both William Honing and Bonner failed in their efforts to discover the identity of the new ambassador. Concurrently, the Imperial ambassador, Chapuys, was revoked before a replacement had arrived, heightening Henry and Cromwell's suspicions that Francis and Charles were plotting to invade England. England was on a state of alert until Castillon's replacement Charles de Marillac arrived on 28 March, with Henry trying to use English trade as leverage to head off the impending crisis.[102]

THE *EXHORTATION*

'TO styrre all Englyshe men to the defence of theyr countreye'[103]

At some point during this crisis, Morison composed another propaganda tract for the government. Morison's *Exhortation to styrre all Englyshe men to the defence of theyr countreye* was another widely distributed piece of polemic, running to three editions in 1539. The content and purpose of the tract indicate it was written to be available by early March at the latest. The *Exhortation* is closely linked to the *Invective* and contains large sections of related material.

The *Exhortation* was primarily written to prepare the country for war. Morison again constructed a narrative in which Henry personally strove to defend his country against invasion and superstition. The king faced unjustified aggression from his neighbours as the pope urged foreign princes to attack England to further his own political and financial ambition. Although 'all good men' should 'desyre peace, concorde, and ernest amitie, betwene nation and nation', when it was unavoidable, rulers could resort to violence for defensive purposes.[104] Morison described a king personally vigilant to ensure adequate military preparations were made. Henry spent 'dayes and nightes devysynge all the wayes, that wytte can invent, for our assuraunce' and had overseen the expansion and modernization of the realm's defences, such that

---

[102] *LP* XIV i 337, 353, 355, 365; Heinze, *Proclamations*, 143–4.
[103] *Exhortation*, Ai[r].   [104] Ibid., Aii[r–v].

England would 'be moch liker a castel, than a realme'. To hammer
home his point, Morison listed some of the fortifications Henry had
commissioned. Such was his concern and dedication to protecting his
whole realm that he was prepared to invest his personal treasure to
finance its defences.[105] Henry's personal involvement in the defensive
campaign is borne out by Morison's contemporaries.[106]

Morison combined his vision of a just, religious war with a return
to anti-sedition material and appeals for obedience, asserting that 'all
men within the reache and dominion of a prince, are by goddis worde
commaunded to be obeysaunt to his hestes and pleasure, not only
for feare of punyshement, but for consciences sake'. Subjects had a
reciprocal responsibility to their prince: just as he owed them physical
and spiritual protection, they owed him obedience. Morison redeployed
the body politic imagery of the *Remedy*, suggesting that England would
be more quiescent if Englishmen were better at diagnosing the ills of the
realm.[107] Even ancient pagans had sacrificed themselves for the good of
their country. Morison also linked the *Exhortation* to the lessons of the
Invective by asking, 'If dedes maye speake, doo not so many exaumples,
as we have had a late, preach shameful death to all traytours, to al
rebels?'[108] Treason and sedition were futile as God would protect the
rightful king, especially when that king was engaged in a struggle for
God's word.

Part of Morison's strategy for galvanizing the country for war involved
reporting the scandalous rumours being spread on the continent about its
military insufficiency. Morison appealed to patriotic sentiment, asking:
'wolde not this contumely, this spytefull tale, make us shewe unto
suche reporters, that as long as Englyshe bodies remayn in Englande,
they shal also fynde Englyshe stomackes, Englysshe handes, Englysshe
hartes?'[109] Designed to prepare the country mentally and practically for
war, the *Exhortation* was closely linked to the muster held in London
on 8 May. By 11 March the muster commissions had been issued,
giving the city plenty of time to prepare for the military spectacle.
Contemporaries viewed the muster as an impressive display of military
strength: 'there was never a goodlyer sight in London, nor the citizens
better besene'.[110] If Hall and diplomatic commentators are correct in

[105] Ibid., Diii[r]–iv[r].
[106] BL Harley 4990, fo. 5[v]; *Hall's Chronicle*, ed. H. Ellis (London, 1809), 826–9.
[107] *Exhortation*, Aii[r]–iii[v].   [108] Ibid., Cii[r].   [109] Ibid., Biv[r].
[110] C. Wriothesley, *A Chronicle of England during the Reigns of the Tudors*, CS 2nd ser. 11
(1875), i. 96–7; *Hall's Chronicle*, 828–30.

their estimates of *c*.15,000 participants, the May musters represent the
largest mobilization of London in the sixteenth century.[111]

'For the warre is not yours, but Goddes'[112]

In the *Exhortation*, as in the *Invective*, Cardinal Pole was central to the
military threat England faced and at the heart of domestic conspiracy.
Morison claimed that although Pole had initially been repelled by
Rome, he had since transferred his allegiance. Now he was collaborating
with, and encouraging, the pope's plans to return England to the papal
tyranny it had so recently escaped.[113] These accusations had a basis
in reality—Pole was involved in papal diplomacy which was aimed at
encouraging foreign powers to ally against Henry.[114] Moreover, Pole
was envisaged as a real focus for treasonous activity, and was cited in
numerous attainders for treason in the 1530s and 1540s.[115] Morison was
not obsessed with attacking Pole, rather he was discrediting a real threat.

The *Exhortation* vilified Reginald Pole as England's arch-enemy,
although the *Invective* was a far more comprehensive condemnation.
Pole was referred to as 'Reynard' (the fox) with all the implications of
sleight and deceit that entailed.[116] In both works, Morison played on
the pronunciation of Pole's name, using watery imagery when referring
to him. Pole's influence was thus portrayed as fluid, insidious, dangerous
and flowing from Rome, creating a distinctive link between the two
tracts. In the *Invective*, Morison lamented: 'o pole, o hurle pole, full
of poyson, that wouldest have drowned thy countrey in bloudde, thou
thoughtest to have overflowed thy prince and soveraygne lorde, thou
thoughteste with thy traiterous streames to have over rounne all to
gether. But god be thanked thou art now a Pole of lytel water, and that
at a wonderfull lowe ebbe.'[117] Morison also used this language to link
Pole to his papal master: 'He that had dwelte in the stynkynge chanal
of Paule Bishoppe of Rome, his bosome, or in the synke of Pole and his
fellowes stomakes.'[118] In the *Exhortation*, Morison used similar language
when referring to Pole's legatine mission, claiming that the pope would

[111] http\senior.keble.ox.ac.uk/fellows/extrapages/iarcher/levies.htm#1539.
[112] *Exhortation*, Bvi^v.   [113] Ibid., Aiv^v, Avi^v.
[114] The best discussion of Pole's missions is Höllger, 'Reginald Pole'.
[115] J. Harris, 'The Use and Significance of Parliamentary Attainder in the 1530s and
1540s', undergraduate thesis (Oxford, 2008).
[116] *Exhortation*, Avi^v.   [117] *Invective*, Bviii^{r-v}. Pole was pronounced 'pool'.
[118] Ibid., Diii^v–iv^r.

'do what he can, to overrunne this way, with a pestyferouse Poole, that
floweth out of course, that seketh ayenst nature, to destroy the heed,
from whense it fyrste dyd sprynge'. Morison's hostility to Pole suffused
the works; in the *Exhortation* he even went as far as advocating violence
against Pole's person, asking, 'shal we … not make this trayterouse
Cardynalles bloudy hat, cover a bloudy pate?'[119] This aggressive stance
towards Henry's enemy went beyond mere polemic: Francis Bryan and
Peter Mewtas had been charged with the task of assassinating Pole earlier
in the year.[120]

Ultimately the pope remained England's arch-enemy and Morison's
characteristic anti-papalism runs throughout the *Exhortation*. The pope
fomented discord among Christian princes and within their realms,
distracting Christendom from its plans to attack the infidel. Papal
contempt extended into the spiritual realm too, where the pontiff had
tried to usurp powers over the remission of sins. The *Exhortation* singled
out indulgences for specific condemnation: they had 'brought us far
from purgatory, even the nexte way to helle'. The pope was a tyrant,
a 'strumpet of babylon', surrounded with 'legions of dyvels', and was
'meter to be a hogherde than a shepherde'; he used custom as an excuse
to maintain abuses and exploit his spiritual position to exact financial
gain.[121] Morison also employed humour to censure the papacy and
ridicule those who supported it. In the *Invective* he had related how
the intellectual elite of the church was founded on a 'whole cloutry
of Carnalles [cardinals]'.[122] The *Exhortation* contained an even more
damaging satire in denunciation of the papacy. Morison told the story of
young, honourable, Italian bishop Gheri, who had died in controversial
circumstances. Rumour attributed his death to his shame after being
raped by Pierluigi Farnese, the captain-general of the Roman church.
Libels on the subject had been circulating in Nuremberg, but it is
most likely that Morison's information came from Edmund Harvel or
another friend in Venice.[123] According to Morison, Gheri's generous
offer of hospitality had been exploited by Farnese, ending in the rape
and poisoning of the young bishop. The reason for Farnese's behaviour
and character? He was the illegitimate son of the pope.[124]

---

[119] *Exhortation*, Avii[v], Ci[v].   [120] Brigden, ' "The shadow that you know" ', 9–10.
[121] *Invective*, Di[r]; *Exhortation*, Avii[v]–viii[v], Bii[v], Ci[r], Cviii[v].   [122] Ibid., Diii[r].
[123] G. B. Parks, 'The Pier Luigi Farnese Scandal: An English Report', *Renaissance News*, 15
(1962), 193, 197–200. Morison's friends were relaying news of Pierluigi's exploits: *LP* XIII
ii 847.
[124] *Exhortation*, Cvi[r]–viii[v].

Morison's earlier rhetoric of the centrality of scripture was now harnessed to provide a justification for war and to quell any consciences that might object to fighting against a papal army. Papists were 'fyghtynge ayenst religyon, ayenste goddes worde, and so ayenst god hym selfe', whereas England was fighting 'for the mayntenaunce of al thre'. Henry would rather face opposition from all other princes, than relinquish God's word from his realm. Morison reassured his readers that England was facing a religious war to defend the true faith and scripture, by relating the stories of figures such as Jehosophat who had waged 'Goddes' war against the Moabites and Ammonites. Anyone who believed the pope's motives were religious was mistaken—he only cared about his financial interests.[125]

'fyghtynge for the defence of religion'[126]

Even more than his other tracts, Morison's *Exhortation* stressed that the adversity Henry faced actually reflected God's favour. He insisted that, contrary to foreign opinion, England was actually in a stronger position than before. Providentially, the Pilgrimage of Grace, which might have been a disaster for England, had instead allowed a new generation of horsemen to be trained, while 'harneys, bowes, bylles, gunnes, with the rest of the furnitures for soudiours, were prepared than', and northerners should be extra keen to prove their loyalty to the crown. Morison cited the battles of Crécy, Poitiers, Agincourt and the Spurs to show the enduring military dominance of the English. The English should also have faith that God would defend them from their enemies: 'god ofte proveth his electe, sendynge them many soore broutes. He leaveth non undefended, that constantlye putte theyr affiaunce in hym.'[127]

At the end of the *Exhortation*, Morison used a prophecy to reinforce his message of an ultimately triumphant England. Many popular prophecies had been circulating in England in the 1530s, and prophesying was a way for those outside the normal political framework to express political concerns. The government had earlier tried to use prophecies in its favour, through the activities of Thomas Gibson and Wilfrid Holme in 1537. Gibson's prophecies had predicted that Henry 'shall wyn victory of the dyvelles mynyster the bysshop of rome' and 'shalbe unto all realms a lanterne of light wherby thay may truly and faithfully se

---

[125] *Exhortation*, Biii[r], Bvi[r]–vii[r], Dii[v]–iii[r].   [126] Ibid., Ciii[r].
[127] Ibid., Biv[r]–v[r], Bviii[v], Civ[r]–vi[v].

the cencerenes of the gospel, whiche is the glorye of god'.[128] In order to counter popular anti-governmental prophecies and the concomitant political dissent, Morison's prophecy drew on a much older and more respected tradition as the basis of his prophecy; Merlin, Bede and Becket were discarded and the Old Testament invoked instead.[129] Jansen has speculated that this passage in the *Exhortation* was a response to a specific prophecy rather than the more vague 'ones lately come from Wales'.[130] Whether or not this was the case, Morison's prophecy was an essential part of his vision of England's destiny and Henry's monarchy in particular. Henry's reign was the fulfilment of 4 Esdras. This was the culmination of Morison's overall providential message that England was a chosen nation with a chosen leader who had rediscovered the purity of religion and was in the process of restoring it. As he had in the *Persuasion*, Morison identified the papacy with the 'kyngdome of Antichriste'; in doing so, he further intensified official anti-papal polemic.[131]

Morison informed his readers that the Old Testament should show them that England, which followed scripture and was God's chosen nation, his new Israel, need not be worried about the superior numbers amassing against it: 'who so dwelleth under the shadowe of the almyghty, hym, as David saythe, god coureth with his wynges, and kepeth safe under his fethers'.[132] With God's favour and his own continued faith, Henry could be a new Abraham and defeat four nations with just his servants. Morison again paralleled Henry to several Old Testament kings who had been protected from external threats due to their faith and their efforts in purifying religion to signal that Henry would enjoy the same favour. Amasias' trust in God's deliverance had ensured him a resounding victory over his enemies. Josiah had destroyed the idols and altars in his realm and instead ensured the true worship of God. He had therefore received God's protection. Morison's use of Hezekiah in the *Exhortation* is even more revealing: Henry, as Hezekiah before him, was 'styll occupied in clensynge his realme of idolatry'. It was Hezekiah's intention to cleanse the realm completely that had warranted his protection.[133] This appearance of Hezekiah after the 1538 Injunctions and the widespread dismantling of notorious shrines indicates that Morison felt that the king had still not gone far enough. He was tacitly

---

[128] S. L. Jansen, *Political Protest and Prophecy under Henry VIII* (Woodbridge, 1991), 147–54; BL, Cotton Cleopatra EVI, fos. 401^r–6^r.

[129] *Exhortation*, Dv^r.   [130] Jansen, *Political Protest*, 152.

[131] *Exhortation*, Div^v–viii^r.   [132] Ibid., Bv^v. A loose rendering of Psalm 91:1–4.

[133] *Exhortation*, Bv^r–Ci^r.

threatening Henry: if the king did not implement wholesale reform God would withdraw his benevolence. In the context of 1539, the loss of God's favour would mean invasion and conquest by a foreign, ungodly power.

The *Exhortation* and the *Invective* shed further light on the direction in which Morison envisaged Henry's church would develop. Morison lauded Henry for removing papal idolatry and allowing the true word of God to be taken to the people. He continued to encourage wide access to vernacular scripture. He praised Henry for promoting biblical reading, urged his readers to 'rede all scripture' and 'look at the sundry histories of scripture', and advocated the 'worthy herynge of the gospell'.[134] Cromwell's 1538 Injunctions meant Morison's advocacy of Bible reading could now explicitly, rather than just implicitly, encompass the New Testament. This expansion was paralleled in Henry's pictorial iconography, particularly in the title page of the Great Bible, as King has vividly shown.[135]

Morison advocated preaching the word to the masses, as 'the onely way to knowledge of faith, to the styckynge unto god his promyses, is heryng his word'. He articulated a vision of Henry as a godly ruler who took good care of his subjects' spiritual and physical well-being: 'he wol venture al thynge rather then the losse of his subiectes sowles'.[136] Yet he combined this with criticism that insufficient effort was being put into preaching, and that Englishmen were not taking enough notice of the available preachers. Although 'people begin to know what they that be curates oughte to preache, and what they ar bound to folowe', Morison opined he 'wolde god some were appoynted to take them for the newe lessons. They have long sithens begon to knowe their duetie toward god . . . and yet they be styll atte the begynning.' Two or three good preachers, he maintained, could change the religious texture of northern England. Morison's frustration with the lack of progress led him to suggest that Henry should investigate just how and where his instructions were having an effect: 'I truste as our moste prudente kynge ceasseth nat to sende his holsome and godly proclamations abrode, that so one day men shall be sent after them, to se what effecte they take, what successe commeth of them, where they worke and where they be ydle, where they have fre passage, and where they be stopped.'[137] Morison

[134] *Exhortation*, Avii[r–v]; *Invective*, Cvii[r–v], Avii[r], Bv[r–v].
[135] King, *Tudor Royal Iconography*, ch. 2.
[136] *Exhortation*, Avii[r], Dii[v]; *Invective*, Avii[r].   [137] *Invective*, Dvi[v]–vii[r].

clearly believed that Henry was moving the theological orientation of England in a Lutheran direction, as is evident from his earlier works, and his theological writings indicate that this is what Morison himself wanted to see. The passing of the Act of Six Articles later in the year highlighted that this was over-optimistic.

The Continuing Campaign

In 1539 Berthelet published Morison's translation of Sextus Julius Frontinus' *Stratagems, sleyghts and policies of warre*.[138] This translation represented as conscious a part of the propaganda effort in 1539 as Morison's translation of Sturm's *Epistle* had in 1538. Morison clearly intended it to help rally England to war. In this case, however, the primary contribution of the work did not lie in the specific content of the tract, but rather in the polemic of Morison's dedication to Henry VIII. Indeed, Morison very deliberately invoked the military preparations and fears of early 1539 and encouraged his readers to link the *Stratagems* with the *Exhortation*. '[I]n another trifle of mine', Morison told his readers, he had 'exhorted my country men, peace laid aside, to prepare for warre'.[139] This dates the publication of the *Stratagems* to between March and late May 1539, but it was most likely printed shortly after the *Exhortation* and intended to be available for the opening of Parliament in mid-April.

   This was the only known printed work that Morison dedicated to the king. He began it by explaining that he had not dedicated any of his previous public works to Henry, as he had felt his previous 'trifles' to be unworthy. Given the gravity of England's position, Morison felt compelled to do his part. His motivation for publishing in 1539 was not primarily the promotion of classical knowledge in England but a contribution to the forthcoming war effort. Frontinus had gathered words of wisdom that were relevant even for Morison's contemporaries. This notion of translation as a form of political action was not unique to Morison, but he was an early exponent of it in England. Thomas Paynell, Thomas North and William Burton were among those who later hoped their translations would benefit the political and moral life of their compatriots.[140]

---

[138] Morison translated Frontinus directly from the Latin.   [139] *Stratagems*, Avi[r].
[140] T. Paynell, *The Conspiracie of Lucius Catiline* (London, 1557), Aii[r]; T. North, *The Lives of the noble Grecians and Romanes* (London, 1579), Aii[r]; W. Burton, *Achilles Tatius the most delectable history of clitiphon and leucippe* (London, 1592), A3[r–v].

The age-old debate over whether military wisdom or sheer force of numbers was most effective on the battlefield had apparently inspired Morison's efforts. He recalled that Homer had praised Ulysses over Ajax, as Ajax had merely possessed strength, whereas Ulysses had wisdom; he also argued that towns that had withstood prolonged sieges had later fallen to ingenious deceits. Thus Morison proposed to set out the 'sleightes and strategies employed by the noblest captains' in English for Henry's and his soldiers' consideration, expressing the hope that whereas he could not provide an army, he could contribute 'wytte understanding, memorie and invention, qualities and ornamentes of the mind'.[141] The comparison was probably chosen in light of the superior numbers thought to be massing against England.

Morison's dedication repeated some of the themes evident in his *Exhortation*. Thus mention was made of the fortification programme pursued by Henry in the later 1530s. Similarly, throughout the dedication Morison was at pains to stress Henry's personal involvement in government and the care he took for the safety not just of his subjects' bodies, but also of their souls. He wished the country no greater joy than to know the extent of Henry's love and activity for his country. Henry spent all his time 'devysynge in tyme of peace mooste godly lawes, statutes and proclamations for the tranquillitie and quietness of your subiectes sowles, in tyme of ware plattes, blockehouses, bulwarkes, walles castelles, with other munitions, ingins and fortresses'. In view of the recent threats, Henry had been even more diligent; he had inspected the sea defences in case of invasion, and had also been 'continually inventing newe sortes of wepons, newe kindes of shyppes, of gunes of armure'. Morison also deliberately evoked the *Invective*. A short discussion of the malice that drove men to treason, and how the fear of God could bring traitors to the truth, introduced the subject of Sir Nicholas Carew's treason. The *Invective*, printed before Carew's trial, had made no mention of him. The *Stratagems* corrected this omission, asking 'Coulde syr Nicolas Carowe have fallen into treason, yf he hadde thought well upon that in his lyfe tyme, whyche he confessed to be trewe, at his deathe?'[142] Thus Morison's dedication followed on from the *Invective*, completing the official news of the conspiracy. In doing so, it overtly politicized a classical text.

---

[141] *Stratagems*, Aiii^v–iv^r–v, Av^v.   [142] Ibid., Aii^r–iii^v.

Frontinus' *Stratagems* were a series of observations on military life and effective military formations drawn from ancient Roman and Greek practices and formed part of a canon of works on military matters, which also included Vegetius' *De re militari* and works by Aelian and Modestus.[143] Morison nodded to this literary tradition as passages from Vegetius' *De re militari* on the 'general rules of war' (3:26) filled a few pages at the end of the book. Only two similar military texts were published in England before Morison's translation, both of which were heavily dependent upon Vegetius. Morison's translation was independent of both Christine de Pisan's text and the *Trayne of War*.[144] During the Hundred Years War, copies of Vegetius' *De re militari* were owned by bishops, knights, kings, princes and soldiers. In the early sixteenth century, it was the only military text more popular than Frontinus.[145] Morison, then, chose a text that was suited to the military climate of 1539 and would probably reach a wide readership.

Morison's works were buttressed by other official publications in the run-up to the Parliament. Cuthbert Tunstall's Palm Sunday sermon was preached before the king on 31 March 1539 and printed shortly afterwards. It was intended as part of the same propaganda campaign and raised many themes familiar from Morison's tracts.[146] The sermon discussed the 'vyce and synne of Disobedience', and 'Howe farre they be from Christ, and howe contrarye to his doctrine' seditious persons and traitors were.[147] In particular Tunstall condemned the treason of Pole and his league with the pope, warned of the threat of papal invasion, and advocated that Englishmen put their faith in God in the face of adversity.[148] The printed text of Tunstall's sermon provides a further indication that Morison's tracts, while attuned to Henry's political disposition, were overly optimistic when it came to his religious inclinations. Thus Tunstall specifically rejected *sola fideism*, serving as a warning that conservative doctrines were met with sympathy at court.[149]

---

[143] H. D. Cockle, *A Bibliography of English Military Books up to 1642 and of Contemporary Foreign Works* (London, 1900), 3–4.
[144] C. de Pisan, *Here begynneth the table of the rubryshys of the boke of the fayt of armes and of chyvalrye* (London, 1489); Anon., *The Trayne of War* (London, 1525–39).
[145] C. Allmand, *The Hundred Years War: England and France at War c. 1300–1450* (Cambridge, 1988), 157–9; Cockle, *Military Books*, 3–4.
[146] McConica, *English Humanists*, 182; C. Tunstall, *A sermon preached before the kinge upon Palm Sunday* (London, 1539).
[147] Ibid., Biv[r].   [148] Ibid., Div[r]–vi[r], Ei[v]–ii[r], Eiv[r].   [149] Ibid., Eviii[r]–Fii[r].

LOST WORKS BY MORISON

There remains the possibility that Morison was responsible for yet more
pamphlets. That Morison's surviving canon is incomplete was suggested
by Morison himself, who claimed in the *Invective* to have 'oft bidden
my contreye menne to marke the procedynges of god'.[150] Yet this was
in only the second English tract to be issued in his own name. If
Morison's statement can be taken at face value, he expected his readers
to be familiar with his name as an author. More conclusively, when
Morison was commissioned to write the *Invective* he had, he claimed,
been drafting another tract, in which he intended 'to have handled a
good sorte of places, whiche I have gathered out of the scripture, &
doctors both, makynge for the mayntenance of the kynges supremytye,
and also shakynge downe that arrogante and usurped power of the
bisshop of rome'. After some consideration, Morison prioritized the
shorter *Invective*. He intended to publish the other eventually, but
no trace of it remains.[151] Zeeveld may be right that Morison penned
more tracts against the Pilgrimage of Grace than just the *Remedy* and
Lamentation.[152] Morison was certainly capable of writing long tracts
full of classical and contemporary references in a matter of days when
necessary, as the *Remedy* and *Lamentation* prove, and so could easily
have combined writing a tract with other duties. His reference to his
other 'tryfles' in the *Stratagems* may also indicate that he produced
a more extensive body of literature than can now be traced and that
he may have produced more shorter pamphlets like the *Lamentation*.
Certainly the men working for Henry were well aware that cheaper
printed material could be turned to their purpose, as the ballads of
William Gray amply demonstrate.[153] Watt's work has elucidated the
low survival rates of pamphlets and other small, relatively cheap, printed
material.[154] Morison's propagandistic 'tryfles' most likely suffered a
similar fate and there may well have been much more than can now be
discerned.

Several works that survive in manuscript bear similar stylistic traits to
Morison's writings and are evidently fair copies, rather than drafts by
the original author, which makes their true authorship difficult to trace.

---

[150] *Invective*, Div^v–v^r.   [151] Ibid., Fiii^v–iv^r.   [152] Zeeveld, *Foundations*, 176.
[153] E. W. Dormer, *Gray of Reading* (Reading, 1923) reprints many of Gray's ballads.
[154] Watt, *Cheap Print*.

Two extant texts may owe something of their composition to Morison.
Elton suggested that Morison composed a tract on the executions of the
abbots of Reading and Glastonbury and the prior of Colchester in 1539.
It bore stylistic similarities to Morison's works and like the *Invective*
placed the commentary of the specific crime within a more general
condemnation of treason.[155] Morison may also have contributed to a
tract which reviewed Henry's religious policy from 1529 to early 1539,
but which was composed of four distinct sections.[156]

ASSESSMENT

Morison played a substantial role in the formation and development of
Henrician ideology in the period 1536–40. He produced more tracts
for the government than any other propagandist of Henry's reign. The
Protestation and *Epistle* can be added to his established canon of works.
Although a connection between Morison and these works has previously
been suggested, there is now no doubt that Morison authored the works,
even if he did draw on a wider pool of opinions in order to do so.

This study helps elucidate how Henrician propaganda was written
and how the government used it. Edward Foxe and Thomas Cromwell
were undoubtedly prime movers in the process and supervised the
writing of some of the tracts. The king seems to have taken an active
role, as 'certeyn epistoles correctyd by the kinges maiestie' featured
in diplomatic correspondence.[157] Polemics were written for a variety
of reasons. Some, such as the *Remedy* and *Lamentation*, were reactive.
Some of the later tracts such as the *Exhortation* were pre-emptive,
while Morison's apparent presence at the Exeter conspirators' trials
indicates that there were plans to write the tract even before unease
at the treatment of the Poles and Courtenays had fully surfaced.
After the Pilgrimage of Grace had subsided, even those tracts that
seem reactive were composed with a degree of premeditation. Tracts
such as the *Comfortable Consolation*, although contributing little to
the legal justification of the Supremacy, did explain and develop the
ideology behind it. The evidential basis of the *Invective* suggests that
the polemicists' approach to propaganda writing was also becoming
more sophisticated. Certainly Morison was consistently sensitive to the

---

[155] Elton, *Policy and Police*, 195; SP1/155, fos. 50ʳ–67ʳ [*LP* XIV ii 613].
[156] SP1/142, fos. 198ʳ–206ʳ [*LP* XIV i 402].   [157] SP1/131, fo. 166ʳ [*LP* XIII i 840].

demands of effective propaganda; he was not just concerned with the polemical thrust of his tracts, but also with their accuracy, consistency and defensibility.

Throughout the 1530s the government considered foreign propaganda and responded to it when necessary. Elton was wrong to think that England was becoming increasingly isolated from the continent, and that Henrician propaganda of the later 1530s reflected this.[158] During the crucial years of the Divorce and Royal Supremacy, Henry's government began to use printed polemics as source books for English diplomats. Tracts such as Gardiner's *De vera obedientia* and Sampson's *Oratio* were concurrently sent to English diplomats at foreign courts, presented to foreign courtiers and sometimes published by continental printers. This ensured a uniformity of rhetoric at home and abroad at the very time when the theory of the Henrician church was being developed and faced its strongest criticisms.[159] Morison's works were also used in this manner: Morison was not just the government's voice at home, but also abroad, and his works provided English diplomats with the information and arguments with which to conduct their diplomatic negotiations. They therefore indicate how Henry wished to be, and was, presented on the international stage.

The assumption in recent scholarship has been that government propaganda was unpopular. However, the sheer number of editions in English (eighteen by 1540) of Morison's propaganda tracts suggests that they were taken up with at least moderate enthusiasm, and as late as 1586, George Whetstone recommended Morison's *Invective against Treason* to his readers.[160] Robert Crowley's *Way to wealth: wherin is plainly taught a most present remedy for sedition* (1550) may have been deliberately titled in order to evoke Morison's *Remedy*, and certainly discussed similar issues. Morison heavily influenced three other government authors. Taverner had adopted Morison's providential understanding of Henry's reign by 1539, Hales had clearly read many of Morison's tracts, and Udall's introduction to his translation of Erasmus' *Paraphrases* had much in common with the *Comfortable Consolation*.[161] Key political figures owned copies of Morison's tracts. Henry VIII, perhaps unsurprisingly, had copies of all of Morison's tracts except the

---

[158] Elton, *Policy and Police*, ch. 4.   [159] Sowerby, 'Henrician Polemic'.
[160] G. Whetstone, *The English Mirror* (London, 1586), 218.
[161] BL Harley 4990; Udall, *Paraphrase of Erasmus upon the newe testamente*, Aii^r–Ci^r; R. Taverner, *A catechisme or institution of the christen religion* (London, 1539), Aiii^v–iv^v.

Comfortable Consolation.[162] Thomas Cranmer owned the *Lamentation* and Cochlaeus' refutation of the *Apomaxis*, while John Dudley probably had a copy of the *Apomaxis*.[163] Morison's tracts were known in the universities too: William Brown, an Oxford scholar, owned a copy of the *Apomaxis*.[164]

Shagan and Gunter have expressed frustration with the stress historians have placed on Henrician obedience literature and show that fruitful insights can be made by examining individual responses to and interpretations of the Royal Supremacy.[165] Yet Morison's tracts demonstrate that 'obedience literature', when appreciated in its complexity, has more to offer us, precisely because they were about much more than the 'cult' of obedience. The tracts all contained a strong evangelical message and so offer us a means of assessing how Englishmen were presented with and encouraged to view the religious reforms of the later 1530s. Bonini highlighted Morison's attachment to Lutheran principles and identified a Lutheran passage in the *Invective*, but did not systematically examine Morison's tracts to see of what his evangelical programme consisted.[166] They very consciously gave sanction to evangelical and Lutheran principles, while appearing to have the approval of the king. Moreover they placed interpretations upon the Royal Supremacy that the king might not have intended and made godly kingship conditional, leaving an ideological space for further interpretations to develop. Similarly, Morison's insistence that Henry order his rule according to the counsel of scripture and for the good of his subjects' souls may have inadvertently encouraged more radical interpretations of the Royal Supremacy. Indeed, Morison's pamphlets may go some way to explain the phenomenon that Shagan and Gunther have outlined.

The religious message of Morison's tracts would undoubtedly have given much encouragement to evangelicals within England. Some men viewed any tract issued with the copyright formula 'cum privilegio regis' as an official publication; Morison's, printed by Berthelet the king's printer, looked more official still.[167] Lutheran sentiments were

---

[162] J. P. Carley, *The Libraries of Henry VIII* (London, 2000), 102, 257–8, 316.

[163] D. Selwyn, *The Library of Thomas Cranmer* (Oxford, 1996), 27; Zeeveld, *Foundations*, 236.

[164] *PLRE*, iii.30.

[165] E. Shagan and K. Gunter, 'Protestant Radicalism and Political Thought in the Reign of Henry VIII', *PP*, 194 (2007), 35–74.

[166] Bonini, 'Lutheran Influences'.

[167] A. W. Reed, 'The Regulation of the Book Trade before the Proclamation of 1538', *Transactions of the Bibliographical Society* (1917–19), 176–7.

also transmitted by the translations of Richard Taverner and William Marshall, who were likewise sponsored by Cromwell.[168] No wonder, then, that many genuinely believed and hoped that Henry would introduce further reform. Morison's tracts help to explain why, as Ryrie has demonstrated, many English evangelicals viewed the period after the Act of Six Articles as one not of catholic resurgence and evangelical decline, but of ambiguity, fluidity and hope and only gradually became disillusioned with their king.[169] If they had read Morison's 1530s pamphlets, they could be forgiven for believing that Henry would continue to purify his church.

Morison repeatedly exhorted Henry's subjects to reform their beliefs and how they worshipped. Yet Morison was not just appealing to the commons. His vernacular tracts articulated Henry's responsibility as king to 'redresse thynges of religion'. By cautiously anticipating official policy in his tracts, Morison put even more pressure on Henry to develop his policies in a more evangelical direction. By making access to scripture essential to salvation, Morison ensured that Henry could not prohibit vernacular Bibles or permit traces of idolatry to remain and still justifiably portray himself as a godly king. Equally Henry's essential duty to care for his subjects' souls could not be met without strenuous efforts to provide religious education for his people.

Henry's role as a providential king was a two-edged sword: although God had sustained Henry thus far, there was no guarantee that he would continue to do so if Henry did not fulfil his half of the covenant and usher in a full reform of his church. By Morison's reckoning, this meant more than merely expelling the pope: Henry had to 'restore his holy worde', 'put downe hypocrysie' and 'banish idolatry'. In using providential rhetoric in this way, Morison pre-empted a strategy later employed by prominent Elizabethan writers. Freeman has shown how Foxe developed his narrative of Elizabeth in subsequent editions of the *Actes and Monuments* in order to warn that though Elizabeth may have been a providential ruler, if she did not implement further reform, she would lose God's favour.[170] Other Elizabethans, including Richard Cox, also employed providence as a means of pressuring Elizabeth to action.

---

[168] J. K. Yost, 'Taverner's use of Erasmus and the Protestantization of English Humanism', *Renaissance Quarterly*, 23 (1970), 266–76; Underwood, 'William Marshall's Protestant Books'.
[169] Ryrie, *Gospel*.
[170] T. S. Freeman, 'Providence and Prescription: The Account of Elizabeth in Foxe's "Book of Martyrs"', in S. Doran and T. Freeman (eds.), *Myth of Elizabeth* (Basingstoke, 2003), 27–55.

Yet Elizabeth found the providential rhetoric so useful, even with its potential barbs, that her government fostered, rather than suppressed it.[171] Henry, too, found political currency in Morison's providential construction of his kingship. It provided a much-needed link between Henry's momentous policies, the slow pace of substantive doctrinal change, and God's will. Morison, however, believed that further reform needed to come if a truly godly commonwealth were to be established in England.

Morison employed this strategy not just in works addressed to Henry personally, but also in public, widely disseminated pamphlets that were issued as official tracts by Henry's government and sometimes in Henry's own name. Morison, then, was not the servile 'pet humanist' of historiographical commonplace. Henry may even have been aware of exactly what Morison was doing. In his *Persuasion*, Morison told the king that 'playes songes and bokes ar to be borne withal, though they payne and vexe some', regardless of their content, if their overall message concurred with the king's anti-papal sentiments. Morison further explained: 'Howbeit best that such bokes therof were made, that shulde be sincere and in all poyntes pure without erroure or doubtfull doctrine, but harde it is to make anythyng ayenst papists so perfect, as som will not fynde faulte in it.'[172] He was recommending Henry utilize authors such as himself because the benefits they offered far outweighed any possible disadvantages.

An analysis of Morison's pamphlets also offers insights into other areas of debate on the Henrician Reformation. McEntegart has suggested that Cromwell, Cranmer and Foxe headed an evangelical group which consistently promoted further reform in England and an alliance with the Schmalkaldic League, sometimes even pursuing this without the king's knowledge or consent.[173] Morison's General Council tracts highlight the importance of continued negotiations to both foreign and domestic policy in 1537–8. Even when Henry knew theological consensus was unlikely, a shared commitment to opposing a 'papal' Council was still politically indispensable. It created the valuable impression of a close alliance, while also helping to legitimize Henry's actions to determine theology within the English church.

---

[171] A. McClaren, *Political Culture in the Reign of Elizabeth I* (Cambridge, 1999), 22–30; A. Walsham, ' "A Very Deborah?" The Myth of Elizabeth I as a Providential Monarch', in Doran and Freeman, *Myth of Elizabeth*, 143–68.
[172] BL Royal 18 AL, fo. 16ʳ⁻ᵛ.   [173] McEntegart, *League of Schmalkalden*.

Bernard has taken issue with interpretations of the religious events of the 1530s and 1540s that depict religious policy as dependent upon the influence of competing factions on the king.[174] Instead, Bernard sees the Henrician Reformation as a tyrannically imposed *via media* conceived of by Henry, who was the 'dominant force in the making of what is best called the king's reformation'. Cromwell, Cranmer and Foxe did not try to manipulate the direction of religious change, but meekly followed Henry's instructions. If Cranmer influenced anything, it was merely the details, not the direction of religious policy. The Henrician Reformation and its formularies of faith were 'not the contingent outcomes of factional rivalries but, consistently and robustly, his [Henry's] own aspirations'. To the question of whether there were any other Henricians, Bernard emphatically answers, 'Thomas Cromwell, rather than pursuing a more radical religious agenda of his own, was one.'[175]

This study of Morison's polemical strategies when constructing Henry VIII's kingship questions Bernard's interpretation. It demonstrates that individuals and groups were seeking to sway the king on matters of religion, even individuals we would not necessarily expect to be acting in such a way. More subtle, yet equally valuable, means of putting pressure on the king were available to the different religious and political groups than large-scale factional struggles. Henry may well, on the whole, have 'harnessed the rhetoric of Erasmian humanists'[176] yet a mere polemicist like Morison (who owned a substantial number of Erasmus' works) could manipulate Henry's propaganda for his own ends. Furthermore, there is no reason to believe that Morison was acting alone. Morison's immediate superiors when composing these tracts were two of the men McEntegart has identified as the prime movers of the evangelical pressure group: Foxe and Cromwell. While the rhetoric of the tracts appears to be Morison's own invention, Cromwell and Foxe were evidently happy to sponsor it, and Morison, and there is every reason to believe that they were well aware of Morison's religious sensibilities. If Cromwell, Cranmer and Foxe did want to put pressure on Henry, then the rhetoric Morison was formulating gave them the perfect opportunity to do so.

---

[174] Including C. Haigh, *English Reformations* (Oxford, 1998) and J. Block, *Factional Politics and the English Reformation* (Woodbridge, 1993).
[175] Bernard, *King's Reformation*, 224–7, 240–3, 512–21, 533–40, 604–6.
[176] Ibid., 225.

Morison was not the first, nor the last English writer to use literature to try to sway the king.[177] He was, however, unique in being the voice of Henry himself at the time.

[177] Walker, *Writing Under Tyranny*; J. F. McDiarmid, 'John Cheke's Translation of Plutarch's *de superstitione*', *JEH*, 48 (1997), 100–20.

4

The Politician

EARLY POLITICAL CAREER

Morison's life of *negotium* entailed much more than writing government propaganda. Upon his return to England he took up a position in Cromwell's household. He was firmly Cromwell's client, receiving a pension of £20 and several other payments from the vicegerent.[1] He soon became one of Cromwell's most trusted servants, serving in a range of capacities. For many men a position serving Cromwell was a route into royal service, and Morison was no exception. Cromwell also employed numerous other humanists, including Morison's friend and patron Thomas Starkey, who composed tracts and translated treatises for the government.

Although Morison's early duties were mostly literary (over the summer of 1536 Morison wrote the first draft of the *Apomaxis* and sat on the commission to examine Pole's *De unitate*) his position in Cromwell's household ensured that he was soon seen as a potential patron and intermediary. Morison was asked to persuade the abbot of Reading to take William Gray back into his service in late 1536. Gray had so offended the abbot that Morison's suit was unsuccessful, but shortly afterwards Cromwell was employing Gray to write polemical ballads.[2] At about the same time, the antiquarian scholar Robert Talbot sought Morison's help in a dispute with New College, Oxford.[3] Soon Morison was being asked to intercede with powerful men he did not know and the range of petitions expanded: Berthelet requested Morison's intercession on behalf of a foreigner trying to become a freeman of London while William Clifton thought Morison could help him secure

---

[1] *LP* XII ii 289, XIII i 430, ii 1249; M. L. Robertson, 'Thomas Cromwell's Servants: The Ministerial Household in Early Tudor Government and Society', Ph.D. thesis (University of California, Los Angeles, 1975), 164–5; E36/256, fos. 125^r, 159 ^{r} [*LP* XIV i 782].
[2] *LP* XI 1270; Dormer, *Gray*, 18–19.   [3] *LP* XI 1185.

a loan from the crown. Such brokerage could be a profitable business for Morison: he was offered a satin doublet by Talbot, while William Clifton proffered a house worth £400.[4] Morison in turn expected, as Cromwell's confidant, to be able to sway figures such as William Castleton, dean of Norwich and unashamedly appealed to Cromwell for help in his own affairs.[5]

Anthony Bellasis may have been Cromwell's main patronage secretary but he was not the only one: Morison also frequently acted as an intermediary between Cromwell and university scholars.[6] Hence in 1536 Morison helped the itinerant scholar Henry Philipps to secure Cromwell's assistance in procuring tuition from England's leading Hebraist, Robert Wakefield, for himself and some friends.[7] Morison also had personal and professional contacts with Master George Day and the fellows of King's Hall, Cambridge and secured Cromwell's aid for the Hall in 1538.[8] Evangelical scholars, in particular, turned to Morison to help advance their suits in their parishes and monasteries.[9]

Morison consistently tried to use his increasing influence to promote his friends. Edmund Harvel, who had housed Morison in Venice, was one beneficiary. Morison helped Harvel to secure a 'licence of wolles' and persistently petitioned that his friend be appointed England's official ambassador to Venice, in recognition of the status the Venetians assumed Harvel already held.[10] Morison realized he might be considered over-zealous, commenting to Cromwell in 1538: 'I myght percase thryve better, if I sued for fewer. I thinke not so: No my prayer is, that I may bynd all my frendes to *your* lordshyp.' He professed strong views on the binding nature of friendship in his letters, telling Cromwell that 'frendshyp shold be lyke a marriage, for better for worse, for richer for porer, til death departe'. He also claimed that 'as I refuse no new, I would never willingly leave my old' friends; a man's continued attachment to his old friends was indicative of his virtue.[11] This may be why Morison

[4] *LP* XV 1029.52, 16; SP1/112, fo. 31ʳ, 1/127, fo. 158ʳ [*LP* XI 1185, XII ii 1330].

[5] SP1/133, fo. 135ʳ, 1/122, fo. 181ʳ [*LP* XIII i 1256, XI 1481]. See also *LP* XII i 212, XI 1404.

[6] C. S. Knighton, 'Anthony Bellasis', *ODNB*, 4.994; Robertson, 'Cromwell's Servants', 182–3.

[7] *LP* XI 1482. Morison may have heard Wakefield's lectures in Oxford in the later 1520s.

[8] SP1/133, fos. 243ᵛ–5ᵛ [*LP* XIII i 1296, 1297].

[9] *LP* XI 1404, XII i 212, XIV ii 437.

[10] SP1/106, fo. 26ʳ, 1/133, fo. 243ʳ [*LP* XI 328, XIII i 1296]; *LP* XII ii 1127.

[11] SP1/133, fo. 245ᵛ [*LP* XIII i 1297].

helped his longstanding friends, for example signing over a pension to Nicholas Lental whom he knew from his days at Cardinal College.[12]

One friend took advantage of Morison's proximity to Cromwell. Throckmorton, who had been a fellow scholar at Padua, paid a great compliment to Morison, claiming that 'where other men gett money, you get mennes heartes'. After Pole's *De unitate* had been delivered to Henry VIII, links to figures such as Throckmorton had the potential to make Morison suspect in the eyes of the king. By the time he was next in England in 1537 Throckmorton was Reginald Pole's agent, but he protested his ignorance of the cardinal's plans and downplayed the importance of Pole's legation, claiming that Pole was simply promoting a general peace and the extirpation of heresy. He suggested that Cromwell meet Pole in Flanders to discuss affairs and tried to elicit information from Morison about Cromwell's intentions. However, in 1538 Throckmorton admitted to a mutual acquaintance that he had deceived Morison and Cromwell and had known of Pole's true plans all along.[13] It seems unlikely that the friendship between the men would have splintered so completely had this betrayal not occurred. Morison believed that when a man fell into vice, his true friends would not abandon him, but rather try to help him amend.[14] His views on friendship were demonstrably informed by Cicero's *De amicitia*, which described friendship as 'the most complete agreement in policy, in pursuits, and in opinions'. Cicero also counselled that men 'must not think themselves so bound that they cannot withdraw from friends who are sinning in some important matter of public concern'.[15] In the case of Throckmorton, as with Pole, this matter of public concern was surely their attachment to the papacy and diplomatic moves against England.

Morison undertook a wide range of activities in Cromwell's service. In March 1538 he was chosen to present a gift of money to Edward Carne at his first child's christening; other menial tasks included delivering money to Alexander Alesius.[16] A surviving list in Morison's hand, which included notes to 'Remember to wryght to my lord of yorke' and to sort out Tanner, surveyor 'for George forde's wyfe' suggests that his duties were even more extensive than can now be traced.[17] Occasionally

---

[12] *LP* XIII ii 1255.   [13] SP1/116, fo. 39[r] [*LP* XII i 430]; *LP* XIII ii 507.

[14] *LP* XIII i 1297.   [15] Cicero, *De amicitia* 4, 21.

[16] E36/256, fos. 121[r], 143[r] [*LP* XIV i 782]. For Carne see L. E. Hunt, 'Sir Edward Carne', *ODNB*, 10.184.

[17] SP1/162, fo. 144[v] [*LP* XV 1029.53].

Morison acted as Cromwell's secretary, although not with the same frequency as Thomas Soulimont, Richard Cromwell or Bellasis. He drafted correspondence between Cromwell and Nicholas Shaxton in 1538 when the two disagreed over an appointment to the divinity lecturership at Reading Abbey.[18] Morison also acted as a scribe in 1538 during the interrogation of John Dove, the prior of the friars in Calais.[19] Dove's dispute with Adam Damplyp, a preacher, over the Eucharist and their subsequent interrogations by Cromwell's agents were part of the run-up to the discovery of sacramentarians in Calais who had been receiving Cromwell's sponsorship.[20] There are also indications that Cromwell may have sent Morison out as an agent. In 1538 John Legh commented that Morison had recently been in the country with him, and Morison acted as an amanuensis for the abbot of Pershore.[21]

Certainly Cromwell involved Morison in many aspects of his work as vicar general. As well as employing Morison in theological debates, diplomatic negotiations with the Lutherans (which will be discussed in the next chapter) and the campaign against the General Council, Cromwell also used Morison in the practical aspects of reform such as the dissolution of the monasteries, no doubt due to Morison's consistent anti-monasticism. In March 1538 Morison translated letters from John Portinari, Cromwell's 'Italian demolition expert', who was dismantling Lewes Priory in Sussex; the priory had been granted to Cromwell and the duke of Norfolk in October of the previous year.[22] Morison's next job was much more involved. In 1540, he was entrusted with the task of dissolving two hospitals of which he was master. He had taken over as master of St James's Northallerton in 1537; two years later he replaced John Bell as Master of St Wulstan's Worcester when Bell was promoted to the bishopric of Worcester.[23] On 17 May, Morison voluntarily surrendered St Wulstan's, which became a residential building. One day

[18] BL Cotton Cleopatra EIV, fos. 81ʳ–5ʳ [*LP* XIII i 571–2]; S. Wabuda, 'Nicholas Shaxton', *ODNB*, 50.134–5.

[19] *LP* XIII ii 248.

[20] P. Ward, 'The Politics of Religion: Thomas Cromwell and the Reformation in Calais, 1534–1540', *Journal of Religious History*, 17 (1992), 152–71.

[21] *LP* XIII ii 1249, 1259.

[22] *LP* XIII i 590.2; J. Youings, *The Dissolution of the Monasteries* (London, 1971), 65.

[23] G. Hynde (ed.), *The Registers of Cuthbert Tunstall . . . and James Pilkington*, Surtees Society 161 (1952), 70; Dugdale, *Monasticum Angolorum*, vi. 780; *VCH Worcestershire*, ii. 176; WRO, MS 716.093/2648/9/iii, fo. 2; *Valor Ecclesiasticus*, v. 85–6, iii. 228–9. After reprises St James's was worth £52. 2s. 2d. and St Wulstan's £63. 18s. 10d.

later, he surrendered St James's which retained its charitable function, at least initially.[24] Later rumours that the dissolution would be reversed were serious enough for Morison to solicit and gain the help of Anthony Denny. By this point Morison had a vested interest as he had been granted most of the hospital's property.[25]

After a few years in Cromwell's service, Morison was experienced in many areas of government. Moreover he now had strong links to many of the Henrician political elite. He worked alongside Ralph Sadler, who helped him gain a licence to act by deputy as late as 1546 and was his tenant in the 1540s.[26] Morison's links to Henry's other principal secretary in the 1540s, Wriothesley, were even stronger. The two worked closely together in the late 1530s and in March 1539 were jointly granted the next presentation to Heathfield Prebend.[27] Yet by the late 1540s, their friendship had deteriorated, as Morison claimed that he suspected Wriothesley's political ambition during Edward's minority.[28]

THE LAWYER

During his time in Cromwell's household, Morison maintained and developed his legal interests. At some point in 1538 or 1539 Morison presented the king with a scheme for the codification of English law, his *Persuasion that the Laws should be in Laten*.[29] The *Persuasion* can be dated to 1538–9 on internal evidence. In it Morison derided the monastic profession, suggesting that it was composed once the surrenders of the larger monasteries were under way. He also discussed Henry's physical fortifying of the realm, a theme resonant with the claims of his 1539 tracts, but absent from the *Comfortable Consolation*.[30]

[24] E322/271; L. Toulmin Smith (ed.), *The Itinerary of John Leland in or about the Years 1535–1543* (Carbondale, 1964), iv. 108; E322/167; C. M. Newman, *Late Medieval Northallerton* (Stamford, 1999), 130.
[25] *LP* XV 726, XVI 678.25.   [26] *LP* XXI ii 199.4, 200.14, XX ii 496.68.
[27] SP1/112, fo. 181ʳ [*LP* XI 1481]; W. D. Peckham (ed.), *Acts of the Dean and Chapter of the Cathedral Church of Chichester 1472–1544* (Lewes, 1951), 58
[28] *CSPFE*, 489.
[29] BL Royal 18 AL. BL Cotton Faustina C II, fos. 5ʳ–22ʳ [*LP* XVII, App. A. 2] is a working draft. The presentation copy only contains two substantive differences: it omits a discussion of the punishment awaiting idle evildoers and expands a passage detailing Henry's liberation of the kingdom from servitude to the pope.
[30] *LP* suggested 1542 without any solid reasoning (*LP* XVII, App. A. 2). Elton dated the tract to 1535–6 based on the deleted phrase 'Mr Cholmely excepted' (*Persuasion*, fo. 17ᵛ) as

The *Persuasion* deserves more sustained scholarly attention than it has received to date, not least because it helps to elucidate the intellectual climate of Cromwell's household. In this treatise, Morison articulated his vision of the relationship between law, society and religion and demonstrated that legal codification was essential to reforming the moral and religious life of the commonwealth. Indeed his scheme for the reformation of the law is, when contemplated in its entirety, a proposal for the regeneration of society along more virtuous Christian lines.

Morison's own knowledge of common law is difficult to measure. There is no evidence that he had any official training, although he was involved in trials in 1538 and 1540 as an observer or commissioner.[31] If he did attend an Inn, he can only have done so briefly, sometime between 1530 and 1532, and his presence there has left no discernible trace. Morison certainly knew many trained common lawyers as Cromwell's household was full of ambitious young men educated at the Inns of Court.[32] Richard Taverner, who translated tracts for Cromwell, was both a trained common lawyer and a notable academic. Indeed it may be from Taverner, who enjoyed rendering common law into classical Greek, that Morison derived his notion that sections of the law were written in that language.[33] Whatever the state of Morison's knowledge, he did present the king with his personal attempt to prove the feasibility of his scheme—a codification of the English land tenure system in Ciceronian Latin. Of these three volumes, only the first instalment, the *Rerum ac muniorum* is known to be extant. This was not a translation of Littleton's tenures into Latin. Rather than running through the different ways in which land could be held as Littleton had done, Morison attempted to treat land law according to his own historical system, looking at issues such as the origins of lordship and tenancy, the division of property and inheritance.[34] This in itself might suggest his actual knowledge of legal processes in England was limited. Elton

Roger Cholmely was promoted from pleader to judge in 1536. Morison's criticisms of monks were stronger in the draft than in the presentation copy. G. R. Elton, *Studies in Tudor and Stuart Politics and Government* (London, 1974–92), ii. 248.

[31] T. Fuller, *History of the Worthies of England* (London, 1662), i. 327; *Invective*, Evii[v], Fi[v]; E101/206/7–8.

[32] Robertson, 'Cromwell's Servants', 368–70.

[33] A. W. Taylor, 'Richard Taverner', *ODNB*, 53.840–1. Alternatively this could be pedantry about Greek words appropriated into Latin.

[34] BL Royal 11 A I.

dismissed the *Rerum* as an inferior effort, but it might be better to view it as part of the historical and humanist influence within English legal culture espied by John Baker.[35]

Morison clearly announced his intentions to Henry VIII, stating:

> my desyer hath ben to attempte if the commen lawes of thys your Realme, that nowe be unwritten, might be written, that nowe lye dispersed and uncerteyn, might be gathered to gether and made certeyn, that nowe be in no tonge, might be reduced into the latten tonge, whyche thing, if it might be compassed as with your graces helpe I am fully persuaded it maye be, me thynketh ther cold [be] nothing more godly, expedient, profitable and necessary for your commen welthe, nothing more honourable to your majestie then thys.[36]

Morison sought to tempt Henry with the prospect of eternal honour: the true and only long-term defence of the realm lay in its internal structure and, more explicitly, its laws. While praising Henry's achievements and diligent military campaigns, Morison warned that these only provided temporary protection. Alexander the Great, Xerxes, Cyrus and Caesar had received renown for their 'victories and triumphs', but Justinian's fame for 'bringing the Roman lawes unto order and certeynte for the welthe of hys subiectes' 'lasteth until this tyme' and it was Justinian's example that Henry was encouraged to emulate. An exemplary legal system that would define English law for generations to come would bring Henry more enduring and greater glory than transient military victories.[37] Here Morison gave new direction to an established figure in Henry's iconographical scheme. In earlier Henrician propaganda, such as Foxe's *De vera differentia*, Justinian illustrated the powers an emperor enjoyed over the spirituality within his empire, an integral justification of Henry's rejection of papal authority.[38] Morison offered Henry an opportunity to match Justinian's magnanimous governance in the legal sphere.

For Morison, law was 'the pyller that sustayneth and holdeth up every comen welthe and cyvyle societe'.[39] Legal codification was therefore essential for civil concord. Before the laws of ancient Athens and Rome had clearly articulated written laws, Morison argued, their citizens' suspicion of injustices had frequently caused disorder and occasionally civil

---

[35] Elton, *Reform and Renewal*, 138–9; J. H. Baker, *Oxford History of the Laws of England*, iv: *1483–1558* (Oxford, 2003), ch. 1.

[36] *Persuasion*, fo. 7ʳ.   [37] Ibid., fos. 18ᵛ–19ᵛ.

[38] J. Guy, 'Thomas Cromwell and the Intellectual Origins of the Henrician Revolution', in Fox and Guy, *Reassessing the Henrician Age*, 160, 171.

[39] *Persuasion*, fo. 7ʳ⁻ᵛ.

war. Only once their laws had been codified and made accessible had the Athenians and Romans begun 'to flourishe in welthe, richesse, lernyng and wysdom'. Moreover God had deemed written laws so essential for mankind, that he not only engraved the law of nature into men's hearts, but also 'with his most blessed hande wrote them in two tables of stone, and delyvred them to Moses'.[40] The implication was clear: if Henry codified his laws, dissension and rebellion would largely be averted.

For Morison, the confusion in the English legal system stemmed from the multiplicity of languages used to express the law: it was an amalgam of English, Saxon, French, Italian, Latin and Greek. On the most basic level, this caused ambiguity as not all lawyers knew all of these languages and the antiquity of some of the terms led to uncertainty as to their precise meaning. This array of languages had occasioned a diversity of legal opinions that impeded the efficiency of the legal system, meaning some suits lasted over forty years.[41] Morison's concerns reflected actual practice in the law courts. The three main languages of the common law were English, French and Latin, all of which had a relatively narrow and quite specific legal vocabulary that was often unrelated to contemporary usage. Lawyers did not need a detailed knowledge of any of the languages in order to practise law, yet grammatical or spelling mistakes could significantly impede the legal process: courts could deliberately exploit such errors in order to clear a defendant while imprecision could mean the failure of a case.[42]

Morison therefore recommended to Henry VIII that the law should be recorded in one 'parfytt tonge', either English or Latin. Ideally the laws would be rendered into English so everyone might have access to them, no matter how superficially. Ultimately, however, Morison advocated Latin as the language for his codification on practical grounds. There were many legal terms that could be easily expressed in Latin, but for which no exact equivalent existed in the vernacular. Consequently, any English codification would necessarily retain some Latinate terms, creating a dangerous hybrid; he predicted there 'shall arise doubts in a tonge that smelleth of the Latynyte but in deade [is] barbarouse and far from it'.[43] Furthermore, most of the existing legal records, testimonies and declarations were in Latin. By 1530, one of the main courts, the

---

[40] Ibid., fos. 8ʳ–9ʳ.   [41] Ibid., fos. 9ʳ⁻ᵛ, 7ʳ.

[42] J. H. Baker, *The Common Law Tradition: Lawyers, Books and the Law* (London, 2000), 228–37.

[43] *Persuasion*, fo. 9ᵛ.

King's Bench, would reverse the judgments of local courts if the legal record contained the vernacular.[44] Yet despite this, in Morison's own codification, some Greek words remained.[45]

Morison's scheme, particularly his choice of language, had a further motivation: the desirability of creating a highly educated layer of lay society. In the early decades of the sixteenth century, it was unusual for common lawyers to be university educated. Morison had friends and acquaintances who were—men like Sadler, Taverner and Wriothesley. Most aspiring lawyers, however, joined the Inns of Chancery or the Inns of Court aged fourteen or fifteen, which excluded the possibility of a university education. Once there, they received a good grounding in the rudiments of the law and participated in moots and readings, but their linguistic training rarely extended beyond the narrow vocabulary of the law.[46] Morison believed that if all lawyers had to undergo a thorough Latin education, they would have to read precisely those texts on 'other sciences and artes liberalle' whose principles they needed to adopt in order to practise law virtuously and effectively.[47] Philosophy, rhetoric and logic were essential skills for any competent lawyer; none of the main texts in these languages were available in the vernacular. Morison pointed out the folly of having lawyers practising who were unskilled in these disciplines—how could they adequately understand legal principles, analyse cases, teach students or make effective orations? Certainly Morison believed in the utility of classical rhetoric and oratory for modern lawyers. He recounted that Cicero had preferred Servius Sulpitius over Scaevola: despite Scaevola's greater legal knowledge, Sulpitius' broad education and use of logic made him a greater orator and expositor of the law, who made 'playne and evydent that that the others handled obscurely'.[48] Morison was arguing quite pointedly here: Scaevola was widely admired in the Renaissance as providing a prototype for the model lawyer, who united legal expertise with a mastery of the *studia humanitatis*.[49]

The ramifications of the Latin education Morison was proposing went beyond the acquisition of oratorical skills: he hoped that a good

[44] Baker, *Common Law Tradition*, 228.
[45] BL Royal 11 A I, fos. 9ʳ, 11ʳ, 56ʳ–7ʳ, 59ʳ, 63ʳ, 84ʳ.
[46] J. H. Baker (ed.), *The Reports of Sir John Spelman* (London, 1977–8), ii. 125–35; *EHD 1485–1558*, 563–73.
[47] *Persuasion*, fo. 10ʳ.   [48] Ibid., fos. 10ʳ⁻ᵛ, 11ᵛ. Cicero, *Brutus* 41.
[49] See for example B. Scala, 'Dialogue on Laws and Legal Judgements', in J. Kraye (ed.), *Cambridge Translations of Renaissance Philosophical Texts* (Cambridge, 1997), ii. 193.

grounding in the arts would instil virtue and an appreciation of the moral concepts underlying the law and so make men less self-seeking in their study and practice of it. He saw money as the primary motivation of the legal professions and the cause of a proliferation of corrupt practices: 'councell requyreth money, no peny, no plea'. Lawyers sought nothing but their private profit, 'making thonely end of ther studie an encrease of richesse'.[50] Contemporary condemnations of the legal profession abounded. Gifts to lawyers and judges were relatively common and in many cases were direct attempts at bribery, while lawyers often charged high fees.[51] In the period 1535–55 figures as diverse as Thomas Becon, Stephen Gardiner, John Hales and Thomas Starkey all criticized the morality and practices of lawyers. While Thomas Audley felt it necessary to exhort the readers in the Star Chamber 'truly and justly to interpret and expound his laws and statutes in the readings and moots', Gilbert Walker disapproved of lawyers' financial extortion, asking, 'think you the laweiers could bee such purchassers if their pleas were short and al their iudgements, iustice and conscience?'[52] Morison also criticized lawyers because many could not adequately draft papers and arguments without clerical help, yet they still charged exorbitant fees. Legal codification was an important means to reform such practices.

Morison's treatise went further than this, however, proposing that lawyers receive religious education as part of their training; this would promote integrity, virtue and morality among the lawyers. The suggestion was also predicated on the basis that man's law should be compatible with God's law, 'for whatsoever lawe is repugnant to goddes lawe, it is not to be maintained for a lawe among christen men', meaning that 'whosoever is desirous to have the knowledge of mens lawes, owght not to be ignorant in godes lawe'. Morison unambiguously informed Henry that 'lawe is the ordynance of god' and that 'nothing more godly' than the codification of the law could be imagined.[53] He paralleled Henry to Moses, who had led the Egyptians out of bondage to Pharaoh and brought God's law to the people. Morison's *Persuasion*, like the vernacular propaganda he composed for Henry VIII, emphasized the

[50] *Persuasion*, fos. 7ʳ, 11ᵛ, 13ʳ–14ʳ.

[51] E. W. Ives, *The Common Lawyers of Pre-Reformation England. Thomas Kebell: A Case Study* (London, 1983), 308–29.

[52] Janelle, *Obedience*, 43; BL Harley 4990, fo. 45ᵛ; Baker, *Common Law Tradition*, 46. T. Starkey, *Dialogue between Pole and Lupset*, ed. T. Mayer, CS 4th ser. 37 (London, 1989), 127; Ives, *Common Lawyers*, 308, 320.

[53] *Persuasion*, fos. 7ʳ, 11ʳ.

importance of instilling true religion in England.[54] That Morison's *Persuasion* also contained a plan for national anti-papal celebrations is indicative of his broader attitudes. Law was a potential means of expressing independence and identity;[55] he could have seen this in action during his years in the Veneto. While Morison's interest in legal education was shared by a number of other Tudor humanists, his view that it was an essential stepping-stone on the path to a godly society was less common.

The implications of Morison's scheme were even more profound: learned lawyers could be employed in other areas of the commonwealth. Latinate lawyers could form the backbone of English government 'in thynges perteyning to your Realme' both in England and 'in foreign and outward causes, mete to be your ambassadors'. English was virtually unknown on the continent, meaning English diplomacy was normally conducted in French, Latin or Italian in the sixteenth century. As legal French had a very restricted vocabulary that scarcely resembled early modern French, there would be little discernible benefit in codifying the law in either French or English.[56] The cohort of talented lay administrators created by Morison's scheme would free Henry's government from its reliance on churchmen, 'who be chiefly ordeyned to preche and teache goddes worde'. Enabling English bishops to pursue their true pastoral vocations unhindered was especially important given Morison's assertion that at present 'a greate nombre of your poore subiectes for lack of teaching be ignorante in the knowledge of god'.[57] Morison's concern that bishops fulfil their pastoral functions was present in his theological writings and was shared by a number of contemporaries including Hugh Latimer.[58]

The Royal Supremacy raised issues of the relationship between church and state that had ramifications for English law. Most obviously, it meant that England had to determine how to treat canon law now that it no longer recognized papal authority; this process culminated in the *Reformatio legum ecclesiasticarum* of 1552.[59] However, secular

---

[54] *Persuasion*, fos. 14ʳ–17ᵛ.

[55] See for example R. Helgerson, *Forms of Nationhood: The Elizabethan Writing of England* (Chicago, 1992), ch. 2.

[56] Baker, *Common Law Tradition*, 245.   [57] *Persuasion*, fo. 13ʳ.

[58] H. Latimer, *A notable sermo[n] of ye reuerende father Maister Hughe Latemer* (London, 1548), Bviᵛ–viiʳ. See below, ch. 5.

[59] On canon law in England see R. H. Helmholz, *Roman Canon Law in Reformation England* (Cambridge, 1990).

law was also rethought as a result of the Break with Rome. Shagan and Gunther have examined how for radicals like Clement Armstrong, Henry Brinkelow and Thomas Derby the Supremacy entailed 'sweeping transformations of the English polity, overriding tradition, law and the ancient constitution in favour of a post-Reformation State built along biblical lines'.[60] Unlike Gunther and Shagan's radicals, Morison did not advocate dispensing with Parliament nor was he suggesting that customary laws should be discarded, merely that the language in which they were recorded, and consequently the laws themselves, should be standardized. Yet he was motivated by the same fundamental principle as Brinkelow's 'rule after the gospel': the commonwealth should be organized in accordance with scripture in order to promote a godly society. And Morison's means of achieving this did not obviously entail parliamentary involvement, but would stem from unilateral action by the king.

One potential criticism of Morison's scheme was that it was a disruptive innovation and would contravene custom; this was a likely critique given the attachment of common lawyers to the principle of custom.[61] Morison pre-empted attacks from this direction, by invoking a stance on custom that owed something to both humanist and evangelical thought. As men recognized that many of the actions of previous generations had been detrimental to the realm, he argued, perceptions of the role of custom and the validity of received wisdom had changed. Consequently, present and future generations of Englishmen had much to undo and to introduce for the first time. Once the arts and sciences had been disparate and digesting the Roman laws had been an innovation, but no one now challenged the wisdom of drawing them together. In the area of law this was also apparent. The efforts of Morison's contemporary humanist Guillaume Budé illustrated the benefits of taking a historical approach to the law. Civil law had changed over time, and by the time Tribonianus codified the laws for Justinian several had fallen into disuse.[62] In the *Persuasion* Morison pointed out that Justinian's codification had shown that custom could corrupt laws, while others were no longer needed.[63] Morison's historical attitude to the law challenged the authority of custom. Such attitudes had an obvious

---

[60] Shagan and Gunther, 'Protestant Radicalism', 37.

[61] R. H. Helmholz, 'Christopher St. German and the Law of Custom', *University of Chicago Law Review*, 70 (2003), 129–39.

[62] D. R. Kelley, *Foundations of Modern Historical Scholarship* (London, 1970), ch. 3.

[63] *Persuasion*, fos. 20ʳ–1ʳ.

parallel in anti-papal literature such as Thomas Swinnerton's *Mutteringe of some papists in corners*, where the challenge to unquestioningly following custom was explicitly religious.[64]

Morison was not alone in government circles in recognizing the need for over-arching legal reform. In the late fifteenth century, a parliamentary petition to the king articulated the need for an authoritative written codification of the law.[65] Many of Morison's colleagues in Cromwell's service also considered legal reform. Taverner published a tract on the *Principal lawes customes and statutes of England* in 1540.[66] Starkey had briefly touched on the reform of English law in his *Dialogue between Pole and Lupset*, but his programme was far different from Morison's. His concern was not the preservation and refinement of English law, but its wholesale replacement with an internationally recognized legal system; England should 'recyve the cyvyle law of the Romaynys the wych ys now the commyn law almost of al Chrystyan natyonys'. If lawyers examined the 'lawys of the romanynys' they would find 'rulys more convenient to the ordur of nature then they be in thys barbarouse tong and old French'.[67] Elton was undoubtedly right that Starkey's *Dialogue* was read by the circle of pamphleteers around Cromwell, and Morison's close association with Starkey would point towards his familiarity with it.[68] But the *Persuasion* was much more than a plagiarized extension of Starkey's ideas: Morison's comprehensive vision rejected the reception of civil law and instead proposed a wholesale, wholeheartedly English reorganization of law and society.

An alternative to Starkey's plan was to take Morison's position and advocate the clarification of the existing English laws. John Hales, Morison's relative by marriage, advocated codification in the vernacular for 'yf the lawes were plainelie sett furth ffewer Sutes, lesse trouble, more quiet and concorde shoulde be emonge people'. His 'Oration in Commendation of lawes' was more a defence of common law and English independence against the threat of civil law than a programme for reform.[69] In Hales's opinion, the reception of civil law contravened the legal practices of the realm, disregarded England's peculiarities and would breed confusion and disorder. He, like Morison, believed

[64] Swinnerton, *Muttering*, Aiv^r. In this case, tradition could not challenge Christ's commandments.

[65] Westminster Abbey Muniments, MS 12235, m. 2. I am grateful to Paul Cavill for this reference.

[66] Baker, *Reports*, ii. 31.   [67] Starkey, 'Dialogue', 11, 80, 127–9.

[68] Elton, *Studies*, ii. 250.   [69] BL Harley 4990, fos. 20^v, 45^r, 5^v–14^r.

those who advocated it were mistaken and unpatriotic: 'if they had any witt they mighte sone perceyve that chaunginge of lawes is veraie pernicious to a commen welthe'. Civil law was simply too inflexible and inappropriate for England, and any problems in the application of existing laws were down to the 'man that professeth yt'. Hales's tract provided a less well-developed version of some of Morison's ideas, some of which he may have borrowed directly.[70] Morison's and Hales's tracts do not mount up to the threat of reception that Maitland espied in 1530s England, but they do suggest that the common law was being assessed against ideas of the civil law.[71] Civil law was certainly encroaching on the legal systems of other territories at this time. In Germany, German law had been converging with Italian and Roman law for some time, but the late fifteenth and early sixteenth centuries witnessed the introduction of Roman law into the central legal courts, and it also gradually encroached upon the local territorial courts.[72]

Cromwell's interest in legal reform was evident by summer 1536 when John Rastell mentioned the 'reformation of the common law' as a projected piece of legislation in a letter to Cromwell.[73] Morison was only one of Cromwell's propagandists who were involved in suggesting legal reforms. In 1539–40, William Marshall drafted a poor law bill that was never enacted while Thomas Gibson penned a bill restricting sales to fairs and markets, and yet other reform-minded individuals with links to Cromwell contemplated how the English legal system might be improved.[74] Their ideas were disparate and did not amount to a coherent scheme for overarching reform.

At some point between 1539 and May 1540 Henry VIII commissioned an investigation into the institutions and practices of the law courts from three barristers (Thomas Denton, Nicholas Bacon and Robert Cary) in preparation for a school foundation. Their surviving reports reviewed contemporary practices in legal education and

---

[70] Ibid., fos. 8ᵛ, 21ʳ–3ʳ, 24ʳ–30ᵛ, 32ʳ–43ᵛ, 45ᵛ–7ʳ. Hales addressed Sir Anthony Browne as Knight of the Garter, dating his tract to after 1540.

[71] Baker, *History of the Laws*, ch. 1 dismisses the idea that there was a threat of reception.

[72] G. Strauss, *Law, Resistance and the State* (Princeton, 1986), 56–84; P. Stein, *Roman Law in European History* (Cambridge, 1999).

[73] A. W. Reed, *Early Tudor Drama: Medwall, the Rastells, Heywood and the More Circle* (London, 1926), 245–6; R. M. Fisher, 'Thomas Cromwell, Humanism and Educational Reform', *BIHR*, 50 (1977), 157–8.

[74] S. E. Lehmberg, *The Later Parliaments of Henry VIII, 1536–1547* (Cambridge, 1977), 253–4; Elton, *Reform and Renewal*, ch. 6.

recommended structural and curricular revisions.[75] One of their main goals was that 'the knowledge of the pure French and Latin tongues, as of your graces laws in the realm should be attained' so that lawyers could serve Henry abroad, as ambassadors' advisers. The highly accomplished lawyers could also be employed as official chroniclers who could follow the king's military campaigns or observe treason trials; they could then 'the more truly and lively in their chronicles set forth the same'. The report shared Morison's conviction that lawyers should receive religious education as part of their training, and that they should be of high moral character.[76] As the focus of the report was the hierarchy and syllabus of houses of legal training the consequences of its suggested reforms were far from fully developed.

Morison's interest in legal reform, then, was not unique. His scheme for the codification of the common law into English, however, was far more complex and developed than those of his contemporaries. Such a digest would involve far-reaching reforms in education and society as well as the law. Latinity would create well-educated, proficient lawyers, with obvious benefits to their clients, and free the episcopacy of temporal affairs, allowing them to concentrate on their pastoral duties. The precision of the law itself would produce a more efficient legal system. This clarity, and the consequent accessibility of the law, was a means not just to establish Henry as Justinian or even Moses the law-giver, but also to reduce popular disorders and disturbances. A sustained propaganda campaign would be needed both to discredit England's arch-enemy, the pope, and concurrently to reinforce governmental policy. However, this was secondary and complementary to Morison's notion of legal reform as the basis for a reformation of English society towards a more Christian ideal.

There is no evidence that Morison's scheme was discussed in Parliament. When Thomas Audley outlined a plan for legal reform to the House of Lords in 1540, over-arching reform of the common law was not part of the agenda. In its place, Cromwell was forced to settle for piecemeal reform of the land law.[77] Bacon, Cary and Denton's recommendations for legal education also fell by the wayside. Morison's vision of a codified and clearly articulated legal code remained an unrealized dream, as did his related hope of a godly society based on law and the gospel.

[75] Fisher, 'Thomas Cromwell', 153–7; *EHD 1485–1558*, 563–73.
[76] Ibid., 568–9, 572–3.   [77] Lehmberg, *Later Parliaments*, 95–104.

THE KING'S SERVANT

In the period 1536–9 Morison was often at court, especially when composing his polemical works. In June 1538 rumours circulated that Morison's career had received a further boost: an appointment to the King's Privy Chamber. This position would have given Morison much greater contact with the king, but it was one he claimed he did not seek. The rumours proved to be unfounded, much to Morison's embarrassment. He complained to Cromwell: 'It hath greaved me not a litel, that I was named of the kinges prevy chambre, and that I had from me frendes lettres [con]gratulatory for it. Every man that knoweth me, toke it for a season to be so.'[78] Morison's failure to gain a post in the Privy Chamber in 1538 need not be taken as a sign that Cromwell's plans to place another of his cronies around the king were thwarted. Rather, the rumours may simply reflect Morison's rise in England's political community and his contemporaries' expectations of where his career would lead next.

There were further factors complicating the issue of Morison's entry into the Privy Chamber. At some point in the 1530s, Morison became involved with Lucy Harper (née Peckham), who was the estranged wife of one of the Gentlemen of Henry VIII's Privy Chamber, George Harper. In 1537 Morison was contemplating marriage, presumably to Lucy, with whom he eventually had at least four children.[79] A rich heiress, she had become embroiled in a property dispute with her husband; she refused to sign over half of her inheritance to her husband as she did not want to disinherit 'the heyers that shall com after me ffor teym off hes [Harper's] lyff'. In the late 1530s, Lucy was hopeful that she would, with Thomas Cromwell's help, be able to secure a divorce and receive restitution.[80] This divorce never materialized, but it may be one of the reasons why Morison's entry into the Privy Chamber, which would have placed him alongside George Harper, was delayed.

Morison's promotion to the Privy Chamber finally came in 1539, making him one of only six of Cromwell's servants to be promoted

---

[78] SP1/133, fo. 243ʳ [*LP* XIII i 1296].   [79] *LP* XII ii 1330.
[80] SP1/162, fo. 122ʳ [*LP* XV 1029.32]; H. Miller, 'George Harper', *HoP 1509–1558*, 303. By 32 Henry VIII c. 72 Harper received Home Place in Kent in fee simple, in right of his wife.

into the primary arena of court politics.[81] His name is not on the list of those gentlemen serving at the start of 1539, when the removal of those involved in the Exeter conspiracy necessitated a reorganization. By Easter he was serving Henry and was receiving wages of £20, which mark him out as a junior member of the chamber.[82] Starkey dramatically claimed that Cromwell 'successfully foisted Morison on the reluctant king', but it is far more likely that Morison earned his place in the chamber with the *Invective* and *Exhortation*, written in the months before his appointment. Certainly Leland, who was in a position to know, believed that Morison enjoyed 'the favour of our prince'.[83]

A further reason for Morison's appointment may have been his skills. The king called upon Morison's linguistic proficiency: he 'dyd reade unto hys hyghenes, and interpreted' Italian letters.[84] Morison was probably considered an Italian expert due to his familiarity with many Italian authors fashionable on the continent and his years in the Veneto when he had kept a keen eye on political developments. Even after his return to England, he received news and printed material on current affairs from friends in Italy. His expertise in this area was undoubtedly why he was chosen to entertain Ferrarese diplomats over Easter 1539.[85] Soon Morison was writing letters out of the Privy Chamber on Henry's behalf, helping to organize the defence of Tilbury Fort and other of the realm's defences.[86] In September 1539 Morison was granted, alongside his associates at court Thomas Thirlby and Thomas Wyatt, the presentation to the next canonry at King's (formerly Cardinal) College, Oxford.[87]

In December Morison was one of the gentlemen of Henry's Privy Chamber sent to Calais to greet Anne of Cleves.[88] As well as providing a formal escort Morison and the other gentlemen were expected to

---

[81] The other five were Philip Hoby, Ralph Sadler, Maurice Berkley, Peter Mewtas and Richard Cromwell (Robertson, 'Cromwell's Servants', 316).

[82] *LP* XIV i 2, 781. Most senior members received £50 and most junior members 50 marks. D. R. Starkey, 'The King's Privy Chamber 1485–1547', Ph.D. thesis (Cambridge, 1974), 214.

[83] Starkey, *Personalitites and Politics*, 95–6; http://www.tertullian.org/articles/petitmengin_malmesbury_eng.htm.

[84] SP1/162, fo. 142 [*LP* XV 1029.51].

[85] See for example *LP* VII 1311, 1318, IX 687, X 320–1, 417, 565, 660–1, 801, XI 328, 513, XII i 430, 763, ii 484, XIII i 1296–7, XIV ii 781.

[86] *LP* XIV i 773, 771.   [87] Ibid., 264.

[88] J. G. Nichols (ed.), *Chronicle of Calais in the Reigns of Henry vii and Henry viii*, CS 1st ser. 35 (London, 1846), 168–9, 175.

entertain her. So when her retinue was delayed at Calais due to bad weather, Morison taught her how to play popular English card games, such as cent. The gentlemen of the Privy Chamber also ate with Anne, as she wished to observe English dining etiquette, but as the most junior member of the chamber Morison did not get to sit at the table.[89] While in Calais, Morison was among the courtiers who heard the case of Geoffrey Loveday, who was accused of defrauding the king by abusing his office of woolbeamer; the earl of Southampton presided over the proceedings between 6 and 8 December.[90]

In 1540 the humanist poet Johannes Stigel presented Henry VIII with a book of poetry celebrating the Cleves marriage. Stigel served on the delegation bringing Anne to England; his volume contained long epigrams on Henry VIII and Anne of Cleves, as well as shorter poems on Anne Boleyn, Thomas Cromwell, Philip Melanchthon, Justas Jonas, Elector John Frederick of Saxony, Polydore Vergil and Étienne Dolet (some of whom Stigel knew well). One of these poems praised Morison's literary skills as evoking 'the eloquent soul of the muses' and expected him to have the king's ear; its inclusion in this volume shows Stigel placed Morison firmly in England's political elite, although Morison was not yet prominent enough for Stigel to know his first name.[91] In Stigel's *Epithalamium*, he celebrated the Cleves marriage as an opportunity for Henry VIII to adopt Protestantism. He believed that kings had a duty to defend the true faith, and that subjects had a duty to obey their kings.[92]

THE COURT POET

Stigel's verses highlight an aspect of Morison's life at court which has passed almost completely without historical commentary: his poetical endeavours. Yet the future imperial poet laureate was far from alone

[89] M. St Clare Byrne (ed.), *The Lisle Letters* (London, 1981), v. 726–7.

[90] E101/206/7–8.

[91] J. Stigel, *Ad Henricum Octavium Angliae et Franciae regem, Carmen elegiacon* (1540); H.-H. Pflanz, *Johann Stigel als Theologe (1515–1562)* (Ohlau, 1936), 31–2. Stigel thought Morison was called Thomas.

[92] R. Mohl, *Studies in Spenser, Milton and the Theory of Monarchy* (New York, 1949), 34–40.

in praising Morison's skills as a poet. John Parkhurst was sufficiently impressed that he positioned Morison as heir to the classical poets:

> The ancient poets created the world in which the ancient Muses lived
> In the mountain, the wood, the well-watered regions
> Let him see if this is true: this I know is true
> They remain, for me, in your soul, Morison.[93]

Even allowing for the superlative nature of the genre, this was strong praise indeed. John Leland, the antiquarian bibliophile who was himself a prolific poet, also praised Morison's poetry. Leland commented that Morison 'might have sung, full of melodious verses and full of Apollo, and you might have outstripped me in gaining the glory of the ivy wreath'; he exhorted Morison to 'keep striving to surpass my Muse in your singing'. Leland's epigram claimed that 'An honorable guest from Oxford gave me your poems, which sing the deeds of heroes in hexameters', providing crucial evidence that Morison's verses were circulating.[94] In composing verse, Morison was engaging in a pastime enjoyed by many members of Henry VIII's court, including Thomas Wyatt, Henry Howard and Francis Bryan.

Very few verified poems by Morison are now extant. The process by which verses became popular was haphazard,[95] so it is unsurprising that Morison's fame as a poet did not last far beyond his own century. What does survive of Morison's verse suggests that it may have contained many evangelical Latinate compositions. At the opening of his *Apomaxis* is an anti-papal poem with strong evangelical overtones. In it, Morison censured the pope for his deceit and trickery, while celebrating the triumph of truth over false religion. He depicted England as a chosen nation which now showed its gratitude with songs and prayers of thanks.[96] Another equally anti-papal poem by Morison also survives. It reads:

> Breathes he still, who so often was believed to have died?
>   He who lay dead for so long still lives?
> Although you now breathe, you will perish, a pope born to die,
>   Behold the one who will place the stones around you. Can you survive?[97]

[93] Parkhurst, *Epigrammata*, 23.

[94] J. Leland, *Principum, ac illustrium aliquot & eruditorum in Anglia virorum, encomia, trophaea, genethliaca, & epithalamia* (London, 1589), 94. I have also used D. F. Sutton's online edition: http://www.philological.bham.ac.uk/lelandpoems/

[95] J. W. Binns, 'The Humanist Latin Tradition Reassessed', in Woolfson, *Reassessing Tudor Humanism*, 186–96.

[96] Morison, *Apomaxis*, Aii^v.   [97] BL Additional 40676, fo. 117^r.

The sentiment of this poem was probably a reaction to the Marian restoration of Catholicism and may have been inspired by a picture in the royal collection: Girolamo da Trevisa's *Four Evangelists Stoning the Pope* (*c*.1542).

Morison's verses 'which sing the deeds of heroes in hexameters' were not confined to the pages of books. He composed at least one poetical inscription for a portrait of Edward VI. The painting was executed by Holbein and was almost certainly presented to Henry VIII as a New Year's gift in 1540. Morison's verses both praised Henry's achievements, and expressed his hopes that Prince Edward would be an even greater monarch than his father:

> Little one, emulate thy father and be the heir of his virtue
> The world contains nothing greater. Heaven and earth could
> Scarcely produce a son whose glory would surpass
> That of such a father. Do thou but equal the deeds of
> Thy parent and men can ask no more. Shouldst
> Thou surpass him, thou has outstript all, nor shall
> Any surpass thee in ages to come.[98]

Seemingly then, this is a glowing encomium for Henry and a model for Edward to follow. Yet Morison also tempted Edward with pre-eminent glory if he went further than his father.

Holbein's portrait inspired further poetical reflection. Among a collection of copies of poems that once belonged to Leland, is a short verse praising Edward's physical perfection with specific reference to Holbein's portrait.

> As often as I direct my gaze to look at your delightful face and appearance,
>   So I seem to see the form of
> Your magnanimous father shining forth in your face.
>   The immortal Holbein painted this pleasing picture with rare dexterity of
> hand.[99]

It is unclear who was responsible for these lines. If the lines were by Leland then it suggests an afterlife for the portrait and Morison's poem among his humanist friends; perhaps such commentaries on Tudor propaganda were more widespread than the extant evidence suggests.

Morison's contribution of verses for Holbein's portrait of Edward VI raises the possibility that Morison worked with Holbein on other

---

[98] Translation from K. Hearn, *Dynasties: Painting in Tudor and Jacobean England 1530–1630* (London, 1995), 41.

[99] S. Foister, 'Humanism and Art', in Woolfson, *Reassessing Tudor Humanism*, 143.

important iconographic projects. In particular, there is circumstantial evidence to suggest that Morison may have composed the verses on Holbein's mural for the Privy Chamber at Whitehall. The mural situated Henry VIII within the Tudor dynasty, and established that his deeds were even greater than those of his father. Central to this message were the verses inscribed on the tablet around which the Tudor kings and queens stand. These employ a rhetoric reminiscent of Morison's printed propaganda tracts of the later 1530s. Indeed the mural was finished at some point in 1537, probably around the time Morison composed his *Comfortable Consolation*, the mural's literary equivalent. Rowlands rightly pointed out that the verses are essential to the mural's meaning and are almost certainly contemporary with the painting, rather than an addition from the next century as Strong suggested. The verses read:

> If you enjoy seeing the illustrious figures of heroes,
>   Look on these; no painting ever bore greater.
> The great debate, the competition, the great question is whether the father
>   Or the son is the victor. For both indeed are supreme.
> The former often overcame his enemies and the fires of his country
>   And finally gave peace to its citizens.
> The son, born indeed for greater tasks, from the altar
>   Removed the unworthy and put worthy men in their place.
> To unerring virtue, the presumption of popes has yielded
>   And so long as Henry the Eighth carries the sceptre in his hand,
> Religion is renewed, and during his reign
>   The doctrines of god have begun to be held in his honour.[100]

Although Henry VII had brought civil peace, Henry VIII had begun to purify religion, a stance taken in the *Comfortable Consolation* and Morison's 1539 tracts. The Whitehall verses are anonymous; to place the name of the author on such a monarchical statement would have been anomalous. In contrast, Morison's name appears on the Edward portrait to associate him with a highly skilled gift. Morison was connected to Holbein and his circle of patrons and friends, including Philip Hoby, Anthony Denny, William Butts and John Leland. Foister has even suggested that Holbein knew enough about Morison's work to alter his

---

[100] J. Rowlands, *Paintings of Hans Holbein* (Oxford, 1985), 225; R. Strong, *Holbein and Henry VIII* (London, 1967), 49–50. Henry VII was praised for overcoming adversity and establishing security in the *Comfortable Consolation* (Di^v–ii^v). For a fuller discussion of the mural see Foister, *Holbein*, 178–91.

own compositions.[101] Moreover, in order to receive praise from Stigel, Morison must have undertaken at least one high profile composition.

THE MP: 'NEVER MORE TRACTABLE PARLIAMENT'

Morison's literary talents were recognized and developed by Cromwell in other areas. In March 1539, when selecting suitable candidates to place in the forthcoming Parliament, Cromwell chose Morison for his learning and eloquence. He informed Henry that he had no doubt that Morison 'shalbe redy to answer and take up suche as wold crake or face with literature or lernyng or by Indirecte wayes'. Appointing men like Morison, Cromwell promised, would ensure that Henry 'had never more tractable parliament'.[102] Cromwell, then, envisaged Morison as a 'parliament man' to act on the crown's behalf.

Numerous aspects of Morison's experience would have suggested his placement in the House of Commons. The parliamentary agenda in 1539 included the largest attainder bill of the Tudor period, which covered over one-third of all those attainted in the sixteenth century. Included among these putative traitors were the Exeter conspirators and Reginald Pole.[103] Morison was excellently placed to discuss both and quieten any opposition. Certainly the publication of the *Invective* in such large numbers suggests that the government was anxious about popular disapproval. However, such opposition did not materialize: the Commons passed the act and even added a 'schedule' of a further six traitors.[104] Cromwell may also have wanted Morison in the Commons in anticipation of a religious debate. As the 1539 Parliament drew closer, it became apparent that a statement on religion was likely to be part of the statutory agenda.[105] Morison's theological expertise and involvement in the *Bishops' Book* meant he could speak with some authority, while Cromwell knew he would promote an evangelical religious programme. Ultimately, though, Norfolk's six questions led

[101] Ibid., 23–40, 165–8.   [102] BL Cotton Titus B I, fo. 266ʳ [*LP* XIV i 538].
[103] S. E. Lehmberg, 'Parliamentary Attainder in the Reign of Henry VIII', *HJ*, 18 (1975), 685.
[104] Lehmberg, *Later Parliaments*, 60–1; HL/PO/PB/1/1539/31H8n15.
[105] G. Redworth, 'A Study in the Formulation of Policy: The Genesis and Evolution of the Act of Six Articles [1539]', *JEH*, 37 (1986), 42–67.

to a more conservative Act than Morison, and presumably Cromwell, would ideally have wanted.

From almost the very start of his parliamentary career Morison was a prominent figure in the Commons. In 1540, when Henry VIII required a peacetime subsidy, the benefits of having an experienced propagandist in the Commons became very apparent. Henry had been granted the first peacetime subsidy in 1534. On this occasion, he had justified his request by emphasizing the benefits of his rule and requesting the money in return for improving the realm's defences. A request for a second peacetime subsidy was likely to be met with some scepticism, especially when there had been not yet been a war.[106] Consequently, Morison wrote and delivered a speech to men 'assembled here in the parlement'.[107] It is the only genuine speech to survive from Henry VIII's Parliaments. Morison first appealed to the Commons' collective identity as 'men chosen to utter the voyce, to expresse the mynd of the hole realme' and 'obeysant subiectes', before recounting the defensive and spiritual benefits of Henry's rule in some detail. He then summarized the nation's duty and articulated the threat it faced before outlining Henry's past expenditure. Finally, Morison pointed out that England could afford to help the king in his religious war. Mack has shown that rhetorical training was certainly evident in Elizabethan parliamentary speeches;[108] there is no reason to think it was any less important in Henry's reign, when trained rhetoricians were at hand. Certainly Morison believed that classical oratory had contemporary relevance.

By redeploying the body politic analogy from the *Lamentation* and the *Remedy* Morison assured his fellow MPs that Henry was a good king. The body that had been diseased and rebellious in 1536 was now peaceful and functioning harmoniously, thanks to Henry, who had also repaired the fortifications of the realm and had personally borne the cost of suppressing the rebels in Ireland.[109] In language reminiscent of the *Exhortation*, Morison failed to see how any subject could ignore the claims of 'reason honesty and duty' and refuse the subsidy. Similarly, Morison deployed the same religious rhetoric in his parliamentary speech as he had in his polemical works. He emphasized

[106] Lehmberg, *Reformation Parliament*, 207–9; *idem*, *Later Parliaments*, 92–5.

[107] *Parliamentary Speech*, fo. 109ʳ. A later copy of the speech can be found at BL Harley 296, fos. 31ʳ–2ʳ. Before Morison delivered the speech Cromwell made a few minor adjustments.

[108] P. Mack, 'Elizabethan Parliamentary Oratory', *HLQ*, 64 (2001), 23–61.

[109] *Parliamentary Speech*, fos. 110ᵛ, 114ᵛ, 115ʳ.

the spiritual benefits Henry's reign had brought to his subjects. Thanks to Henry's care for his subjects' souls, 'most fortunate England' was now 'delyvered from false errors, delyverd from bondage, superstition, Ipocrisie and Idolatrie, of England, restored to knowlege fredom, ryght religion, ryght worshypyng of god'. Morison's providential warnings were also present: God had recently favoured England for its 'rytely restored religion'; if England were to forsake true religion, she would be forsaken in turn: England was only 'assured of godes favour as longe as we favour treuthe'.[110] England's arch-enemy, the pope, posed an even more terrifying threat than the infidel: the Turks only captured men's bodies, whereas the 'tyrant of Rome' was determined to bring men's souls from 'light and libertie' into the 'dark dungels of errors'.[111] The link between the maintenance of the commonwealth and the welfare of Christ's doctrine was most strongly articulated through a discussion of the Catholic conspiracy, orchestrated by the pope and Reginald Pole against England. As he had in the *Invective* and the *Exhortation*, Morison told his audience that the 'archtraytor' Pole and the 'stronge strompet of babylon' were plotting with other countries to bring down England. A lesser king would have capitulated under pressure from the ungodly pope and converted back to his corrupt religion, bringing his subjects into everlasting, not just earthly, peril. Instead, Henry had taken on 'the defence of godes cause' and would fight for 'the mayntenance of Christes religion and pure doctrine'. Morison therefore appealed to his fellow MPs to pass the subsidy for the maintenance of 'our safetie, the staye of christes religion, the defence of godes cause'.[112]

The subsidy passed successfully with a preamble that closely resembled Morison's speech.[113] In Henry's reign, for the first time, statute preambles explained in detail the reasons behind grants of taxation. In the late 1530s, Henry's care for his subjects' souls was to be found among these justifications for the first time. The printed preamble placed this before the traditional defensive needs of the monarch for two reasons: first to justify defensive costs during peacetime and secondly to spell out the priorities of Henry's government more clearly.[114] As the preambles became more polemical, deploying the services of a propagandist in parliamentary business made sense not only from the point of view of

---

[110] Ibid., fos. 111ʳ, 112ʳ, 116ʳ.   [111] Ibid., fos. 113ᵛ–14ʳ.

[112] Ibid., fos. 110ᵛ–11ᵛ, 114ʳ.

[113] Drafts can be found at SP1/159, fos. 19ʳ–20ᵛ, 23ʳ–6ʳ [*LP* XV 502.1–2].

[114] D. Grummitt, ' "For Divers and Great Charges": Justifying Taxation in Late Medieval and Early Modern England', unpublished paper. HL/PO/PU/1/1540/32H8n78.

debates, but also when thinking about drafting of legislation. Cromwell may have envisaged that Morison, like Sadler and Wriothesley before him, would become involved in drafting parliamentary bills and editing drafts of statutes. Whether Morison did fulfil this role is impossible to tell, as so few traces remain of his parliamentary career. He probably sat in the remaining Henrician Parliaments, but would, however, have been absent for the second session of Henry's last Parliament, which coincided with Morison's mission to Denmark.

COURT IN THE 1540S

Morison professed his continued loyalty to Cromwell throughout the late 1530s, even after his appointment to the Privy Chamber, when he continued to act as a messenger between Henry and Cromwell.[115] He praised Cromwell's attachment to Christ's gospel and truth; this is probably why he remained a devoted client of the vicegerent.[116] Morison dedicated his translation of Juan Luis Vives' *Introduction to Wisdom* to Cromwell's son Gregory, demonstrating that Morison continued to view Cromwell as a patron. He professed his wish to repay his gratitude to Thomas Cromwell, whom he placed within the overarching vision of England's destiny articulated in his propaganda tracts. Not only had Henry rediscovered true religion, but he had also been blessed, as God had granted him Cromwell to assist his godly purposes: 'truthe and religion may hold their hands up to heaven, that God hath sente to so gracious so prudent & wise a prince so good so wise and so faithful a councillor, to so noble a master so diligent a minister, to so highe courageous and virtuous a kinge, a subjecte of so noble an harte and stomacke'.[117] Morison had chosen Vives, he claimed, because he was 'excellentlie wel sene in all kindes of learnyng' and his book 'introduceth wisedom into you, rootyng the love and desire of vertue in your hert'. As Cicero had before him, Morison believed that merely by reading suitable authors, one could become imbued with the moral values their works contained.[118] Through reading the *Introduction to Wisdom* Gregory would become endowed with 'such precepts of vertue, as may make you most like your noble father'.[119]

[115] SP1/127, fo. 158ʳ, 1/162, fo. 142ʳ [*LP* XII ii 1330, XV 1029.51].

[116] SP1/133, fo. 245ʳ [*LP* XIII i 1297].

[117] J. L. Vives, *Introduction to Wisdom* (London, 1540), Aviiʳ⁻ᵛ.   [118] Ibid., Aivʳ⁻ᵛ.

[119] Ibid., Aiiiᵛ.

The *Introduction to Wisdom* contained advice on all manner of issues, from avoiding the idolatry of gold down to one's diet and dinner companions.[120] It shared Morison's belief that only the selfless practice of virtue would ever confer true honour on a man. Nobility too, in its purest sense, was dependent upon virtue: men of non-aristocratic blood could lay claim to nobility through 'some excellent acte', while those with aristocratic forebears still needed to show 'vertue and worthy qualities' in order to be considered truly noble.[121] The dedication and even the tract itself, which was to become a popular educational text, served to reinforce Morison's strong attachment to Cromwell in the months preceding the minister's fall from grace.

By the time of Cromwell's fall in June 1540 Morison was well established at court. Starkey has stated that of all Cromwell's servants, only Morison was so loathsome to the king that he was expelled from the chamber on the death of his master.[122] This supposition is based on a list of gentlemen of the Privy Chamber in which Morison's name has been scored through, which is dated by both Starkey and *LP* to 1540.[123] While it is true that Morison's name does not appear on Henry's household accounts as a gentleman of the Chamber in the 1540s, some of Henry's other Privy Chamberers are also absent from at least some of the 1540s accounts. If Morison did fall out of favour he did not fall far or fast. On 16 June 1540, only six days after Cromwell's arrest, Morison was again granted the properties of the hospitals of St James and St Wulstan; the grant described him as a gentleman of the Privy Chamber.[124] There are other indications that he was not excluded from royal favour. Throughout the 1540s, Morison was able to purchase large quantities of land from Augmentations on favourable terms, while in July 1541, one year after Cromwell's arrest, the king trusted Morison sufficiently to give him a diplomatic mission at court.[125] Morison also received a favourable description in John Leland's *Antiphilarchia*, a treatise on the Royal Supremacy presented to Henry in the 1540s, as 'a young man with elegance . . . and among the most clever you could be acquainted with'.[126] It is unlikely Leland would have done this had Morison been disgraced.

[120] Ibid., Biii[v], Civ[r]–v[r].   [121] Ibid., Biv[v]–v[r], Bvii[r–v].
[122] Starkey, 'Intimacy and Innovation', 114–15.
[123] *LP* XVI 394.6. It is unknown when the deletion was made or who made it.
[124] C66/679, m. 1; *LP* XV 831.64.   [125] *LP* XVI 992; E315/338, fo. 32[r].
[126] CUL, MS E.e.5.14, fo. 184[v]. Carley dates the tract to after 1541. J. P. Carley, 'John Leland', *ODNB*, 33.297–301.

During the 1540s, Morison was consistently styled the 'king's servant' on land grants, his appointment to the post of petty customer and the Augmentations accounts for 1546,[127] but it is unclear exactly what Morison's status and duties at court were. He does not appear to have written any propaganda tracts for Henry, but he did continue to write for the king: it was almost certainly in the 1540s that Morison wrote a history of Henry's reign. Among the books Henry VIII had in the royal library was Morison's 'historia de rebus gestis ab Henrici octavi'. Carley suggested that this work was in fact Morison's *Apomaxis*, a sensible attribution given the scope of the *Apomaxis*.[128] However, a separate text bearing this title did exist. Tanner's *Biblioteca* attributes Morison with the *Apomaxis* and a work entitled 'Historiam rerum gestarum Henrici Octavi' and the location of the entry suggests it was a manuscript.[129] Furthermore a manuscript in the Folger Shakespeare Library, headed 'Ex oratione cardinalis Campegij ad Henricii octavii Anno regni decimo', was apparently copied from 'morisoni de rebus gestis h 8^i', which rules out the *Apomaxis*.[130]

One possibility is a volume from the Cotton collection entitled 'Historia de gestis reg. Henrici Octavi' by an anonymous author. The watermark in the paper is of a sort in use between 1544 and 1558, while the manuscript is a fair copy with several small annotations and corrections that bear a strong resemblance to Morison's hand.[131] The volume relates and glorifies the major events of 1519–22. It is sometimes written with the king as the authorial voice, suggesting at least tacit official sponsorship. The only occurrence from these years that might indicate the religious persuasion of the author is Henry's campaign against Luther. Here, however, the work is studiedly neutral, without the outright condemnation of Luther and his ideas that one would expect. Henry wrote against Luther due to his excessive piety and zeal for his subjects' souls, not because he was indebted to the pope. If the Cotton manuscript was by Morison, it was only one of several volumes: Campeggio gave his speech in 1518, the year before the 'Historia de gestis' opens. Certainly Vespasian B XVII was part of a series: it jumps straight into describing a Garter event, without any

[127] *LP* XVIII i 226.33, XX ii 266.6, 266.12, 496.98, 910.67, XXI ii 200.14; E164/33, fo. 57^v, C82/778/15, C82/857/6.

[128] Carley, *Libraries of Henry VIII*, 257.   [129] Tanner, *Biblioteca*, 532.

[130] Folger Shakespeare Library, MS X.d.207.

[131] E. Heawood, *Monumenta Chartae Papyraceae Historiam Illustratia* (Hilversum, 1950), i. 119, 328.

explanation of what came before.[132] However, any identification of the work with Morison remains speculative.

By the end of Henry's reign Morison was seemingly back in Henry's Privy Chamber, as in 1546, when he was chosen for an embassy to Denmark, the French and Imperial ambassadors in England all believed he was a gentleman of the Privy Chamber. There is, then, the possibility that Morison was never formally expelled from the Chamber. If he was, then it was only a temporary setback.[133] Morison's long and varied experience in politics provided essential preparation for diplomatic service, which was to be the next advance in his political career.

Humanists recognized the problems faced by any scholar engaged in the *vita activa*, and Morison was no exception. In book I of Utopia, Hythloday explained that, as far as he could ascertain, the counsellors of kings merely 'endorse and flatter the most absurd statements of the prince's special favourites' and even those counsellors who were initially virtuous eventually succumbed to the evil influences of their fellow counsellors.[134] The problem of how to counsel a king effectively was one that confronted any humanist who entered royal service. Thomas Elyot's solution was to recount to Henry an anecdote from Diogenes Laertius which highlighted Henry's own descent into bad governance. Plato warned Dionysius that he was becoming a tyrant; he was rewarded with banishment.[135]

In the 1530s, Morison's novel solution to the problem of counsel was to use his propaganda tracts and treatises dedicated to the king to articulate what he believed were the duties of a good prince. He appealed to Henry's attachment to scripture and may have genuinely believed that Henry would further reform the English church. Openly praising Henry for feats he had not yet achieved was a means of counselling where his policies should lie and was especially potent when combined with the providentialist royal image Morison offered. In adopting this strategy, Morison subverted flattery in the interests of the commonweal and, in doing so, he circumvented the Platonic charge that flatterers worked for their own gain to the disadvantage of the state. He may have been the first English humanist working for the crown to employ this method and particularly the providential model, but he was not the only

---

[132] BL Cotton Vespasian B XVII.   [133] *LP* XXI ii 662, 679.

[134] T. More, *Utopia*, ed. G. M. Logan and R. M. Adams (Cambridge, 1999), 13–14.

[135] A. Fox, 'Elyot and the Humanist Dilemma', in Fox and Guy, *Reassessing the Henrician Age*, 70–3.

one. In 1543 or 1544 Morison's friend John Cheke presented Henry VIII with a translation of Plutarch's *De Superstitione*. Cheke's preface praised Henry for returning 'parts of religion that have been obliterated and suppressed back to the light', so that 'the very salutary things you cause to appear may drive away these miseries of ignorance and error, and true religion, gradually growing up, may at last reach a full and perfect maturity'. This was far more than the removal of the corrupting papal influence: it was the construction of a pure church founded solely on scripture.[136] For Cheke however, this counsel remained within the semi-private world of the court.

When writing the *Remedy*, Morison had praised Henry for choosing virtuous advisers (Cromwell, Cranmer) who had England's best interests at heart, but at some point in the 1540s, he became disillusioned with Henry's rule. It may well be the case that Morison, like many English evangelicals, saw the *King's Book* and Act for the Advancement of True Religion as an irrefutable sign that no further reform would come under Henry's auspices.[137] In his *Discourse* he complained that many of his erudite friends had grown tired during the 'drie and barren years' they had spent 'giving counsel' to Henry 'in keeping no good to serve his sonne'. Rather, Morison believed, 'England should have known the difference between these that give counsel because they are called and those that are called because they give such counsel as they should.' He also stressed the importance of the moral integrity of a king's advisers to the good governance of the commonweal: 'in vaine is a king good himself if his councillors be not so too'.[138] Morison's picture of late Henrician politics, then, was one where a belligerent but well-intentioned king would not listen to his wisest councillors and was surrounded by many bad ones.

LANDED GENTLEMAN

Although little evidence remains of Morison's political activities in the period 1541–6, there is ample evidence of his continuing ambition. During this time Morison built up a substantial property portfolio. Only in 1540, one year after his appointment to the Privy Chamber, did Morison start to receive substantial grants of land, in the form of

---

[136] McDiarmid, 'John Cheke's Translation', 100–20.
[137] Ryrie, *Gospel*, 44–58, 252–6.   [138] *Discourse*, fos. 132ʳ, 134ᵛ.

modest tenements in St Margaret Moses, London (Friday St), St Mary without Bishopsgate, and Honey Lane, All Hallows, all of which he had sold by the end of Mary's reign.[139] One year later Morison was granted his main London property, the house of the former White Friars; by this point Morison was well on the way to being a man of some wealth, as he was assessed for the subsidy there at £200.[140]

In 1540 Morison was granted the properties belonging to the two hospitals he had surrendered to the crown, giving him a not inconsiderable landed base in Worcestershire and Yorkshire.[141] He sold many of these properties at a profit. Whereas Morison had paid £587. 5s. for the full rents of all the properties belonging to St Wulstan's and St James's, he sold the property belonging to the hospital in Worcester city to Thomas Wylde, a wealthy Worcester clothier, for £498. Even after selling three more of the properties, those remaining were valued at £154. 2s. 7d. per annum.[142] Some of Morison's other property deals were evidently an opportunity to turn a quick profit. He sold Lustby within a month of purchasing it, and also quickly sold Bromley Hall to his friend William Clifton.[143]

Morison mainly conducted business with friends and members of his extended family. He had extensive property transactions with his brother-in-law's brother, John Hales, who had also been one of Cromwell's clients in the 1530s, and was to be a prominent member of Protector Somerset's affinity in Edward's reign. They jointly owned property in Coventry and in 1545 Morison helped Hales purchase the Priory of Coventry and its tenements, which gave them both substantial property based in the centre of the town. By the time of his death Morison had passed his interest in these properties on to Hales.[144] Morison also had extensive dealings with John Combes, a distant relative by marriage, who was a man of some standing in Coventry and Stratford, and acted as John Dudley's surveyor in Edward's reign. Morison sold

[139] *LP* XV 613.3, XVI 678.5, 780.5, XVIII i 226.33; LR 2/262, fos. 6ʳ, 12ʳ; *CPR P&M*, i.356. Morison did not live in these properties.
[140] *LP* XVI 678.24; R. G. Lang (ed.), 'Two Tudor Subsidy Assessment Rolls', *London Record Society*, 29 (1993), no. 114.
[141] *LP* XV 831.64, XVI 678.25. He was re-granted the properties with a lower rent, in April 1544. *LP* XIX i 444.10.
[142] *LP* XIX i 444.10, 610.116, ii 690.27; WRO, MS 899:749/8782/45/J1/1. Wylde had previously been renting the property from Morison for £40.
[143] *LP* XIX ii 266.6, 266.36; HALS MTD/XVI/1.
[144] Coventry Archives, MS PA/101/138/17; SBTRO, MS DR10/416; E315/337, fo. 78ᵛ, E315/338, fos. 39ᵛ, 58ᵛ. Hales also bought property from Morison (*LP* XVI 780.5).

members of Combes's family properties in Worcestershire; Combes's son Richard was Morison's tenant, and another son, John, received a pension of £5 from him. Combes in turn granted Morison properties in Coventry and mentioned him in his will.[145]

Over the next decade, Morison bought lands in Suffolk, Gloucestershire, Somerset, Worcestershire, Wiltshire, Hampshire, Nottinghamshire and Lincolnshire. From 1546, he had more money with which to do so, as in that year he was appointed a collector of the petty custom, a well-paid sinecure.[146] Like many of his contemporaries, Morison concentrated his lands in certain areas by selling off some of the lands granted to him by the king and using the capital to buy other properties in places where he was interested in building up a landed base. Initially his lands were concentrated in Worcestershire, Warwickshire and Yorkshire, but in 1545, Morison exchanged most of his remaining ex-hospital properties with the crown for manors in Somerset (East Chinnock, Clowesworth and Whitesbury) and Warwickshire (Snittersfield). He also bought lands with William Ford, the Winchester evangelical, some of which were in Lincolnshire.[147] By the time of his death his main estates were in Lincolnshire, Middlesex and Somerset.

On 13 November 1546 Morison received a licence to marry Bridget Hussey, the daughter of John Lord Hussey of Sleaford.[148] In preparation for this marriage Morison settled Snittersfield on his mistress Lucy Harper to be divided between their sons after her death; one month later he granted her the reversion of part of his property in White Friars, London.[149] As Bridget's father had been attainted for treason in 1537, she had to rely on her independently wealthy mother, who left Bridget half her estate.[150] Morison's marriage to Bridget catalysed his reorientation of his landed possessions. Perhaps in anticipation of the

[145] Birmingham City Archives, MS 3279/351597, 3279/351598; *VCH Worcester*, iii. 332; *LP* XVIII ii 690, XIX ii 690.67; WRO, MS 899:749/8782/45/J1/1; Coventry Archives, PA/101/138/17; SBTRO, MS DR10/416; C142/94/98; PROB 11/39, fo. 216ʳ.

[146] J. Alsop, 'Nicholas Brigham (d.1558), Scholar, Antiquary and Crown Servant', *SCJ*, 12 (1981), 54. The salary was £10, but Morison was entitled to £4 of every £100 of custom collected on alien cloth. H. S. Cobb (ed.), *The Overseas Trade of London Exchequer Accounts, 1480–1* (London, 1990), pp. xxii–iii.

[147] E315/339, fo. 17ᵛ; *LP* XX ii 266.32, 266.6. Morison eventually sold the properties in Worcestershire and Suffolk (C1/1220/28–31; *VCH Worcester*, iii. 512).

[148] D. S. Chambers (ed.), *Faculty Office Registers 1534–49* (Oxford, 1966), 284.

[149] *LP* XXI ii 200.50; BL Additional 40631A, fos. 28ʳ–30ʳ. Morison also provided for his illegitimate children in his will. PROB 11/39, fos. 214ʳ–17ʳ.

[150] G. E. Cockayne (ed.), *Complete Peerage of England* (London, 1910–59), vii. 17–18. Anne Hussey died in March 1545. Her will was proved on 11 December 1545.

marriage, he had already begun to purchase properties in Lincolnshire
that had once belonged to her father, including parcels of Hussey's
main manor of Sleaford. In 1549 Morison paid £1685. 5s. 10d. into
Augmentations for the reversion of several more manors previously
owned by Hussey in Lincolnshire.[151]

Morison consistently tried to consolidate his properties. He purchased
the right to farm these properties and those which had formerly belonged
to St James's Northallerton. Morison requested the farm of several of his
manors, including Quenington, East Chinnock, Clowesworth, Whitesbury, Snittersfield, Boyton and Berwick as well as of his lands in
New Sleaford.[152] He was prepared to pay an extra £154. 17s. 8d.
for the woods, stock and store let out with the manors of Whitesbury, Clowesworth and Eshingby and consolidated his properties at
White Friars, buying further parcels after William Butts's death in
1545.[153]

Cashiobury in Hertfordshire was to become Morison's main manor;
it was granted to him with some other properties in August 1545 for
a fee of £176. 15s. 5d. He obtained the lordship of the manor and
other profits, including the tolls from the markets and fairs.[154] Although
Morison started the process of turning the house into a country seat,
in 1557 most of the outhouses and the gate to the property were still
seriously dilapidated. Some work had been done on the main building,
but the oven and the baking house were about to fall down, perhaps
the best indication that Morison's plans had not progressed far.[155] On
the evidence from Cashiobury, Morison did not take an active role in
governing his properties. He did retain the medieval court books of the
manor and does appear to have consulted them, but has left little trace
other than notes of his ownership (in Greek and Latin).[156] Court leets
were regularly held in Morison's name, but it seems likely that it was
his local agents, his brothers-in-law Stephen Hales and Thomas Hussey,
who oversaw them.[157] A court case from shortly after Morison's death
also suggests that he was not a conscientious landlord, as it contains
several references to houses which had been allowed to fall into ruin

[151] *LP* XX ii 266.12; *DKR*, x.240; *CPR Edward VI*, iii.209.
[152] *DKR*, x.240.   [153] E315/339, fos. 27ʳ, 95ʳ; *CPR Elizabeth*, i.79.
[154] *LP* XX ii 266.32; W. R. Saunders, *History of Watford* (Watford, 1931), 15.
[155] HALS, MS 6576.   [156] BL Additional 40626, fos. 15ʳ, 7ᵛ.
[157] HALS, MS 6547, 6565–7, 6570–3, 6575. The lawyer Robert Bell may have been
acting in this capacity at Whitesbury (*Cal. Dom. Elizabeth I 1601–3, Addenda 1547–56*,
445).

and decay by the Morisons.[158] Morison's credentials as a social reformer are further undermined by his ambitions to become a sheep farmer of some note. In 1538, he requested the stock of sheep at Sedgeworth, Lincolnshire from William Castleton, dean of Norwich.[159] Morison certainly had the potential to be a large-scale sheep farmer as his main properties had over 1250 acres of pasturage attached.[160] However, without any of Morison's accounts it is impossible to assess further his ambitions in this area.

EVANGELICAL CONTACTS

Morison's political survival after Cromwell's fall despite his open Protestantism is not surprising. He had proven himself a useful servant to Henry VIII, who continued to use him for minor diplomatic duties. As Ryrie has shown, the Act of Six Articles did not lead to a sustained attack on evangelicals, nor did Cromwell's execution in the following year. Instead, the religious picture was not one of Catholic dominance and Protestant retraction, but one which held a degree of ambiguity and uncertainty. In this atmosphere, evangelicals actually received a surprising degree of toleration and protection at court.[161] Morison was no exception. In the 1540s he was part of a powerful evangelical clique at court, which no doubt helps to explain his political survival. Anthony Denny, William Butts and William Parr were at the heart of a group of courtiers committed to Protestantism. The royal physician Butts was Morison's neighbour at the Whitefriars and patronized Morison's friends Latimer, Cheke, Thomas Thirlby and William Gray.[162] Anthony Denny, one of Henry's chief Gentlemen of the Privy Chamber from 1538, used his position at court to promote religious reformers including Morison's friends Cheke and Hales;[163] he also patronized Morison. The two were so closely associated by 1544 that one of Denny's clients, John Caius, praised Morison in a dedication to him. After Denny's death in 1549,

---

[158] C1/1423/55.   [159] SP1/133, fo. 135 [*LP* XIII i 1256].

[160] C142/110/170; C142/118/65; HALS 8753.   [161] Ryrie, *Gospel*, ch. 6.

[162] BL Additional 35831, fo. 171ʳ; C. T. Martin, 'Sir William Butts', *ODNB*, 9.278–9; Dormer, *Gray of Reading*, 18.

[163] P. C. Swenson, 'Patronage from the Privy Chamber: Sir Anthony Denny and Religious Reform', *JBS*, 27 (1988), 34–42; Dowling, *Humanism*, 62–4; P. S. Needham, 'Sir John Cheke at Cambridge and Court', Ph.D. thesis (Harvard, 1971), 164–5; M. K. Dale, 'John Hales II', *HoP 1509–1558*, ii.276.

'his frende' Morison was appointed to oversee his will, alongside John Dudley, earl of Warwick and the Lord Chancellor.[164] This was a circle which also included William Paget and extended into the secretariat.[165] Morison had other powerful patrons: in 1544 Queen Catherine Parr granted Morison, Nicholas Udall and Richard Stringfellow an advowson.[166] His connections to Udall may have dated back to Oxford, as in 1527–8 Udall had lectured at Corpus Christi and had been one of the evangelicals. Parr was Udall's patron, overseeing the translation of Erasmus' *Paraphrases* of 1543–5 in which Udall had a leading role, the introduction to which was heavily influenced by Morison's *Comfortable Consolation*; she also patronized other evangelical scholars at court.[167]

Although he does not feature prominently in Franklin Harkrider's study of Katherine Willoughby, Morison was closely connected to the duchess of Suffolk. In 1546–7 she gave him three gifts from her stables and by the 1550s he knew her sufficiently well to comment upon her temperament.[168] Morison was surely the master 'M' Cheke expected to find at Grimsthorpe, the duchess's house, in 1549; he was certainly resident there in April 1550.[169] He even entrusted the duchess with the education of his son, Charles, and also named her overseer of his will in 1550, expressing his wish that she gain his son's wardship. If this happened, Morison was confident that she would 'se hym brought up according to my trust'; his illegitimate daughters, meanwhile, were to follow the duchess's advice in all matters.[170] Morison's properties in Lincolnshire were close to the duchess's main seat at Grimsthorpe and he appears to have spent quite a lot of time there in the late 1540s and 1550. In 1549 his son was baptized in Stamford.[171] This places Morison within an important community of evangelicals in the east Midlands.[172]

In Edward's reign the renowned Italian preachers Bernardino Ochino and Peter Martyr Vermigli became members of Morison's evangelical

[164] *LP* XX 706.82; Caius, *Pergameni nobilissimi medici*, Aa2r; PROB11/32, fo. 286r. HALS, MS 6985 suggests Morison took an active role, at least initially.

[165] Johnston, 'William Paget', 188–203.

[166] W. L. Edgerton, *Nicholas Udall* (New York, 1965), 51–2; BL Additional Charter 8937.

[167] S. E. James, *Kateryn Parr* (Aldershot, 1999), 227–33; Ryrie, *Gospel*, 196–7.

[168] S. C. Lomas (ed.), *Report on the Manuscripts of the Earl of Ancaster Preserved at Grimsthorpe* (Dublin, 1907), 456; *CSPFE*, 338.

[169] BL Additional 46367, fo. 7r; CCC Parker MS 119, 44.

[170] PROB 11/39, fo. 214r.   [171] WARD 7/12/72.

[172] M. Franklin Harkrider, *Women, Reform and Community in Early Modern England: Katherine Willoughby, Duchess of Suffolk and Lincolnshire's Godly Aristocracy, 1519–1580* (Woodbridge, 2008).

clique. They arrived in England at the invitation of Cranmer in 1547 escorted by Morison's friend, John Abel, and were given positions by Somerset.[173] Morison soon became Ochino's friend and patron, lodging Ochino in his London house at the Whitefriars from 1548 to 1553. Ochino spent most of his time ministering to the Italian stranger church in London and writing anti-papal polemics.[174] Among Ochino's influential supporters were Morison's associates the duchess of Suffolk and William Parr. His works were read by enthusiastic reformers within England, including John Bradford and John Clement, while Princess Elizabeth and the king himself were also familiar with at least some of his works.[175] Morison's friendships with Ochino and Vermigli also placed him within a loose group of scholars who helped to introduce new religious ideas and texts such as the *Beneficio di Cristo* (translated by Edward Courtenay) into England.[176] Martin Bucer also became part of this godly crowd after his arrival in England in 1549. The duchess of Suffolk apparently tended him in his final illness and Morison corresponded with him about imperial politics.[177]

Morison's evangelical credentials were sufficiently strong that he was chosen to serve on a number of Edwardian religious commissions, which will be discussed in the next chapter. It is indicative that when John Parkhust composed an epigram on the Edwardian political elite, he placed Morison firmly in their midst.[178] Morison was also a member of Edward's Privy Chamber until his appointment as ambassador in the summer of 1550.[179] By 1548 he was sufficiently influential that Princess Elizabeth requested her 'frende' Morison help her acquire two properties and Morison later claimed to have pleaded for mercy to be shown to Somerset after the Privy Council seized power from the Protector in October 1549.[180] He was also charged with local government, serving on the commission of the peace for Middlesex in 1547; in 1550, when he

[173] N. H. Nicholas, 'The Bill of Expenses . . . of Peter Martyr and Bernardinus Ochin', *Archaelogia*, 21 (1827), 469–73; *CPR 1547–8*, 265–6.

[174] Benrath, *Bernardine Ochino*, 157; *CSPF Elizabeth, 1561–2*, 454. Morison made provision for Ochino and his wife's continued residence at Whitefriars in his will (PROB 11/39, fo. 214ᵛ).

[175] *CSPS 1547–9*, 253; M. A. Overell, 'Bernardine Ochino's Books and English Religious Opinion, 1547–1580', *Studies in Church History*, 38 (2004), 201–11.

[176] M. A. Overell, 'Edwardian Court Humanism and *Il Beneficio di Cristo*, 1547–1553', in Woolfson, *Reassessing Tudor Humanism*, 151–73.

[177] CCC, Parker MS 119, 43–4.   [178] Parkhurst, *Epigrammata*, 55.

[179] E101/426/5, fos. 25ʳ, 42ʳ, 60ʳ, 81ʳ, 96ʳ, 108ᵛ; 426/6, fos. 27ᵛ, 44ʳ, 62ᵛ, 76ʳ; *CPR Edward VI*, iii.208; BL Additional, 33581, fo. 30ʳ.

[180] *A Collection of State Papers*, ed. S. Haynes (London, 1740), 97; *CSPFE*, 489.

was not even in the country, he was appointed to collect the subsidy.[181] Elevation to the Privy Council followed in July 1550, but this was predominantly titular in anticipation of his embassy to the Imperial court. On 5 July he was knighted; the crest he chose (a Pegasus) reflected his enduring literary ambitions.[182]

During this time, Morison continued to sit in Parliament. His appointment to Wareham in 1547 was probably due to crown patronage, as David Seymour, the borough's other MP, was probably preferred by Thomas Seymour, Lord Admiral, or Catherine Parr.[183] A lack of evidence makes it impossible to reconstruct Morison's activities in the Parliaments of the 1540s, but it is possible that he continued to act as the king's orator in the Commons and Davies is probably right to link Morison to the Vagabond Act of 1547 (1 Edward VI, c. 3). This Act certainly reflected Morison's earlier distaste for the idle poor and his belief that all men should be profitable members of the commonwealth.[184]

Even when on embassy, Morison maintained close friendships with leading figures at court such as Thomas Wroth, who were also part of the duchess of Suffolk's affinity. He relied upon his friends Nicholas Throckmorton, John Cheke and William Cecil and Richard Cotton to advance his interests while abroad and was apparently on friendly terms with Cecil's accomplished wife Mildred Cooke.[185] These friendships, and his family links to John Hales, tie Morison into the evangelical affinity surrounding first Protector Somerset and later John Dudley, duke of Northumberland.[186]

ASSESSMENT

Morison's political career was much more varied than previous treatments of him would suggest. He was viewed, and acted, as a potential

[181] *Cal. Pat. Edward VI*, i.86, v.356.

[182] W. H. Rylands (ed.), *Grantees of Arms* (London, 1915), 177.

[183] H. Miller, 'Richard Morison', *HoP 1509–1558*, ii.634; H. Miller, 'David Seymour', *HoP 1509–1558*, iii.290.

[184] C. S. L. Davies, 'Slavery and Protector Somerset: The Vagrancy Act of 1547', *EcHR*, 19 (1966), 533.

[185] *CSPFE*, 338, 427, 450, 489, 536, 543, 550, 558.

[186] S. Alford, *Kingship and Politics in the Reign of Edward VI* (Cambridge, 2002), 80–5, 122–8, 152–3.

patron within months of arriving on English soil. Cromwell involved him in many aspects of government life: diplomacy, Parliament, the court and the work of the vicegerency. When a friend surmised Morison was 'contyn[ually] occupied in things of great moment', he was not exaggerating.[187] Morison was prized equally for his evangelical beliefs and scholarly abilities, but it was the latter that most interested the king. He earned his position in the Privy Chamber through long and varied service to the crown and was not foisted on a reluctant Henry. Cromwell's fall from power did not halt Morison's political career as has previously been suggested. Rather, Morison was part of, and probably protected by, a powerful evangelical clique who were influential at court. He continued to serve the king and became a wealthy man, amassing an impressive portfolio of properties that eventually centred in Middlesex, Somerset and Lincolnshire. In 1548, Morison was again assessed at £200, which seems a low figure given the valuation of his lands at nearly £400 per annum after his death.[188] Evangelical beliefs and humanist activities dominated Morison's political activities in England, just as they were to dominate his diplomatic activities abroad.

[187] *LP* XIII ii 847.   [188] *CSPDE*, 171; HALS, MS 8753.

5

The Theologian

EARLY CAREER AND REPUTATION

Morison had promised Cromwell that he would return from Padua 'not unskilled in theology'[1] and he certainly enjoyed a reputation as a talented theologian. Among his admiring contemporaries was Thomas Swynnerton, a highly educated client of Thomas Cromwell who, in 1537 or 1538, composed an evangelical examination of the New Testament. Swynnerton only recognized three modern authorities in his 'Tropes and figures of scripture': Melanchthon, Barnes and Tyndale. These were among the more acceptable evangelical authorities in the late 1530s. Explicit references to more controversial authors, such as Luther, Oecolampadius and Zwingli, were omitted, probably deliberately. Swynnerton protested his unworthiness to examine scripture in such detail, asserting that the task was better suited for a 'man of more rype learning' such as 'good master Moryson'.[2]

Morison soon became a figure to whom evangelical scholars appealed when seeking patronage. His proficiency in theology and respect for the gospel were invoked, both in requests for patronage from Morison himself, and to Cromwell. William Dynham wrote to his friend Morison to report deficiencies in implementing the king's 'Christian Elements and Articles' near Lyfton in Cornwall; later, when he required Cromwell's help, he invoked this role as informer and praised Cromwell's 'christen enterprises'.[3] Robert Huicke, a scholar at Merton College, Oxford, believed that Morison would be sympathetic when, in 1537, he revealed that it had been five years since his conversion to gospel truth. Eager

---

[1] BL Cotton Nero BVI, fo. 161^r [*LP* X 320].

[2] R. Rex (ed.), *A Reformation Rhetoric: Thomas Swinnerton's Tropes and Figures of Scripture* (Cambridge, 1999), 1–10, 21, 32–3, 70–2; E36/193, fo. 8^r. Morison's name was later crossed out.

[3] SP1/110, fo. 92^r [*LP* XI 936].

to convert others, Huicke was facing strong opposition in Oxford. He hoped that Morison, who combined evangelical beliefs with a political career, would be able to help him do the same and 'for the sake of the name of Christ and the propagation of the gospel' protect him from his detractors.[4] These undoubtedly included his fellow Mertonian Robert Smith, who had defended purgatory and the value of works over faith for salvation in the previous year.[5] Robert Testwood, a committed evangelical openly opposed to shrines and the worshipping of saints, praised Morison's attachment to gospel truth. He asked for Morison's help dealing with a priest at Windsor who had preached blasphemous and seditious sermons against 'godes worde' and demarcated the local 'shavelynges' as the instigators.[6] At the dissolution of Evesham Abbey in 1539 one of its monks, Thomas Coventree, appealed to Cromwell to save his exhibition. Coventree assured Cromwell he had taken 'great paynes in hebrewe greke and Latyne' in order to practise 'pure teaching of the holy lettres and scripture of god' and expose 'all thoos whiche have paynted a papisticall and sophisticall dyvinytie and myered the clere vayne of goddess word', to all of which Morison could testify.[7] Morison's reputation as a theologian persisted. In 1550, the Imperial ambassador Scheyfve concluded that Morison was 'well thought of for his proficiency in theology'. Scheyfve, however, also included warnings about Morison's theological persuasions. He was a great heretic, an enemy of the pope and it was the new, Protestant, theology in which he was skilled.[8]

Morison does not appear to have been ordained but he did hold lay appointments within the church. In 1537, he was appointed to be a lay prebendary of Salisbury Cathedral, a post he held until 1539, when he was succeeded by his friend Henry Cole. His appointment was probably political—he replaced Reginald Pole at the time when Morison was rising in the king's favour and Pole was in open opposition. The prebend of Yatminster secunda was a sinecure; Morison was given licence to be absent during his tenure.[9] Morison also received, as we have seen, the mastership of two hospitals. Despite Morison's lay status,

4 SP1/115, fo. 31ʳ⁻ᵛ [*LP* XII i 212].
5 J. Loach, 'Reformation Controversies', in McConica, *Collegiate University*, 365.
6 SP1/113, fo. 60ʳ [*LP* XI 1404]; 'Robert Testwood', *ONDB* 54.178–9. Testwood was executed for heresy in July 1543.
7 SP1/154, fo. 74ᵗ [*LP* XIV ii 437].   8 *CSPS 1550–52*, 187, 169.
9 J. le Neve (ed.), *Fasti Ecclesiae Anglicanae 1300–1541 III, Salisbury Diocese* (London, 1962), 103; WSRO, D/1/2/16 i, fo. 7ʳ, ii, fo. 1ᵛ.

Thomas Cromwell drew upon his expertise in the period 1536–40; Morison drafted theological treatises, translated theological works and participated in theological discussion at the vicegerent's behest.

THE *BISHOPS' BOOK*: THE SEVEN SACRAMENTS

Background

In early 1537, Morison became involved in the theological determinations that led to the *Institution of a Christian man*, otherwise known as the *Bishops' Book*. These debates began sometime after 18 February, and continued well into July. The *Ten Articles* of 1536 had proved an unsatisfactory doctrinal statement for evangelicals and conservatives alike. Consequently, the bishops were instructed to discuss the main articles of the Christian faith: the Creed, the Ten Commandments, the nature of justification and the number and nature of the sacraments. They were not told to reach a particular theological conclusion although Cranmer and Cromwell did hint at what theological agreement they might reach.

It was probably Cromwell's decision to engage Morison as a vicegerential aide in these discussions, even though Morison did not have a formal position in convocation. Cromwell, whose own informal education left him poorly qualified on paper to participate in detailed theological discussions, used theologians to argue for him during the *Bishops' Book* debates. He brought Alexander Alesius to the opening sessions and later used another clergyman, Thomas Starkey, to hurry the process along. Cromwell also employed laymen during the determinations, including Christopher St German and Thomas Wriothesley.[10]

During the talks, two main sides emerged: the evangelical bishops of Salisbury, Ely, Hereford and Worcester and Archbishop Cranmer were opposed by the conservative bishops of Chichester, Bath, Lincoln, Norwich and London and the archbishop of York.[11] John Stokesley of London, for example, was outraged by Alesius' argument that there were only two true sacraments. The difference emerged because the conservatives believed that the meaning of a sacrament should not be limited to the remission of sins and should also include the giving of

[10] McConica, *English Humanists*, 162; Mayer, *Starkey*, 245; *LP* XII ii 1151.2.
[11] A. Alesius, *Of the auctoritie of the word of god* (Strasbourg, 1544), Avi[r].

divine grace.[12] As the debate continued, Stokesley and Cuthbert Tunstall found precedents in Basil, Chrysostom and other Greek patristic writers for their defence of traditional ceremonies.[13] A theologically sensitive humanist such as Morison was, therefore, a useful addition to Cromwell's side.

The main evidence for Morison's involvement is a determination on one of the first items the bishops tackled.[14] His *Treatise on the Seven Sacraments* used biblical and patristic sources to justify openly reformist views. In 1537, English evangelicals were optimistic. Henry had been negotiating with the Lutherans, and the opportunity for reform seemed to be at hand. Morison's *Treatise on the Seven Sacraments* reflects this optimism—he clearly did not expect to encounter any difficulties as a result of his reformist doctrine. The *Treatise* has received very little scholarly attention, but bears examining in some detail, as it is the only coherent statement of Morison's own theological beliefs still extant.[15]

Morison first clarified how England could make an autonomous theological determination. He did so by reference to one of the other major concerns of the year, the General Council. Despite the emperor's good intentions, the pope wished to oppress by 'strengthe and armes' all those who 'do reprehende any thynge in the old doctrine' leaving no hope of a 'franke consayl' to settle matters of religion. Consequently, regional churches were compelled to hold regional councils to settle doctrinal matters locally. Morison thus cast the assembly of English bishops and divines as precisely the type of provincial council envisaged in his General Council tracts.[16]

Morison's treatise was closely connected to the *Bishops' Book*, the second section of which discussed the seven sacraments in the order: matrimony, baptism, confirmation, penance (contrition, penitence and confession), the Eucharist, orders and finally, extreme unction. It discussed the traditional sacraments in a different order (baptism, penitence, the Eucharist, mass, the sacrament of orders, communion,

[12] MacCulloch, *Thomas Cranmer*, 188.   [13] Strype, *Ecclesiastical Memorials*, i. 326.
[14] Alesius, *Word of god*, Avi[r-v]; *LP* XII ii 405.2. Morison's treatise probably dates from late February or early March. A fair copy, in Sadler's hand, can be found at SP6/2, fos. 130[r]–54[r].
[15] Christie mistakenly assumed the *Treatise* was a draft of the *Bishops' Book*. S. K. Christie, 'Richard Morison: An Analysis of his Life and Work', Ph.D. thesis (West Virginia, 1978), 77–85. The notes on the Old Testament, attributed to Morison by *LP* are in fact by Starkey (BL Royal 7 CXVI, fos. 212[r]–26[r] [*LP* XII ii 904]; Mayer, *Thomas Starkey*, 248–64).
[16] *Sacraments*, fo. 137[r-v].

marriage and extreme unction) but divided penance into the same three parts. It is one of several determinations on the seven sacraments that survive from this period.[17] This suggests Morison was among the theologians whose opinions were sought (perhaps by a fellow evangelical such as Edward Foxe or Thomas Cranmer), even though his name does not appear among those who subscribed to the final printed version of the *Bishops' Book*. Further evidence of the semi-official genesis of Morison's treatise is to be found at its end, where he stated he had 'loste no labour if your lordshyp unto whom I howe, as moch as I can performe, take it thankefully'; that Morison did not translate all of the Latin passages would suggest he composed the tract for a learned audience.[18]

In his initial address to the assembled divines, Cranmer outlined their brief. They were to consider those ceremonies omitted from the *Ten Articles* and decide whether rites such as confirmation and anointing were comparable to baptism and the Eucharist. Cranmer strongly intimated that the divines should find that there were only two true sacraments, stating that some other ceremonies could 'not be proved to be institute of Christ nor have any word in them to certifye us of remission of sinnes'. Indeed, Cranmer emphasized the lack of consensus as to what a sacrament was, stating that the first matter for agreement should be: 'what a sacrament doth signify in the holy scripture'. Cromwell conveyed Henry's wishes that all opinions be based solely on scripture not on 'any glosys/ any papistical lawes' or rites 'approved only by continuance of tyme and old custome and by unwritten verytes'.[19]

Echoing Cranmer's speech, Morison opened his treatise by noting that there was great controversy over the number, use and efficacy of the sacraments. He juxtaposed 'Scholastical doctors', who believed there to be seven sacraments that conferred grace 'by our workes', with an unnamed group who believed 'that ther be but iii necessarie whych muste be gotten with feythe'.[20] Morison's opinion was in line with the *Ten Articles*, which had only treated baptism, penance and

---

[17] For example SP6/2, fos. 158^r–72^r, 6/3, fos. 5^r–10^r; *LP* XII ii 407.

[18] *Sacraments*, fo. 150^v. 'Your lordshyp' was probably Cromwell or Foxe.

[19] Alesius, *Word of god*, Aviii^{r-v}, Avi^r. For the debate on unwritten verities, see P. Marshall, *Religious Identities in Henry VIII's England* (Aldershot, 2006), 81–99.

[20] *Sacraments*, fo. 137^r. Morison agreed with Cranmer that 'sophisters . . . delight in the debate and dissencyon of the world and in the miserable state of the church' (Alesius, *Word of god*, Avii^v).

the Eucharist as sacraments 'necessary to our salvation'.[21] Significantly Morison located the difference as lying in the matter of faith. He briefly discussed two modern authors who had proposed solutions to doctrinal disagreements. The first was Erasmus, who had 'shewde the way, how this dissention myght be ended'.[22] The second author, Philip Melanchthon, had also proposed a solution that Morison found favourable: 'the controversie . . . was rather in wordes then in thynges'.[23] Even patristic authors, Morison went on to state, had not always agreed on the number of sacraments. Dionysius stated there were three in his *Ecclesiastica hierarchia* while St Augustine, in several works, had only accorded baptism and the Eucharist full sacramental status.[24]

Morison then tackled Cranmer's instruction to define a sacrament. The problem, he felt, lay in how people had interpreted the term 'sacrament'. He cited Peter Lombard on the nature of a sacrament: 'a sacrament is taken for a figure of an holy thynge, either of invisible grace, visible in forme, excepte they take grace, for grace that sanctifieth and iustifieth'. He then further narrowed his definition using St Augustine's injunction that a ceremony or rite could only be a sacrament if 'remission of sinnes is promised us, by expresse wordes'. For Morison, a sacrament needed three features. First, it had to be 'instituted of Christe' and must be found in the New Testament. Men could not change or create a sacrament, or absolve another man from one. Christ had reserved these powers for himself alone. Morison would not give church traditions that were not in the Bible, the so-called 'unwritten verities', full sacramental status. Secondly, a sacrament was the precept of God. Thirdly, a sacrament had to 'be adioyned with promise of remission of sinnes'. Morison explicitly denounced the 'Judaical' belief that 'sacramentes by our workes or our belefe Justifie'. Saint Paul was invoked for support: his writings showed that faith was the essential component, not works. This reliance on Pauline texts, and insistence on the centrality of faith, lent Morison's *Treatise* an

[21] *Ten Articles*, Aii[v]–Ciii[r].

[22] *Sacraments*, fo. 137[v]. Erasmus had asserted that in the New Testament 'sacrament' was sometimes merely a translation from the Greek and did not always represent a Christian sacrament more narrowly defined. J. B. Payne, *Erasmus: His Theology of the Sacraments* (Richmond, VA, 1970), 99, 277 n. 13.

[23] *Sacraments*, fo. 137[v]. See P. Melanchthon, *Loci Communes, 1543*, trans. J. A. O. Preus (St Louis, 1992), Locus 13.

[24] *Sacraments*, fo. 137[v].

evangelical flavour. Before discussing the sacraments in turn, Morison summarized his definition of a sacrament as: 'a ceremonie instituted of Christe, and com*m*anded of hy*m*, unto the whych he hathe added hys promyse. Whych assuredly, signifieth remission of sinnes.'[25] His definition therefore conformed to the limits defined by Cromwell and Cranmer at the opening disputation.[26]

Baptism

Morison's treatment of baptism concurred with that put forth in the *Bishops' Book*, but he produced a more developed refutation of Anabaptism.[27] As all Christians agreed on baptism's sacramental status, Morison tackled the debate over paedo- versus anabaptism. He strongly defended infant baptism, linking his contemporary opponents, the Anabaptists, to a longer line of baptismal heretics—Donatists and Pelagians—who also believed Christ had not instituted infant baptism. Morison relied heavily on patristic evidence, using Augustine's assertion that paedobaptism had been the 'tradition of thapostles', Origen's claims that the apostles had known of original sin and so had baptized infants, and Cyprian's arguments that baptism superseded circumcision.[28] Paul had described circumcision as a 'signale' of justifying faith; Morison claimed baptism was a similar sign. He met with scorn the Anabaptists' argument that infants should not be baptized as they were too young to have faith, asking whether the Anabaptists if they had been born before Christ, would have denied the efficacy of circumcision. His emphatic belief was that infants were capable of receiving the 'fre giftes of god' and the benefits of baptism.[29]

Penitence

The second sacrament Morison discussed was penance, treating each of the scholastical components of penitence (contrition, confession and satisfaction) in turn. Even before he started a full exposition of the

[25] Ibid., fos. 138ʳ–9ʳ. Book 4 of Lombard's *Sentences* gives a general discussion of the sacraments.
[26] Alesius, *Word of god*, Aviiiʳ.   [27] *Formularies*, 93–4.
[28] *Sacraments*, fos. 139ʳ–41ʳ. Augustine, *On Genesis*, 10.23; *idem*, *Against the Donatists*, Book 4; *idem*, *Epistle on the Origin of the Human Soul to Jerome*; Origen, *Commentary on the Epistle to the Romans book 6*; Cyprian, *Eighth Epistle to Fidus*.
[29] *Sacraments*, fos. 140ʳ–1ʳ.

sacrament, Morison stressed that grace was contingent upon faith: 'in [the] penitence of a Christe*n* ma*n*, ther must be, not o*n*ly co*n*tricion, but also feithe, that receyvith remission of synnes'. On contrition Morison's point of departure was 2 Corinthians 7: contrition was a sorrow and fear that God would punish man for his sins. This was corroborated elsewhere in scripture, including the Psalms. Morison consistently elucidated the role of faith in contrition, stating that 'in Christen penitence, co*n*trition and feith ar verry wel joyned, evy*n* as Christe bad, that paenitence and remission of synnes shold be preachid in hys name'. Faith and belief allowed a penitent sinner access to grace.[30]

Morison believed confession was necessary, but disagreed with the official line, found in both the *Bishops' Book* and the *Ten Articles*, that this must take the form of auricular confession to a priest. Both texts implied that priests had the power to absolve sins. People were to give 'no less credence to the same words of absolution' than they would to the 'very words and voice of God himself'. However, this was one of the many areas in which the message of the *Bishops' Book* was fudged—absolution by a priest gave men 'certain comfort and consolation of their consciences'.[31] People were told to believe they were absolved by the priest, but simultaneously they were not promised salvation.

Morison also invoked church history to criticize theologians who defended auricular confession using Lombard's writings, claiming that only under Innocent III, after Lombard's death, had private confession to priests replaced the public confession commanded by Christ.[32] He invoked theological luminaries who had not believed in the necessity of private confession to a priest: Bede, Ambrose, Chrysostom and Prosper.[33] If confession were taken to be 'that, by the whych we acknowleg o*ur* sinnes before god', then Morison believed there would be no controversy. Absolution belonged to God alone so priests could merely offer advice, not judgement. Although he supported public confession, Morison was not opposed to keeping private confession in the English church, provided it was divorced from the notion of priestly absolution.[34] Underpinning these views was an adherence to the Lutheran notion that 'we are all priests, as many of us as are christians'.

---

[30] *Sacraments*, fos. 141ᵛ–2ʳ.   [31] *Ten Articles*, Bivʳ; *Formularies*, 98.
[32] *Sacraments*, fos. 142ᵛ–3ʳ. The reference was to Cassiodorus-Epiphanius' history.
[33] Ibid., fo. 143ʳ⁻ᵛ. Bede, *Commentary on Luke*; Ambrose, *Sermon Forty-Six*; Chrysostom, *Homily 31 on the Epistle to the Hebrews*; Prosper, *Commentary on Psalm Fifty-one*.
[34] *Sacraments*, fos. 142ᵛ–3ᵛ, 144ᵛ.

Morison's position that 'pristes regal, be all they that ar me*m*bres of the churche [of Christ]' negated the intermediary function of a priestly caste.[35]

Meanwhile, Morison's discourse on satisfaction attacked the idea that 'the pope may remitte all pey*n* and delyv*er* sowles out of purgatory', because, he wrote, powers of dispensation had been unknown to the 'auncyau*n*t fathers' of the church. Purgatory was a gross fault, a Roman fiction. Referencing Mark 16C Morison clarified the ambiguity of Matthew 18C–D, the key biblical passage used by Catholics to justify purgatory. Once a man was condemned to hell, stated Morison, he would go straight there.[36] Morison was not alone in government circles in condemning purgatory: in 1536 Robert Singleton and John Salcot both preached sermons against it at Paul's Cross while Hugh Latimer produced a thorough refutation of the doctrine in 1537.[37] Henry VIII, however, believed purgatory existed, but that the system of release developed by the late medieval church was flawed.[38] Morison's views also differed from Henry VIII on the related notion that men could achieve salvation through good works. Although the gospel taught that a change of lifestyle was part of penitence, Morison believed that '*ou*r workes can not be called satisfaction, but rather examples'. Men were only 'sanctified by faith, sanctified by Christes blode'.[39] Henry, in contrast, never accepted the notion of justification *sola fide*.

This exposition of penance was significantly more Lutheran than that found in the *Bishops' Book* or the *Ten Articles*. Both official statements asserted that 'a certain faith, trust and confidence of the mercy and goodness of god' was an essential component of penitence, but they also retained the necessity of good works for salvation.[40] More specifically, the *Bishops' Book* placed a strong emphasis on good works, claiming that 'precepts and works of charity be necessary to our salvation'. If men did not perform 'works of mercy and charity and express their obedient will in the executing and fulfilling of God's commandment

---

[35] Ibid., fo. 148ʳ; *Luther's Works*, 36.112.

[36] *Sacraments*, fos. 144ʳ–5ʳ. The text of Matthew is 'non remittetur ei in hoc seculo, equae in futuro'. Mark adds 'in eternum'. All New Testament references are to the Tyndale Bible.

[37] BL Cotton Cleopatra EVI, fos. 130ʳ–3ʳ; M. MacLure, *Register of Sermons Preached at Paul's Cross, 1534–1642* (Ottawa, 1989), 20.

[38] G. W. Bernard, 'The Making of Religious Policy, 1533–1546: Henry VIII and the Search for the Middle Way', *HJ*, 41 (1998), 334.

[39] *Sacraments*, fos. 144ʳ–5ʳ.   [40] *Formularies*, 97; *Ten Articles*, Biiᵛ–Ciiʳ.

outwardly . . . they shall never be saved'.[41] This undermined attempts
to introduce the Lutheran doctrine of *sola fide* elsewhere in the book,
such as the passage in the article on baptism that Henry VIII was so
keen to amend.[42]

The Eucharist

In the introduction to his *Treatise*, Morison identified a large, amor-
phous group of people who held erroneous beliefs about the Eucharist
but did not specify exactly what these dangerous beliefs were.[43] His
own views focused on the words, 'do this in my memory, remember
that my body is betrayde for yow, and my blodde shed for your sinnes'
(Luke 22B). The phrasing of this passage suggests Morison may have
been influenced by the Swiss theologians' position that the Eucharist
was a commemorative act. Although he had apparently been exposed
to Swiss theology in Oxford in 1527–8, and may have read more
during his travels in the early 1530s, no connection can be made
between Morison and any of the Swiss reformers at this time. That
said, Foxe and Cromwell, the two men who oversaw most aspects of
Morison's first years in government service, were certainly in contact
with Bucer in the 1530s.[44] Morison's further exposition of the Eucharist suggests that he did not at this point hold Reformed views
on the Eucharist. Interestingly, he did not specifically condemn them
either.

The Eucharist was a 'confirmation of our faith' whereby Christians
professed their belief that Christ had died for the remission of their sins.
Although Morison stated that Christ's words 'hoc est corpus meum,
hic est calyx sanguinis mei' were to be believed, he did not advocate
transubstantiation. The key belief for Morison was, again, *sola fideism*.
Men needed to take the Eucharist in faith or they would receive no
benefit; equally they would receive no harm. Provided one approached
the sacrament with faith, one would receive 'the same fleshe and blod
that he [Christ] had when he sufferd, when he gave satifaction for
our sinnes'. Morison's position was close to that of some Lutherans:
there was a real and spiritual presence in the Eucharist, but only true

---

[41] *Formularies*, 96–9. Essentially the same position is taken in the *Ten Articles*, Biv^{r-v}, Ci^r, Cii^v.

[42] F. Heal, *Of Prelates and Princes* (Cambridge, 1980), 199–200.

[43] *Sacraments*, fo. 137^v.   [44] McEntegart, *League of Schmalkalden, passim*.

believers would receive it and this was not reliant upon any action by the officiating priest. Like many of his evangelical contemporaries in England, he seems to have believed in some form of true presence, but avoided discussing the thornier matter of in what form Christ was present.[45] In contrast, Morison's support for communion in both kinds was unambiguous. Whereas in contemporary religious practice laymen only received the wafer, Morison's discussion consistently assumed that communicants were receiving both bread and wine during the Eucharist. Hence Morison could talk of men taking 'the chalice of the blod of the newe testamente from the wyne that every man drinketh'. Morison also opened his discussion with the scriptural passage Luther took as proof of communion in both kinds: 'my blodde [is] shed for your sinnes'.[46]

Morison's views on the Eucharist contrasted with those in the *Bishops' Book*, which explicitly asserted a belief in the real presence during the Eucharist for everyone using the traditional language of transubstantiation: 'under the form and figure of bread and wine . . . is verily, substantially and really contained and comprehended the very selfsame blood and body of our saviour Christ'. Anyone who received communion in bad conscience 'eateth and drinketh it to his own damnation'.[47] In this theological schema, the sacrament, once consecrated, became Christ. The faith of the individual was not the key to receiving grace during communion.

This notion was even stronger in Morison's separate discussion of the mass. In the *Bishops' Book*, the mass was not treated as a separate matter, as it was considered part of the Eucharist. For Morison, however, the mass was an unimportant periphery to the Eucharist that did not confer satisfaction for sins. Only taking communion in faith oneself conferred any spiritual benefit. Morison thus believed the mass was commemorative: 'Christe commandith that it shold be don in remembrance of hym'. For Morison there was only ever one propitiatory sacrifice, and no further propitiatory sacrifice was necessary or possible: Christ could not suffer every time a man asked for forgiveness of his sins. The benefit of Christ's passion was only applied 'by our faith and not by an other mans wyll', meaning that officiating priests had no power to

---

[45] *Sacraments*, fos. 145^{r-v}; Ryrie, *Gospel*, 138–44.

[46] *Sacraments*, fos. 145^{r-v}. In the *Babylonian Captivity* Luther combined Matt. 26C and Luke 22B: 'this is my blood, which is poured out for you and for many for the forgiveness of sins' (*Luther's Works*, 36.22).

[47] *Formularies*, 100–1.

offer sacrifices for men's sins.[48] Morison's rejection of the propitiatory aspect of the mass was in line with some official thinking on the matter and was shared by a number of fellow evangelicals. Denying this aspect of the mass was an important step on the road to the dissolution of the monasteries. However, any comprehensive rejection of the mass went far beyond what Henry VIII was prepared to accept.[49]

The Sacrament of Orders

Orders set the tone for Morison's discussion of the 'sacraments' that had not been covered in the *Ten Articles*. Only the Eucharist, baptism and penance were 'necessarie sacramentes of the newe testament'. He grudgingly asserted that he would 'be contente that ordre be called a sacremente', because many divines saw the origins of orders to lie in the New Testament and to have been ordained by Christ (John 20E). Morison, however, did not believe that orders fitted his initial definition of a sacrament. Using Paul's Epistles and 'th'acte of th'apostols' he argued that the first ministers of the church were in fact ordained 'per impositione manuum'. Furthermore, Morison explicitly noted that even 'scholastical doctors' did not consider orders to remit sins.[50]

Unlike the *Bishops' Book*, Morison's *Treatise* did not use a long discussion of orders to bolster the Royal Supremacy. Instead Morison emphasized the responsibilities of those in orders to educate and prevent heresy; a bishop should 'teache that he may and can exhorte by holesome doctrine and convince them that be in error'. Morison also used Chrysostom to criticize avaricious bishops, the lack of relief for poor benefices and the baseless payment of tenths. All of this had subverted the true purpose of the church: 'avarice hathe slayn the æternal word of god'. According to Cyprian, priests were originally 'wonte to be chosen in the presence of the people, bycause he myght be judged worthie by publike testimonye'. Morison supported this with Acts 6A–B on the early selection of deacons but he did not explicitly suggest that this practice should be reintroduced.[51] This emphasis on the pastoral duties and morality of the priesthood pervaded Morison's literary output. It was also to be found

---

[48] *Sacraments*, fos. 145ᵛ–6ᵛ.

[49] G. W. Bernard, 'The Piety of Henry VIII', in Amos, Pettegree and van Nierop, *Christian Society*, 79–80.

[50] *Sacraments*, fos. 146ᵛ–7ʳ.   [51] Ibid.; Cyprian, letter 67, 4.1.

in the writings of many of Morison's contemporaries, including Colet, Latimer and Hooper, irrespective of their confessional attachment.

Confirmation

Morison also denied confirmation full sacramental status. This was easily done as no one claimed that confirmation conferred remission of sins. Previous theologians and the *Bishops' Book*, however, recognized the usefulness of the ceremony.[52] Morison paraphrased Peter Lombard and Rabanus Maurus: 'the vertue of thys sacramente is the gifte of the holy goste, unto the strengthenyng of that, whych is gyven in baptime' and cited Chrysostom and Jerome on its benefits. In particular, Morison believed confirmation could be useful in the battle against erroneous doctrines such as Anabaptism.[53]

Marriage

Although marriage was 'institute of god' Morison denied it full sacramental status. However, he took the opportunity to promote clerical marriage, as marriage was 'allowed of god in all states and ordres of men'. Invoking St Paul and Bernard in support, Morison asserted that banning clerical marriage condemned the church to concubinage and incest.[54] In supporting the notion of a married clergy Morison was going far beyond officially accepted doctrine. Henry VIII was adamantly opposed to priests' marriage, which proved one of the sticking-points in the negotiations with the Schmalkaldic League in 1538.[55] The *Bishops' Book* denied any precedent for married priests by claiming that the apostles had been given the continence to 'abstain from the works of marriage' while a proclamation of 1538 upheld clerical celibacy.[56]

Extreme Unction

For Morison extreme unction was merely a 'ceremonie' instituted by St James, not Christ, that did not confer remission of sins. However,

---

[52] *Formularies*, 94–6.
[53] *Sacraments*, fo. 148^{r-v}. The references are probably to Jerome's *Dialogue against the Luciferians* (8–9) and Chrysostom's *Letter to the Tribucians*.
[54] *Sacraments*, fos. 148^{v}–9^{r}.
[55] See for example BL Cotton Cleopatra EV, fos. 123^{r}–9^{r}; McEntegart, *League of Schmalkalden*, 139–40.
[56] *Formularies*, 88–9; *TRP*, i.270–6.

he conceded that extreme unction was a 'signe of an holy thy*n*ge and of
a gifte that healeth' and was a useful means of bringing sick men into
charity with their neighbours.[57] Morison's interpretation of the origins
of extreme unction was in line with the *Bishops' Book*, but his theology
was more evangelical. The *Bishops' Book* asserted that provided the sick
man was in faith with God and in charity with his neighbours, extreme
unction would be a 'visible sign of an invisible grace', which included
'the remission of his sins if he be then in sin'.[58]

Summary

Morison's *Treatise on the Seven Sacraments* was a predominantly
Lutheran exposition of the sacraments, and one that drew on Luther's
early thoughts more than his most recent. Morison only allotted true
sacramental status to baptism, penitence and the Eucharist. He made
this clear at the start of his discussion of orders: 'It is evident that
baptime, the sacrame*n*t of th'altar [and] penitence do be assured signes
of remission of sinnes, instituted and comma*n*ded by the gospel and
therefore to be necessarie sacraments of the newe testament.'[59] However,
Morison allowed other 'sacraments', such as that of orders, to be called
sacraments to avoid disunity. He was prepared to fudge his language,
but not his theology. *Sola fideism* informed Morison's entire treatise,
placing him at odds with a king who remained opposed to the doctrine
throughout his reign.[60] Like Swynnerton, Morison avoided any mention
of banned continental authors; the only modern theologians he directly
cited were Melanchthon and Erasmus. This, and his attack on the
Anabaptists, were probably designed to dissociate him from continental
thinkers and movements that Henry VIII deemed radical.

The *Bishops' Book*, meanwhile, became such a series of compromises
that it was forced to make a distinction between the 'dignity' of different
sacraments. Essentially Catholic doctrine coexisted alongside Protestant
terms and ideas. Thus the article on baptism contained a brief statement
of justification by faith that was undermined by the article on penitence.
Of the sacraments, only the Eucharist, baptism and penitence were
instituted by Christ as 'remedies necessary for our salvation, and the
attaining of everlasting life' and through them 'our sins be remitted and
forgiven, and we be perfectly renewed, regenerated, purified, justified

---

[57] *Sacraments*, fos. 149^r–50^r.   [58] *Formularies*, 123–9.
[59] *Sacraments*, fo. 146^v.   [60] Bernard, 'Piety of Henry VIII', 84–6.

and made the very members of Christ's mystical body'. As such they were of a higher dignity than the remaining four, which had the sanction of tradition and 'conferred some certain and special gifts of the Holy Ghost'.[61] This essentially allowed Catholics and Protestants to read their own doctrine into the *Bishops' Book*.

Morison consistently cited Lombard throughout the treatise, probably because the traditional view that there were seven sacraments stemmed from Lombard's writings. He took issue with 'scholastical' opinions on a regular basis, arguing against them using their own core texts (Aquinas and Lombard) and occasionally from subsequent commentaries: 'thes sententiaries do iniurie unto the m*aster* of the sentences'.[62] His main sources, however, were the Bible and church history. Morison drew on a wide range of authorities, including Nectarius, Dionysius, Zosimenus, Cassiodorus-Epiphanius, Rabanus Maurus, Bede and Bernard.[63] He was heavily dependent upon the church fathers and cited Cyprian's *Letters*, at least two works by Chrysostom and at least five works by Augustine. Drawing on these texts helped him sidestep some scholastic works that contained centuries of glosses on both the Bible and earlier theological works. Morison probably admired patristic authors as they were considered more reliable doctrinally, and more accessible stylistically, than medieval commentators. Within England, patristic texts were becoming more widely available and were being deployed with increasing frequency.[64] The church fathers were also being treated to the humanist philological method, just as their classical secular counterparts were. In particular, Morison turned to authors such as Chrysostom, Cyprian and Augustine and their accounts of the earliest practices of the church to support his interpretation of scripture. In doing so, Morison appears to have been sympathetic to Josse Clichtove's belief that patristics helped to illuminate the New Testament.[65]

INTRODUCING THE *BISHOPS' BOOK*

Morison had at least one further task in relation to the *Bishops' Book*. His literary talents were called upon to produce a potential

---

[61] *Formularies*, 128–9.   [62] *Sacraments*, fo. 142ᵛ.   [63] *Sacraments, passim*.

[64] W. P. Haugaard, 'Renaissance Patristic Scholarship and Theology in Sixteenth Century England', *SCJ*, 1 (1979), 37–41.

[65] E. F. Rice, 'The Humanist Idea of Christian Antiquity: Lefevre d'Etaples and his Circle', in W. L. Gundersheimer (ed.), *French Humanism, 1470–1600* (London, 1969), 163–80.

preface to the work. Foxe, who was given the task of overseeing the composition of the preface, did not know until late July if the book would officially represent the opinion of the king or the bishops. He approached several scholars, soliciting prefaces that accounted for either possibility.[66] Morison's preface was probably only rejected once Henry's sentiments became known, but it did have several points in common with the version chosen. Both stated the bishops' intention to discuss the four sacraments that had not been covered by the *Ten Articles* and explained that they had been left out because at the time the Articles were issued they had only wished to discuss those sacraments known to be necessary to salvation. Morison's preface and the final version also shared an emphasis on the importance of marriage and a declaration that the bishops' determinations were based on scripture or ancient custom.[67]

Morison's draft preface emphasized Henry's efforts to protect his subjects' souls. Henry intended 'nothinge so ernestley, as to sette forthe emonge all his subiectes, the light of scripture, which alone showith men the right pathe to cum to god'. He had instructed the bishops to fulfil their pastoral duties and provide spiritual instruction for his people who previously had been ignorant in matters of the faith: lay people 'shold now knowe more, in mattiers of ther feith, then they have don in tymes paste, which in very deade, was nothing at all or so litel, that almost nothing could be lesse'. Doctrinal reform was not the sole aim of the king, he also wished to 'change the hartes of the people'. Indeed, Morison stated, Henry's subjects were showing themselves eager for such religious education.[68]

THE SCHMALKALDIC DELEGATION

In 1538, Morison's theological talents were called upon once more. A delegation from the Schmalkaldic League arrived in England in May to determine theological differences between England and the League. This was preparation for a future embassy to discuss Henry's entry into the League. Friedrich Myconius, the chief theologian delegated to the mission, impressed Henry, who suggested that Myconius debate with

---

[66] *LP* XII ii 289, 330, 404.   [67] SP6/6, fos. 3ᵛ–4ʳ [*LP* XII ii App. 33].
[68] Ibid., fo. 3ʳ⁻ᵛ.

English divines. For these debates Henry deliberately ensured a theological balance, choosing a mixture of conservatives and evangelicals. John Stokesley, Richard Sampson, Nicholas Heath, George Day, Thomas Cranmer, Robert Barnes and Nicholas Wilson formally debated with the Schmalkaldic delegation in June and July on such issues as images, ecclesiastical rites, free will, justification, original sin, the Creed, and the nature of the sacraments and their use.[69] During these discussions, Morison was entrusted with keeping John Stokesley in line. A leading conservative only recently cleared of praemunire charges, Stokesley was hostile to English scripture and any compromise with evangelical doctrine.[70] Although he felt unable to comply with the king's wishes and compromise with the Lutherans, he offered to absent himself from the discussions rather than openly oppose the king. Cranmer, however, informed Morison that although progress would be much quicker if Stokesley were absent, it would ultimately damage the cause, as 'Men woll talke, or at the lest, thinke evyl if he shold be taken from their assemble'.[71] Morison, given his own theological opinions, was not the subtlest choice of messenger.

Morison may have been used unofficially in the negotiations with the Schmalkaldic delegation. The evidence for this comes in the form of a Latin tract on the seven sacraments which discusses each in turn, giving a 'concordia' or summary for most of them. Crucially, the discussion of matrimony ends with the assertion that 'agreement is easy over this sacrament since the Lutherans themselves honour it more than the priests'. Consequently Jeanes has concluded that 'De sacramentis' was drafted for use in the Anglo-Schmalkaldic theological discussions of 1538.[72] 'De sacramentis' shares many features of Morison's own *Treatise on the Seven Sacraments* written in the previous year. Its two-page introduction is almost identical to Morison's own introductory passages. In Morison's tract, it is clearly part of the original composition; in 'De sacramentis', evidently a later addition.[73] Jeanes's assertion that Morison's work is secondary to and a freer rendition of 'De sacramentis' is erroneous, as the correspondence between Morison's work and the

[69] McEntegart, *League of Schmalkalden*, 95–7, 99–105, 108–13.

[70] A. A. Chibi, *Henry VIII's Conservative Scholar, Bishop John Stokesley, the Divorce, the Supremacy and Doctrinal Reform* (Frankfurt am Main, 1997), 99–100, 104–6.

[71] SP1/133, fo. 234^v [*LP* XIII i 1296].

[72] G. Jeanes, 'A Reformation Treatise on the Sacraments', *Journal of Theological Studies*, 46 (1995), 149–90.

[73] Ibid., 150; *Sacraments*, fos. 137^r–8^r.

Bishops' Book demonstrates.[74] It is more likely that sections of Morison's tract were adopted, probably in conjunction with the determinations of other divines, into 'De sacramentis', making the latter a statement of concord within the English church which could be shown to the Lutherans. If derivative, Morison's discussion of ecclesiastical orders would surely expand upon the examples given in 'De sacramentis', yet it does not. Instead its texts and focus are different. Morison's discussion of extreme unction also maintains a truly independent position and is not derived from that in 'De sacramentis' in any way.[75] The differences between the two works are best explained by the different audiences for which they were intended. Morison's *Treatise* was part of a national theological discussion; 'De sacramentis' part of an international one. Consequently, it had to represent opinions which Henry VIII would not dismiss out of hand and had to represent a viable theological consensus of the English clergy (although it might give the most Lutheran spin possible to doctrines that Henry was prepared to tolerate). This, in turn, would explain differences in tone between the two works such as Morison's strong support for clerical marriage.[76] At the very least, 'De sacramentis' indicates that many of Morison's religious views were being used in the Anglo-German theological debates.

Morison also entertained the Schmalkaldic delegates during their stay in England. He conveyed their books to them and tried unsuccessfully to tempt them with the 'pleasur of huntyng'. Cromwell and Cranmer, keen to portray England and Henry as more Lutheran than they actually were, probably chose Morison because they knew him to be theologically sympathetic. Morison certainly believed the ambassadors would return to Germany as witnesses of Cromwell's personal efforts to purge England of idolatry and his 'love toward religion'.[77] If many of Morison's ideas, in their slightly adapted form in 'De sacramentis', were debated formally, it is likely that he informally discussed doctrine with the delegates. Morison's expertise on the General Council was probably another reason he was asked to attend to the delegation as this was one of the topics the Schmalkaldeners were commanded to discuss.[78] It is not clear when Morison learnt German, but he would

---

[74] Jeanes, 'Reformation Treatise', 151. No palaeographic trace of Morison is to be found in Lambeth Palace 1107.

[75] *Sacraments*, fos. 149^r–50^r; Jeanes, 'Reformation Treatise', 190.

[76] Ibid., 188–9; *Sacraments*, fos. 148^v–9^r.

[77] SP1/133, fo. 245^v [*LP* XIII i 1297]; McEntegart, *League of Schmalkalden*, 98–9.

[78] *LP* XIII i 1305.

have had the opportunity in Edmund Harvel's household in the 1530s, and by 1536 he had travelled through the Empire. If he did know the language by this date, it gives another potential reason for his part in the discussions.

Morison had a further link to the Schmalkaldic League in September 1538. Philip of Hesse and John of Saxony wrote to warn Henry VIII that they had recently uncovered information indicating that significant numbers of Anabaptists existed in England, and Morison translated the letter for the king.[79] It warned that 'th'errors of that secte, ar by secrete meanes, dayle spred abrode' in England, while emphasizing the Schmalkaldeners' total rejection of Anabaptist ideas. The events of Münster were briefly recounted to illustrate the dangers before the Schmalkaldeners' own treatment of Anabaptists was outlined for Henry's instruction. Once found, an effort should be made to convert Anabaptists using preachers and scripture. Only contumacious Anabaptists should be imprisoned or suffer physical hardship, while death should be reserved for those with no hope of amendment. The persecution of the Lutherans by popish magistrates was lamented.[80] Henry was evidently meant to realize the same distinction and not treat Lutherans within his kingdom as heretics—the Schmalkaldic delegation had been shocked that a Lutheran was made to bear faggots and do public penance at St Paul's during their stay in England.[81] Henry was to adduce a further lesson from the translation. Morison juxtaposed two religious options: those who are 'popishe' and those who are 'proffessors of the doctrine of the gospell'. If Henry was not one, he had to be the other.[82] As a result of the Schmalkaldeners' letter, a commission was set up during the following month to investigate the extent of Anabaptism in England and punish any Anabaptists found. This was followed in November 1538 by a proclamation commanding all Anabaptists, whether or not they had recanted, to leave the realm within twenty-one days.[83]

FURTHER WRITINGS AND INVOLVEMENT

Morison's combination of literary talent and theological knowledge was called upon on other occasions. He was involved in the drafting of

[79] *LP* XIII ii 264. [80] SP1/137, fos. 19^r–22^v, 24^{r-v} [*LP* XIII ii 427].
[81] MacLure, *Register*, 22. [82] SP1/137, fo. 22^v [*LP* XIII ii 427].
[83] *LP* XIII ii 498, 890.

at least one religious proclamation, which he corrected and annotated. The pattern of these corrections indicates that Morison was working on the middle stages of the drafting process: one more person annotated the document after Morison and this early draft was more evangelical than the eventual proclamation.[84] The draft proclamation, an early version of the proclamation issued on 26 February 1539, was written sometime after October 1538, and was intended to explain the official stance on several rites and ceremonies.[85]

Morison also wrote sermons during the 1530s. Only notes for one of these have survived, a sermon on Proverbs 17:1: 'Better a dry morsel, and quietness therewith, than a house full of feasting with strife.' This fragment could be read as his parable on the English Reformation. Although momentous advances had been made, not everyone could be satisfied. Using the language of a sumptuous feast, Morison argued that anyone in their right mind would prefer to eat only vegetables than to corrupt their mind by too much exposure to the pleasures of the flesh. Those who were only given a little to eat were more likely to strive after virtue; giving people too much in one portion could cause disorder. He also emphasized that all of Christ's elect had strong and faithful souls and would receive salvation. It was, then, preferable to have a slow-moving and piecemeal reformation achieved peacefully than to incur violence and confusion.[86]

LUTHERAN TRANSLATIONS

Morison authored one further theological work. His *Treatise on Faith and Justification* survives in the Harleian manuscripts in the British Library among papers which once belonged to John Foxe. It is possible that it was connected to the *Bishops' Book*, perhaps representing Morison's opinion on justification. As Morison is not among those known to have provided determinations on justification for the *Bishops' Book*, and as the manuscript is undated, this remains a matter for conjecture.[87]

Morison's *Treatise of Faith and Justification* has been taken as evidence that Morison and other evangelicals at Henry's court did not have an advanced Protestant understanding of faith by continental standards.[88]

[84] SP6/4, fos. 267ʳ–79ʳ.   [85] *TRP*, i.188.   [86] SP1/123, fos. 168ʳ–9ʳ.
[87] *LP* XII ii 1122.ii.   [88] Wooding, *Rethinking Catholicism*, 101–3.

Wooding was right: Morison's position was not advanced Protestant theology, and the theologians who criticized Luther's position on justification would have been able to make the same criticisms of Morison's tract. Yet this is because Morison's *Treatise on Faith and Justification* was not an original composition but a non-literal translation of Luther's *Freedom of a Christian Man*.[89] Its theology was not advanced Protestantism, because it was Luther's theology.

Morison omitted Luther's prefatory open letter to Leo X. At no point did he acknowledge that he was translating a Lutheran tract. By obscuring its origins, he may have hoped to make it more acceptable for publication, or for Henry VIII's consideration. Morison translated Luther's seminal *Freedom of a Christian Man* with respect to the meaning of Luther's tract and using language he deemed suitable. He included in his translation the alliteration that proliferated in his other works, ornamenting Luther's prose with such phrases as 'far felt fond phantasies' and 'soch a pomp of power, to so terrible a tyrannie'.[90] He did not attempt to add passages to make Luther's work more relevant to the English situation, nor alter the theology of the original. A comparison with Luther's work shows Morison's translation was faithful to the meaning of the original.[91]

Sturm's *Epistle*

Morison's 1538 translation of Johann Sturm's tract on the papal commission investigating the state of the church was primarily intended as part of the government's anti-conciliar campaign.[92] However, Morison probably also had theological motives for picking this tract. Sturm's *Epistle* explicitly defended Lutheranism and was littered with condemnations of Roman Catholic ceremonies and doctrines. Instead of removing or glossing over those passages that did not agree with English doctrinal statements, Morison retained them, signifying he agreed with Sturm doctrinally.

Sturm's *Epistle* strongly emphasized the importance of scripture for salvation. '[W]e have no hope of salvation' without 'the true knowledge of scripture'.[93] This was safe ground as scripture was the

---

89 Christie also did not realize it was a translation. Christie, 'Richard Morison', 85–95.
90 BL Harley 423, fos. 12^v, 19^v.
91 The text used for comparison was that in *Luther's Works*, 31.333–77.
92 See above, pp. 79–6.   93 Sturm, *Epistle*, Avi^r–Bv^r, Dvi^r.

professed foundation for Henry's church. However, the *Epistle* moved on to more extreme territory. Sturm attacked the sacramental practice of the Roman church as 'wonderfully defyled', 'depravate' and 'perverted'. By suppressing scripture, successive popes had been 'leaving unto wycked fowle and inveterate custome, the rule of religion', a situation which had been exacerbated by the commission's condemnation of Erasmus' writings.[94] Sturm questioned the administration of specific sacraments, claiming the Eucharist had been 'abused' for financial gain: communion was being sold as a 'faire marchandyse' and people were wrongly encouraged to believe that the mass was more beneficial than Christ's passion. Similarly, Sturm's tract held it that the Catholic practice of confession was introduced and maintained for purely financial reasons.[95] Sturm vilified many other aspects of traditional devotion, such as worshipping images and the Roman doctrine that good works contributed towards salvation. Although good works were useful and should not be discouraged, one could not 'opteyne heven by masses, by oure good dedes'. Indulgences and pardons were also decried as having no basis in scripture and were 'fainid, vain, and very foolysshe'.[96] Monasticism was flawed as it encouraged the monks to live in sin and separated men called to serve God from those to whom they should be spreading God's word. Moreover, monasticism was symptomatic of a larger error: the papacy actively discouraged preachers and impeded the teaching of God's word. Sturm also singled out the prohibition of clerical marriage for opprobrium.[97]

Morison did nothing to hide Sturm's consistent defence of Lutheranism. Sturm refuted the papists' accusation that the Lutherans' primary motivation in pressing for church reform was financial. He emphatically assured his readers that Lutheran writings contained nothing 'contrarye to the honour of Chryste, nor the mynde of thapostels, nor yet against auncient councilles'.[98] Morison also retained Sturm's assertion that Luther and his followers had received 'many and great tokens that god favoureth them'. One passage implied Lutheran doctrine was purer than Roman doctrine, claiming that the pope could 'never make the name of Luther so hated, but that whan your falshod is knowen, the trouth woll appere'.[99] Luther's theology, then, was truth. Morison's translation was

94 Sturm, *Epistle*, Bi^v–iii^v, Bviii^r, Cii^r, Dii^r, F^r–iv^r.   95 Ibid., Evii^v, Bviii^v, Ciii^v.
96 Ibid., Cii^r–v, Dvii^v, Ei^v.   97 Ibid., Ei^r–v, Civ^r–v^v, Evii^v.
98 Ibid., Bvii^r–v, Eviii^r, Eiii^v.   99 Ibid., Dv^v, Eiii^v–iv^r, Fiv^r–v.

part of an official propaganda campaign. By retaining these passages, he made Henry's government appear to be sponsoring Lutheranism.

Morison's religious efforts in the period 1540–7 have left no trace. He retreated into life in the country and at court, where he was part of a strong evangelical network. As Ryrie has suggested, the court was one of the most propitious places for evangelicals in England after Cromwell's fall.[100] Here, Morison's strong links to some of the country's leading evangelicals placed him among what became the godly political elite of Edwardian England. It was in Edward's reign that he once more became an active reformer.

THE EDWARDIAN REFORMATION

Royal Commissioner, 1547

Cranmer's sermon at Edward's coronation indicated the direction in which he saw the English church heading. As England's Josiah, Edward would cleanse the realm of superstition and idolatry.[101] As part of this process the government in August 1547 issued commissions to investigate the religious state of the parishes, which were to take the recently printed *Homilies* and royal injunctions with them. Men known for their reforming zeal were deliberately chosen to fill these commissions.[102] Morison was among them, appointed to investigate the dioceses of Worcester and Hereford as well as those in Wales.[103] His fellow commissioners were also committed to further reform. Richard Tracy had composed several evangelical works on topics such as *Sola fideism* in Henry VIII's reign; in Edward's reign he penned attacks on the mass.[104] Robert Ferrar was a trained theologian, who, having been one of the Oxford heretics in 1528, became an enthusiastic evangelical preacher in the 1530s.[105] George Constantine was a veteran evangelical and Henry Siddall was a canon lawyer who was to become a strong

---

[100] Ryrie, *Gospel*, ch. 4.   [101] Aston, *England's Iconoclasts*, 247–8.
[102] MacCulloch, *Church Militant*, 72.
[103] J. Strype, *Memorials of Cranmer* (Oxford, 1840), i. 209. Morison's Worcestershire properties probably explain his appointment.
[104] Tracy was heavily involved in the dissolution of the Worcestershire monasteries and held several positions in local government in Worcestershire and Gloucestershire (A. Ryrie, 'Richard Tracy', *ODNB* 55.195).
[105] G. Williams, 'Robert Ferrar', *ODNB* 19.419.

supporter of Peter Martyr Vermigli.[106] The active members of the commission appear to have been Morison, Tracy, Siddall and Ferrar, who investigated and confirmed the statutes of the recently re-founded Worcester school.[107]

The 1547 Injunctions instructed the commissioners to ensure 'the suppression of idolatry and superstition', to 'take down, or cause to be taken down and destroy' abused images and 'utterly distinct and destroy all shrines'. Sufficient ambiguity remained for the visitors to exercise their personal judgement. They might allow images that were not abused to remain, or exploit the phrasing of the twenty-eighth injunction to remove all images (including those which had not been abused).[108] Many of the commissions were strongly iconoclastic, prompting the Grey Friars' chronicler to note: 'alle imagys pullyd downe thorrow alle Ynglonde att that tyme, and alle churches new whytte-lymed, with the commandmenttes wryttyne on the walles'.[109] In some areas visited by Morison's commission, the destruction of images was fairly comprehensive. At St Michael's in Bedwardine, Worcester, after noting the visitation and the books bought as a result, the churchwarden noted the 'hewinge downe' of the images, the 'whytelymynge' of the church, the painting of the altars and expenses for re-glazing the church windows. Elsewhere in the locality images were destroyed and lights taken down in 1547–8, most likely due to the visitation.[110] The visitors forced the removal of images in Halesowen, the burning of local saints' bones in Much Wenlock in Shropshire, and held a bonfire in Shrewsbury marketplace to burn images and statues from the local parishes.[111] In the Welsh dioceses, despite the efforts of the commissioners, many images were simply hidden. In late 1551 Bishop Bulkley of Bangor was concerned that there were images left in his diocese and many were later resurrected in Mary's reign.[112]

[106] E. I. Carlyle and A. A. Chibi, 'Henry Siddall', *ODNB* 50.511; A. Hope, 'George Constantine', *ODNB* 13.35.

[107] A. F. Leach (ed.), *Documents Illustrating Early Education in Worcester* (Worcester, 1913), 134, 147.

[108] Aston, *England's Iconoclasts*, 254–9.

[109] J. G. Nichols (ed.), *Chronicle of the Grey Friars of London*, Camden 1st ser. 53 (London, 1852), 54.

[110] J. Amphlett (ed.), *Churchwardens' Accounts of St Michael's in Bedwardine, Worcester* (Oxford, 1896), 19–20; D. MacCulloch and P. Hughes, 'A Bailiff's List and Chronicle from Worcester', *Antiquaries' Journal*, 75 (1995), 245.

[111] F. Somers (ed.), *Halesowen Churchwardens' Accounts, 1487–1582* (London, 1952–7), 90; MacCulloch, *Church Militant*, 72–3.

[112] M. Gray, *Images of Piety* (Oxford, 2000), 75–8; G. Williams, *The Edwardian Reformation in Wales* (Bangor, 1991), 24.

Chantry Commissioner

The 1547 Injunctions had gone a long way towards converting the chantries into charitable institutions. The Chantries Act of November 1547 provided for their dissolution and the reallocation of chantry funds for educational purposes.[113] In February 1548, Morison was appointed a commissioner to enquire what colleges, chantries and other obits had come into the crown's hands since the Chantries Act had been passed on 4 November 1547, in Middlesex, London and Westminster. Morison's fellow commissioners included three common lawyers (Sir Roger Cholmely, Sir Nicholas Hare, Richard Goodrich), two experienced administrators (Sir Wymond Carew, Sir John Godsalve), the local surveyor, Hugh Losse, and John Carrell. Morison's inclusion added to the mix a civilian with some theological training.[114] During this time, Morison was based in London, as the commissioners sat at the Saddlers' and Haberdashers' Halls. The commissioners' return was not as detailed as some of the others, probably because three months was insufficient time to complete their task and write a substantial document. The return listed the many 'superstitious' activities and bodies associated with the various companies and corporations in the metropolis, but did not detail their secular endowments.[115] As a result of the commissioners' recommendations, the curates of St Botolph Aldersgate and St Sepulchre without Newgate acquired assistants, while a new priest was appointed to the chapel at Stratford le Bow. Meanwhile, the alms at St Stephen's College, Westminster, were protected, as was the future of the free school at Ashwell.[116]

Royal Visitor

In 1548, Morison was appointed a visitor of the king's free chapel and college at Windsor Castle, Winchester College and the Diocese

---

[113] 1 Edward VI, c. 14; A. Kreider, *English Chantries: The Road to Dissolution* (London, 1979), ch. 6.

[114] *Cal. Pat. Edward VI*, ii.137; J. H. Baker, 'Sir Roger Cholmley', *ODNB* 11.505–6; J. H. Baker, 'Sir Nicholas Hare', *ODNB* 25.258–9; P. N. Carter, 'Richard Goodrich', *ODNB* 22.803; P. R. N. Carter, 'Sir Wymond Carew', *ODNB* 10.68; D. Hoak, 'Sir John Godsalve', *ODNB* 22.604; C. J. Kitching (ed.), *London and Middlesex Chantry Certificate, 1548* (London, 1948), p. x.

[115] Ibid., *passim*; Kreider, *English Chantries*, 200–3.

[116] E319/15/10, E319/15/14.

and University of Oxford. Although an active member, Morison's exact role in the commission is difficult to ascertain. The commission's remit, combined with one issued for Cambridgeshire, covered those institutions exempted from the Chantries Act. Morison's fellow visitors were the earl of Warwick, Henry Holbeach, Nicholas Ridley, William Paget, William Petre, Richard Cox, Simon Haynes and Christopher Nevinson.[117] The religious agenda of the commission is suggested by its composition: Paget and Petre were civilians; Cox, Haynes and Nevinson theologians; Morison could claim to be both. Warwick, meanwhile, was not an active member.

John Bale claimed that Winchester College was full of obdurate papists.[118] Reforming Winchester was essential to reforming Oxford, as Winchester acted as a feeder school for New College. In 1548, the college received new injunctions, stipulating that religious services be performed in English. The warden of the college, John White, was hostile to Protestantism and opposed to Peter Martyr Vermigli's theology. However, his second in command, William Ford, was an evangelical who may have been responsible for an act of iconoclasm in the school in the later years of Henry's reign and certainly propagated reformed doctrines within the school.[119]

Morison had earlier connections to some of the Windsor reformers, including Robert Testwood and Simon Haynes, who were both canons there in the 1530s.[120] Sadly, the Windsor accounts do not permit any detailed assessment of the visitation. The chapel did sell much of its church plate and had, by 1550, lost its organist.[121] Probably at the same time that Morison and the commissioners visited Windsor Castle, Thomas Cranmer and the 'Windsor commission', a group of divines debating the doctrine contained in Cranmer's proposed *Book of Common Prayer*, relocated to Windsor for the consecration of Robert Ferrar as bishop of St David's. They then continued their eucharistic debates prior to a wider disputation in the House of Lords. Among those known to have been at Windsor participating in the deliberations

[117] *Cal. Pat. Edward VI*, ii.251.

[118] J. Bale, *Expostulation or complaynte agains the blasphemies of a frantic papiste in Hampshire* (London, 1552), Ciiiᵛ.

[119] P. McGrath, 'Winchester College and the Old Religion', in R. Custance (ed.), *Winchester College: Sixth Centenary Essays* (Oxford, 1982), 238–41.

[120] *LP* XI 1404.

[121] M. F. Bond, *The Inventories of St George's Chapel, Windsor Castle* (Windsor, 1947), 16; Bodleian Library, Ashmole 1123, i, 187ᵛ, ii, 41ʳ.

were Holbeach, Ridley, Haynes, William May, Thomas Goodrich, Cranmer, Thomas Thirlby, Thomas Robertson and John Redman.[122] Thomas Fuller added John Skip, George Day, Richard Cox and John Taylor. Goodrich and May were on the commission to visit Cambridge University, which also had responsibility for Eton, while Holbeach, Ridley, Haynes and Cox were on the Oxford/Windsor commission. It seems likely that the two commissions gathered at Windsor for Ferrar's consecration and that all the visitors were involved in the eucharistic debates. This certainly would have been a pragmatic move, as both commissions were mandated to supervise disputations on the Eucharist in the universities.[123] As a theologian of some reputation, Morison probably participated in these discussions.

OXFORD

Notice of an impending royal visitation had been given to Oxford University in April 1548. The colleges were instructed to refrain from making any appointments and their statutes were effectively suspended until the visitation occurred. It soon became apparent that the visitation had been postponed until the following year. Some colleges petitioned for and gained the right to elect fellows in the meantime.[124] Morison and the other visitors were instructed to investigate fully all the colleges and halls. They were given powers to correct any transgression by colleges and adjudicate disputes. Every college was to have its statutes examined, enforced and, where appropriate, reformed by the visitors. Reforms were necessary, as some colleges had been using their foundation statutes as a reason not to conform to Edwardian liturgical reforms. Such allegations were made against Owen Oglethorp, president of Magdalen, although Oglethorp maintained his innocence.[125] The visitors were also to bring the finances of the colleges in line with the Edwardian reformation—chantry income was to be reallocated to purely educational pursuits, while money previously used for grammar schools or to support traditional religion was

[122] Strype, *Cranmer*, i. 261.

[123] F. Procter and W. H. Frere, *A New History of the Book of Common Prayer* (London, 1902), 46–7. Strype, *Cranmer*, i. 261; W. K. L. Clarke, *Liturgy and Worship* (London, 1932), 152.

[124] *VCH Oxfordshire*, iii. 86–7.

[125] H. A. Wilson, *Magdalen College* (London, 1998), 91.

instead to be used to promote the study of arts. From a pedagogical point of view, the visitors were to encourage the study of civil law, establish All Souls as a civilian college, designate one college for the study of medicine and amalgamate colleges when this would prove beneficial.[126]

The visitation officially opened in St Mary's Church on 24 May, with an indication of what was to come: Peter Martyr Vermigli, whose theological views had been causing unrest in Oxford, delivered the opening sermon.[127] After the sermon, the visitors read out their commission to the assembled academics. In Cambridge the visitors opened by inviting scholars to bring matters that needed redressing to their attention; the same probably happened in Oxford. Certainly members of individual colleges such as Magdalen brought their complaints to the attention of the commission.[128]

Colleges tried to clean up before the arrival of the visitors. Lincoln, a largely conservative college, laid new rushes, bought new tapers and ensured a new, legible copy of the college statutes was available for the visitors' inspection.[129] Merton meanwhile sold £70 of plate in order to buy new books.[130] This was a politic move—there are indications that at Balliol and All Souls the visitors assessed the colleges' libraries, while Magdalen bought new books following the visitation.[131] Colleges such as Balliol and Lincoln ensured the visitors were remunerated for their efforts and the process was eased along by gifts and wine.[132]

At Lincoln, All Souls and Magdalen the visitors redrafted the college's statutes, while other colleges also expected to have their statutes revised.[133] On 4 June it was the university's turn. The commissioners presented new statutes, which, although they were not intended to be permanent, attempted educational reforms. The allocation of prescriptive texts within the arts course reflected a change of focus:

---

[126] T. Rymer, *Syllabus of 'Rymer's Foedera'* (London, 1885), vi. 171.

[127] Wood, *History*, ii. 99.   [128] CUL, M.m.1.42, 13.

[129] V. H. H. Green, *The Commonwealth of Lincoln College 1427–1977* (Oxford, 1997), 88.

[130] Cross, 'Oxford', 136.

[131] J. Jones, *Balliol College: A History* (Oxford, 1997), 54; N. R. Ker, *Records of All Souls College Library* (Oxford, 1971), 117; *idem, Books, Collectors and Libraries* (London, 1985), 381.

[132] Ibid., 54; Green, *Lincoln*, 88.

[133] Green, *Lincoln*, 88; W. H. Frere, *Visitation Articles and Injunctions of the Period of the Reformation* (London, 1910), 197–203; CUL, M.m.1.42, 15–16.

logic, for instance, now encompassed oratory and sophistry.[134] The study of medicine was to be refined by making practical anatomical examinations mandatory. Canon law was removed from the syllabus, but the study of common law was introduced. The visitors also used their powers of amalgamation to suggest turning All Souls into a college of civilians: they were to swap their arts students for New College's lawyers. Although this scheme had its roots in Henry's reign and Cox had been an avid exponent of a similar scheme in 1546, the idea was so unpopular that it was quietly dropped once the visitors had left Oxford. Regulations governing Greek studies in the university made their first appearance in the statutes, which set the times for public lectures in Greek and Hebrew. The visitation also encouraged a greater centralization of facilities: lecturers were instructed to publicize details of their courses at the start of each term and contribute to the general university disputations.[135]

The new statutes also ensured that the Edwardian religious reforms would be integrated into university practice. Anything in the existing college statutes that conflicted with the Edwardian church was removed. The visitors left students with a minimum of communion at the start of each term and mandatory daily Protestant worship.[136] Another means of reforming the university was controlling college appointments. The visitors were given the power to remove heads of colleges but they seemingly did not remove conservative college heads.[137] Wood's claims that the visitors expelled many Catholics from the colleges and installed 'such that were rigid Calvinists' and cronies of Richard Cox in their place are exaggerated.[138] Some Catholics left of their own accord upon hearing of the visitation. At Lincoln the visitors probably removed the conservative Hugh Weston from his professorship; they certainly extended William More's term of office as rector of Exeter College.[139] It appears that Morison and the other visitors did appoint scholars, but with limited success—a complaint against Oglethorpe was later made because he had been 'refusing toward young men appointed by the visitors'.[140]

---

[134] Wood, *History*, ii. 99; L. Jardine, 'The Place of Dialectic Teaching at Cambridge', *Studies in the Renaissance*, 21 (1974), 34.

[135] Rymer, *Foedera*, vi. 171–2.   [136] Cross, 'Oxford', 136.

[137] G. D. Duncan 'The Heads of Houses and Religious Change in Tudor Oxford 1547–1558', *Oxoniensia*, 45 (1980), 227.

[138] Wood, *History*, ii. 96, 100.

[139] Green, *Lincoln College*, 88; Duncan, 'Heads of Houses', 227.

[140] CUL, M.m.1.42, 12.

The Oxford visitation exercised similar powers to its Cambridge counterpart to remove vestiges of popery from the university.[141] Several colleges witnessed the destruction of images during the visitation. Although All Souls had pulled down the crucifixion group and other images over the high altar in 1548, the visitors caused the removal of the reredos, images of saints, stained-glass and the organ from the college chapel.[142] At Magdalen statues of saints were removed from the chapel and images painted over; Balliol paid 8*s.* for 'obliterating the images beside the altar' and employed two workmen to remove the altars.[143] Images were also removed from New College; Merton lost its minor altars, and payments to its organist ceased. However, the 1549 visitation did not eradicate all vestiges of Catholic worship. Altars were allowed to remain in several college chapels, including All Souls, Magdalen and Merton.[144] Similarly, the organ at Balliol was not removed until 1551, the same year in which the college library was purged.[145] The second Edwardian visitation, with which Morison was not involved, was far stricter with regard to images and papistical books, targeting especially Thomas Aquinas' and Peter Lombard's writings.[146] Wood's influential image of the 1549 visitation as one of wanton destruction needs to be revised. In 1549, the visitors forced the removal of images and superfluous altars, and imposed new reading matter on the colleges. But they were not responsible for the wholesale purge of Catholic material—that was to come later.

Some of the requirements of the visitation proved impracticable for the colleges. Magdalen, which proved particularly difficult, objected to the reallocation of its choristers' emoluments, arguing that the choristers were also scholars and opposed moves to sever its links with its grammar school, arguing that the school provided scholars for the college and benefited the city too. In one respect the visitors did successfully introduce reform at Magdalen: they converted all payments for masses into exhibitions for poor scholars.[147] They probably did the same at other colleges.

---

[141] Cross, 'Oxford', 136.

[142] C. G. Robertson, *All Souls College* (London, 1898), 59; *VCH Oxfordshire*, iii.177.

[143] Wilson, *Magdalen*, 91; Jones, *Balliol*, 54.

[144] *VCH Oxfordshire*, iii.146, 177; J. M. Fletcher and C. A. Upton, 'Destruction, Repair and Removal: An Oxford College Chapel during the Reformation', *Oxoniensa* (1983), 123–4; Wilson, *Magdalen*, 96.

[145] Jones, *Balliol*, 54.   [146] Wood, *History*, ii. 106–8.

[147] Wilson, *Magdalen*, 91.

The 1549 visitation had one further purpose: to oversee a theological debate between Peter Martyr Vermigli and his conservative detractors. Vermigli had begun lecturing on 1 Corinthians 10D in 1548. This text contained several passages at the centre of doctrinal debates, in particular a section on the nature of Christ's presence in the Eucharist. He was challenged to debate this issue by Richard Smith, but refused to stray from his planned lecture. Cox, hoping to avoid any further disruption, arranged for the scholars to debate privately and set the date for May 1549; the Privy Council then stipulated that it would take place in the visitors' presence.[148] The new liturgy, recently approved by Parliament, was not yet introduced into the parishes. It was essential that the government retain control over public statements on the nature of the Eucharist, not least as they had not issued their own exposition of official doctrine on the matter. In the meantime, however, religious unrest continued in Oxford with some colleges, such as Magdalen, witnessing disruptions to the eucharistic service.[149]

By the time the debate took place, Smith had fled Oxford. From 28 May to 1 June his fellow conservatives Chedsey and Tresham disputed with Martyr in his stead on whether the medieval doctrine of transubstantiation could be proven. Such a debate was possible, as the 1549 *Book of Common Prayer* did not contain any officially sanctioned eucharistic theology, a point Cox made when concluding the debate.[150] The royal commissioners did not play a very active role in the debate. Cox occasionally intervened on Martyr's side and Morison merely made a few interjections designed to move the discussion along.[151] Vermigli opposed the doctrine of ubiquity, maintaining that Christ was spiritually present in the Eucharist to those who believed: he was physically present only in as much as Christ was present in all things.[152] Vermigli's eucharistic theology refuted a physical presence in the host and rejected any notion of sacrifice, concluding that the body and blood of Christ were only joined to the bread and wine sacramentally. Ab Ulmis, for one, believed that Vermigli's position was very close to that of Bullinger.[153] In concluding the debate, the commissioners praised the learning of all of the disputants with sufficient vagueness that both sides claimed

148 Cross, 'Oxford', 135–6.
149 OUA WPβ/B/24. Townsmen were apparently present.
150 MacCulloch, *Church Militant*, 91.   151 BL Harley 422, fo. 14ʳ.
152 J. C. McClelland, *The Visible Words of God* (London, 1957), 203–5.
153 S. Corda, *Veritas Sacramenti: A Study of Vermigli's Doctrine of the Lord's Supper* (Zurich, 1975), 73. *OL*, clxxxviii.

victory, but Cox made it clear that he supported the Italian reformer.[154] Vermigli published his account of the debate in the following year, dedicating it to Cox, Morison and the other visitors. This work was produced in English and Latin editions, and was popular abroad.[155]

CLERICAL PATRONAGE

As a substantial property owner, Morison controlled the patronage of over thirty parishes in the 1540s and was also granted the presentations to several higher-ranking benefices. However, Morison does not appear to have exercised this patronage very extensively. In part, this was because many of the incumbents did not die or vacate their benefice until after Morison's own death in 1556. Such was the case with the nominations Holbeach had granted Morison to the archdeaconry of Huntingdon and the prebend of Nassington.[156] In some parishes, including Croule Hackett, Worcestershire, Morison sold his lands and his advowsons before the position became vacant.[157] Certainly his exchange with the crown of many of the lands he had received from St Wulstan's and St James's Hospitals severely reduced his potential as a patron of clerics.[158] In still more cases, there is simply no record of a presentation to the benefice during the time that Morison controlled the advowson. This makes it impossible to determine Morison's clerical patronage. One can infer, however, from his patronage of continental evangelicals that he would have appointed men cut from the same religious cloth as himself if given the opportunity.

ASSESSMENT

Morison's theological career demonstrates the importance of the training and enthusiasm of laymen for the Reformation. His reputation as a reformer in the 1530s was deserved. He was actively engaged in the English Reformation, composing theological determinations in Henry's

---

[154] P. M. Vermigli, *The Oxford Treatise and Disputation on the Eucharist*, ed. J. C. McClelland (Kirksville, MO, 2000), p. xl.

[155] MacCulloch, *Church Militant*, 91–2.

[156] R. E. G. Cole (ed.), *Chapter Acts of the Cathedral of St Mary of Lincoln, 1536–47*, Lincoln Record Society, 15 (Horncastle, 1917), 46, 48. Anthony Draycote and William Tailboys held the posts throughout the 1550s (ibid., 172, 176).

[157] C1/1394/31–5.   [158] HALS, 6593.

reign and acting on commissions in Edward's. Throughout the 1530s Morison was openly Lutheran. He was closely associated with two of the leaders of the evangelical group at court: Cromwell and Foxe. He participated in both national theological debates and international negotiations of a religious character. His doctrinal position seems to have moved closer to that of the Swiss in the 1540s, if his favourable opinion of Peter Martyr Vermigli is indicative. However, Morison's exact position in the 1540s and 1550s is difficult to pin down, as he maintained friendships with continental reformers whose theological beliefs covered quite a wide spectrum, from the Lutheran stalwart Johannes Sturm to John Calvin. Even Bernardine Ochino, whose theology was becoming increasingly radical in the 1550s, thought Morison's beliefs lay close to his own in 1554.[159]

Despite Morison's strong religious views, he was able to reconcile himself to the lack of progress after 1539. His brief sermon on Proverbs 17:1 is perhaps the best indication of his views on the Henrician Reformation: he would have preferred further reform, but was content to wait until the reign of Edward VI if Henry VIII and his country were not yet ready to countenance it. Henry's own theological position remains unclear. He may well have remained attached to traditional religion.[160] Bernard has suggested Henry's attachment, such as it was, was limited, and as McEntegart has convincingly shown, Henry approached theology in the 1530s from an inquisitive point of view and only gradually made up his mind.[161] This allowed even committed Protestants, like Morison, to survive. Morison could be open about his evangelicalism in the 1530s because Henry's own religious views were not yet solidified. After Henry's death, Morison's commitment to the evangelical cause was harnessed by the Edwardian regime, who viewed him as an appropriate member of several religious commissions and a suitable figure to represent Edward and his church abroad.

---

[159] I have used the German edition. B. Ochino, *Des Hochgelehrten und Gottsäligen mans Bernhardini Ochini. . . seiner Apologen* (Augsburg, 1559), Aii[r].

[160] R. Rex and C. D. C. Armstrong, 'Henry VIII's Ecclesiastical and Collegiate Foundations', *HR*, 125 (2002), 390–407; F. Kisby, ' "When the King goeth a procession": Chapel Ceremonies and Services, the Ritual Year, and Religious Reforms at the early Tudor Court, 1485–1547', *JBS*, 40 (2001), 44–75; C. Haigh, *English Reformations* (Oxford, 1993), ch. 9.

[161] McEntegart, *League of Schmalkalden, passim*; Bernard, 'Piety of Henry VIII', 62–88.

6

The Diplomat

TRAINING

Early Diplomatic Duties

Morison's diplomatic career spanned nearly twenty years, beginning in 1535 when he joined Edmund Harvel's household in Venice. Here Morison gained experience in gathering intelligence and insight into the workings of a diplomatic household.[1] In the period 1536–40 Morison regularly translated and deciphered letters from foreign dignitaries and English ambassadors.[2] He mistakenly believed he might be sent as part of an embassy to Germany in 1537–8. However, his role in the diplomatic corps was extended considerably when Cromwell employed him to entertain the delegates of the Schmalkaldic League in 1538.[3] A brief mission hosting Ferrarese ambassadors followed in 1539. At about this time, Morison claimed to be well informed about the opinions of ambassadors at Henry's court, suggesting that his duties probably included more diplomatic activities than can now be traced.[4]

Throughout the 1540s Morison continued to serve in the capacity of diplomatic host. In July 1541 he served and conveyed plate to an evangelical Polish potentate, Stanisław Ostroróg, part of a Polish delegation mainly interested in visiting Henry's palaces. In February 1546 Morison and Richard Shelley together escorted another Polish ambassador, Stanisław Lasotta, from palace to palace. Lasotta's mission was to negotiate a dynastic alliance between one of the English princesses

[1] BL Cotton Nero BVI, fos. 151ʳ–2ʳ; *LP* X 372, 418, 565.
[2] *LP* XIII i 571–2, 590.2, ii 427, XV ii 51, 1029.51.
[3] BL Cotton Cleopatra EVI, fo. 323ʳ [*LP* XII i 1311]; SP1/133, fo. 253ᵛ [*LP* XIII i 1297].
[4] BL Arundel 97, fo. 63ᵛ [*LP* XIV ii 781]; *LP* XIV i 370; *Exhortation*, Biiiʳ.

and the recently widowed king of Poland. Later that year, Morison again acted as a diplomatic host: he and Richard Shelley gave attendance upon a 'certen Italyon sent in embassedge'.[5]

In December 1546 Morison received his first official embassy. He was appointed to represent Henry at the Diet of Holstein and to mediate a jurisdictional dispute between Frederick, the count Palatine and Christian II of Denmark. The Palatine had requested Henry's intercession; later he sent Henry wines, probably in thanks. At the start of December rumours circulated of a conference between ambassadors from several nations to resolve the dispute. Henry's Privy Council were anxious that the English broker the peace and not the recently despatched French emissary. This competition probably stemmed from Anglo-French rivalry over access to Danish mercenaries in the 1540s. Morison's instructions to visit Hamburg, Lingen, Lübeck and Bremen also suggest a military purpose for his mission — it was to the countryside around these towns that Henry increasingly looked when retaining mercenaries after 1544. Morison stayed with Conrad Courtpfennig, a former mercenary captain under Henry VIII who became the foremost recruiter of German mercenaries for Edward VI, and was even approached by one captain, Peter van Utrecht, with offers of troops for the king.[6] Morison was also instructed to inform the king of Denmark and the Hanse towns of Henry VIII's death. Despite Morison's efforts the Danish king would only confirm the existing Anglo-Danish agreement orally and was not prepared to renegotiate. Meanwhile the French suspected that Morison was instructed to arrange a truce between Charles V and the Lutherans, though this was unfounded.[7] On his way back to England, Morison was also expected to reclaim some monies owed to the crown. By 16 April 1547 he was back in England to receive reimbursement for his mission without having achieved much.[8]

---

[5] *LP* XVI 992, 954, 1011, XXI i 234, 289, 478; *CSPS 1545–6*, 310, 318; SP68/6, fo. 133ᵛ [*CSPFE*, 316]; E315/255, fo. 85ᵛ [*LP* XXI ii 775].

[6] *LP* XXI ii 484, 640, 647, 662, 679, 684, 707, 758; *CSPFE*, 7, 19; *APC 1547–1550*, 23; G. J. Millar, *Tudor Mercenaries and Auxiliaries 1485–1547* (Charlottesville, 1980), 162–6; D. Potter, 'The International Mercenary Market in the Sixteenth Century: Anglo-French Competition in Germany, 1543–50', *EHR*, 111 (1996), 24–58.

[7] SP68/1, fo. 23ʳ [*CSPFE*, 11]; *LP* XXI ii 662, 707.

[8] *APC 1547–1550*, 23; E315/256, fo. 79ᵛ. He had received three months' pay in advance: E315/255, fo. 120ᵛ.

THE KING'S REPRESENTATIVE

In 1550 Morison's old friend Edmund Harvel, the English ambassador in Venice, died. Morison, who was eager to continue in
diplomatic service, petitioned to replace Harvel, but the post went
to the Italian Peter Vannes. However, when Philip Hoby asked to
be relieved as resident ambassador to the Imperial court, Morison
was chosen as his replacement. He received his letters of introduction to Charles V on 8 August 1550.[9] At this point, Morison
was a well-trained diplomat. He had experience of diplomatic entertainment, ciphering and had served overseas. His career therefore
appears to contradict Gary Bell's notion that until Elizabeth's reign
English diplomats received very little training before they were appointed.[10]

According to contemporary diplomatic theory, an ambassador was
the king's representative abroad and his every action reflected and commented upon the attitudes and accomplishments of the king himself.
Ludovico Sforza had believed that the excellence of a prince could
be gauged by the distinction of his diplomatic representatives. This
attitude was just as firmly held in the mid-sixteenth century.[11] The
choices a king or his council made when appointing his diplomats
were therefore taken as an indication of what sort of prince he was:
they could tell another court whether he was learned, interested in
cultural trends, philosophically skilled, linguistically adept or militarily
capable. Morison's appointment and his subsequent actions will have
been scrutinized by the Imperial court and other ambassadors there
and taken as an indication of the intentions of the Edwardian government. His embassy will have shaped perceptions of England and its
king.

Diplomatic service in the sixteenth century was both a political and
social activity. Consequently ambassadors needed a wide skill set in
order to be suitable for overseas service. Sir Francis Thynne, when

[9] S. Brigden (ed.), 'The Letters of Richard Scudamore to Sir Philip Hoby, September
1549 to March 1555', *Camden Miscellany XXX*, CS 4th ser. 39 (1990), 122–3; BL Additional
5395, fo. 84ʳ.
[10] Bell, 'Elizabethan Diplomacy', 267–89.
[11] J. G. Russell, *Peacemaking in the Renaissance* (London, 1986), 75.

attempting to describe the perfect ambassador in the 1570s, articulated
that such a person should be:

learned, well born, free, no bond-man, of good credit in respect of his honesty, of
good estimation in respect of his calling . . . wise, valiant, circumspect, furnished
with divers Languages, eloquent of quick capacitie, of ready deliverance, liberall,
comly of person, tall of stature, and briefly that he be adorned with all vertues
required, or commendable, in a good man, and unfurnished of any vice to
blemish his credit, or that may win him the Surname of a wicked man.[12]

Morison's career suggests the idealism of Thynne's description, in
contrast to the complex qualifications needed in an ambassador serving
in a Europe politically and religiously divided.

The position of ambassador was eminently prestigious, not least
because of the prevailing assumption that a close relationship with the
monarch was a necessary qualification. As a gentleman of both Henry
VIII's and Edward VI's Privy Chambers Morison already had diplomatic
credibility, but his knighthood in early July and subsequent admittance
to the Privy Council gave him the essential additional political clout
required to be taken seriously at the status-conscious Imperial court.[13]
Even the physical paraphernalia available to an ambassador on his
mission were designed to reflect his association with the king. At the
imperial court Morison used expensive plate bearing the king's arms.[14]

Morison received many honours thanks to his status as ambassador.
On his mission to Denmark, the cities of Bremen, Utrecht and Hamburg
offered him money and escort, while Courtpfennig entertained him in
his own house and also offered a twenty-five horse escort. The embassy to
Charles was even more prestigious. Thus Morison was given honourable
escorts at several points on his journey to Augsburg to the emperor's
court. Morison's retinue was accompanied by Cranmer from Canterbury
to Dover; his old friend Richard Brandsby wanted to escort him from
Antwerp to Louvain; at Ulm he was 'presented solemnly by the states of
the town' and given a tour of the armoury and grain stores; and Philip
Hoby 'with a great number of horse' ensured that his replacement's

---

[12] F. Thynne, *The perfect ambassadour treating of the antiquitie, priveledges, and behaviour
of men belonging to that function* (London, 1652), fos. 18ᵛ–19ʳ.
[13] For the problems low status ambassadors could face see G. M. Bell, 'John Man, the
Last Elizabethan Resident Ambassador in Spain', *SCJ*, 7 (1976), 81–6; Brigden, 'Richard
Scudamore', 140.
[14] BL Additional 5756, fo. 239ʳ; *CSPFE*, 270.

arrival at Augsburg was suitably impressive.[15] Even during Morison's later disgrace, the German towns continued to treat the ambassador of the reforming King Edward with great honour. At Nuremberg, Morison was greeted by two senators and fifteen town officials, who presented him with thirty-two vessels of wine and fish and showed him the town's artillery and granaries. Morison interceded for two men banished from the city, after being petitioned by a townsman. For Edward's sake, the senate granted Morison's request. Morison subsequently received several other petitions for intercession, but due to the nature of the crimes committed—including wilful murder—Morison refused: he did not want to sully his and consequently Edward's reputation by helping obdurate criminals.[16]

Diplomacy held a strong attraction for Morison, who viewed it as an extension of his humanist career. He has been attributed with the saying that one of the three things that made a man was 'travel wherby they saw whith they read; and made it a solid apprehension and observation, which was before but a fluid notion'.[17] Morison used his embassy as an opportunity for practical education and endeavoured to visit several interesting sights and people on his way to Augsburg. He took in the traditional coronation site of the king of the Romans at Aachen, pointedly visited the imprisoned Philip of Hesse in Mechelen and spent one night lodged with Philip Melanchthon's brother-in-law in Melanchthon's hometown. Morison had hoped to visit scholars in Basel and Strasbourg, in particular Johannes Sturm and Johannes Sleidan, but Hoby wanted him at court immediately.[18]

Morison's embassy occurred during a time of transition for England's diplomatic corps. England had introduced resident ambassadors to Spain in 1505, while Wolsey's direction extended the network to include Venice and France.[19] Ecclesiastics predominated in English diplomacy under Henry VIII, as they possessed the necessary linguistic skills. Furthermore, theological training became important during the ideological and theological shifts of the 1530s. Clerical dominance slowly waned through the mid-Tudor years as more demanding standards were applied to the pastoral responsibilities and residence of the

---

[15] *LP* XXI ii 758; BL Additional 35841, fos. 3ᵛ, 6ʳ; *Whole Works*, I.ii.211, 263–4, 405.
[16] SP68/8, fos. 25ᵛ–6ʳ [*CSPFE*, 405].   [17] BL Sloane 1523, fo. 29ᵛ.
[18] Brigden, 'Richard Scudamore', 145–6; A. Katterfeld, *Roger Ascham: Sein Leben und seine Werke* (Strasbourg, 1879), 127; BL Additional 35841, fo. 5ʳ; *Whole Works*, I.ii.244, 257, 259–60.
[19] G. Mattingly, *Renaissance Diplomacy* (London, 1955), 159–61.

clergy, and a new generation of highly educated professionals rose in the diplomatic ranks. Bell contends that this was engendered by a new professional ethic that emerged to spawn the highly integrated diplomatic profession that he sees in Elizabeth's reign. However, MacMahon posits another explanation: the ideology of Protestant clergy chosen to be ambassadors was incompatible with successful residence at a court with a clearly defined Catholic identity and ideology.[20] This was particularly problematic in the Holy Roman Empire, as its iconographic heritage had suffused the imperial crown with a Catholic philosophy so as to distinguish it, alongside the papacy, as a defender of Catholic doctrine. This became even more pronounced under Charles V, who was faced with the threat of Lutheranism.

In 1550 the exact role and behaviour of a resident ambassador from a Protestant England to a Catholic emperor was not yet established, nor were the boundaries within which one could operate. Despite his own secular status, Morison's embassy was to highlight many of the issues that propelled the personnel of English diplomatic missions into an increasingly secular composition. Once the Book of Common Prayer had finally removed England's quasi-Catholic façade, Protestant bishops were potentially problematic. So too were humanist ambassadors with theological training such as Morison, who in many respects resembled Bell's 'professional' diplomats.

THE SCHOLAR-DIPLOMAT

A diplomat needed to possess several skills in order to operate effectively. Linguistic proficiency was one such prerequisite. Latin, the international language of diplomacy, was essential, as English was virtually unknown on the continent. Even in the late sixteenth century, English was not mentioned in a list of languages essential for the continental diplomat. Italian, French, Spanish and German were also increasingly important in English diplomatic negotiations. A lack of such key languages could seriously impede an ambassador's success. Morison mostly conducted

---

[20] G. M. Bell, 'Tudor–Stuart Diplomatic History and the Henrician Experience', in C. Carlton et al. (eds.), *State, Sovereigns and Society in Early Modern England* (Gloucester, 1998), 25–45; *idem*, 'Elizabethan Diplomacy', 267–89; L. MacMahon, 'The Ambassadors of Henry VIII: The Personnel of English Diplomacy', Ph.D. thesis (Kent, 2000), 74–9, 113–15. Mattingly previously made the same point for European diplomacy in *Renaissance Diplomacy*, ch. 21.

negotiations with Charles in Italian, a language with which the emperor was more comfortable than Latin.[21] Meanwhile his fluency in Latin, Greek and German ensured that he could interact effectively with the other diplomats and agents at Charles's multi-lingual court.

Delivery and eloquence were also prized.[22] Morison's oratorical skills were finely tuned in 1550: the imperial ambassador in England, Scheyfve, who elsewhere was quite critical of the 'great heretic' Morison, described him as a 'learned and lettered man'.[23] Roger Ascham was struck by Morison's mastery of the linguistic arts:

> His conversations are sprinkled with the salt of humanity, and are so remarkable for the marks of his prudence. And if some debate crops up, his arguments are so pointed and have such force and strength, to which he adds an extensive knowledge of affairs and a strong memory, that I seem not to be torn away from my studies, but rather not to have lived in them until now.[24]

Morison's long career in several areas of government service was in itself a qualification. In 1550, he appeared to combine the ideal qualities of a successful diplomat: considerable knowledge and political experience, and the linguistic ability and oratorical finesse to use them effectively.

Literary considerations played a large part in the compilation of Morison's early reports. 'Merry Morison' employed witticisms and stylistic form to add personal interest to his professional duties. He referred to the pope as 'his holowness' or '*our* hollow father' and to the 'Popistants' (Catholics). As he explained: 'I made them a peece of my*n* exercise, and thought it my game, to lose som*e* labo*u*r in wryting them.' After a rebuke from an exasperated secretary Cecil, Morison explained that he was merely writing in his accustomed manner: 'they be morosiores . . . that can not allow me more mirthe than I at any tymes hetherto have used'.[25] His reports also frequently adopt biblical imagery and references, a further indication that he continued to write in a similar style to the distinctive one he had employed in his 1530s tracts. Such stylistic considerations detracted from the accessibility of

[21] Ottaviano Maggis' *De legato* (1596) listed Latin, Greek, Italian, French, Spanish, German and Turkish (Burke, *Languages and Communities*, 115). *CSPFE*, 611 gives the best description of the language used in audiences. For Charles's attitudes see J. Russell, *Diplomats at Work: Three Renaissance Studies* (Stroud, 1992), 8.

[22] Ibid., p. xv; Thynne, *Perfect Ambasador*, fo. 21^{r-v}.

[23] *CSPS 1550–52*, 187, 169.   [24] *Ascham Letters*, 136.

[25] SP68/5, fos. 110^r–11^r, 68/6, fo. 112^r, 68/7, fo. 84^r [*CSPFE*, 268, 308, 363]; BL Additional 40629, fo. 15^r; *CSPFE*, 358. Morosiores—hard to please/pernickety people.

Morison's reports, as did his concern to report as much intelligence as possible.[26]

Morison used Greek both to showcase his learning and for more practical purposes. Ambassadors' letters were frequently intercepted and the official cipher was cumbersome. After an early reprimand for over-ciphering, the cautious Morison wrote sections of his reports in Greek, or with passages in English transliterated into Greek characters. This protected the politically sensitive contents of the letters without recourse to time-consuming codes. Greek was not a widely known language, and foreign agents would have been hard pressed to translate the Greek/English sections of text. Meanwhile, the English principal secretaries William Cecil, Thomas Smith and John Cheke, all distinguished Grecians, would have understood the letters with ease.[27]

Just as Morison continued to exercise his pen, he ardently pursued the study of Greek and Latin whenever possible. Ascham paid testament to his master's academic dedication in his letters back to his former Cambridge colleagues, claiming that a man on embassy with Morison 'might have learnt as much Greek and Latin and perhaps more than at St John's [College]'. The Strasbourg humanist and pedagogue Johannes Sturm was warned to write carefully to Morison, for Ascham had never met anyone who judged scholarly discourse 'with more seriousness'. Ascham also noted that Morison, 'whenever he is free from his public duties, takes long, daily excursions into the Greek language'; at the start of the embassy this was five days a week. Although it appears that Morison's Greek was a bit rusty, Ascham acknowledged his superior ability in a letter to John Cheke, predicting that it would not be long until 'he catches up to you Olympians, which he will, even if you are on guard'. He claimed to have 'talked over all the best Greek authors' and seriously studied 'whole Herodotus, three orations of Isocrates and seventeen orations of Demosthenes' with Morison in just six months.[28] John Hales and William Darrell, who were also resident in Morison's ambassadorial household at this point, probably joined them. Although the texts studied after the early months of the embassy are more difficult

---

[26] SP10/13/39, 10/15/1 [*CSPDE*, 538, 711]; *CSPFE*, 272, 443; BL Cotton Galba BXI, fo. 58ᵛ.

[27] SP68/6, fos. 28ʳ–9ʳ, 213ʳ–14ʳ, 68/10, fos. 24ʳ, 37ᵛ, 87ʳ–8ʳ, 68/11, fo. 53ʳ⁻ᵛ, 68/12, fos. 26ʳ, 169ʳ [*CSPFE*, 287, 331, 536, 541, 569, 620, 652, 700].

[28] BL Additional 35841, fos. 6ᵛ, 7ᵛ, 15ᵛ; *Ascham Letters*, 206, 142, 136. Ryan, *Roger Ascham*, 135 adds five tragedies to the list. The 'Olympians' Ascham referred to were Cheke and Thomas Wilson, England's most accomplished Grecians.

to determine, Homer's Odyssey and Xenophon's works were certainly among them as Aeschines' may have been.[29]

Morison's educational pursuits did not stop there. He taught his household Italian, perhaps motivated by a desire to provide them with extra diplomatic skills. By Morison's own confession this was achieved using the choice material of Bernardino Ochino's *Prediche* and unspecified texts of Machiavelli, which he defensively claimed to have chosen only 'for the tongue' when criticized.[30] Yet Morison clearly had strong sympathies with the sentiments expressed by these authors. He had cited Machiavelli favourably in three of his 1530s tracts. Ochino was a friend living in Morison's London house at this time. To Charles, however, the apostate Ochino was 'one of the greatest heretics of our time', whose sermons were unsuitable reading material in any language.[31] Even private didactic activities could create diplomatic tensions.

THE RESIDENT AMBASSADOR

Early Duties and Altercations

On 9 November Morison's appointment was formally acknowledged. In the handover audience, Morison and Hoby tentatively put out feelers to determine how Charles felt about France's recent aggression towards England. They did not manage to persuade Charles to take England's side, as he felt he had not been sufficiently informed of recent Anglo-French relations.[32] After Hoby's departure Morison began the meetings with Charles's chief minister, Antoine Perrenot sieur de Granvelle, and other of Charles's courtiers that were customary for the minor suits associated with resident diplomacy. Christopher Mont, the English agent in Germany, also joined Morison at court, to brief him on occurrences elsewhere in the Empire and to attend the Diet of Augsburg. One of Morison's early tasks was to acquire the licences necessary to

[29] *CSPFE*, 569; *Ascham Letters*, 137; M. Toxites, *Commentarius Michael Toxites . . . in orationem . . . Ciceronis pro C. Plancio* (Strasbourg, 1551), Aiii[v].

[30] *Ascham Letters*, 142; BL Additional 35841, fos. 7[v], 15[v]; *Whole Works*, I.ii.266; SP68/10, fos. 12[r]–13[r] [*CSPFE*, 530]. In 1554 Ascham recommended Machiavelli to Petre, but warned that 'to many good men he seems to disparage impudently the religion of the Lord Jesus Christ and to mock impiously' (*Ascham Letters*, 253).

[31] *Cal. For. Elizabeth 1561–2*, 454; *CSPS 1550–52*, 349; *CSPFE*, 436.

[32] *CSPFE*, 256; BL Additional 5756, fo. 239[r]; *CSPS 1550–2*, 187, 189–91.

purchase specific military supplies. In this area, Morison was hampered by his lack of military experience. Hoby, as Master of the Ordnance, had been an ideal candidate for such tasks. Once Morison took over, the Council's instructions included definitions of various artillery and munitions to ensure that Morison did not make any mistakes.[33] The Council were vague in their requests and not officially at war. Charles, whose military position was unclear, was therefore not very obliging.

On 3 March 1551, Morison attended his first audience with the emperor since Hoby's departure. This audience was to have lasting implications for Morison's diplomatic career, and belied his apparent suitability for the post. It also went some way towards establishing the boundaries within which representatives from an explicitly reformed England could operate when at a stalwartly Catholic court. Morison first thanked Charles for his recent good advice to Edward VI and made several minor suits. He requested a licence to purchase military supplies and complained about a Jacobin monk who was preaching slanderous rumours that the English had turned Jewish and were awaiting the new messiah. The focus then shifted to two extremely contentious issues, resulting in a heated debate between Morison and the emperor. The one singled out by Charles as of most importance was Morison's suit that English ambassadors serving at Charles's courts be granted permission to worship according to their native practices. The other question was whether Charles's cousin Mary might continue to hear mass in her household in England.[34] These two issues not only concerned the legitimacy of the moves made to forward religion during Edward's reign, but also raised issues of diplomatic reciprocity and tested the limits of ambassadorial rights of reply.

Charles and Mary claimed that Van Der Delft, the late imperial ambassador, had been promised that Mary could worship unmolested as in the latter years of Henry VIII's reign. Charles further asserted that Paget and the Lord Treasurer had personally guaranteed him the safety of Mary's masses. The Privy Council argued that Henry VIII's grant had not been permanent, and denied giving any assurances to Charles or Mary in Edward's reign.[35] Meanwhile, Edward personally insisted on Mary's obedience. Mary's refusal to conform publicly to Edward's religious practices had long been a source of tension. It became a

---

[33] *Whole Works*, I.ii.140; SP68/6, fos. 65ʳ–7ʳ [*CSPFE*, 294].

[34] *CSPS 1550–52*, 238–41.

[35] SP68/6, fos. 65ʳ–7ʳ, 139ʳ–40ʳ [*CSPFE*, 294, 317]; *CSPS 1550–52*, 312.

more pressing issue after she publicly celebrated the (now outlawed) mass at Whitsun in 1549; such deliberate agitation made any further tolerance untenable.[36] Yet Mary and Charles insisted that she enjoy the same treatment as she had in the latter years of Henry's reign. They questioned the legitimacy of moves made during Edward's minority and the legality of their application to Mary, arguing that any alterations to church services and doctrine had occurred as a result of the interests of Edward's evil councillors, as Edward himself was too young to introduce any significant changes. Mary's approach did not recognize Edward's or his Council's power to legislate on religion before he reached his legal majority and thus disclaimed her culpability for any overt disobedience. Rather, she presented herself as the champion of her father's wishes.[37]

Mary's defiance could no longer be tolerated. It set a dangerous precedent of granting 'license to violate a lawe' that might be taken to extremes by others. First and foremost, Mary was Edward's subject and bound to behave as such. Morison was charged with relaying the Privy Council's stance to the emperor, but felt that he was being asked to treat an insoluble issue. As he explained retrospectively, the Privy Council wanted 'to gratefie the Emperor wher he and they might', but were sorry that the emperor 'should seeke at his and their handes a thing wherein the kinge was forced to saye him naye'.[38]

On the issue of ambassadors' communion the Privy Council resorted to effectively empty rhetoric, asserting that they 'differ[ed] not in any substance of religion from our said good brother but only in the forme of certen ceremonyes and usages, having the same Christ and saviour, the same bookes and scripture ... which the rest of Christendome have'.[39] The rather tired assertions that England differed from the Empire merely in terms of ceremonial were considerably weakened by the doctrine contained in the Book of Common Prayer, which demarcated the English form of worship as undeniably doctrinally distinct from that of the Roman Catholic Church. Charles was forced to recognize a heretical king, but could reconcile himself to Edward's unorthodoxy by presenting Edward as an impressionable minor at the mercy of his heretical councillors. To Charles, the English service was also an innovation, and he would not go so far as to permit it to be used

[36] *CSPS 1550–52*, 248; D. M. Loades, *The Reign of Mary Tudor* (London, 1979), 13.

[37] H. Ellis, *Original Letters Illustrative of the English Reformation* (London, 1846), ii. 154, 176–82; *CSPS 1550–52*, 213.

[38] Ibid., 294; SP68/6, fos. 65ᵛ–7ʳ [*CSPFE*, 294]; *Discourse*, fo. 130ᵛ.

[39] SP68/6, fo. 140ʳ⁻ᵛ [*CSPFE*, 317].

anywhere in his domains, for this would be: 'to grawnt a thynge that is new, never used, never heard of before and such a thing as is not good'. Charles deemed the English requests an inequality, and one which was also personally offensive. Thus he was adamant that he would not grant Morison 'or anyone else, whoever he might be' freedom of conscience within his or her own quarters or anywhere else 'within our dominions'.[40]

The Privy Council, conversely, viewed both forms of religious worship as native customs. English ambassadors' right to hear English communion was a privilege reciprocating that of the Imperial ambassador to use his country's rites in England.[41] Moreover, their form of service was not novel, but a restoration of ancient worship. Thus to the English, requesting permission to use the Book of Common Prayer in private was merely a courtesy; to refuse such a request was a diplomatic slight and belittled England's international prestige. If Charles could permit Jews freedom of conscience, why not English ambassadors? To accept such an insult unchallenged would be to acknowledge English inferiority.[42]

Morison had a personal stake in the outcome of the debate. His position compelled him to observe Catholic custom, a practice he found abhorrent and one that greatly offended his conscience. The emperor's perception of Morison may have been aggravated by Morison's evident disgust that he was 'forced to be of th'old sorte to please this courte'. Morison's concern that England be a truly godly nation, so prevalent in his treatises and tracts, also permeated his political opinions. He requested that he be allowed to return home if the Privy Council were to tolerate Charles's massing ambassador, whom he feared would 'bi foule and hatefull Idolatrie . . . provoke godes wroth upon the realme'.[43] Morison was expressly forbidden the English service in his lodgings and was in fact commanded by the Privy Council to attend mass as before.[44]

Morison's first audience with Charles compelled him to defend the integrity of the English church against the emperor's incessant attacks on its doctrines, decisions and personnel. He remained true to his humanist training, and disputed the matter forcefully. In defending his king, country and confession, Morison had little option but to demonstrate

[40] SP68/7, fos. 145ʳ–7ᵛ [*CSPFE*, 436]; *CSPS 1550–52*, 239.
[41] Ibid., 311; *APC 1550–52*, 330; SP68/6, fos. 138ʳ–51ʳ [*CSPFE*, 317].
[42] *CSPFE*, 338; BL Cotton Galba, BXII, fos. 221ʳ–4ʳ.
[43] Ibid.; SP68/7, fo. 179ʳ [*CSPFE*, 392].   [44] BL Cotton Galba BXII, fos. 221ʳ–3ʳ.

a deep lack of respect for Charles's person and office. Moreover, his theological knowledge and commitment to reform propelled him into dangerous territory. Not only did he presume to debate religion with Charles, he also outspokenly claimed that the English faith was the only true faith and cited scripture extensively in proof. Charles's assertion that by heretic he meant 'you and others who believe the same as you' led the discussion into personal territory, and did nothing to abate Morison's proselytizing. Only Charles's order that Morison depart ended the debate. Morison had far overstepped the bounds of diplomatic protocol, by refusing to desist when commanded. Charles had provoked him, but in his eagerness to defend the English church Morison had disrespected Charles's political position. Such impudence could not be seen to emanate from official channels, especially when Charles believed that diplomatic privilege had been deliberately exploited.[45] The Privy Council thus repudiated their involvement in the incident and besought Charles 'to impute it to the ernestnes and affection of the man'. Morison was reprimanded by the Privy Council for his manner; in future, he was pointedly told to 'modestlie and conveniently defend the honnor of us and our Realme'.[46]

Morison consistently denied any personal transgression: 'the faute was in the matier' and was not his. He merely bore the brunt of the ageing emperor's wrath at his impotence in the matter: 'the Emperore was so angrie, the Ambassador doinge his message earnestly unto him that he writ a verie hot lettre to the Kinge against him'.[47] Charles himself later acknowledged his overreaction. He had been reminded of the earlier evangelistic efforts of Thomas Wyatt, who had reputedly tried to persuade the emperor to revoke the Donation of Constantine and 'with dishonourable words was urging many to study certain pamphlets of his, full of heresies'.[48] Such dissatisfaction with the manner of English ambassadors in the first few months after their appointment was not uncommon—in 1538 Francis I had rebuked Francis Bryan for his use of 'intemperate and high flown language [which] at first required correction'.[49] More unusual, however, was the scale of displeasure Charles exhibited towards Morison and the political consequences of the dispute.

[45] *CSPS 1550–52*, 239–41, 253–5.
[46] SP68/6, fos. 138ᵛ–9ʳ [*CSPFE*, 317]; BL Cotton Galba BXII, fo. 222ᵛ.
[47] SP68/7, fo. 179ʳ [*CSPFE*, 392]; *Discourse*, fos. 130ʳ–1ʳ; *CSPS 1550–52*, 238–41.
[48] Ibid., 311–12; *LP* XII ii 1031. At least one of these pamphlets was written by Morison.
[49] *CSPS 1538–42*, 7.

The aftermath of this incident was further exacerbated by Morison's reputation at Charles's court and fears that he might try to indoctrinate others. Shortly after the audience, Charles had been informed that Morison 'habitually indulges in heated arguments on the subject among his friends, and whenever anyone is present who will listen to him, as if his mission here were to convert others to his religion by predication'.[50] Morison had been betrayed by a member of his own household. John Bernardine, an occasional agent Morison had inherited from the established diplomatic network, had been playing on the preconceptions of the emperor's men. Morison later discovered that Bernadine had 'uttered al my talkes and doings to al men, with as many disadvantages to me as he cold' and had reported him as having daily preached to his household. When Morison uncovered the extent of Bernardine's slander, he wrote, 'I do not marvel, why themperor wrote I was an apostle'. These rumours were probably inflamed by Morison's use of Ochino's sermons in his household. However, there is no other evidence that Morison was conducting religious services or preaching to his retinue. Rather the evidence points to Morison's household attending Protestant services in the churches of Augsburg where Charles's court was based at this time.[51]

DISGRACE

Morison's first audience had seriously strained Anglo-Imperial relations. Scheyfve had simultaneously requested Mary's freedom to worship; Edward noted in his journal that Charles threatened war because 'I wold not suffer his cosin the princesse to use hir masse'. Initially, the Privy Council decided to temporize, sending Cranmer, Ridley and Ponet to persuade Edward that 'to give licence to sin was sin; to suffer and wink at it for a time might be borne'.[52] Meanwhile, Scheyfve was informed that he and Mary would both be allowed to continue to attend private masses for the time being. The Privy Council announced Morison's revocation, appointing Dr Nicholas Wotton special ambassador to

[50] *CSPS 1550–52*, 240.

[51] SP68/6, fo. 199ʳ, 68/10, fos. 52–3ʳ [*CSPFE*, 328, 550]. BL Additional 35841, fos. 3ʳ–10ʳ, 18ʳ–25ᵛ.

[52] *CSPS 1550–2*, 235–6; W. K. Jordan (ed.), *The Chronicle and Political Papers of Edward VI* (Northampton, 1966), 56. Morison ascribed their actions to concern for Edward's safety, *Discourse*, fo. 131ᵛ.

resolve the matter.[53] Yet Wotton did not leave with sufficient papers to replace Morison as resident and the Council were assured that Charles would be happy for Morison to remain, provided he refrained from debating religion and other sensitive topics. By appointing a special embassy, the Council acquired precious time—three months elapsed between Morison's audience in March and Wotton's arrival at the imperial court in June. These delaying tactics paid off as the worsening situation in Germany and Italy ensured that Charles became powerless to follow through on any threats of military reprisals. Meanwhile, England pursued closer ties with France. The size of the English legations aroused Charles's suspicions and although Henry II had not openly declared war, he was practising against the emperor. Charles could not risk an Anglo-French military alliance.[54]

Rumours spread as far as Rome that Morison, shamed, had left the imperial court. Although disgraced, Morison was not formally revoked and so remained in Germany. He continued suing for gunpowder while the regent tried to smooth over the diplomatic rift.[55] His lack of success with even standard requests convinced the Privy Council that the emperor held Morison in disfavour. Wotton's attempts at a resolution were no more successful than Morison's, but the matter could now be debated more dispassionately. Nothing had essentially changed; Wotton was instructed to pursue the same objectives as Morison had. He was also to refute rumours that England was pursuing an Anglo-French League, cemented by a marriage between Edward and a French princess, assuring Charles that it was the French who wished for the marriage and that the Council had yet to make a decision.[56]

Morison exploited Wotton's presence, gaining valuable experience of the world outside the court and indulging his own curiosity. He spent eight or nine days touring the nearby villages and cities, including Nuremberg, where the simple piety of the city impressed him.[57] Upon his return, the need for a conciliatory approach was apparent: the

---

[53] *CSPS 1550–52*, 255–6; BL Cotton Galba BXII, fos. 222^r–5^r.

[54] SP68/6, fos. 128^r–31^r, 68/7, fos. 177^r–9^r [*CSPFE*, 314, 392]; M. J. Rodriguez-Salgado, *The Changing Face of Empire* (Cambridge, 1988), 41–5; W. A. Wright (ed.), *The English Works of Roger Ascham* (Cambridge, 1984), 136–7.

[55] J. Strype, *Ecclesiastical Memorials* (Oxford, 1822), II. i. 468; *CSPFE*, 370i, 316. Strype was wrong to believe that Morison returned to England. J. Strype, *Life of John Cheke* (Oxford, 1821), 70. Morison's London residence was used for a eucharistic debate by senior politicians in his absence.

[56] BL Cotton Galba BXII, fos. 222^r–5^v, BXI, fo. 47^r.

[57] SP68/8, fos. 25^r–7^r [*CSPFE*, 405].

Council had instructed Wotton to converse with Charles in front of Morison in French, which Morison could 'barely understand', but a concession to the disgruntled emperor, who felt most at ease conversing with foreigners in that language. The Council restored Morison as resident ambassador, despite domestic speculation over the matter, recalling Wotton in September with Charles's consent. This indicated that whilst the councillors clearly felt Morison had overstepped the mark, the overall position he had stated concurred with their own.[58]

Charles still refused to grant Thomas Chamberlain, the English ambassador to the Netherlands, freedom of conscience. Edward stepped up pressure on Mary and denied Charles's ambassadors the right to hear mass. Nevertheless, no further affront to the emperor's honour could be risked. The Netherlands was England's trading partner and the Empire the main source of England's mercenaries and military supplies. Furthermore, officials in the Netherlands had seized Protestant literature that an Englishman had mistakenly imported in May, highlighting that religious developments in England were not isolated from the continent.[59] Thus the Councillors who had, Charles claimed, promised Mary her mass, were questioned before the Privy Council and the imperial ambassadors. Consequently, the Council sacrificed William Paget, giving credence to Charles's insistence that he had received personal reassurances from Paget in 1549, despite Paget's consistent denials. He was placed under house arrest in October, making the arrest of Mary's chaplains slightly easier to swallow. To Morison, this did not represent a convenient political coup, but the fitting punishment for Paget's duplicity.[60]

FINANCES

Morison was to suffer severe financial difficulties in the latter months of 1551 that interfered with the efficacy of his mission. He believed that he should be the principal ambassador at Charles's court, but felt that his place had been usurped by the pope's nuncio. Yet he could not

[58] SP68/6, fo. 213ᵛ [*CSPFE*, 331]; Russell, *Diplomats*, 8; BL Additional 35841, fo. 18ᵛ: 'Mr Wotton cometh home and we tarry; and me thinketh I know what your Papists at home have talked of that matter.'

[59] SP68/7, fo. 20ʳ; SP68/8, fos. 113ʳ–17ᵛ, 145ʳ–7ᵛ [*CSPFE*, 343, 429, 436].

[60] SP68/9, fos. 22ʳ–3ʳ [*CSPFE*, 461]; *Discourse*, fo. 130ᵛ.

afford to provide himself with basic essentials when it became apparent that the court was to move. Consequently Morison had to walk a fine line between liquidity and reducing his household expenses to the point where his penury would become glaringly apparent and bring dishonour on the king.[61]

Morison had arranged his personal finances before his embassy began, appointing his brother-in-law Stephen Hales as his proctor. Richard Warner, Morison's deputy as collector of the petty custom, was renewed in the post and Morison made a will in case he died overseas.[62] Morison's official diets amounted to six hundred pounds per half-year, not far short of the £1,216. 11*s*. 8*d*. a year given to Elizabeth's resident ambassadors.[63] Residence in Germany proved prohibitively expensive, as the emperor's military campaigns and the sheer number of people at court pushed up prices. Meanwhile official diets arrived late. Only in February 1552 did Morison receive payments for his previous year's diets. Similarly, reimbursements for Morison's posting charges were not made until well into his embassy.[64] Recent debasements and revaluations of the English coinage meant that even the exchange rate exacerbated the problem as Morison's diets did not stretch as far as they were supposed to. This led Morison to ask for his diets in French crowns, a more stable currency. Despite Morison's frequent pleas for his diets and the actions of his solicitor, Richard Goodrich, no further money was forthcoming, culminating in his reminder to the Privy Council that 'while the skies here afford frost, cold and snow, they as yet afford no manna'.[65] Morison frequently asked Hales to sell his lands, but Hales was either unable or unwilling, leading Morison to comment in 1552 that Hales merely kept him in coals and small billets.[66]

From almost the very onset of his embassy, Morison was 'wonderfully cumbred for lack of mony' as essential expenditure outstripped his allowance.[67] On the outward journey, Ascham noted the expense and

[61] SP68/6, fos. 28ʳ–9ʳ, 74ᵛ; 68/9, fo. 43ʳ⁻ᵛ; 68/10, fo. 4ᵛ [*CSPFE*, 287, 296, 467, 544].

[62] *Cal. Pat. Edward VI*, iv.345; PROB11/39, fos. 214ʳ–17ʳ.

[63] G. M. Bell, 'Elizabethan Diplomatic Compensation: Its Nature and Variety', *JBS*, 20 (1981), 3.

[64] SP68/5, fo. 7ʳ, 68/6, fo. 199ʳ [*CSPFE*, 271, 328]; *CSPDE*, 714; *APC 1550–2*, 421; *APC 1552–4*, 75; BL Cotton Galba BXI, fo. 67ʳ; E315/260, fo. 64ʳ; E315/261, fos. 103ʳ–4ʳ; E315/262, fo. 70ʳ. By May, his diets were overdue again [*APC 1552–1554*, 41, 46].

[65] SP68/7, fo. 114ʳ⁻ᵛ, 68/8, fos. 170ʳ–3ʳ, 187ᵛ [*CSPFE*, 376, 443, 450]; SP10/13/39 [*CSPDE*, 538].

[66] SP68/8, fos. 107ʳ–8ʳ, 175ʳ–6ʳ, 68/9, fos. 41ʳ–2ʳ [*CSPFE*, 427, 445, 544, 550].

[67] SP68/5, fo. 70ʳ, 68/6, fos. 14ʳ⁻ᵛ, 28ʳ–9ʳ, 74ᵛ [*CSPFE*, 271, 279, 287, 296].

attempts at economy: 'Careful supervision and moderate caution are being applied, but expenses overflow, converging from unexpected sources along multiple lines of expense, so that they can readily absorb and exhaust even an immense supply of resources.'[68] Morison struggled even to afford the basic standards of entertainment that were expected of him. As he complained to the Council, 'the reast of my callinge, be able to lashe and laye on, and I pore sowle, muste ofte lose my nyghtes reast, for that I can not day it, as others do'. Yet certain basics were required if Morison were not to allow his king's poverty to show: 'the minstrels wol playe spite of my teethe, and then I muste paye them, or do as no body else dothe'. By late 1552, Morison had even been forced to sell some of the king's plate.[69] This had important consequences, as Morison's impoverished state and inability to entertain to the same standards as his fellow ambassadors reflected badly on his king's honour, suggesting the king too was in pecuniary straits.

Morison's predicament was not unusual. His predecessor with the emperor, Hoby, had also experienced problems receiving timely payment. That Morison was not overspending is confirmed by Wotton's inability to live on his appointed diets.[70] Bell has asserted that by Elizabeth's reign, at least, ambassadors' complaints of poverty were dramatically exaggerated. Although the later financial rewards of diplomatic service undoubtedly compensated for any financial hardship during the embassy, Bell underestimates the potential extent of that hardship during the embassy itself.[71] Moreover, England's low credit rating in the early 1550s created even greater problems for the payment of ambassadors, as ambassadors who served on a long-term basis often received their diets through foreign bankers.

Morison sought alternative sources of income to help support the rising costs of his ambassadorial entourage, requesting a licence to export leather hides, an idea he probably got from the service he had rendered Edmund Harvel years earlier. He petitioned Nicholas Throckmorton, William Cecil, Warwick and Northampton in writing after earlier hints were ignored, while Stephen Hales petitioned Cecil in person and even drafted a bill. The Council felt any such arrangement would be injurious

[68] *Whole Works*, I.ii.108; *Ascham Letters*, 136.
[69] SP68/6, fo. 146[r]; BL Cotton Galba BXI, fos. 57[r], 95[r].
[70] Bell, 'Henrician Experience', 36; Brigden, 'Richard Scudamore', 123, 134, 138, 143–4; SP68/8, fo. 105[r] [*CSPFE*, 426].
[71] Bell, 'Diplomatic Compensation'.

to Edward's prerogative, so no licence materialized.[72] At court, Morison was forced to borrow increasing amounts, becoming reliant upon the bankers and imperial agents, the Schorers and the Fuggers. Even this was not enough: he asked Cecil to arrange a loan in England for him and borrowed money from his own agent John Hales. These problems climaxed in the latter part of 1551 as the imperial court moved to Innsbruck, where victuals were twice as expensive. Morison could not afford to take his pregnant wife with him, yet equally could not bear the financial strain of maintaining two households.[73]

RECONCILIATION

Meanwhile, the issues at stake in March remained unresolved. Charles frequently referred to Mary's need for masses in the months following Wotton's departure. After Somerset's fall, Morison reassured the emperor that Mary would receive fair treatment from the Council. He was not kept abreast of developments in England, throwing doubt on his assertions, hindering his ability to operate and depriving him of information to trade with other ambassadors. As relations remained cool with the emperor, Edward was invited to join a League of Protestant Princes, which he declined.[74]

The intense disfavour with which Morison and England were still viewed by the emperor culminated in Morison's expulsion from his lodgings at the imperial court in Innsbruck in favour of the bishop of Cartagena in December 1551. This was a huge insult to Edward, and Morison was forced to take accommodation at Halle more than four miles from the court.[75] It also had serious implications for the effectiveness with which Morison could do his job. One of a resident ambassador's main tasks was to gather news about foreign politics. Ambassadors and courtiers traded information during casual visits, over dinner and in the gardens. Morison found the Venetian ambassador

---

[72] SP68/6, fos. 4ʳ, 112ᵛ, 199ʳ⁻ᵛ, 213ᵛ, 68/7, fo. 7ʳ, 68/8, fos. 153ʳ–4ʳ [*CSPFE*, 274, 308, 328, 331, 338, 437]; BL Additional 35831, fo. 171ʳ; *LP* XII ii 1127.

[73] *APC 1550–52*, 421; *CSPDE*, 688; SP68/9, fo. 43ʳ⁻ᵛ, 68/10, fo. 43ᵛ [*CSPFE*, 467, 544]; BL Cotton Galba BXI, fos. 65ʳ, 67ʳ.

[74] Ibid., fo. 116ʳ [*CSPFE*, 490]; *CSPS 1550–2*, 396–7; SP68/9, fos. 119ʳ⁻ᵛ, 151ʳ [*CSPFE*, 492, 509].

[75] Ryan, *Roger Ascham*, 152; SP68/9, fos. 3ʳ, 12ʳ [*CSPFE*, 525, 530]; *CSPS 1550–2*, 533–4.

in particular a valuable source of intelligence. By denying Morison the opportunity to interact socially at court, the imperialists severed him from his sources of information. Instead he had to rely solely on friends and agents to gather information from a distance. Bernadine, who had formerly poisoned the minds of the imperialists against Morison, strove to ensure that he at best received inaccurate reports.[76]

In March 1552 notification that Morison's lodging at court was available once more signalled a return to amicable relations. The divisions within Germany flared up again and by April the imperials were pursuing their old alliance with England, hoping to procure an ally against the French king.[77] Consequently, Granvelle flattered Morison, referring to him as his countryman, and offered the assistance of the burgomasters of Innsbruck to find the most honest matrons to wait on Bridget Morison. The Spanish at court now held him in high estimation and even shook him by the hand. Nonetheless, through the summer of 1552, as Charles's court converted itself into a military camp, Morison became suspicious that he was being kept in the dark about developments and that Charles was slighting him in favour of other ambassadors. Granvelle had to reassure him that the Portuguese ambassador at the camp was present for a practical reason. Furthermore, the continued isolation of Morison and his fellow ambassadors from Charles's military court created an atmosphere of speculation and conjecture. Charles wished to preserve the secrecy of his plans, meaning concrete information was hard to come by, even when agents were permitted within the military cocoon, as Ascham and Weston found.[78]

In such a situation, the framework within which England's envoys were expected to act impeded their performance. The Royal Supremacy and consequent anti-papalism created an atmosphere in which even discreetly canvassing papists for information unavailable by other means was shunned lest it be misconstrued. Morison had avoided the problem in the past, drawing on his fellow ambassadors for information.[79] In the summer of 1552 Morison was seriously ill. This combined with Charles's withdrawal into his military camp and the court's geographical

[76] Wright, *Ascham*, 127, 147; SP68/7, fo. 84^r, 68/8, fos. 76^r–8^r, 68/9, fo. 12^r [*CSPFE*, 363, 415, 530, 659]; BL Cotton Galba BXI, fos. 94^v–5^r.

[77] SP68/10, fo. 37^v [*CSPFE*, 541].

[78] BL Cotton Galba BXI, fos. 94^r–5^r, 103^r,123^r.

[79] SP68/10, fos. 52^r–3^r [*CSPFE*, 550]; *Nuntiaturberichte*, 124. Previously Ascham had received information from his friend Lazarus von Schwendi, a servant of the duke of Alba (BL Cotton Galba BXI, fo. 136^r).

fragmentation to create further difficulties. In September the only reliable source of information in Charles's military camp was the papal nuncio. Ascham officially requested permission to converse with the pope's men, explaining that he had been uncertain as to the official reaction to any contact. The fate of Germaine Gardiner in 1544 warned of the danger inherent in such communication.[80] Ascham's uncertainty had been denying him, and thus the Privy Council, a valuable source of information on which every other ambassador was free to draw. Ascham reassured the Privy Council that it would be possible to talk to the nuncio's men without anyone thinking that England was considering converting.[81]

THE ANTI-TURKISH LEAGUE

In September, Morison was instructed to treat with the emperor on the matter of a league against the Turks, to ensure amicable relations continued between England and the Empire and clarify that recent tensions had been transitory. This league was to be kept secret from the French king.[82] Charles hoped to use the league to embroil England in his latest dispute with France. Many of the German princes had broken with him during the course of the year. Not least of these was Albert, margrave of Brandenburg, whose book declaring why he had broken with Charles was as damaging to Charles as his military opposition.[83] Morison was consequently shown increased marks of favour, to the extent that an order was issued that his former slanderer Bernadine be apprehended if he returned to the court. Morison advocated that the Council bide their time: they would soon be able to attain 'what ye well can ask' as Charles's brother Ferdinand, Duke Maurice of Saxony, the Palsgrave Otto Heinrich and the duke of Württemberg were believed to have formed a great league against the emperor.[84] By mid-October Charles was starting to believe that Morison's repeated protestations of English neutrality were genuine, but he desperately continued to hope that England would send military aid. Edward's

[80] G. Redworth, *In Defence of the Church Catholic: The Life of Stephen Gardiner* (Oxford, 1990), 205.

[81] BL Lansdowne 3, fo. 3ʳ. The Privy Council's solution was to order Mont to join Morison (*APC 1552–1554*, 43).

[82] BL Additional 4106, fo. 8ʳ; *CSPFE*, 564.   [83] Wright, *Ascham*, 144–5.

[84] *CSPFE*, 566; BL Cotton Galba BXI, fos. 129ʳ–30ʳ.

league against the Turks was at best a platform for a general truce, and definitely not a covert offer of an anti-French alliance.[85] The time was seemingly propitious for English involvement as Charles held the other potential intermediary, the papacy, in mutual suspicion. Yet Morison's endeavours had yielded only limited harvests and by November Charles ceased his efforts towards a 'closed amity', a bilateral Anglo-Imperial pact. Morison feared that this heralded that an acceptable offer had been received directly from the French. Combined with inside information from the count of Nassau's man, Dr Bruns, that Charles desired a favourable peace, this provoked Morison to recommend the immediate dispatch of a special envoy to proffer English mediation. Letters from Rome had indicated that the pope wanted to broker the peace, but had not yet sent an envoy, as he hoped that Charles would regain Metz, have his pride somewhat sated and be more inclined towards a settlement.[86]

The Privy Council had reached a similar conclusion based on Morison's reports. Andrew Dudley was dispatched in late December as special representative to mediate a peace. Dudley's mission raised Charles's hopes of English military aid; this meant Morison received markedly more honourable treatment than at any other time during his embassy. Sumptuous rooms were prepared for Dudley and Morison, while Monsieur du Rie, a chief gentleman of Charles's Chamber, accompanied by eight horsemen escorted them to their first official audience on 25 January 1553. No firm commitment from Charles was received, merely the promise of a further audience with Dudley once Charles had reached Brussels. However, Charles's ill-health postponed the conference until 11 February. Charles treated Dudley favourably, casting his arm about Dudley's neck, but he adamantly refused to discuss the details of the peace until he knew his enemy's mind and was offered reasonable restitution. Thus Dudley departed on 12 February, after Charles reiterated his position: the attacks on his territories were unprovoked and without warning, the opening suit for a truce would therefore need to come from the initial aggressor.[87] As France appeared intent on hostilities, the impasse was obvious. It is tempting to concur with Thomas Hoby's assessment

---

[85] BL Additional 4106, fo. 8ʳ; *CSPS 1550–52*, 573–4.

[86] BL Cotton Galba BXI, fos. 110ʳ–17ʳ.

[87] SP68/10, fos. 161ʳ–6ᵛ, 68/11, fos. 26ʳ–8ʳ, 49ʳ–51ʳ [*CSPFE*, 599, 611, 619]; *CSPS 1553*, 8–9.

that Dudley 'returned again into England without having done anie thing in the matter', but the scene was set for further negotiation and England's claim staked for the prestigious position of mediator ahead of its rival, the papacy. Morison was to keep the possibility of English mediation alive for when the parties were more amenable to reconciliation.[88]

Charles's failing health was an important factor in diplomacy during 1553. Negotiations lengthened as ambassadors waited months for an audience, leading to some suspicions that Charles was merely using his ill-health to buy time for secret negotiations. Furthermore, it suggested the advisability of ensuring the extension of the 'Turkish league' to include the German princes. The worsening military and financial plight of the emperor presented the possibility of an alliance with 'other princes of power according with us in the matter of Relligion', which Morison was also to pursue.[89] This 'Protestant league' remained linked to the 'Turkish league'. It was not yet considered an independent objective.

Throughout March there seemed little hope of achieving a lasting peace between Charles and Henry II. Morison was convinced that the German princes wished to continue the wars, while Henry offered unrealistic terms for peace. Yet the financial predicament of both powers and the French preparedness to offer terms, however unreasonable, indicated that a temporary armistice might be within reach. Morison was determined to ensure that England received recognition for any peace agreement and was troubled by rumours of papal mediators.[90]

In an audience on 24 March, Regent Queen Mary of Hungary, the major figure in the Netherlands in the 1550s, gave Morison what had become the conventional formula: Charles desired the weal of Christendom and should France offer peace, he would be ready to negotiate. Granvelle and the queen jokingly denied rumours that a monk was at court to broker the peace when Morison broached the matter.[91] Yet the dispatch of papal intermediaries stirred the Privy Council into action. Charles had indicated his desire for independent arbitration, so on 2 April, papers were issued appointing

[88] E. Powell (ed.), 'The Travels and Life of Sir Thomas Hoby, Knight, of Bisham Abbey', *Camden Miscellany X*, CS 3rd ser. 4 (London, 1910), 91; SP68/11, fo. 47ʳ [*CSPFE*, 618]; BL Cotton Galba BXI, fo. 147ʳ.

[89] Ibid., fo. 148ᵛ; BL Cotton Galba BXII, fos. 236ʳ–8ʳ.

[90] SP68/11, fos. 92ʳ–3ʳ, 98ʳ–9ʳ, 105ʳ–6ʳ [*CSPFE*, 631, 633, 636].

[91] *Cecil Papers*, 431.

Morison, Thomas Thirlby and Philip Hoby special commissioners to treat of the peace. Other ambassadors at court thought Morison would depart at this juncture and viewed his continued residence with suspicion.[92]

By April, Morison was certain that the regent's support was essential to their quest for peace. He was personally attracted to the notion of a defensive league of Protestants. Overtures under Henry VIII had tentatively established amicable relations with the German princes. Having Morison, a committed evangelical, as ambassador in the Empire further encouraged links with Protestant princes. Morison had certainly used his position to cultivate links with them. In 1552–3 he dined and hunted with Otto Heinrich and John Frederick and received presents from the count of Nassau. In August 1552 he hosted the baron of Holnersteng, the count of Schwartzenburg and the duke of Saxony. By the end of the year Morison was even planning to escort John Frederick's eldest son back to England. Morison encouraged this amity at an official level too. He advocated that Edward write a congratulatory letter to Duke John Frederick of Saxony when Charles freed him from captivity, fully aware that the duke was intending to write to Edward. When John Frederick did so, he congratulated Edward on his expulsion of the antichrist.[93] Morison therefore advocated that the league with the German princes be pursued for its own sake if necessary.

THE NORTH EUROPEAN LEAGUE

On 24 April 1553 Morison, Hoby and Thirlby received explicit instructions to include the princes of Germany in the league with the 'House of Burgundy' and determine Charles's plans for the succession of the Low Countries. It was on this that the direction of English diplomacy hinged. The commissioners promptly responded that despite the popularity of Charles's nephew Maximillian, his son Prince Philip was the more likely heir to the Low Countries. This cemented the alliance with

---

[92] SP68/12, fos. 11ʳ–17ʳ [*CSPFE*, 646]; BL Additional 5498, fo. 63ʳ; *Nuntiaturberichte*, 222.

[93] *Var. Coll.*, 337; *Cecil Papers*, 436; BL Additional 4106, fo. 8ʳ; BL Cotton Galba BXI, fos. 109ʳ, 119ʳ, 123ʳ; *CSPFE*, 548, 583, 586, 639; SP68/10, fos. 52ʳ–3ʳ, 68/11, fos. 57ʳ–8ʳ [*CSPFE*, 550, 558]; *Whole Works*, I.ii.76.

Charles over his brother Ferdinand, yet did not rule out the possibility of concurrently pursuing an independent league with the princes. In May, Charles's deteriorating health led the commissioners to conclude that they should confer with Ferdinand and the German princes, even if Charles or his successor were to be, with Edward, a central member of the league.[94]

Thomas Chamberlain was instructed to join the commissioners and advise them before returning to London. As resident ambassador to the regent, his particular area of expertise was the affairs of the Low Countries, on which he submitted a report to the Council.[95] Indeed Chamberlain's knowledge of affairs proved so instructive that the commissioners initially refused to revoke him. The separate matter of France and the Empire reaching a truce was incorporated into England's scheme. In the event of a peace, the French king would be permitted inclusion in the league, under such conditions as were thought convenient by its members.[96] This left the commissioners free to pursue both issues simultaneously without any apparent conflict of interests.

The commissioners further suggested that Mont be consulted over the likely alliances of the German princes, who, divided by personal and confessional motives, had been fighting regularly over the previous two years.[97] Political and religious grievances had alienated certain of the princes from Charles, leading them to ally with France. Albert, margrave of Brandenburg, deserted the Imperial cause after financial slights in 1552; Duke Maurice of Saxony revolted due to the continued imprisonment of his kinsman, and the two eventually came into conflict with each other as their alliances changed. Indeed the coalitions of the princes shifted as circumstances changed, occasioning the comment from Morison that 'the Princes of Germany are about many Leagues; what will ensue it will hardly be guessed till it be done'.[98] Charles was making conciliatory moves towards the renegade princes and attempting to heal the rifts between them, as their united support was vital for the defence of the Low Countries against France. Consultation with Mont was also advocated because Morison and the commissioners feared the consequences if Charles disapproved

---

94 SP68/12, fos. 53^r–5^r, 63^r–6^r, 87^r–8^r [*CSPFE*, 663, 668, 673].
95 BL Cotton Galba BXII, fos. 238^r–43^r.
96 SP68/12, fos. 51^r, 59^r–60^r, 69^r–70^r, 73^r [*CSPFE*, 662, 665, 669, 671].
97 Ibid., fos. 53^r–5^r [*CSPFE*, 663].
98 *Cecil Papers*, 427, 436; Wright, *Ascham*, 149–63.

of their proposed league. This also led to their suggestion that they gauge the emperor's reaction by presenting the idea as their own; this was approved as a 'very wyse discourse'. If Charles objected, they might then officially pursue another league without disgracing Edward. Meanwhile, the commissioners were to ferret out 'by all wayes and meanes' as much information as possible regarding the intentions of Ferdinand.[99]

Little progress was made in the remaining months of Morison's embassy. Henry II continued to name unreasonable terms, which the emperor would not consider. Charles's continuing ill-health disrupted the mediations: he wished to consult the commissioners personally, while the commissioners were hesitant to entrust the matter to any of Charles's delegates. Only one major success was achieved by the mission: the English contingent were met more favourably than their papal rivals. They were heard before the papal embassy and it soon became common currency at court that Dandino, the papal legate, was more concerned with his own affairs than with the mediation of the peace, despite Granvelle's apparent interest.[100]

The commissioners continued to pursue a league with Charles, though no concrete alliances were formed. The original concept of a 'Turkish league' evolved, expanding to encompass other northern European powers. In April it seemed that Poland, Sweden and Denmark also desired inclusion in any league.[101] The commissioners therefore set about the not insubstantial task of determining with which German princes it would be best to ally, and noted that most of the princes would prefer a general league including Charles to a purely Protestant league. Security was paramount, which left the commissioners in doubt as to how to proceed.[102] Charles alleviated the problem by summoning the German princes to Frankfurt to resolve their various disputes, a scheme which evolved into the notion of a grander German league. The commissioners recommended that Edward send a man to the Frankfurt conference, aware of the potential opportunity to gather more information and opinions regarding the league should Charles's measures prove ineffective. Meanwhile the Privy Council sent an envoy to confer with Ferdinand, informing the commissioners of the terms of

[99] SP68/12, fos. 60ʳ, 88ʳ [*CSPFE*, 665, 673]; BL Harley 523, fo. 37ʳ⁻ᵛ; BL Cotton Galba BXII, fo. 240ʳ.

[100] Ibid., fos. 33ʳ–4ᵛ, 39ᵛ–40ʳ; SP68/12, fos. 110ʳ–11ʳ, 135ʳ⁻ᵛ, 153ʳ [*CSPFE*, 680, 688, 696]; Powell, 'Sir Thomas Hoby', 94.

[101] SP68/11, fo. 59ᵛ [*CSPFE*, 665].   [102] BL Cotton Galba BXII, fos. 238ʳ, 85ᵛ–93ʳ.

his mission.[103] However, the league never progressed further than this initial investigatory phase.

The commissioners were officially ignorant of their king's ill-health. As late as 1 July the Council claimed that rumours of Edward's illness were the work of 'a lewd sort of man'. However, in private letters to Hoby, Cecil revealed the dire situation. Ten days later, Richard Shelley conveyed letters from Queen Jane to Charles's court.[104] Morison and his companions avoided associating themselves with the transitory regime of Queen Jane in public, as Shelley fortuitously arrived during an audience with the emperor. They could thus inform Charles of Edward's demise whilst simultaneously pleading ignorance of domestic politics, giving themselves personally and England diplomatically some leeway. They even tried to tempt Charles away from supporting Mary, by proffering a revival of the old league or the formation of an altogether new one. The commissioners' report of 15 July indicates that they knew much more than they were later willing to reveal, if only through unofficial sources. Morison and his colleagues deftly asserted that they would 'conforme *our*selves most willingly' to Mary's wishes, once her triumph was assured. As late as 20 July, the commissioners requested further news from the Council, to amplify what little they had heard unofficially. In the same letter they warned of the danger from the French inherent in 'our sovereign' Lady Jane's monarchy, and relayed the unlikely news that Charles wanted Mary to marry within the realm, thus helping to allay one of the fears that had initially united the Council against her.[105]

ACADEMIC AND EVANGELICAL CONTACTS

During their service overseas, English ambassadors engaged in a range of cultural activities. Morison was no exception. His ambassadorial household maintained a high level of scholarly activity even beyond his efforts to ensure that they studied Italian, Latin and Greek. Morison undoubtedly came into contact with many of the scholars attendant upon Charles, including such figures as the anatomist Vesalius, who was

---

[103] BL Cotton Galba BXII, fo. 243^r; SP68/12, fos. 91^r–2^v, 119^r–21^r, 127^{r-v} [*CSPFE*, 686, 674, 684]; BL Harley 523, fos. 38^r–9^v.

[104] Ibid., fos. 40^v–5^r.

[105] Powell, 'Sir Thomas Hoby', 95; BL Harley 523, fos. 1^r–5^r, 11^v–12^v, 13^v, 46^v; Haynes, *State Papers*, 152–3.

serving as the court physician, and the philologist Vitus Polandus.[106] The most active scholar in Morison's entourage was Ascham, whose letters provide evidence that the most recent scholarship was being read in Morison's ambassadorial household, including Paolo Giovo's *Historia sui temporis*, a new edition of Polybius and the works of Pietro Bembo and Peter Ramus. Ascham struck up a literary acquaintance with Christopher Froben about Erasmus' increasingly rare *Antibarbarorum . . . liber unus*, which Ascham wished to see reprinted. With his servant Vaughan, Ascham engaged in a number of scholarly enterprises, including reading Petrus Nannius' translation and commentary upon Philo Judaeus, and transcribing Johann Sturm's edition of Aristotle's rhetoric. Meanwhile, Ascham's correspondence with Sturm on the education of nobility was published in Conrad Heresbach's *De laudibus Graecarum literarum oratio*.[107] It is highly unlikely that Ascham could have undertaken such work without the consent and involvement of Morison. The consequence of this, and of Morison's own activity, was to cast both the ambassador and his king as scholars of some note.

During the embassy, Morison was in contact with and promoted a wide range of continental scholars outside the Imperial court, from different areas of the Empire and who were theologically eclectic. One such scholar was Hieronymus Wolf, an evangelical pedagogue who translated classical Greek texts into Latin and acted as the curator of the Fuggers' library.[108] Ascham's interest in some of the Fuggers' rarer volumes had led to a friendship with Wolf, whom he introduced to Morison. In 1551 Wolf dined with the ambassador in his lodgings on at least two occasions. Soon, Morison was sufficiently impressed by Wolf's abilities to act as a patron. He 'conducted himself with great friendship and condescension' towards Wolf, whom he tried to place as tutor to the young duke of Suffolk with a 'considerable royalty'.[109] The duchess of Suffolk's house at Grimsthorpe oversaw the education of about a dozen children, including Catherine Parr's daughter and Morison's

[106] SP68/6, fo. 182ᵛ [*CSPFE*, 323]; BL Cotton Galba BXI, fo. 121ᵛ; *CSPFE 1558–9*, 329.
[107] Ryan, *Roger Ascham*, 130–49; BL Lansdowne 98, fo. 66ʳ.
[108] H.-G. Beck (ed.), *Der Vater der deutschen Byzantistik: das Leben des Hieronymus Wolf von ihm selbst erzählt* (Munich, 1984), *passim*; H.-J. Künast, 'Entwicklunglinien des Augsburger Buchdrucks von 1468 bis zum Augsburger Religionsfrieden von 1555', in J. Brüning and F. Niewöhner (eds.), *Augsburg in der frühen Neuzeit* (Berlin, 1995), 232–3; Ryan, *Roger Ascham*, 130.
[109] Beck, *Hieronymus Wolf*, 73. The deaths of the Brandon dukes of Suffolk put paid to Morison's plans.

son Charles. Wolf also provided information on the latest imprints by scholars such as Martinus Borrhaeus and Johannes Camerarius and gave at least one book to Ascham—a copy of Aeschines.[110]

In April 1551, Morison informed the Privy Council of his admiration for Pier Paulo Vergerio, the former bishop of Capo d'Istria, for leaving his Italian bishopric and for his diligent and prolific production of tracts.[111] These tracts were Protestant pamphlets designed to induce conversions in Italy and many were dedicated to Edward VI. By October 1551 Morison was corresponding with Vergerio and had secured the Italian a safe haven in England. Ministering to the Italian Protestant community in London was mooted, and Vergerio was encouraged by his friends there. Expecting to be revoked in the summer of 1552, Morison suggested Vergerio travel to England with him.[112] Although Morison's revocation failed to materialize he maintained contact with Vergerio. They even planned to travel to Zurich together to visit Heinrich Bullinger. By March 1552 the friendship between the two men was close enough that Vergerio dedicated a short Italian pamphlet to the ambassador. His dedication praised Morison's virtues and principles as bringing honour to his country and portrayed England as a truly godly realm. A response to a tract by Frederick Nausea on the Council of Trent, Vergerio's pamphlet was highly critical of the Council, denying that it was a true, free council that represented the universal church; consequently it would not mend the divisions in Christendom or produce adequate reform within the Roman church. His dedication described the struggle between the papal antichrist and his followers and those who based their church on scripture and defended pure doctrine. Edward VI and his ambassador Morison were in the latter category, whereas the Council of Trent, the most recent sessions of which had been debating doctrine, was not. Vergerio's dedication therefore located Morison within the group of evangelicals who were highly critical of Trent not long after Thomas Cranmer had mooted the possibility of a Protestant General Council.[113]

---

[110] SP68/10, fos. 52ʳ–3ʳ [*CSPFE*, 550]; *CSPDE*, 332; BL Additional 35841, fos. 14ᵛ, 16ᵛ; *Ascham Letters*, 193.

[111] SP68/6, fo. 166ʳ⁻ᵛ [*CSPFE*, 319].

[112] R. A. Pierce, *Pier Paulo Vergerio the Propagandist* (Rome, 2003), ch. 3; *Bullingers Korrespondenz*, 163, 185, 187.

[113] F. Hubert, *Vergerios Publizistische Thätigkeit* (Göttingen, 1893), 284; MacCulloch, *Thomas Cranmer*, 394, 448, 478–9. P. P. Vergerio, *Risposta del vescovo vergerio/al libro del nausea vescovo di Vienna scritto in laude del concilio tridentino vicosoprano* (Poschavio, 1552), a2ʳ–3ᵛ.

Morison's other academic contacts while ambassador also had a distinctly evangelical flavour. He corresponded with Johannes Sleidan and Johannes Sturm and passed on greetings to other Strasbourg humanists including Simon Grynaeus, Erythraeus, Michael Toxites and Conrad Hubert. When Morison and Ascham visited Strasbourg in September 1552 they were welcomed at the Protestant historian Sleidan's house. Sleidan later mentioned Morison's stay at Speyer in his *History of the Reformation*.[114] Morison was also in contact with Bullinger during the embassy, although none of this correspondence has survived. He was probably introduced to Bullinger by his brother-in-law Christopher Hales, who corresponded with Bullinger in the 1540s. Bullinger would have known Morison by 1549, at least by reputation, as ab Ulmis forwarded him a transcript of the Oxford eucharistic debates Morison had helped to adjudicate.[115]

At least one Strasbourg humanist dedicated a tract to Morison. Michael Schutz, alias Toxites, had written a commentary on Cicero's oration for C. Plancio. His dedication to Morison provides further evidence, not only for a blossoming friendship with Morison, but also for Morison's relationship with Johannes Sturm. In 1547 Toxites had composed a poem for Edward VI which outlined his duty to purify religion. Toxites' 1551 dedication praised Morison's learning in languages and literature as well as commending religion in England and Morison's knowledge of divine letters and theology. The effect, then, was to cast Morison as a worthy evangelical from a godly country.[116] Toxites also dedicated another commentary on a work by Cicero to Morison's secretary Ascham, praising his scholarly abilities and appealing to him to correct the text.[117] He had initially sent Ascham a manuscript copy for which he was thanked with cash. Toxites then asked Ascham to convey another work to Princess Elizabeth. In the following year, Morison met Toxites during his stay in Strasbourg and

---

[114] J. Rott and R. Faerber, 'Un anglais à Strasbourg au milieu du XVIᵉ siècle: John Hales, Roger Ascham et Jean Sturm', *Études anglaises*, 21 (1968), 390–4; *Ascham Letters*, 187, 299; J. Sleidan, *Histoire de la Reformation* (Le Havre, 1767), iii. 225.

[115] *Bullingers Korrespondenz*, 193; T. Kirby, 'Vermilius absconditus? The Iconography of Peter Martyr Vermigli', in E. Campi, F. A. James and P. Opitz (eds.), *Peter Martyr Vermigli: Humanism, Republicanism, Reformation* (Geneva, 2002), 296–8; *OL*, clxxxviii.

[116] Toxites, *Ciceronis pro C. Plancio*, Aiiʳ–viᵛ.

[117] M. Toxites, *Commentarius Michael Toxites . . . in orationem . . . Ciceronis pro P. Quintio* (Strasbourg, 1551), Aiiʳ–viʳ, Oviiᵛ–viiiᵛ. This was actually a revision of Johannes Sturm's commentary of 1538.

it is probable that the poet visited Morison's ambassadorial house-hold.[118]

Morison's attempts to have similar personal contact with Johannes Sturm were unsuccessful. Ascham had initiated correspondence with Sturm six months before going on embassy and remained in regular correspondence with him throughout, aided by Morison's frequent posts to Strasbourg. When Morison had discovered their correspondence he had apparently asked Ascham 'to greet you cordially in his name', as he 'wanted very much to become closer friends with you, whom for years he has loved very much'. Morison had translated a tract by Sturm in 1538, and claimed to have admired his writings for years. He may have briefly met Sturm, or heard reports about him, during Sturm's embassy to England in 1546. Although the pressures of diplomatic service prevented Morison from writing to Sturm as often as he would have liked, their correspondence made a significant impression on Morison: he reported Sturm's virtues back to England.[119]

Morison also tapped into the continental academic community through his agent John Hales. Hales had followed Morison to Augsburg in 1550. After several months in Morison's household Hales relocated to Strasbourg to continue his studies. He reported to Morison on a regular basis, although few of these letters survive. Through Hales, Morison corresponded with John Aurifaber, the duke of Saxony's preacher, and possibly also Erasmus Sarcerius, the superintendent of Leipzig. Hales also kept Morison informed of Sturm's progress on an edition of Aristotle.[120]

ASSESSMENT

In 1550, Morison appeared to be the model humanist ambassador. His long education at Oxford, Cambridge and Padua and continued contact with the academic community ensured that Morison possessed Thynne's first quality. He received many encomia attesting to his eloquence and wit. He may not have been from aristocratic stock, yet by the time of his death, Morison had acquired sufficient status and property that

[118] Ryan, *Roger Ascham*, 143.
[119] *Ascham Letters*, 187, 206. For details of Sturm's embassy see McEntegart, *League of Schmalkalden*, 212–13.
[120] *CSPFE*, 625.i.

his wife could take £600 to her next marriage.[121] His loyalty and obedience to his prince had been amply demonstrated by the prominent role he had played on many government commissions. Morison also had a long apprenticeship before he became a resident ambassador, so had had plenty of opportunities to hone his skills in a diplomatic context. However, Morison's apparent qualifications combined with the political climate to complicate his mission. His concern for literary aestheticism decreased the utility of his reports, while his abilities as an orator and debater could create, rather than solve problems. Morison's loyalty to the crown and the religious system established by it over the previous twenty years created an antagonism that greatly compromised his diplomatic endeavours. His secretary ardently defended his master's efforts, leaving little doubt of Morison's earnestness: 'my lord is surely a witty man and serves his God, his King and his Countrey nobly here. If ye hear any thing to the countrary, be bold . . . of my word to reprove it.'[122]

Morison's embassy experienced in microcosm the paradox of the English diplomatic corps: service to one's God demanded higher scruples than service to one's king permitted. Yet for many evangelicals such as Morison, failure to serve one's God adequately abroad could lead to the loss of providential favour for one's country. The religious sensibilities of committed Protestants with a personal stake or involvement in the religious side of the Reformation were increasingly becoming incompatible with a diplomatic career representing a Protestant England abroad. Confessional lines had hardened. England's diplomats at Catholic courts could no longer be religious controversialists of any description if their missions were to succeed.

Morison's embassy has further significance. His activities on embassy will have affected continental perceptions of England and its king, as contemporaries judged Edward, at least in part, by the merits of his diplomatic representatives. In Morison, they were presented with a scholarly, humanistic political culture. Concurrently, if continental reformers looked to English diplomacy to determine the state of England's religious health, they will have seen in Morison a committed reformer who actively defended his country's faith. Morison's patronage of and extensive contacts with continental evangelicals will have bolstered the

[121] *Manuscripts of . . . the Duke of Rutland . . . Preserved at Belvoir Castle* (London, 1888), i. 71.
[122] BL Additional 35841, fo. 13[r].

perception of England as a safe haven for Protestants under a magnanimous Josiah. As well as cultivating links with the Protestant princes, Morison also pursued contacts with reformers and scholars within the Strasbourg–St Gall axis, particularly in Strasbourg and Zurich. Such contacts and Morison's conduct while on embassy may ultimately have helped the Marian exiles by helping to create the impression that Edward and his subjects really were the co-religionists of the Protestant princes and territories of the Empire, even if their exact confessional identity did not fully cohere. All of which might prove influential once Morison's Josiah was succeeded by his Jezebel.

7

The Exile

BACKGROUND

The End of the Embassy

Morison's public career and his vision of a Northern European League effectively ended with Mary I's accession. A confirmed and prominent Protestant, Morison had too actively pursued the cessation of Mary's private masses to entertain any hope of accommodation with the new regime. Thirlby was appointed resident ambassador. Morison and Hoby were recalled and were soon in trouble. To Mary's disbelief, they claimed that Charles wished her to marry an Englishman, and had recommended that England's civil and religious policies remain unchanged. The Queen asked the Imperial ambassador in England, Scheyfve, to check their information. Charles substantiated some of their account, but concluded that Morison and Hoby had elaborated for their own purposes. From this point, their reports were not accepted without verification.[1]

Morison had his final audience with Charles V on 21 August. He insisted on receiving the standard letters of credence given to departing ambassadors, much to the Imperialists' disgust. Granvelle warned Renard that Morison, the 'great preacher and persuader, one of the most obstinate heretics in the world' might 'spoil all in England' on his return, ascribing to Morison an exaggerated degree of political influence. He urged that Morison be detained at Calais, at least until after Northumberland's execution, and that he be watched closely afterwards.[2] Despite the intense distrust with which Morison was viewed, no moves were made against him. Instead he was grudgingly issued *pro forma* letters of recommendation. Before their departure Morison and Hoby were sumptuously feasted by the queen regent, probably unaware that

---

[1] *CSPDM*, 5, 7; *CSPS 1553*, 133–4, 152, 155, 159–60.   [2] Ibid., 183.

they were suspected. In England, Morison briefly attended Mary's court, proudly displaying two gold chains, gifts from the emperor, each worth one thousand crowns.[3] Although expensive gifts were usually presented to departing ambassadors, Morison was so disliked that these collars seem incongruous. They may simply represent a covert attempt to buy his support, or to hide the Imperialists' dislike.

Morison continued to be intensely distrusted and soon retired from public life. In September the Imperial ambassadors were reassured to hear that Mary knew his seditious and heretical character. Meanwhile, they blamed Morison and Hoby for a perceived increase in resistance to the restoration of Catholicism in England. It is possible that they were galvanizing their friends at court to withstand Mary's pressure to return to Roman Catholicism, as the queen issued the summons for the first Parliament of her reign, which was to repeal her brother's religious legislation and pave the way for England's return to Roman jurisdiction. In October the Imperialists further demolished Morison's political credibility—he was accused of deliberately antagonizing Anglo-Imperial relations by reporting 'lying and invented stories' from Germany.[4] However, Morison appears to have sidestepped any real threat, as on 29 October he was granted a general pardon.[5] He was not returned to the first Parliament of Mary's reign, which opened three weeks earlier. It seems likely that, like Thomas Cawarden, Morison was prevented from sitting as an MP by the crown.[6]

In January 1554 Thomas Wyatt raised troops against the queen. The aims of the rebels were varied: some were motivated by religion, others rose under the pretext of protecting the realm from the Spanish. Some of the key conspirators sought to replace Mary with Elizabeth, whom they hoped to marry to Edward Courtenay. Morison was evidently among them. Courtenay later confessed that Morison and Hoby had persuaded him to commit such 'ingratitude' against Mary.[7] Despite Morison's apparent support for Wyatt's rising, he played no active part in it. Many of his associates were implicated in the rebellion including Nicholas Throckmorton, Peter Carew and Nicholas Arnold. The rebellion itself was intended to be much more widespread than Wyatt's rising in Kent suggests. Its true leadership never materialized, in part due to Stephen

[3] Powell, 'Thomas Hoby', 95–6.   [4] *CSPS 1553*, 240, 242, 257, 324, 307.
[5] HALS, 8752; *Cal. Pat. P&M*, i.454.
[6] W. B. Robison, 'The National and Local Significance of Wyatt's Rebellion in Surrey', *HJ*, 30 (1987), 769–90.
[7] *CSPS 1554*, 267.

Gardiner's desire to protect his protégé Courtenay, so the exact role of more senior politicians such as Morison remains obscure.[8] Wyatt's failure removed the evangelicals' hope that they might be able to secure some form of religious compromise and led many, including Morison, increasingly to view exile on the continent as their only option, rather than remain in an increasingly Catholic England. Although Morison's involvement was not discovered until June, he was repeatedly suspected of conspiring against the queen in the immediate wake of the rebellion. In April, the Imperial ambassador was convinced that Morison and Hoby were plotting a new insurrection and that their planned exile was thought to be a tactical retreat in case it went awry. Hoby was sufficiently suspected that he was dropped from the list of dignitaries who would escort Philip of Spain to England.[9] Yet on the cusp of his exile, the government took no action against Morison; he even stood surety for family friend William Warner, who replaced Morison as collector of the petty custom in February 1554.[10]

EXILE

Preparations

Morison was a more significant figure in the history of the exile than has been appreciated. As a former member of Henry VIII's and Edward VI's Privy Chambers, a former ambassador and titular Privy Councillor, Morison was one of the most senior politicians to seek religious refuge on the continent during Mary's reign. Yet his activities in exile have failed to attract much scholarly attention. A scarcity of evidence explains this gap: Morison's death in exile means that there are none of the anecdotes or extant correspondence with fellow émigrés during Elizabeth's reign, which in the case of figures such as Thomas Wilson provide otherwise elusive information. No list of Morison's household members exists, so there is no possibility of reconstructing his entourage in the same detail as Bartlett has for Francis Russell.[11] Instead, the course of his exile and the scope of his

---

[8] D. Loades, *Two Tudor Conspiracies* (Cambridge, 1965), 15–24; E. J. Harbison, *Rival Ambassadors at the Court of Queen Mary* (Princeton, 1940), 111–12.

[9] *CSPS 1554*, 157, 214; Powell, 'Thomas Hoby', 97.

[10] C82/980/2; Alsop, 'Nicholas Brigham', 54.

[11] K. R. Bartlett, 'The Household of Francis Russell, Second Earl of Bedford in Venice, 1555', *Medieval Prosopography*, 2 (1985), 66–85.

social circle have to be patched together from frustratingly fragmentary evidence.

Many of the Marian exiles found it difficult to justify their flight from England. Initially Morison was in an awkward position as he could not yet claim to be facing persecution: Gardiner had not yet introduced the heresy bill into Parliament.[12] Tertullian and other church fathers with whom Morison was familiar condemned those who went into exile, especially if they held benefices. As Morison was a layman who was not abandoning a vulnerable flock, there were fewer objections to the legitimacy of his flight. Morison could find ideological justifications for fleeing the realm in scriptural passages such as Matthew 10C, 'when they persecute in this city fly into another', as well as in the works of Athanasius, Gregory of Nazianzen and Clement of Alexandria.[13] Thomas Cranmer and other leading English clerics openly advocated their co-religionists leave the realm, fearful that persecution would not be far off.[14] Many continental theologians, some of whom had fled to England in Edward's reign, also recommended exile. Vermigli's letter *On flight in persecution* condoned flight for spiritual reasons, but condemned anyone whose motives were material.[15] There was little sympathy for concealing one's true faith and equivocating with a Catholic regime: even those who had advocated this policy under Henry VIII now labelled it unacceptable, as the true church had flourished under Edward VI.[16] Indeed Thomas Cottisford, John Olde, Henry Bullinger, Guillaume Farel, Pierre Viret, Calvin, Vergerio and Vermigli all produced tracts against 'Nicodemites' (evangelicals who conformed with the Marian regime), whom they believed were numerous. Martin Bucer's arguments in favour of Nicodemism were rare.[17] This made flight the safest option for committed evangelicals. Morison clearly viewed Mary's accession as a divine punishment, yet he still felt justified fleeing persecution, perhaps believing that his own efforts to purify the realm excused him from divine retribution.[18]

[12] J. Loach, *Parliament and the Crown in the Reign of Mary Tudor* (Oxford, 1986), 98.

[13] For Morison's familiarity with these authors see ch. 8.

[14] J. Wright, 'Marian Exiles and the Legitimacy of Flight from Persecution', *JEH*, 52 (2001), 232.

[15] P. M. Vermigli, *Life Letters and Sermons*, ed. J. P. Donnelly (Kirksville, MO, 1999), 67–95.

[16] A. Pettegree, *Marian Protestantism: Six Studies* (Aldershot, 1996), 90–1, ch. 4; M. A. Overell, 'Vergerio's Anti-Nicodemite Propaganda and England', *JEH*, 51 (2000), 296–313.

[17] Wright, 'Marian Exiles', 233.   [18] *Discourse*, fos. 130ʳ–4ʳ.

Morison's departure from England was designed to be fully in accord with the law. He and three other men (probably John Cheke, Anthony Cooke and Thomas Wrothe) together petitioned for permission to leave the realm in March. The Imperial ambassador wrongly suspected that Morison valued money over his faith, believing that he would remain in England rather than lose his property. Renard's remark suggests that either he knew of plans to seize the exiles' property or he believed Morison would be forced to flee the country illegally.[19]

Before Morison left England, he did his best to raise funds to support his travels, selling all of his remaining properties in London except Whitefriars. He also arranged his financial affairs so that it was difficult for the Marian government to seize his lands. On 2 April Morison signed over most of his remaining properties to his brothers-in-law Stephen Hales and Thomas Hussey, who were to hold them in trust for Morison and his wife for life.[20] Both men had previously acted as agents for Morison; they were able administrators who would forward him the money necessary to fund his exile. Morison probably hoped that this would protect his property if the Marian government did decide to move against the exiles, as the exact position of enfeoffed lands was still a matter of legal debate.[21] Other exiles also enlisted family members to look after their property: Anthony Cooke had Nicholas Bacon safeguard his interests.[22] They were right to take such protective measures. On 31 October 1555 a bill was introduced into Parliament that would have punished those who refused to return from exile with the loss of profits from their lands, although there is evidence to suggest the bill might have been amended so that it only applied to those who had gone abroad without licence. The bill was defeated in December. In 1556, the crown sought legal opinions on whether it could seize the goods of those exiles who had departed without permission and refused to return, but these opinions were not favourable.[23] Some exiles, such as James Haddon and Katherine Brandon, had their property confiscated regardless, but properly enfeoffed property would have been much more difficult to sequester.[24] The government was not the only threat to the exiles' lands: some of Morison's neighbours forcibly took some

[19] *CSPS 1554*, 157, 214.
[20] *Cal. Dom. Elizabeth I 1601–3, Addenda 1547–56*, 445–6; *Cal. Pat. P&M*, i.356, 368.
[21] Baker, *History of the Laws*, 672–86.
[22] R. Tittler, *Nicholas Bacon: The Making of a Tudor Statesman* (London, 1976), 54.
[23] Loach, *Parliament*, 138–43.
[24] E163/13/4; C. S. Knighton, 'James Haddon', *ODNB*, 24.413.

of his lands after his death, perhaps trying to exploit their uncertain status.[25]

The rental income from Morison's properties should have been sufficient to sustain his travels: Cashiobury alone was generating over £100 in rent at this time.[26] It is unclear what money Morison did receive from his lands during his exile. Morison did not have his full portfolio of properties at his disposal as he had been involved in a property deal with Northumberland in the summer of 1553; these lands in Worcestershire were confiscated by the crown.[27] In April 1555 he talked of his hope to be restored to his affairs and in September the Strasbourg council recorded that Morison and Cooke hoped to recover their lands soon; the following month they noted that Morison's means of subsistence was unclear. Yet there is no record of Morison's lands being seized and Morison was able to pay the extra financial securities demanded of him in return for citizenship at Strasbourg and to buy sufficient supplies for the winter.[28] Morison's embassy had given him other resources upon which he could draw. He knew the posting routes and how to move money around, and was friendly with two of the leading German banking families, the Fuggers and Schorers, and prominent foreign dignitaries. Meanwhile back in England were friends such as William Cecil, whose experience in government administration meant that they knew how to send money abroad. Morison was certainly acting as a financial conduit to other exiles. Nicholas Tremayne, a scholar companion to Nicholas Arnold's son, reported that 'the moni is alwais sent to Mr Morysin' and was having problems as he had to collect it in person.[29] Morison's diplomatic experience and contacts meant that he probably acted in this capacity for other exiles.

Initial Stay in Strasbourg

Morison's first year in exile was peripatetic. On 4 April, Cheke, and presumably Cooke, Wrothe and Morison, reached Calais.[30] Later that month, Morison's friend Johannes Sleidan noted that the Marian exiles

---

[25] STAC 7/4/18.   [26] HALS 6576.   [27] *Cal. Pat. Elizabeth*, i.79.

[28] C. Garrett, *The Marian Exiles: A Study in the Origins of Elizabethan Puritanism* (Cambridge, 1938), 230, 366, 368; *OL*, lxxiv, lxxv. Morison is not mentioned in E387.

[29] SP11/6, fo. 90ᵛ [*CSPDM*, 268]. Morison had probably known Arnold since he entered Cromwell's service in 1537 and certainly since Arnold was appointed one of the Gentlemen Pensioners in 1539.

[30] *Nugae Antiquae*, i. 49–53.

began to arrive in Germany, singling out for notice Morison, his travel companions Cooke and Cheke, and John Ponet, another of Morison's close contacts.[31] Strasbourg was Morison's first port of call. Here he could draw upon existing friendships with Sturm, Sleidan and the other Strasbourg humanists, as well as links with English merchants like John Abel, with whom he had been in regular contact during the 1550s.[32] Abel had been a resident in Strasbourg since the 1540s and Morison used him as an intermediary with the city council.[33] Strasbourg was on one of the main transit routes south to Italy and had established trade links with England. It was, then, a logical and safe place from which to plan his next move.

During his exile, Morison's itinerary owed much to the contacts he had developed during his embassy and his friendships with several continental reformers who had earlier emigrated to England. Many of these, including Peter Martyr and Bernardino Ochino, also emigrated to Strasbourg in the first instance. Ochino's friendship with and debt to Morison ran sufficiently deep that he dedicated a tract to Morison in 1554. He did so, he claimed, because he knew no one else who would appreciate the book's anti-papal polemic quite so much or grasp the underlying truth of the stories so clearly, and because he 'wanted to be joined with firm ties' to Morison. Ochino paid tribute to Morison's godly zeal and to the generosity Morison had shown to him, protesting that 'Nothing that I do with such things satisfies in any way your extremely generous charity [and] friendship/or discharges me of the countless duties with which I am joined to your lordship'.[34] Ochino's *Apologi* satirized numerous aspects of Roman Catholic doctrine and dogma. By 1559 it had appeared in German, Latin, French and Italian editions.[35] The dedication clearly cast Morison as a former supporter of a religious exile: it may, then, have eased his stay on the continent and encouraged others to show Morison and his compatriots the generosity he had once shown Ochino.

Morison's first stay in Strasbourg was brief. While there, he may have lodged with John Burcher, as did his travelling companion Anthony Cooke.[36] He soon decided to travel to Basel. In April and again in May 1554 Morison, Cooke and Cheke requested the services of two native Baselers to guide them there. They left at some point in June or July.[37]

---

[31] Sleidan, *Histoire*, iii. 272.   [32] SP68/10, fo. 12[r] [*CSPFE*, 209].

[33] Garrett, *Marian Exiles*, 362–3.   [34] Ochino, *Apologen*, Aii[r].

[35] Benrath, *Bernardine Ochino*, 218–19.   [36] *OL*, cccxxvii.

[37] Garrett, *Marian Exiles*, 362–3. On 26 July Vergerio, who was in Strasbourg, reported that he had not seen Morison. Hubert, *Vergerios Publizistische Thätigkeit*, 115.

On their way to Basel, they stayed at Neuburg with Otto Heinrich, the Palsgrave, who had been closely linked to Morison in 1552. This journey provoked further imperial distrust. In May, news of Hoby's intention to meet with Morison in Italy had provoked imperial suspicions that they were again plotting. More seriously, in June Courtenay revealed Morison's and Hoby's part in persuading him to support Wyatt's failed rebellion. By the end of June the scope of the supposed conspiracy had broadened to include Paget, Mason and Lord Cobham, among others. Granvelle believed they were scheming against Mary's marriage to Philip and were plotting against the emperor. Morison was thought to be recruiting Otto Heinrich, while Hoby embroiled the duke of Savoy.[38] If Morison and Hoby were trying to raise support against Mary they do not appear to have been successful. It is more likely that as former ambassadors with personal and professional ties to many of the German princes, they were trying to secure financial aid and refuge for their fellow exiles.

Basel, Zurich, Geneva, Brussels

Morison's next verified port of call was Basel, where his presence was recorded by one of its premier humanists and professor of rhetoric, Celio Secondo Curione. Morison probably knew Curione's works before he went into exile; they were certainly circulating in England, as John Philpot translated his 'Defence for the trew and olde authoritie of Christ his churche', which he dedicated to the duke of Somerset.[39] Curione was also in contact with two of Morison's close friends, Cheke and Ochino. Curione and Morison shared an interest in the fifteenth-century humanist Marc Antonio Sabellico, whose history Curione edited and expanded using Paulo Giovio's history to fill in the period up to 1545. For the period after 1545 he evidently received information from the English exiles, including Morison, on recent events in England, as he included an account of the 1549 rebellions and Lady Jane Grey's short reign.[40] In the mid-Tudor period many Basel intellectuals dedicated tracts to influential men and women within England, demonstrating a wider interest in English affairs and contact between the two centres,

[38] *CSPS 1554*, 231, 267, 269–70, 278–9, 281; *CSPFM*, 323, 625. Renard suggested that they should be watched.
[39] BL Royal 17 CIX.
[40] R. A. Chavasse, 'Humanism in Exile: Celio Secondo Curione's Learned Women Friends and Exempla for Elizabeth I', *Parergon*, 14 (1986), 165–86.

which perhaps explains why so many English exiles were drawn to the city and why a sizeable proportion of them worked in the printing industry while there.[41]

Cheke stayed at the university in rooms provided by the rector, Ulrich Iselin. Morison may have been with him, or may have stayed with Curione, who lodged other English exiles including Elizabeth Sandys and Dorothy, the daughter of Morison's friend Henry Stafford. At this time there were twenty-nine English scholars registered at the university.[42] During their stay in Basel, Cheke left the manuscript of his *De pronuntiatione Graecae* with Curione, who decided to publish it with a dedicatory letter to Anthony Cooke.[43] Morison may also have associated with Sebastian Castellio, who knew many of his fellow exiles and friends. Castellio was at the centre of the propaganda campaign for religious toleration in this period in response to the burning of Michael Servetus in Geneva.[44] Basel was a city already inundated with refugees, mainly from Italy, and the city council had, from 1541, given priority to rich and skilled refugees in the granting of citizenship.[45] Morison's stay there, like his stay in Strasbourg, was temporary.

Exactly where Morison was in the months between September 1554 and February 1555 is difficult to ascertain. He probably moved to Zurich next as his travel companion Anthony Cooke was preparing to visit this city in September 1554 and Morison probably still wanted to meet Bullinger. He also spent some time in Geneva with John Calvin, seemingly in the reformer's house. In April he wrote to Calvin, thanking him for the hospitality shown to him and Cheke and apologizing for taking several months to do so.[46] After Geneva, however, Morison parted ways with Cheke and Cooke, who journeyed on to Padua. He may then have briefly visited Frankfurt where his brother-in-law Christopher Hales and good friend John Hales were based.[47] By 13 February 1555 Morison was in Brussels dining with his old friend John Mason, resident ambassador to the Imperial court. It is unlikely that he stayed long.

[41] Including Laurence Humphrey, John Foxe and John Banks. M. E. Welti, *Der Basler Buchdruck und Britannien* (Basel, 1964), 176–87.

[42] H. R. Guggisberg, *Basel in the Sixteenth Century* (St Louis, MO, 1982), 50; H. G. Wackernagel, *Die Matrikel der Universität Basel* (Basel, 1951), ii. 507; Chavasse, 'Humanism in Exile', 171; E. Bonjour, *Die Universität Basel, von dem Anfängen bis zur Gegenwart 1460–1960* (Basel, 1960), 235.

[43] J. Cheke, *De pronuntiatione Graecae* (Basel, 1555).

[44] H. R. Guggisberg, *Sebastian Castellio, 1515–1563* (Aldershot, 2003), ch. 5.

[45] Guggisberg, *Basel*, 39–45; *OL*, cccxxvii.   [46] Ibid., cccxxvii, lxxiv.

[47] Garrett, *Marian Exiles*, 171–4.

Morison had been in touch with Mason earlier in his exile and was thought to be plotting with Mason and Hoby.[48] The Imperialists thought that Morison would ask for a position serving Charles V, but it seems unlikely that his petition to Granvelle was about this. It is much more probable that he was trying to secure some form of protection for the English exiles, or trying to elicit sensitive information from Mason.

Strasbourg

Morison's movements over the next five months are difficult to trace. He was in Strasbourg in April, when he believed himself in the greatest danger, and again in August. There are no compelling reasons to think he left the city where he was to spend the remaining months of his life. Morison had originally intended to stay a short while before moving on to Zurich, where he had business with the chief magistrate, but decided to postpone his journey until the spring, in part because he had heard that Zurich was inundated with refugees. Morison and Bullinger remained in contact, though, and their friendship was much closer than the survival of only one letter from their correspondence would suggest.[49] Claiming the status of religious refugees, Morison, Cooke and Edwin Sandys petitioned the Strasbourg council for permission to stay. In October, Morison and Cooke requested citizenship. This was granted, despite the fact that Morison's means of subsistence was unclear and the intense Imperial suspicion that he was a political dissident, but Morison did have to pay twice the normal financial guarantee.[50]

In the 1550s, Strasbourg was still recovering from the effects of the Interim, which recognized only Lutheranism and Catholicism as legitimate faiths. Four of the city's seven parishes were Lutheran, and refugee ministers were only permitted to preach if they accepted the Augsburg Confession, despite the growing number of Calvinists entering the city after 1550.[51] Although Vermigli and Bucer had helped Swiss

[48] *CSPFM*, 324; *CSPS 1554–8*, 68–9.   [49] *OL*, lxxiv, xc; Zurich ZB, S85, no. 187.
[50] Garrett, *Marian Exiles*, 366, 368; L. J. Abray, *The People's Reformation: Magistrates, Clergy and Commons in Strasbourg 1500–98* (Ithaca, 1985), 51. Morison and Cooke initially applied for temporary residence, Sandys for the right to reside there permanently. As only immigrants who carried or purchased property over £10 were expected to purchase citizenship Morison was probably carrying cash.
[51] Ibid., 89–120, 126–33.

theology make some inroads, after they left for England the religious texture of Strasbourg had swung back in favour of Lutheranism, which was firmly re-established under the directorship of John Marbach. When Vermigli returned to the city from England, he was asked to sign up to the Wittenberg Concordat. Although Vermigli refused, Sturm persuaded the senate to appoint him to his former post at the school.[52] Morison appears to have been attracted to Vermigli's theology, so the tolerant attitude taken towards non-Lutherans in Strasbourg would have appealed.

Morison's existing links to the academic community in Strasbourg eased his exile considerably. Despite the pressures on the city from the influx of refugees, a house with a garden was put at Morison's disposal.[53] Here he presided over a household engaged in educational endeavours. Among those staying in Morison's house was John Aylmer, Lady Jane Grey's former tutor. Aylmer continued to function as a pedagogue, tutoring Thomas Dannet, whose father was a friend of Aylmer and Cecil.[54] Robert Beale lodged in 'myne uncle morisines house' in Strasbourg under Aylmer's tutelage and, while there, frequently attended the lectures of Peter Martyr and Sturm.[55] More of Morison's household, including Morison himself, were probably linked to Sturm's grammar school and it is possible that Cheke and Morison also lectured there. It seems likely that they attended Vermigli's lectures on Aristotle's *Ethics* in 1555. At the very least, Morison socialized with the Strasbourg humanists he so admired. Indeed, twelve years after Morison's death, Sturm recalled how much his learning and friendship had delighted him. Morison was also spending time in the company of 'Bernardine'—probably Ochino.[56] His household was undoubtedly a centre for other English refugees, including Thomas Wrothe, James Haddon and Humphrey Cornwell. Anthony Cooke and Edwin Sandys may have resided in Morison's house, which is suggested by their earlier travels together and joint petitions for citizenship, while John Hales may also have enjoyed Morison's hospitality during his time in Strasbourg. Two other Englishmen, named by the Strasbourg council as Thomas Fracht and Fredus Torvellus, lodged there in 1556, although it is not clear

[52] Vermigli, *Life, Letters and Sermons*, 122.   [53] Zurich ZB, S85, no. 137.
[54] PROB11/32, fo. 217ʳ; J. Strype, *Historical Collections of the life and acts of . . . John Aylmer* (Oxford, 1821), 7, 23.
[55] BL Additional 48039, fo. 48ᵛ. Beale was the son of Morison's sister Amy and Robert Beale, a London merchant (Hasler, *HoP*, 41–2).
[56] *Whole Works*, I.ii.173; Zurich ZB, S85, no. 137.

if this was thanks to Morison or his wife, who continued to dispense 'charitable almes' after his death.[57]

Many of Morison's English friends and associates resided elsewhere in Strasbourg. John Jewel lodged with Vermigli from spring 1555; the duchess of Suffolk passed through Strasbourg in the same year and John Cheke spent the winter of 1555–6 in Strasbourg among his old friends, including Morison.[58] Among the other English exiles, Morison certainly associated with Peter Carew, and in December 1555, his wife stood as godmother to John Ponet's son alongside Abel, suggesting the three men were close. The Englishmen in Strasbourg were undoubtedly more tightly knit than John Brett was later led to believe when he tried to serve writs against many of the wealthier exiles.[59]

Imperial and Marian suspicions of Morison were fuelled by his associates during the exile. Cooke, Cheke and Wrothe had been involved in Northumberland's attempts to install Lady Jane Grey as queen and Sandys had preached in her favour.[60] Peter Carew was complicit in Wyatt's rebellion; Thomas Becon and Edmund Grindal were heavily involved in the exiles' vernacular propaganda. Thomas Sampson, who informed Bullinger of Morison's death, translated a tract by Rudolph Gualther. Meanwhile Morison himself was handling money from one of the key players in Wyatt's conspiracy.[61] When John Brett was commissioned to serve writs against many of the leading exiles, Morison was not among them, perhaps indicating that Mary's government knew of his death already. Many of his friends and associates were, however, including Hales, Cooke and Katherine Brandon.[62]

---

[57] PROB11/37, fo. 217ʳ; Garrett, *Marian Exiles*, 13, 368–9; *Melanchthons Briefwechsel*, ed. H. Scheible (Stuttgart, 1977–), vii. 7554; J. Woolton, *Treatise of Immortatlitie of the soul* (London, 1576), ¶¶ ivᵛ. Woolton may have personally experienced the Morisons' generosity.

[58] W. M. Southgate, *John Jewel and the Problem of Doctrinal Authority* (Cambridge, MA, 1962), 20–1; *OL*, lxxiii.

[59] J. Vowell, *The Life and Times of Sir Peter Carew*, ed. J. MacClean (London, 1857), 60–2; Hudson, *Ponet*, 73; I. S. Leadam, 'A Narrative of the Pursuit of English Refugees in Germany under Queen Mary', *TRHS*, 11 (1897), 131–2.

[60] P. Collinson, 'Edwin Sandys', *ODNB*, 48.915–16; S. E. Lehmberg, 'Thomas Wrothe', *ODNB*, 60.541–2.

[61] Loades, *Two Tudor Conspiracies*, 15–16, 35–46; Garrett, *Marian Exiles*, 84–5; W. Nicholson (ed.), *Remains of Edmund Grindal* (Cambridge, 1864), 221–4; *OL*, xc; A. Ryrie, 'Thomas Sampson', *ODNB*, 48.802–3; *CSPDM*, 268.

[62] Leadam, 'English Refugees', 113–32.

THE PROPAGANDIST IN EXILE

Anti-Marian Propaganda

The Marian exiles produced large quantities of polemical material designed to be sent into England to bolster the faithful and vilify the government. These were not, as Loach argued, aimed at scholarly audiences, but were designed to appeal to a wide spectrum of society.[63] Indeed those writing the propaganda noted the need for literature with broad appeal. Hence John Ponet believed that John Bale and the other exiles should focus their efforts on producing 'Ballets rymes and short toyes that be not deare, and will easily be born away' as they could 'doe much good at home amonge the rude peple'.[64] Pettegree is undoubtedly correct to think there was no coordinated campaign to direct.[65] That does not mean that there was no discussion among the disparate groups of exiles over what to produce. While Ponet advised Bale to change the type of book he was writing, Grindal advised John Foxe on where to publish.[66] Nor does it preclude the possibility that smaller campaigns were coordinated: it seems likely, for instance, that the *Supplicacyon to the Quenes majestie* was designed to work alongside the English translation of Gardiner's *De vera obedientia*. More broadly, the idea that highlighting the earlier works of Gardiner, Pole, Bonner and Tunstall would undermine their credibility was shared by a number of Marian exiles and their evangelical contacts on the continent.

Emden, Wesel, Basel and Strasbourg were all important printing centres for the Marian exiles. Strasbourg had the advantage that it was a convenient place to produce propaganda. Its magistrates only infrequently imposed the city's censorship laws, and were generally more concerned with slanderous or libellous works than with theological or

[63] J. Loach, 'Pamphlets and Politics', *BIHR*, 48 (1975), 36–7; J. W. Martin, 'The Marian Regime's Failure to Understand the Importance of Printing', *HLQ*, 45 (1981), 231–47.

[64] E. J. Baskerville, 'John Ponet in Exile: A Ponet Letter to John Bale', *JEH*, 37 (1986), 442–6.

[65] Pettegree, *Marian Protestantism*, ch. 5. Garrett's claim (*Marian Exiles*, 49) that John Cheke directed a concerted propaganda campaign seems unlikely: by 1553 Cheke had little experience of polemical writing and his literary activities in exile seem to have been more scholarly endeavours (Zurich ZB, B171).

[66] Baskerville, 'John Ponet', 442–6; W. Nicholson (ed.), *Remains of Bishop Grindal* (Cambridge, 1843), 221–4.

political tracts.[67] During the period 1553–8, at least nine tracts were published there by the English exiles.

Morison was by far the most experienced polemicist in exile and had knowledge of how both domestic and international campaigns of persuasion had been waged by Henry VIII. His role in the Marian exiles' propaganda has been neglected. His household may well have been a base for the production of exile propaganda and certainly contained men involved in the production of polemical tracts. In 1554 Aylmer had overseen the publication of Lady Jane Grey's letter to Harding at Strasbourg. James Haddon funded John Banks, who smuggled Jane Grey's papers out of England, although he decided against publishing them. John Ponet, another Englishman associating with Morison, penned tracts which justified active resistance to a tyrannical monarch and defended clerical marriage.[68] As Pettegree has convincingly shown, the English exiles were well aware of the Latin polemic of the Marian government and sought to counter it, producing forty different works that were openly polemical. Foreigners who had taken refuge in England, such as Vallerand Poullain, Vermigli and Ochino played a significant role in these efforts.[69] In 1555 another of Morison's former clients, Pier Paulo Vergerio, issued an edition of Pole's *Pro ecclesiasticae unitatis defensione* with 'scholiis Athanasii' appended to highlight Pole's errors.[70] Of the English exiles, Morison was most closely linked to Vergerio, and may have encouraged both his and Ochino's polemical endeavours. At the very least, his earlier patronage and continued correspondence seems to have aroused in Vergerio an interest in England's religious path. This is apparent in many of the Italian's letters of the 1550s, including some written to his newer patron, Christopher duke of Württemberg, who donated money to the English refugees.[71]

Morison's earlier activities as a government propagandist gave him an understanding, not only of the need for vernacular propaganda in

[67] M. U. Chrisman, *Lay Culture, Learned Culture* (New Haven, 1982), 28–9, 244.

[68] Strype, *Aylmer*, 7–8; Knighton, 'James Haddon', *ODNB*, 24.413; W. S. Hudson, *John Ponet (1516?–1556), Advocate of Limited Monarchy* (Chicago, 1942), ch. 4. The claims for Morison's authorship of *A Defence of Priests' Marriage* stem from John Strype. Recent scholarship on the *Defence* has established Parker's role in the composition of the work.

[69] Pettegree, *Marian Protestantism*, ch. 5.

[70] P. Simoncelli, *Il caso Reginald Pole* (Rome, 1977), 122–6. The publication was also designed to undermine Pole's credentials as a peacemaker, as he was trying to negotiate a truce between the emperor and the French king at the time.

[71] E. von Kausler and T. Schott (eds.), *Briefwechsel zwischen Christoph, Herzog von Württemberg und Petrus Paulus Vergerius* (Tübingen, 1875), nos. 15, 19–22, 24.

England, but also for Latin anti-Marian propaganda. He may also have had links to the Strasbourg printer Wendelin Rihel, who was closely connected to Sturm and Sleidan and had produced imprints of tracts by Morison (the *Protestation*) and Gardiner (*De vera obedientia*) in the 1530s.[72] Two decades later, he printed at least three works for the English exile community. Rihel was also approached by Grindal about printing Cranmer's controversy with Gardiner on the Eucharist, but was too committed to Lutheranism to agree.[73] Morison, then, had the skills and contacts to prove useful to the exiles' polemical efforts.

MORISON'S INTERPRETATION OF EDWARD'S REIGN

During Mary's reign, Morison composed at least one treatise which may have been intended for publication. In it, he expressed the hopes of the evangelical community for Edward's reign, and their disappointment at the godly king's death. He may have written it before he went into exile, as the transcriber of the extant copy dated it to Edward's reign. The treatise later ended up in the possession of John Foxe, who used it in his *Acts and Monuments*.[74] Morison was not present in England to witness the events he described. Although he had previously put a speech into dead Jane Seymour's mouth, he had been clear that this was his invention and his other polemical efforts were marked by a concern for accuracy. This suggests that Morison had a source at court. Most probably this was in the form of letters addressed to him as ambassador. Other possibilities include his fellow exiles Thomas Wrothe and John Ponet.

Morison's treatise began with the Privy Council's attempts to make Mary conform to the Book of Common Prayer, with which Morison had been involved during his embassy to the Imperial court. He consistently portrayed Mary as easily tricked and flattered into a particular course of action. A central theme of the treatise was the political manipulation of which John Dudley was capable. Morison described him as a wily politician, who 'seldom went about anythinge but he conceaved first three or four purposes beforehand'. Dudley deliberately deceived the Imperialists and Mary, knowing that Edward would prove

[72] Chrisman, *Lay Culture*, 25–6.
[73] H. Robinson, *The Zurich Letters* (Cambridge, 1842), i. 219–21.
[74] *Discourse*, fo. 130^v; *AM*, ix.1484–5.

intransigent.[75] The other villain of the piece was the Lord Treasurer, William Paulet. Paulet, according to Morison, was forever fawning over whichever Privy Councillor appeared to be dominant, rather than giving due attention to the welfare of the country. Morison even included what was, for him, one of the worst of insults: he could not 'devise' what Paulet had said, as the Treasurer 'could never skill of learned talke, [n]or of plaine simplicitie'.[76] As a result of the politicians' self-interest, important policies were neglected.

Morison consistently emphasized Edward's godliness. Cranmer and Ridley, whom the Privy Council asked to determine if the king might overlook Mary's masses for the sake of political expediency, had decided that he might. Morison had Edward, unprompted, deliver a detailed, scholarly and stinging rebuke to the bishops' suggestion that he 'wink' at Mary's masses a while longer. In Morison's opinion, Edward was, by 1551, capable of making decisions and judging people and situations accurately in his own right.[77] He refuted the bishops' arguments from scripture, refusing to relent unless the bishops could produce a direct scriptural precedent. Instead, he suggested that his councillors join with him in putting true worship before a contemporary threat, in terms suggesting that Edward literally believed in many contemporary writers' identification of England as Israel. They should be more afraid of provoking God's wrath by sanctioning idolatry than of Charles V, a papal puppet, who was known to be critically ill. Edward's first duty to his country was to fulfil his obligations to God and only this would ensure that England continued to enjoy divine protection.[78] Morison's Edward, then, was a more religiously committed king than Loach has described.[79] If Morison had any intention of publishing his *Discourse* as anti-Marian propaganda, Cranmer's and Ridley's imprisonments would have halted such plans. Although he described a 'plaine, tractable, ientill, milde, loath to displease' archbishop who 'so loved the king', he still accused both Cranmer and Ridley of insufficient faith in God's providence.[80]

The *Discourse* clearly demonstrates that Morison, in common with many of his co-religionists, viewed Mary's reign as a punishment for

[75] *Discourse*, fos. 130ᵛ–1ʳ. Morison shared Ponet's views in the *Short Treatise of Politic Power* that Dudley possessed vast political skills, but was less critical of his methods.

[76] Ibid., fo. 132ʳ.

[77] Ibid., fos. 131ʳ–2ʳ. Interestingly, Morison's account leaves out one figure that Edward places at the scene: John Ponet.

[78] Ibid., fo. 133ʳ⁻ᵛ.   [79] J. Loach, *Edward VI* (London, 1999), 158.

[80] *Discourse*, fo. 131ᵛ.

England's sins. God's chosen nation had failed on two counts: its leaders had been corrupted by Mammon and the people had not embraced true religion when it had been re-established. Morison, as many Edwardian writers had, criticized the Edwardian gospellers for not embracing the true spirit of reform, and instead using the façade of reformation to line their own pockets.[81] Later the greed of England's politicians gave Morison cause to hope they would reject the restoration of papal authority for fear of losing their lands.[82] The punishment of which Morison had warned in his 1530s tracts was finally being exacted on an ungrateful England: 'Was there ever countrey better plied with daily examples than England hath bin ever sithens it was Realm . . . O for faith O Israel thou hast sinned as Gabor did, shall not the battle come upon thy wicked Children as it did upon the wicked Gaborites, when man leste to sin as these did.'[83] Mary's reign and the enforced idolatry it brought was no more than England deserved.

FURTHER WRITINGS

In June 1554, a seditious ballad was printed and scattered on the streets of London. The Imperial ambassadors in England, who sent a copy to Charles V, described it as the most scandalous and seditious ballad they had seen. The author, they believed, was Morison.[84] Sadly this ballad no longer survives. But the fact that Morison was suspected of being the author of propaganda against Philip is indicative. Many of the Marian exiles published tracts either under pseudonyms or anonymously. As a result, the authorship of many of the exile tracts may never be determined with any certainty.[85] It seems highly unlikely that Morison did not pick up his pen once more.

One tract that was probably from Morison's pen was the *Supplicacyon to the Quenes Majestie*, printed by Wendelin Rihel in 1555. The style

---

[81] Ibid., fos. 133^r–4^r; Shakespeare, 'Plagues and Punishment', 107–9; Davies, *Religion of the Word*, 204–9.

[82] *OL*, lxxv.   [83] *Discourse*, fo. 136^v. Referring to Hosea 10.

[84] *CSPS 1554*, 267.

[85] Further complicating the matter is the fact that many of the stylistic features which scholars such as Garrett and Pineas have used to identify John Bale as the author of some of the exile works were actually shared by a number of Tudor writers, including Morison. See for example C. Garrett, 'The Resurrection of the Masse, by Hugh Hilarie or John Bale?' *Library*, 4th ser. 21 (1940), 143–59; R. Pineas, 'Some Polemical Techniques in the Nondramatic Works of John Bale', *Bibliothèque d'humanisme et Renaissance*, 24 (1962), 583–8.

of the *Supplicacyon* is reminiscent of Morison's own and its author demonstrated a good knowledge of the polemics of Henry's Divorce, the English Parliament and the business of Charles V. It sought to discredit Mary's ecclesiastical counsellors by reproducing sections of their Henrician works, including Gardiner's *De vera Obedientia*, Bonner's preface to this work and Cuthbert Tunstall's 1539 sermon.[86] The latter had been part of the same campaign as Morison's *Invective* and *Exhortation*. The *Supplicacyon* went on to cast Mary as a tyrant who was neglecting her duty to Christ's gospel and forcing idolatry on the realm, and Gardiner as the evil butcher of godly Englishmen.[87] Morison had blamed Gardiner for the Marian persecution in a letter to Bullinger, but he was far from alone in this.[88] Also included were petitions to the commons and to laymen, which appealed to their sensibilities as property owners: if the queen had broken her word over the marriage treaty, then she could not be trusted on the matter of ex-monastic property. England was still in danger of becoming an abused Spanish satellite state like Milan or Naples.[89] Morison may also have been involved in conceiving of *A Copye of a verye fine and witty letter*. This was purportedly a translation by Michael Throckmorton, Pole's servant and Morison's one-time friend, of letters from Luigi Lippomano, a papal nuncio in Poland. Throckmorton would not have produced a tract that undermined the reforming credentials of Pole and Contarini and appeared to show a papal nuncio discussing the possibility of executing leading Protestant figures. Morison had known both Throckmorton and Pole well and had grudges against both. However, as he died before the tract was issued, someone else must have put it into execution.[90]

ASSESSMENT

Morison died in Strasbourg on 20 March 1556, leaving his estates to his wife and son Charles.[91] Although Morison's grave is unknown, his son's

---

[86] *Supplicacyon to the Quenes Majestie* (Strasbourg, 1555), Av^r–vi^r, Aviii^r–Bii^r, Biii^r–v^r.
[87] Ibid., Aiv^v, Bvii^r, Cviii^r.
[88] Zurich ZB, S85, no. 137; M. Riordan and A. Ryrie, 'Stephen Gardiner and the Making of a Protestant Villain', *SCJ*, 34 (2003), 1039–63.
[89] *Supplicacyon*, Ci^r–v^r, Cvi^r.
[90] *A copye of a verye fyne and vvytty letter . . . translated . . . by Michael Throckmerton* (false imprint: Rome, 1556).
[91] PROB11/32, fos. 114^r–17^v. His illegitimate children were provided with Snitterfield, Warwickshire. Although Morison had initially bequeathed his library to John Hales, the

epitaph commemorated Morison as universally respected for his literary skills and as a successful ambassador.[92] Shortly after Morison's death his household dispersed. Aylmer and those under his tutelage retired to the house of Morison's old friend Abel, before eventually removing to Zurich.[93] For a while, at least, Morison's wife remained in Strasbourg and continued to lodge English refugees. John Hales called on the aid of William Cecil 'for the love ye bare to mr moryson' to help her gain custody of her son Charles. She was unsuccessful: John Throckmorton, a stalwart conservative, was granted Charles's wardship.[94]

Morison's exile was largely peripatetic, and his long final stay in Strasbourg was not initially planned. He sheltered or forwarded money to many other exiles and was a central figure in the exile community. His household in Strasbourg reflected the overriding interests of his life: education and literature. Young exiles were tutored there while the older residents helped in the polemical efforts against the Marian regime. For much of this time, Morison was probably immersed in the Strasbourg humanist community he had cultivated when ambassador. His peripatetic lifestyle in the first year of his exile seems to have largely been determined by his desire to visit scholars and reformers across continental Europe. The contacts Morison had made in the years leading up to his exile shaped its course, particularly those political and religious contacts he made during his three years at the Imperial court. It was no doubt this experience that made him so useful to the exile community as a whole.

addenda to his will left all his moveable goods to his wife, which she interpreted as including the library: BL Additional 35831, fo. 173[r].

[92] H. Chauncy, *Historical Antiquities of Hertfordshire* (Dorking, 1976), ii. 363.
[93] BL Additional 48039, fo. 38[v].
[94] Garrett, *Marian Exiles*, 368–9; Hatfield House, 520; *Cal. Pat. P&M*, iv.192.

8

The 'Renowned Man of Letters'

'THAT RENOWNED MAN OF LETTERS'[1]

By the time of his death Morison had a reputation both within
and beyond England as a humanist of some note. Although not all
of Morison's works were issued in his own name, the *Apomaxis*,
Comfortable Consolation, *Exhortation* and *Invective* were, and even some
of his anonymous works were associated with him during his lifetime
by scholars such as Bale and Leland. Morison's renown in England
was undoubtedly enhanced by the classical and biblical references
with which his writings were laden. Here he was seen as a source of
patronage for aspiring scholars and he moved in scholarly circles at
court.

Morison's continental reputation is rather more intriguing and is an
aspect of his life that has been almost entirely overlooked by historians.
It undoubtedly began with the publication of the *Apomaxis*, which
displayed his humanist credentials, and was aided by his involvement
in English diplomacy. In part, Morison's reputation was spread in the
letters of his scholarly friends. Leland described Morison as 'remarkable
for his genius [and] his culture' to Rhenanus in 1540, while Roger
Ascham frequently praised his erudition and eloquence to continental
humanists in the early 1550s.[2] In 1544 John Caius described him
as one of England's 'ornaments of literature' in a text published at
Basel; four years later Bale praised both his writing and his learning
in a tract printed in Wesel.[3] Morison's international reputation was
boosted by his mention in a treatise on the eucharistic debate at
Oxford in 1549, which was popular on the continent[4] and no doubt

---

[1] Sleidan, *Histoire*, iii. 225.

[2] http://www.tertullian.org/articles/petitmengin_malmesbury_eng.htm

[3] Caius, *Pergameni nobilissimi medici*, Aa2^v; Bale, *Illustrium Maioris Britanniae scriptorium*,
NNii^r.

[4] Vermigli, *Disputation on the Eucharist*, 129.

developed as a result of his prominence and scholarly activities during his embassy. In 1552 Petrus Bello-Poelius lauded Morison's erudition and eloquence in his tract celebrating the Anglo-French peace.[5] After 1550 Morison received dedications from Michael Toxites, Pier Paulo Vergerio and Bernardine Ochino.[6] This marks Morison out as a much more prominent international humanist than has previously been thought.

MORISON'S BOOKLIST

Perhaps the greatest testament to Morison's scholarship is the library that he assembled across his lifetime. Morison's extensive and extraordinary library reveals the true depth of his learning. It was one of the largest and most eclectic collections of books in England in the first six decades of the sixteenth century for which evidence has survived. Morison has often been labelled unoriginal or derivative.[7] Yet his library suggests that he was more than just a minor scholar; he was an avid collector of books and part of wider book-sharing circles that included major figures such as John Cheke, Thomas Thirlby and Anthony Cooke.

A list of books that belonged to Morison can be found in the British Library. The list is bound with a separate, but possibly related, dictaminal collection and is followed by a few short notes and a poem. The texts were almost certainly bound together at an early date. Many of the works plundered for extracts appear in the booklist, including excerpts from Diodorus Siculus, Plutarch's *Life of Alcibiades*, and Procopius of Caesarea's *De Bello Gottorum*. However, other texts in the dictaminal selection were extracted from works which are not included in the inventory, such as Palladius' *De Gentibus Indiae* and the *De Gestis Friderici*. This collection of transcripts was concerned with the nature of monarchical rule and was most likely assembled either by someone educating a prince, or by someone writing on behalf of one.[8]

Although the booklist is not specified as Morison's in the manuscript, there are compelling reasons to believe that the manuscript, and the

[5] P. Bello-Poelius, *De Pace inter invictissimos Henricum Galliarum, et Eduardum Anglii, reges oratio* (London, 1552), 43.

[6] See above, ch. 6.

[7] Elton, for example, designated Morison 'an eager scholar of little originality of mind': Elton, *Reform and Renewal*, 59.

[8] *Booklist*, fos. 114ᵛ, 115ᵛ; *Additional MS Catalogue, 1921–25* (London, 1950), 121–3.

books it listed, were his. In 1566 the manuscript seemingly belonged to Francis Russell, earl of Bedford, who married Morison's widow, Bridget Hussey, that same year.[9] The booklist itself and the folios surrounding it also point to the identity of its owner. Anthony Cooke and John Cheke are both noted as having borrowed books, placing the owner within their scholarly circle and providing a terminal date for the list, as Cheke died in September 1557. A number of laymen and scholars in the 'Athenian' circle had sufficiently broad concerns to warrant such an impressive collection of books; Morison was one of them. Both Cooke and Cheke were close friends of Morison, and travelled with him during their years in exile. More conclusively, the peripheral folios contain a short antipapal epigram in Morison's hand.[10] The subject of the epigram fits with Morison's known literary output; its emphasis on the renewed activity of the pope would fit the circumstances of the restoration of papal authority in England and echoes Morison's disappointment at Mary's succession.[11] Also included in the peripheral folios is a laundry list in a hand that closely resembles Morison's and a list of goods that 'Weston' was to buy. One of Morison's most trusted household servants was William Weston, who acted as a courier during his embassy in 1550–3 and was present when he organized his affairs in 1554.[12] Cumulatively, this evidence places the manuscript in Morison's hands in the 1550s; that Morison himself noted Cheke's loans confirms that the books it listed were his.

Two possible owners have been suggested for the library in the past: Cuthbert Tunstall and Richard Pace, both of whom had expansive intellectual interests and could viably have possessed such a collection. Herendeen and Bartlett, who believed the library belonged to Cuthbert Tunstall, mistakenly assumed that only a churchman could have the extensive interests represented in the list, but this is not the only problem with their circumstantial identification.[13] The list does not

---

[9] *Additional MS Catalogue*, 122; Cockayne, *Complete Peerage*, ii. 76; W. T. MacCaffrey, 'Russell, Francis, Second Earl of Bedford', *ODNB*, 47.239.

[10] *Booklist*, fo. 117ʳ. Herendeen and Bartlett believed this to be a late sixteenth-century addition.

[11] See for example, Morison's *Discourse*.

[12] *APC 1550–1552*, 480; *APC 1552–1554*, 44, 75, 111, 123, 124, 199, 214, 228, 246. *Booklist*, fo. 119ʳ. The key features of Morison's hand are present, but the writing is less fluid than usual, perhaps suggesting he was ill at the time.

[13] W. H. Herendeen and K. Bartlett, 'The Library of Cuthbert Tunstall, Bishop of Durham', *Papers of the Bibliographical Society of America*, 85 (1991), 235–96. This article contains the only edition of the booklist. Unfortunately, their edition is flawed in places. For

fit with Sturge's reconstruction of part of Tunstall's library.[14] Most damagingly, Tunstall was trained as a canon and civil lawyer, yet law does not seem to be a guiding concern behind the arrangement of the list, as books on civil law appear elsewhere in the collection: Guillaume Budé's *Pandecta* was placed in the section on Latin history, while Alexander Alexandro's *Genialium dierum* was designated as Latin philosophy. Additionally, legal texts are not very well represented in the list and the glossators one would expect a prominent lawyer to own are noticeable by their absence. This organization might make sense to someone with an interest in, and even some training in the law, but seems nonsensical for a leading civil lawyer. Similarly, mathematics is not strongly represented as one would expect in the library of the author of a major work on the subject. Curtis, who accepted Herendeen's and Bartlett's identification, believed that the library had first belonged to Richard Pace. The booklist contained a large number of titles that Pace drew upon in his own literary endeavours or that were written by friends or dedicated to him, and Pace was known to have owned a formidable library. This is not sufficient grounds for ascribing the list to Pace; a small number of other scholars were also capable of putting together such a remarkable collection of books. Another strong reason to doubt Pace's ownership of this particular library lies in the simple fact that some of the titles in the list were not published until after Pace's library was confiscated and some were only printed after his death. It seems unlikely, for instance, that Pace possessed a manuscript volume of the *Bibliotheca Eliotae* over three years before it was published.[15]

How and when did Morison acquire such a large library? During his time in Italy, Morison was keen to collect as many Greek texts as possible. Admittedly he was impoverished for much of this time, but it is possible that his requests for money for books were met before his departure.[16] Although he has sometimes been credited with receiving

---

a more accurate edition of the list and the rationale underpinning it, see Sowerby, 'Morison', 352–66, 372–414.

[14] C. T. Sturge, *Cuthbert Tunstal: Churchman, Scholar, Statesman* (London, 1938), 392–5.

[15] C. Curtis, 'Richard Pace on Pedagogy, Counsel and Satire', Ph.D. thesis (Cambridge, 1997), 312–21. *Booklist*, fo. 113[r]. Morison's ownership of the list does not preclude some of the books on it having once belonged to Pace, as there is a strong likelihood that Morison's former patron, Cromwell, appropriated at least some of Pace's books and may have passed copies on to his client.

[16] See above pp. 29–30.

the library of the White Friars in London, this appears to have been the building and not the books. An anonymous life of John Fisher suggests that Morison received many of Fisher's books via Cromwell, which may well be the case.[17] Most of Morison's books, however, were probably imported from the continent. The question of when the list (and indeed the library) was compiled is almost impossible to answer, but it can be narrowed down to between 1548, when Morison's edition of Budé's *De linguae Grecae* was printed by Robert Estienne, and his death in March 1556.[18]

In addition to *De linguae Grecae*, six other printed books known to have belonged to Morison are extant. These comprise a four-volume edition of Cicero, a Greek Lexicon published by Craston, and Pliny's *Natural History*, all of which contain an autograph inscription. Both the Pliny and Cicero apparently had at least one owner before they came into his hands.[19] Morison's textual contribution to these volumes was editorial—he annotated passages which he felt were in incorrect Latin grammar, or could be rephrased more elegantly. Although there are also many markings in the margin, singling out specific passages for more attention, there is no indication who made them. Sadly this means these volumes give us little sense of anything other than Morison's pedantic temperament.

MORISON'S LIBRARY

Morison's library was unusually large for its time, containing more volumes than any of the libraries surveyed by Jayne.[20] Although in the second half of the sixteenth century a number of Tudor men would assemble libraries of over 1,000 printed books, a collection of over 500 would have been worthy of note in the 1550s.[21] It was also remarkable for the care taken in documenting it: the list was arranged according to language (Greek and Latin) and then divided by class.

---

[17] BL Arundel 152, fos. 68ʳ, 253ʳ, 284ʳ. This suggestion is made very tentatively, as the drafts of the life contain inaccurate information about Morison.

[18] The copy is in St John's College, Cambridge (I.3.29).

[19] Unfortunately I have been unable to see the Craston *Lexicon*.

[20] S. Jayne, *Library Catalogues of the English Renaissance* (Berkeley, 1956).

[21] J. Roberts, 'Extending the Frontiers: Scholar Collectors', in E. Leedham-Green and T. Webber (eds.), *Cambridge History of the Library in Britain and Ireland*, i: *To 1640* (Cambridge, 2006), 292–321.

The organization of a booklist was not necessarily the way in which the library it represented was organized,[22] and there are reasons to believe that the library itself was not physically divided on a rigidly linguistic basis. At the end of the Latin theology section nine theological works in Greek are crossed through before three final Latin works are noted. Eight of these nine works then recur when the Greek theology section commences, implying that some, at least, of the scholar's Greek books were kept amidst his Latin tomes.[23]

Very little information is given in the list as to the physical condition of the individual books. However, it is likely that the vast majority of the works were printed editions. Only two items (both works by Chrysostom) are noted as manuscript volumes, suggesting that manuscripts were distinctive within the context of the library. Printed editions exist for all the other titles it is possible to identify, with the possible exception of Hypparchus Bythnius' *Comentarii in Aratus Phaenomena*, which was seemingly not printed as a separate title until 1567. The enthusiastic collection of printed books was not unusual in England at this time.[24] A handful of books in the collection were noted as being of an unusual size: six were described as especially large and six as small. Only five items on the list were apparently noteworthy for their gilded decoration, a further indication that the books belonged to a scholar like Morison. A royal or aristocratic library could be expected to contain a significant proportion of luxurious items, bound in materials such as velvet, silk, cloth of gold or decorated with precious gems.[25] The only other indication of the physical condition of the books lies in annotations that some titles were bound together.

Morison's library was even more extensive than the substantial booklist suggests. A number of items are listed 'cum aliis operibus', indicating that they were either bound with, or the print edition included, other titles. In some instances it is possible to suggest what these works might be. So the items grouped under the heading 'Oppiani poetae cu*m* multis operib*us*' were almost certainly a collection of works on fish published together in 1534, which included Oppian's work *De*

---

[22] D. McKitterick, 'Libraries and the Organisation of Knowledge', in Leedham-Green and Webber, *Cambridge History of the Library*, i. 592–615.

[23] *Booklist*, fos. 112[r], 115[r].

[24] See for example M. H. Smith, 'Some Humanist Libraries in Tudor Cambridge', *SCJ*, 5 (1974), 16; Roberts, 'Extending the Frontiers', 292–321.

[25] M. M. Foot, 'Bookbinding in England, 1400–1557', in Hellinga and Trapp, *History of the Book*, iii. 116–24.

piscibus; Lorenzo Lippi's translation of Oppian and a poem; book two of Pliny's *Natural History* on fish; Paulo Giovio's *De piscibus*; and a life of Oppian. In other instances the unnamed works were most likely other works by the same author. Faustus' *De Gratia Dei et humanae mentis libero arbitrio* is also described as being bound with 'alijs ope*ribus*'.[26] This title was frequently printed alongside three of Faustus' other works (*de fide adversus Arianos*; *opus insigne, cum. D. Erasmi . . . praefatione*; *ad Flaccillam Imperatricem*) so the entry probably represents a more extensive range of Faustus' works than might initially be supposed. Many of the items described 'cum aliis' or 'et aliis' were one text in a series of controversial literature. It may well be the case that the other works were the very texts that were relevant to the controversy. Thomas Murner's *Caussa Helvetica orthodoxae fidei* is noted as being bound 'with with other works of the same assembly'; this implies that Murner's work was bound with works by the very authors—Luther, Zwingli and Oecolampadius—it criticized.[27] Consequently, Morison probably had access to a much more complete collection of recent controversial literature than the booklist at first suggests. There is also the possibility that in other cases the headings may have concealed works of a more reformed nature. So, for instance, at least five editions of Bernard de Lutzenberger's *Catalogus haereticorum omnium* were printed with a tract by Martin Luther against purgatory appended.[28] There is another reason to suppose that Morison's library contained more volumes: the booklist very self-consciously itemized Latin and Greek volumes, or texts which were predominantly Latin and Greek. He definitely owned books in Italian and English, and possibly other European vernacular languages, which were not noted by the person who compiled the surviving booklist.

The sheer quantity of Greek works in Morison's library marks it out as unusual: eighty-one volumes, or 17.2 per cent of the list, were Greek and several titles in the Latin section also included some Greek, making this a considerable collection by contemporary standards. Indeed, Morison owned considerably more Greek works than a number of other large English scholarly libraries of his day. Nearly a quarter (23.8 per cent) of Master Bisley's books contained some Greek, but this still only amounted to 29 out of 122 volumes. Edward Beaumont owned a similar proportion of works wholly or partially in Greek: 23 out of 117

---

[26] *Booklist*, fo. 112ʳ. [27] Ibid., fo. 111ʳ.
[28] Cologne, 1522, 1526, 1529, 1537; Strasbourg, 1527. *Booklist*, fo. 111ᵛ.

volumes (19.7 per cent). Even William Brown, who had somewhere between 42 and 65 Greek or partially Greek works in his library of 223 books (18.8–29.2 per cent) could not match Morison's collection.[29] The presence of Greek books in such numbers signifies a serious and enduring interest in the language. Although Greek studies in England were on the increase in the first half of the sixteenth century, many of the authors—Thucydides, Aristophanes, Sophocles, Pindar—were demanding, meaning only a very small group of scholars could have used such a library. Of these, most were fellows of an Oxbridge College.[30] Bale's and Ascham's praise of Morison's ability in Greek, then, seems well placed. Morison's more unusual interest in Hebrew is most apparent in his collection of dictionaries, which included three trilingual dictionaries by Sebastian Munster, but he also owned a small number of other texts that included some Hebrew.[31]

A concern for language and its correct usage is clear in Morison's library. He owned eleven dictionaries and lexicons, as well Budé's seminal work the *Thesaurus linguae graecae*, and key works on Greek grammar by Thomas Magister, Constantinus Lascaris and Theodore Gaza. Morison was the owner of works by important Greek writers including Demosthenes, Isocrates, Aristides, Lucian, Aphthonius and Hermogenes, and also owned commentaries by Ulpian and Syrian.[32] Unsurprisingly, Cicero dominated the section of the library concerned with Latin oratory and grammar. His *Opera*, *De Oratore* and *Epistles* were all there, some in multiple copies. In addition, Morison had three commentaries on Cicero, as well as a Ciceronian dialogue by Petri Alcyoni. Quintilian was well-represented at five titles, as was Erasmus at six. These latter included Erasmus' work on composition, *De copia*, and two copies of his edition of Lucian's *Dialogues*. Morison's library contained many of the standard texts on Latin grammar: Perotti's *Cornucopia*, William Horman's *Vulgaria*, Dionysius Nestor's *Vocabularius*, Georgius Trapezuntius' *Rhetorica*, the *Rhetorica ad Herennium* and Despauterius, as well as the more exacting grammars of Thomas Linacre and Aldus Manutius.[33] There were two dictionaries by Thomas Elyot

---

29 *PLRE*, ii.171–97, iii.1–35, 204–221.

30 A. Tilley, 'Greek Studies in the English Renaissance', *EHR*, 53 (1938), 221–39. I am grateful to Alastair Blanshard, who has been extremely generous with his knowledge of Greek texts.

31 *Booklist*, fos. 110ʳ, 111ᵛ.   32 Ibid., fo. 115ʳ⁻ᵛ.

33 N. Orme, 'School and Schoolbooks', in Trapp and Hellinga, *History of the Book*, iii. 461–4. *Booklist*, fo. 113ʳ.

and Grapaldus. Several humanists, such as Francesco Filelfo, Étienne Dolet and Christophe Longueil, were evidently valued as stylists.[34] Lorenzo Valla's *Opera* was presumably acquired both for style and for content: it would have contained his *Elegantiarum linguae latinae libri sex*, an influential work on Latin usage, as well as *Disputationes dialecticae* which were highly critical of scholastic methodology.[35] Morison's ownership of works such as Angelo Poliziano's *Miscellanea* and Guillaume Budé's *De asse et partibus* also demonstrates a keen interest in philology.

The majority (over two hundred) of Morison's books were theological in nature. Herendeen and Bartlett categorized the theological works on the list as those of a Catholic, most likely an Erasmian reformer,[36] but this is misleading. Thomas Aquinas, Denys the Carthusian, Peter Lombard and St Bernard were in the library, but beyond this there are few of the medieval authors one would expect to find in a Catholic library. An interest in scripture was central to the theology section of the library. Morison owned numerous Latin editions of the New and Old Testaments, including a polyglot Bible, while Greek theology was comprised mainly of scriptural works: four Bibles (including one polyglot), two New Testaments, and Erasmus' commentary on the New Testament. Other books on scriptural translation also appear, including those of Lorenzo Valla and Sante Pagnini.[37]

The evangelical tenor of the library is also evident in the large collection of patristic works it contained. Although these texts were not widely available in England at this time,[38] Morison owned several volumes by Chrysostom, Basil, Eusebius and Gregory of Nazianzen, although only Chrysostom's and Basil's *Opera* and works by Dionysius Areopagiticus and Gregory of Nazianzen were owned in Greek as well as Latin editions.[39] Such authors were important to men like Morison who sought to reform the church, as they showed the progression of church history and the customs of the primitive church. Moreover, many of the sixteenth-century editors of patristic texts were Protestants, and used their marginalia to demonstrate these texts' support for Protestant doctrines.[40]

---

[34] D. Robin, *Filelfo in Milan* (Oxford, 1991), ch. 1.

[35] J. B. Trapp, 'The Humanist Book', in Hellinga and Trapp, *History of the Book*, iii. 302–3.

[36] Herendeen and Bartlett, 'Library', 257–9.   [37] *Booklist*, fos. 110ʳ–12ʳ, 115ʳ.

[38] Trapp, 'Humanist Book', 311. Morison owned works by eighteen church fathers.

[39] *Booklist*, fo. 115ʳ⁻ᵛ.

[40] Rice, 'Humanist Idea of Christian Antiquity', 163–80; Haugaard, 'Renaissance Patristic Scholarship', 37–41.

Other theological works also signal an interest in church reform. Thus many of the authors such as Girolamo Savonarola and Berthold Pürstinger were late fifteenth- or early sixteenth-century critics of abuses within the church. One of the most remarkable features of the list is the almost complete collection of Erasmian texts, particularly his theological works. There are numerous Erasmian commentaries on the psalms and editions of church fathers, as well as Erasmus' controversy with Peter Sutor over biblical translation and his debate with Luther over free will. Erasmus' paraphrases, catechism and New Testament are also present, as are his tracts on marriage, purgatory and Christian education. Many of these were critical of the practices of the late medieval church.[41]

Controversial theological literature was well represented. This included numerous works against Luther, by prominent Catholic controversialists such as Erasmus, Cochlaeus and Fisher. Ironically, Cochlaeus' works were also a useful means by which to access Luther's ideas, as he reproduced large sections of the reformer's tracts. Many of these Catholic controversial texts were bound with other, unspecified works. If these were, as seems likely, the reformist texts that the Catholic polemicists attacked in the named volumes, then the religious complexion of the library changes quite considerably. Openly Protestant works such as the *Unio dissidentium* are present, but rare.[42]

Unsurprisingly, given Morison's extensive use of historical texts, his library contained a large number of histories. He owned multiple copies of Plutarch's *Parallel Lives*, which he used so extensively in his propaganda tracts. At least one copy of almost all of the other classical authors he referenced appears on the booklist. The collection of historians included many of the classical authors one would expect: Livy, Valerius Maximus, Sallust, Quintus Curtius, Polybius, Eutropius, Xenophon, Suetonius, Diodorus Siculus, Aelian, Thucydides and Julius Caesar.[43] However, it also included some figures who were much less common, such as Philostratus, Pausanias and Strabo. Morison owned a selection of medieval historians, including Froissart, Giovanni Boccaccio, Werner Rolewinck and the anti-papal Burchard von Ursberg. More recent historians also found their way into the library, including Pius II, Robert Gaguin, Polydore Vergil, Platina, Sabellicus and Robert Barnes.[44] The interest in church history, which is clear here, is also

---

[41] *Booklist*, fos. 110ʳ–12ʳ.   [42] Ibid.
[43] Burke, 'Ancient Historians', 136–43.   [44] *Booklist*, fos. 114ᵛ, 115ᵛ.

reflected in the theological section, which included works by Bede and Eusebius.[45]

Morison owned works by the classical poets one would expect a first-rate humanist to own: Vergil, Homer, Ovid, Lucan, Horace, Ausonius, Martial, Claudian, Pindar and Statius. For the two most prominent of these, Vergil and Homer, Morison also owned commentaries, as well as a scholia for the *Iliad*. A fair selection of Latin and Greek dramatists were in his library, including Terence, Plautus, Sophocles, Aeschylus, Aristophanes, Euripides and Theocritus. Nor were Morison's interests limited to the ancient poets. He owned a copy of the *Opera* of Johannes Joviales Pontanus, the fifteenth-century Italian poet, which contained his love poetry.[46] Such an extensive collection of poets was relatively rare in sixteenth-century private collections,[47] but fitted Morison's own poetic ambitions.

Greek philosophy was dominated by Aristotle: Morison owned nine individual works or collections of works as well as commentaries by Alexander of Aphrodisias and Simplicius; two more works appear in Latin translation as does a commentary by George Valla. Morison's claim to want to read all of Aristotle does not seem to have been an exaggeration. His library also contained Plato's works in Latin and Greek, which is indicative of the intellectual influences he encountered at Padua and the increased importance being placed on Platonic thought at this time. Plutarch's moral works and book on education were clearly also prized for their philosophical content. Rather unusually for an English library of this time, there are several works on occult philosophy by figures such as Henry Cornelius Agrippa, Giovanni Pico della Mirandola and Mercurius Trismegistus as well as some of the ancient Neoplatonists whose ideas influenced Agrippa: Jamblichus, Plotinus and Gemistus Plethon.[48] Works by other Neoplatonists can be found elsewhere in the booklist; for instance Johann Trittheim and Marsilio Ficino can be found in the theology section.[49] Natural history was represented in the philosophy section, which included three works by or about Pliny: his *Natural History*, a commentary by Barbaro and

[45] *Booklist*, fos. 110^r, 112^r.

[46] Ibid., fos. 114^r, 115^v; C. Kidwell, *Pontano: Poet and Prime Minister (1426–1503)* (London, 1991).

[47] Herendeen and Bartlett, 'Library', 246–7.

[48] C. G. Nauert, *Agrippa and the Crisis of Renaissance Thought* (Urbana, 1965), 201–2.

[49] Ficino was a relatively uncommon author in English libraries until after 1600. S. Jayne, 'Ficino and the Platonism of the English Renaissance', *Comparative History*, 4 (1952), 221.

Rabirius' *Index*. In addition, the philosophy section also contained Seneca's *Naturalium Questionum*, two works by the influential Paduan Leoniceno, a herbal and a work on anatomy.[50]

Although the list contained a short section dedicated to Latin law books, including the *Decretals*, the basic source texts for canon law, there is no Panormitanus or any of the other commentaries and medieval texts one would expect a canon lawyer to own.[51] Similarly the basic text of the civil law, Justinian's *Digest*, was listed, but the authors one would expect to find in a dedicated civil lawyer's library were absent. There were none of the standard works by Odofredus, Bartolus or Baldus, nor were there more recent commentators such as Zasius, Oldendorp or Alciati.[52] Where books on the civil law did occur, their position on the list suggests that they were valued for other interests. Guillaume Budé's *Annotationes* on the Pandects and Peter Crinitus' works were apparently prized for their historical approach, rather than their legal content, as they were designated as Latin histories.[53]

Morison's collection of medical texts was both sizeable and eclectic for a non-medic. Only two of these were Greek, both by Galen. Galen was also well-represented among the Latin works, as were Celsus, Dioscorides, Oribasius and Psellus. However, Hippocrates and Avicenna, two of the most widely used authors of the day, only featured in composite volumes. The basic university medical text, Joanniti's *Isagogue*, is on the booklist, as are a number of herbals and Vegetius' work on veterinary science.[54] Moreover, there is evidence that Morison was reading even more medical texts in manuscript.[55]

As befitted an ambassador, Morison's intellectual interests also embraced cosmography, astrology and mathematics.[56] This section of the list also included several standard works, such as Strabo, Ptolemy, Julius Solinus and the *Cosmographia* of Pomponius Mela and Pius II. Arithmetic was covered by Euclid as well as more recent volumes by Luca Paccioli and Cuthbert Tunstall. More unusually, works by Peter Martyr Anghillera and Alvise Ca' da Mosto point to a curiosity about the

---

[50] *Booklist*, fos. 113^{r-v}, 115^{r-v}.

[51] R. H. Helmholz, 'Canon Law', in Hellinga and Trapp, *History of the Book*, iii. 387–98. *Booklist*, fo. 115^r.

[52] A. Wijfels, 'Civil Law', in Hellinga and Trapp, *History of the Book*, iii. 399–410.

[53] *Booklist*, fo. 114^v.   [54] Ibid., fos. 114^r, 116^r.

[55] Caius, *Counseill*, Avi^{r-v}.

[56] For the technological interests of sixteenth-century ambassadors see J. D. North, *The Ambassadors' Secret* (London, 2002).

exploration of the New World. Perhaps unsurprisingly for an eclectic propagandist, Morison also owned works by Leon Battista Alberti, Albrecht Dürer and Vitruvius which indicate an interest in architecture and aesthetics.[57]

ET AMICORUM

The books in Morison's library were read not only by him, but also by his friends. His ownership inscription reflects the communal nature of his library: 'Ricardj Morysini et Amic*orum*' (Richard Morison and friends).[58] This links Morison to a humanist sentiment, popular in Italy in the fifteenth century, which was becoming more widespread within the European humanist community in the early sixteenth century.[59] In Morison's case though, 'et amicorum' was no mere posturing, it was also true of the practical working of his library. The library list contains annotations indicating where other scholars had borrowed volumes. William Darrell, who resided in Morison's household in the winter of 1551–2, had borrowed a Greek Old Testament, which would have been suitable reading material for someone who was probably only just beginning his Greek studies.[60] Cheke apparently had Morison's copy of Aphthonius' *Rhetores*, a text he used to teach Edward VI, the *Variae historiae* of Aelianus, and Porphyry's *De abstinentia*, while Cooke left a note indicating his borrowing of works by Ammonius and Simplicius.[61]

This pattern of book-sharing fits with what can be discerned about Morison's library from other sources. Anthony Rous had, by 1540, been exchanging books with Morison for some time, and Morison expected it to continue: 'I send yow a boke I desire a booke for it, not as a recomp[ense], but as a matier to make forth th'obligation, that y*our* ge*n*til nature, longe sithins wold me to make.'[62] Morison was also connected to the same scholarly book-sharing circle as John Caius, John Skip, Thomas Thirlby, John Taylor and Thomas Smith.[63]

[57] *Booklist*, fo. 114^v.

[58] For example in New College Ω 32.10, Ω 32.1; Morison's volumes of Cicero and Pliny's natural history. Morison also inscribed his copy of Budé with the motif in Greek (St John's, Cambridge I.3.29).

[59] G. D. Hobson, 'Et amicorum', *The Library*, 5th ser. 4 (1949), 87–99.

[60] *Booklist*, fo. 115^r; CUL, MS Dd.9.14; *CSPFE*, 486.   [61] *Booklist*, fos. 115^v, 119^v.

[62] SP1/162, fo.144^r [LP XV 1029.53].   [63] Caius, *Counseill*, Avi^{r-v}.

A number of entries on Morison's booklist were later crossed through. Some deletions no doubt reflect mistakes on the part of the cataloguer, but others (particularly the more detailed ones) may represent books borrowed and then returned, books sold, or books given to friends.[64] Morison certainly did give his friends books as in 1548 Henry Stafford translated Foxe's *De vera differentia* using a copy which had been given to him by Morison.[65]

ASSESSMENT

Morison was the owner of a library which must have been among the best in England at the time. Remarkable both for its size and for the range of topics it covered, it testifies to the diversity of Morison's intellectual interests and the enduring pull they exerted upon him. Meanwhile the communal aspect of Morison's library also highlights his importance within English scholarly networks. Unsurprisingly, his scholarly abilities were lauded by his contemporaries and he deserves to be recognized as a Tudor scholar of some distinction and importance.

[64] See for example *Booklist*, fo. 113^r.
[65] Stafford, *True difference*, Aii^v. The copy of *De vera differentia* seems not to have been returned by the time the list was made, unless it was one of the 'other' works.

Conclusion

Richard Morison was a far more influential figure in Tudor England than has previously been recognized and this influence extended well beyond his role as a propagandist in the 1530s. Morison emerges as a scholar of some importance. No wonder, then, that Zeeveld felt Morison a sufficiently gifted scholar to use as evidence to challenge the theory that English humanism had died with More and Fisher in the summer of 1535.[1] But Morison was an even more accomplished scholar than Zeeveld, Berkowitz and other historians have thought. The considerable range of exempla he deployed in his literary compositions is ample testimony to this, as is the collection of books that he amassed across his lifetime. The communal nature of Morison's library means it has further implications: not only did Morison have access to a vast array of classical, humanist and controversial literature, but his friends did also. Throughout his life he was in contact with a large number of scholars in England and acted as the patron of many; concurrently, he maintained links to important figures in the European intellectual community and acted as a patron on the international stage. All of which indicates that English humanism was more vibrant and cosmopolitan than even recent corrective works have suggested.[2]

Given Morison's evident status as a scholar of some distinction, it is worth pausing for a moment to consider why he was not appointed one of Prince Edward's tutors. Perhaps the simplest explanation lies in the fact that Morison had not previously held a formal educational post: there is no evidence that he was ever a fellow of an Oxford college and while he may have informally tutored students at Padua, this was not on the same scale as Anthony Cooke's private educational endeavours. Richard Cox and John Cheke, on the other hand, were both respected

---

[1] G. W. Zeeveld, 'Richard Morison, Official Apologist for Henry VIII', *PMLA*, 60 (1940), 406–25.

[2] Woolfson, *Reassessing Tudor Humanism*.

and experienced pedagogues. Another explanation may lie in Morison's religious attitudes. As he was open about his commitment to the gospel, Henry will have been aware that Morison promoted views with which he did not agree, such as clerical marriage and justification by faith, and may not have wanted his son exposed to such ideas.

Another theme that emerges very strongly is the originality that Morison brought to his intellectual and literary endeavours. Like many of his contemporaries, he was heavily dependent upon Ciceronian and Aristotelian precepts. He clearly did not derive his ideas from contemporaries such as Thomas Starkey: when they contemplated the benefits of Roman law for Henrician England, Morison and Starkey reached radically different conclusions. On a practical level, Morison was a more significant figure than Starkey simply by virtue of the fact that more men in Tudor England read his works than those of Starkey. Meanwhile Morison's humanism cannot be characterized as Erasmian; it was much more eclectic, embracing a range of contemporary Italian ideas and always focused on the welfare of the commonwealth. For Morison, though, the spiritual health of the realm was as integral to the purposes of civil society as its political well-being.

The greatest originality Morison displayed was in the writing of government polemics. Contrary to Zeeveld's influential contention that 'all the evidence argues for the complete subservience . . . of a newly hired servant',[3] Morison's tracts were far more than mere obedience literature; instead they worked on a number of levels and projected a number of discrete, but complementary messages. He constructed a view of Tudor monarchy that placed conditions on the king. The most important of these was the king's duty to protect his subjects' souls and to provide for their spiritual welfare. Indeed the nature of Tudor kingship as articulated by Morison was unmistakably evangelical, tied to scripture and religious education. Central, too, was a sense of England as a providential nation ruled over by a providential king destined to witness the establishment of the true church. Such ideas were to flourish and become formative to the rhetoric of Edward VI's church. Drawing out the implications of Morison's tracts, however, is only one part of the story; the next will be to see how people responded to them, though that is beyond the scope of the present study.

As well as promoting Henry VIII and his policies, Morison's tracts also advocated evangelical initiatives ahead of official policy, thereby

---

[3] Zeeveld, 'Richard Morison', 410.

offering hope to other evangelicals. This explains why, as Ryrie found, many evangelicals did not despair of further reform until after 1543. In adopting this polemical strategy, Morison was trying to manoeuvre Henry towards further reform of the church. Shagan and Gunter have suggested that 'support for the Royal Supremacy became . . . not an ideology in itself, but a site where ideological differences of many sorts were canvassed'.[4] The government was eager to ensure that they controlled the direction in which opinion would go, but Morison's tracts undoubtedly help to account for the phenomenon that Shagan and Gunter describe. His vision of a godly magisterial Reformation contained elements which were not embodied in the official doctrinal statements of the government. So while Morison praised Henry for establishing a church based on scripture, the *Bishops' Book* allowed unwritten verities to remain. Consequently his tracts may well have created an ideological space within which divergent interpretations of the Royal Supremacy could develop.

The international context was crucial in determining the content and use of English polemical literature. In the late 1530s England faced rebellion and the threat of invasion by combined foreign powers. Henry VIII was all too aware of the dire nature of the situation and used propaganda to counter it. Morison's *Protestation* and *Epistle* reinforce McEntegart's view that members of Henry VIII's government pursued an ideologically determined foreign policy in the 1530s.[5] The core evangelical group focused on Cromwell, Cranmer and Foxe that McEntegart identified as key to foreign policy developments was as strong within domestic religious politics and was also closely involved with Morison's polemical endeavours. This may well explain why the government deliberately used the General Council tracts to suggest that England had firm allies on the continent: foreign policy goals could have domestic political advantages. More surprisingly, these tracts reveal a moment where English polemic was seemingly popular in Protestant territories.

As a leading early English evangelical, Morison highlights the importance of Lutheran ideas within government circles in the 1530s. Converted to the evangelical cause while at Oxford, Morison expressed

[4] Shagan and Gunther, 'Protestant Radicalism', 35.

[5] R. McEntegart, 'Towards an Ideological Foreign Policy: Henry VIII and Lutheran Germany, 1531–1547', in S. Doran and G. Richardson (eds.), *Tudor England and its Neighbours* (Basingstoke, 2005), 74–105.

his theological views openly during the key religious debates of 1537, even those which supported positions that Henry VIII would never countenance such as justification *sola fide*. Nor did Morison hide the Lutheran tenets in the two religious works he translated. This does not appear to have had any significant negative impact on his political career. At least in part this is because, as McEntegart has demonstrated, there was a surprising degree of room for religious debate in government circles in the 1530s; on many issues Henry VIII only gradually made up his mind, not least through the process of negotiations with the Schmalkaldic League (in which Morison was employed).[6] Morison worked closely with those men—Cranmer, Cromwell and Foxe—who were promoting a Lutheran alliance, sometimes without the knowledge of their king, and he did so in domestic religious politics too. The Henrician Reformation involved much more than an Erasmian 'rethinking' of English Catholicism, just as it was the Reformation of more men than the king.

Determining religious identity and allegiance can be a difficult task, not least because clear confessional lines had not yet been drawn.[7] Although his position was broadly Lutheran, Morison's intolerance of images was more pronounced than that of the king or the Lutherans. It seems likely that he became attracted to Reformed theology at some point in the 1540s, and in this he would have been far from alone. Morison's experiences after the Act of Six Articles reinforce Ryrie's argument that evangelical momentum remained strong, even if it was beginning to change direction.[8] His religious views remained sufficiently porous (or tolerant) that he could maintain close links with reformers whose doctrinal stance ranged from Lutheran to Reformed in the 1550s.

Morison became a politician of some note. Although his official appointments may have been few, those he received were significant. His career does not point to specialization, but rather to a diversity of service, throughout which runs the common strand of his humanist credentials. He was an orator, poet, courtier, and theorist on law and the commonwealth who serves as a reminder that there was a vibrant

[6] McEntegart, *League of Schmalkalden*.
[7] The best discussions of this issue are: Marshall, *Religious Identities*, ch. 2; A. Ryrie, 'Counting Sheep, Counting Shepherds: The Problem of Allegiance in the English Reformation', in P. Marshall and A. Ryrie (eds.), *The Beginnings of English Protestantism* (Cambridge, 2002), 84–110.
[8] Ryrie, *Gospel*, ch. 4.

intellectual culture at the heart of the court. Morison's career also casts doubt on Starkey's conclusions about how men gained admission to the ranks of the Privy Chamber. Cromwell did not foist his crony on the king; rather, Morison earned his position through years of loyal and prolific service. He was definitely in the Privy Chamber in June 1540 and was there again in January 1547 and there is the possibility that he did not leave—he certainly was not expelled when Cromwell fell. Ultimately, the evidence is too fragmentary to be sure; Morison's description in land tenure grants suggests that some degree of hiatus is likely, but this did not mean exile from court. Morison came to be frustrated with Henry's style of rule in the 1540s; certainly he was concerned that life at court was corrupting at this time, criticizing those of his friends who sacrificed their principles 'in keeping no good to serve his [Henry's] sonne'.[9]

Strikingly, there is no evidence that Morison was targeted by a faction, despite his close association with Cromwell in the 1530s and his links to leading evangelicals in the 1540s. This must lead us to question the burden historical analyses have placed upon factional struggles at court. Equally, Morison's career would suggest that a tyrannical Henry is unlikely: if even the king's propagandists, indeed the king's most used propagandist, could inject his own agenda into the king's official statements, and if he could pursue a successful career despite his open evangelicalism, can Henry really be termed a tyrant?

The political networks in which Morison participated suggest a degree of continuity across his lifetime. By the 1540s, he was a member of a godly circle which included Henry's last queen and his physician, the duchess of Suffolk, Anthony Denny and many more influential figures, and came to include reformers such as Bernardine Ochino and Martin Bucer. He remained within this circle in Edward's reign and wrote to its members from the Imperial court, and it was with many of these figures that he went into exile.

Only in the summer of 1550 was Morison appointed to the Privy Council. That Morison was not appointed earlier is not surprising: William Paget, John Baker, Anthony Denny and Philip Hoby were far from alone in accumulating over a decade of crown service before being named Councillors. Although his promotion was undoubtedly designed to give Morison more weighty political credentials for his embassy to Charles V, Morison clearly felt that he could use his new

---

[9] *Discourse*, fo. 132[r].

position to offer advice on foreign (and occasionally domestic) policy. In this he was not alone; as Potter has demonstrated, a number of other English ambassadors also felt that they were in a position to dispassionately discuss the state and offer political advice from their embassies.[10] This may well be because for the most part they too were Privy Councillors and, like Morison, they did not conceive of their positions as honorific.

Even in Henry VIII's reign an organized and systematic diplomatic corps was emerging. The supplying of ambassadors with printed polemics as diplomatic aids indicates that the government was considering the way in which it presented itself, and doing so in a sophisticated manner. Morison's career also suggests that the diplomatic service was subject to substantial consideration even in these formative years of permanent diplomacy. Before receiving his first embassy, he was used in a variety of diplomatic roles, from information-gathering to hosting foreign missions in England, and he served on a special mission before being trusted with a resident posting. Ambassadorial selection was based on skill and experience long before Elizabeth's reign.

Morison's activities while serving at the Imperial court illuminate an often neglected cultural angle to Tudor diplomacy. His passion for learning and commitment to education made his ambassadorial household an active intellectual environment. The evangelical and scholarly networks he cultivated while ambassador placed English diplomacy firmly within the Strasbourg–St Gall axis and were to prove crucial during Morison's years as a religious exile. Here, Morison acted as a focal point for many of his fellow refugees and oversaw a household engaged in educational and polemical activities. Looking at the English Reformation through the lens of Morison's life and careers, we can see that it was a truly European event. Not only were the Lutheran princes in Germany and the Swiss reformers influential, but so too were the Italian reformers who sought exile first in Swiss and Imperial cities, and then in England. Such connections influenced perceptions of the English church at critical moments, while also aiding the transfer of religious ideas between the various territories. Morison vividly illustrates the benefits of looking at Tudor lives in a European context. Each of his remarkable and wide-ranging 'careers' was informed by continental ideas and events, while he cultivated

---

[10] D. Potter, 'Mid-Tudor Foreign Policy and Diplomacy: 1547–63', in Doran and Richardson, *England and its Neighbours*, 106–38.

and maintained links with European scholars and reformers across his lifetime. He was an intellectual, evangelical and politician on the European stage as well as the domestic, whose ideas and connections helped to shape the course of the English Reformation and English politics.

Bibliography

MANUSCRIPT SOURCES

Birmingham: Birmingham City Archives
3279/351597 Lease of lands
3279/351598 Lease of lands

Cambridge: Cambridge University Library
D.d. 9.14 Miscellaneous Papers
E.e. 5.14 John Leland's *Antiphilarchia*
M.m. 1.42 Miscellaneous Papers

Cambridge: Corpus Christi College
Parker MS 119 Reformers' Letters

Coventry: Coventry City Archives
PA/101/138/17 Transfer of property in Coventry

Gloucester: Gloucestershire Record Office
MS 9531/10 Cuthbert Tunstall's Register

Hatfield: Hatfield House
MS 46 Treatise on General Councils
MS 47 Treatise on General Councils
MS 520 John Hales to William Cecil

Hertford: Hertfordshire Archives and Local Studies
6547 Court roll
6565–7 Court rolls
6570–5 Court rolls
6576 Survey of the Manor of Cashiobury, 1557
6593 Draft of Exchange
6594 Letters patent
6596 Lease
6985 Rental Book for Cheshunt 1543
8752 General Pardon
8753 Court of Wards Papers
MTD/XVI/1 214 Letters Patent

London: British Library
  Additional 4106, 5498, 5796, 5935, 33271, 35831, 35841, 40626, 40629, 40631A, 40676, 46367, 48039
  Arundel 97, 152
  Cotton Nero B VI, VII
  Cotton Galba B XI, XII
  Cotton Titus B I, II
  Cotton Cleopatra E IV, V, VI
  Cotton Faustina C II
  Cotton Vitellius B XIV
  Cotton Vespasian B XVII
  Cotton Appendix L 82
  Harley 282, 283, 296, 353, 422, 423, 523, 4990
  Lansdowne 2, 3, 98
  Royal 7 C XVI, 11 A XVI, 17 C IX, 18 A L
  Sloane 1523

London: The National Archives: Public Record Office
  C1 Chancery: Early Proceedings
  C3 Chancery: Pleadings, Series II
  C66 Chancery: Patent Rolls
  C82 Chancery: Warrants for the Great Seal
  C142 Chancery: Inquisitions Post Mortem
  C148 Chancery: Ancient Deeds
  E36 Exchequer: Treasury of the Receipt: Miscellaneous Books
  E101 Exchequer: King's Remembrancer: Various Accounts
  E115 Certificates of Residence
  E122 Particulars of Customs Accounts
  E150 Inquisitions Post Mortem
  E159 Exchequer: King's Remembrancer: Memoranda Rolls and Enrolment Books
  E163 Exchequer: King's Remembrancer: Miscellanea of the Exchequer
  E164 Exchequer: King's Remembrancer: Miscellaneous Books
  E179 Exchequer: Particulars of Account and other records relating to Lay and Clerical Taxation
  E301 Court of Augmentations: Certificates of Colleges, Chantries and Similar Foundations 1540–1552
  E315 Court of Augmentations and Predecessors and Successors: Miscellaneous Books
  E319 Court of Augmentations: Particulars for Grants to Schools etc. 1548–1564
  E322 Court of Augmentations: Surrenders of Monasteries and Other Religious Institutions 1518–1552

E387 Exchequer: Lord Treasurer's Remembrancer: Extents of Lands and Goods, of Traitors, Outlaws and Fugitives 1554–1558

KB8 Court of King's Bench: Crown Side: Baga de Secretis

LR2 Office of the Auditors of Land Revenue and predecessors: Miscellaneous Books

PROB 11 Prerogative Court of Canterbury: Will Registers

SP1 State Papers Henry VIII: General Series

SP6 Theological Tracts Henry VIII

SP10 Secretaries of State: State Papers Domestic, Edward VI

SP11 Secretaries of State: State Papers Domestic, Mary I

SP68 Secretaries of State: State Papers Foreign and State Papers Calais, Edward VI

SP69 Secretaries of State: State Papers Foreign, Mary I

STAC7 Court of Star Chamber: Proceedings, Elizabeth I, Addenda c1558–c1603

WARD7 Court of Wards and Liveries: Inquisitions Post Mortem

London: Guildhall
9531/10 Bishop Tunstall's Register

London: House of Lords Record Office
HL/PO/PU/1/1540/32H8n78 Subsidy Act 32 Henry VIII, c. 50

London: Lambeth Palace Library
1107 Thomas Cranmer's Booke on the Lawe

London: Westminster Abbey
12235 Petition for legal reform

Oxford: Bodleian Library
Ashmole 1123 Misc. papers

Oxford: New College
Ω32.1–4, 10 MS annotations in printed books belonging to Morison

Oxford: Oxford University Archive
WPβ/B/24 Note on the Reformation at Magdalen, 1548
WPβ/S/1 Vice chancellor's accounts 1547–59
University Register H

Trowbridge: Wiltshire and Swindon Record Office
D/1/2/16 i Bishop Shaxton's Register
D/1/2/16 ii Bishop Capon's Register

Worcester: County Record Office
  716.093/2648/9/iii Bishop Bell's Register
  899:749/8782/45/J1/1 Documents relating to properties in Worcester

Washington DC: Folger Shakespeare Library
  X. d. 207 'Ex oratione cardinalis campeggio' an extract from Morison's
  De rebus gestis Henrici Octavi

Zurich: Zurich Zentralbibliothèque
  Simmler Sammlung S85 Reformers' letters
  B171 Reformers' letters

PRINTED SOURCES

ALESIUS, A., *Of the auctorite of the word of god* (Strasbourg, 1544; STC 292)
AMBROSE, ST, *Theological and Dogmatic Works*, ed. R. J. Deferrari (Washington DC, 1963)
—— *Seven Exegetical Works*, ed. M. P. McHugh (Washington DC, 1972)
AMPHLETT, J., *Churchwardens' Accounts of St Michael's in Bedwardine, Worcester* (Oxford, 1896)
ANDRICH, A., *De Natione Anglica et Scotia Iuristarum Universitatis Patavinae* (Padua, 1892)
ANON., *The Trayne of War* (London, 1525–39; STC 18841.7)
Ansvvere made by the kynges hyghnes to the petitions of the rebelles in Yorkeshire (London, 1536; STC 13077)
Ansvvere to the petitions of the traytours and rebelles in Lyncolneshyre (London, 1536; STC 13077.5)
AUGUSTINE, ST, *The Works of Augustine*, ed. M. Dods (Edinburgh, 1871–6)
—— *Letters*, ed. R. N. Eno and W. Parsons (Washington DC, 1951)
—— *Great Books [Confessions, De Doctrina Christiana and De civitate dei]*, eds. R. S. Pine-Coffin, M. Dods and J. F. Shaw (Chicago, 1990), 2nd edition
BAKER, J. H. (ed.), *The Reports of Sir John Spelman* (London, 1977–8), vol. ii
BALE, J., *The Image of bothe churches* (Antwerp, 1545; STC 1296.5)
—— *Illustrium Maioris Britanniae scriptorum* (Wesel, 1548; STC 1295)
—— *Expostulation or complaynte agaynste the blasphemyes of a franticke papyste of Hamshyr* (London, 1552; STC 1294)
BARKER, W., *The Bookes of Xenophon* (London, 1552; STC 26066)
BECK, H. G., *Der Vater der deutschen Byzantinistik: das Leben des Hieronymus Wolf von ihm selbst erzählt* (Munich, 1984)
BEDE, *Complete Works*, ed. G. A. Giles (London, 1843–4)
—— *Ecclesiastical History of the English People*, ed. B. Colgrave and R. A. B. Mynors (Oxford, 1969)

BELLO-POELIUS, P., *De Pace inter invictissimos Henricum Galliarum, et Eduardum Anglii, reges oratio* (London, 1552; STC 1849)

BETHAM, P., *The precepts of warre, set forth by Iames the erle of Purlila* (London, 1544; STC 20116)

'The bill of expenses . . . of Peter Marytr and Bernardinus Ochin', ed. N. H. Nicholas, *Archaelogia*, 31 (1827), 469–73

Bullingers Korrespondenz, ed. T. Schiess (Basel, 1904–6)

BURTON, W., *Achilles Tatius the most delectable history of clitiphon and leucippe* (London, 1597; STC 90)

BURY, J., *A Godly Advertisement or good counsel of the famous orator Isocrates* (London, 1557; STC 14276)

CAIUS, J., *Pergameni nobilissimi medici libri aliquot Graeci . . .* (Basel, 1544)

—— *A boke or counseill against the disease commonly called the sweate, or sweatyng sicknesse* (London, 1552; STC 4343)

Calendar of the MSS of the . . . Marquis of Salisbury . . . preserved at Hatfield House, HMC v.9, Cecil Papers (London, 1883–1976)

Calendar of Patent Rolls, Edward VI, ed. R. H. Brodie (London, 1924–9)

Calendar of Patent Rolls, Mary I, ed. M. S. Giuseppi (London, 1936–9)

Calendar of Patent Rolls, Elizabeth I, ed. J. H. Collingridge (London, 1939)

Calendar of State Papers Domestic, 1547–1553, ed. C. S. Knighton (London, 1992)

Calendar of State Papers Domestic, 1553–1558, ed. C. S. Knighton (London, 1998)

Calendar of State Papers Domestic, 1601–1603, Addenda 1547–65, ed. M. A. Everett Green (London, 1872)

Calendar of State Papers Foreign, 1547–1553, ed. W. B. Turnbull (London, 1861)

Calendar of State Papers Foreign, 1553–1558, ed. W. B. Turnbull (London, 1861)

Calendar of State Papers Spanish, 1547–9, 1550–1552, 1553, 1554, 1554–8, ed. P. de Gayangos (London 1862–1954)

Calendar of State Papers Venetian, ed. R. L. Brown (London, 1864–1940)

Calendar to the Feet of Fines for London and Middlesex, ed. W. J. Hardy and W. Page (London, 1892, 1893)

CHAMBERS, D. S., *Faculty Office Registers 1534–49* (Oxford, 1966)

CHEKE, J., *De pronuntiatione Graecae* (Basel, 1555)

—— *The Gospel According to St Matthew*, ed. J. Goodwin (London, 1843)

Chronicle of Calais in the Reigns of Henry VII and Henry VIII, ed. J. G. Nichols, CS 1st ser. 35 (London, 1846)

Chronicle of King Henry VIII of England, ed. M. A. S. Hume (London, 1889)

CHRYSOSTOM, J., *Homilies*, ed. J. H. Parker (Oxford, 1851–2)

CICERO, *De natura deorum; Academica*, ed. H. Rackham (London, 1951)

—— *De Officiis*, ed. M. T. Griffin and E. M. Atkins (Cambridge, 1991)

CICERO, *De Legibus*, ed. and trans. N. Rudd (Oxford, 1998)

——— *De Oratore*, ed. and trans. J. M. May and J. Wise (Oxford, 2001)

CLARKE, G. W. (ed. and trans.), *The Letters of St Cyprian of Carthage* (New York, 1989)

COCHLAEUS, J. DOBNECK, *De matrimonio serenissimi Regis Angliae, Henrici Octavi, Congratulatio disputatoria* (Lipsiae, 1535)

——— *Scopa . . . in araneas Richardi Morysini Angli* (Lipsiae, 1538)

COLE, R. E. G., *Chapter Acts of the Cathedral of St Mary of Lincoln 1536–1547*, Lincoln Record Society, 15 (Horncastle, 1917)

Concilium delectorum cardinalem ac aliorum Paelatorum de emmendanda (Strasbourg, 1538)

COOPER, C. H., *Annals of Cambridge* (Cambridge, 1862)

A copye of a verye fyne and vvytty letter . . . translated . . . by Michael Throckmerton (false imprint: Rome, 1556; STC 15693.5)

The Correspondence of Reginald Pole, ed. T. F. Mayer (Aldershot, 2002)

CORVINUS, A., *Ein Unterredung zwishen dem Pasquillen und Deutschen von dem zukunfftigen Concilio zu Mantua* (Wittemberg, 1537)

COVERDALE, M., *The causes why the Germanes wyll not go, nor consente unto that council, which Paul iii . . . hath called to be kepte at Mantua* (London, 1537; STC 17262.5)

DASENT, J. R. (ed.), *Acts of the Privy Council, 1547–1550, 1550–1552* (London, 1890–1964)

DEMOSTHENES, *Olynthiacs, Philippics and Minor Public Speeches*, ed. J. H. Vince (London, 1954)

Documents Illustrating Early Education in Worcester, ed. A. F. Leach (London, 1913)

DUGDALE, W., *Monasticon Anglicanum: A History of the Abbeys and other Monasteries* (Farnborough, 1970)

EDWARD VI, *The Chronicle and Political Papers of Edward VI*, ed. W. K. Jordan (London, 1966)

ELLIS, H., *Original Letters Illustrative of the English Reformation* (London, 1846)

ELYOT, T., *The boke named the Governor* (London, 1531; STC 7635)

English Historical Documents 1485–1558, ed. C. H. Williams (London, 1967)

An epistle of the moste myghty [and] redouted Prince Henry the .viii. by the grace of God Kyng of England and of Fraunce, lorde of Irelande, defender of the faithe, and supreme heed of the churche of England, nexte vnder Christe, writen to the Emperours maiestie, to all Christen princes, and to all those that trewly and syncerely professe Christes religion (London, 1538; STC 13081.3)

L'Epistre du roy d'Angleterre, Aux princes & peuple Chrestien: touchant le Concile à venire . . . Auec vn liuret composé par maniere de Protestation (London, 1539)

Formularies of Faith, ed. J. Lloyd (London, 1856)

FORREST, T., *A perfite looking glasse for all estates* (London, 1580; STC 14275)

FRERE, W. H., *Visitation Articles and Injunctions of the Period of the Reformation* (London, 1910)

FRONTINUS, S. J., *The stratagems, sleyghts and policies of warre* (London, 1539; STC 11402)

GOUGH, J. (trans.), *An abbrevyacyon of all generall councellys* (London, 1539; STC 15453)

HALL, E., *Hall's Chronicle*, ed. H. Ellis (London, 1809)

HARWOOD, T., *Alumni Etonienses* (Birmingham, 1797)

HAYNES, S. (ed.), *A Collection of State Papers* (London, 1740)

Henrici octaui . . . ad Carolum Caesarem Augustum, caeterosq[ue] orbis Christiani monarchas, populumq[ue] Christianum, epistola, qua rex facile causas ostendit & curis Vincentiam, ad concilium falso nomine generale appellatum non sit uenturus (London, 1538; STC 13080.3, 13080.5)

HISTORICAL MANUSCRIPTS COMMISSION, *Report on the Manuscripts of Wells Cathedral* (London, 1885) MMC 12

—— *Various Collections* (London, 1940), 7

HOBY, T., *The courtier of Count Baldessar castilio* (London, 1561; STC 4778)

HOLFROD-STEVENS, L. (ed.), *Aulus Gellius* (London, 1988)

HOWARD, N., *A briefe chronicle . . . gathered first by Eutropius* (London, 1564; STC 10579)

HUGHES, P. L. and LARKIN, J. F. (eds.), *Tudor Royal Proclamations*, i: *The Early Tudors (1485–1553)* (New Haven, 1964)

Illustris. ac potentis. regis, senatus, populique Angliae, sententia, et de eo concilo, quod Paulus episcopus Roma Mantuae futurum simulauit, et de ea bulla (London, 1537; STC 13082)

JANELLE, P., *Obedience in Church and State* (Cambridge, 1930)

JEROME, ST, *Principal Works*, ed. G. Lewis and W. G. Martley (Oxford, 1893)

—— *Dogmatic and Principal Works*, ed. J. N. Hritzu (Washington DC, 1965)

KAUSLER, E. VON and SCHOTT, T. (eds.), *Briefwechsel zwischen Christoph, Herzog von Württemberg und Petrus Paulus Vergerius* (Tübingen, 1875)

KER, N. R., *Records of All Souls College Library* (Oxford, 1971)

KITCHING, C. J., *London and Middlesex Chantry Certificate, 1548* (London, 1948)

KRAYE, J. (ed.), *Cambridge Translations of Renaissance Philosophical Texts* (Cambridge, 1997)

LANDI, O., *Delectable demaundes, and pleasant questions* (London, 1566)

LATIMER, H., *A notable sermo[n] of ye reuerende father Maister Hughe Latemer* (London, 1548)

LEADAM, I. S. 'A Narrative of the Pursuit of English Refugees in Germany under Queen Mary', *TRHS*, new ser. 11 (1897), 113–32

LELAND, J., *Principum ac illustrium aliquot et eruditorum in Anglia virorum, encomia, trophia, genethliaca & epithalamia* (London, 1589; STC 15447)

—— *The Itinerary of John Leland in or about the Years 1535–1543*, ed. L. Toulmin Smith (Carbondale, 1964)

Letters and Papers, Foreign and Domestic of the Reign of Henry VIII, ed. J. S. Brewer (London, 1862–1932)

Letters of Roger Ascham, ed. and trans. M. Hatch and A. Vos (New York, 1989)

'The Letters of Richard Scudamore to Sir Philip Hoby September 1549 to March 1555', ed. S. Brigden, *Camden Miscellany XXX*, CS 4th ser. 39 (London, 1990), 67–148

'The Letters of William Paget', ed. B. L. Beer and S. M. Jack, *Camden Miscellany XXV*, CS 4th ser. 25 (London, 1974), vii–viii, 1–141

The Lisle Letters, ed. M. St Clare Byrne (London, 1981)

LIVY, *Decades*, ed. B. O. Foster and F. G. Moore (London, 1919–59)

Luther's Works, ed. J. Pelikan (St Louis, 1955–86)

MacCULLOCH, D., and P. HUGHES (ed.), 'A Bailiff's List and Chronicle from Worcester', *Antiquaries' Journal*, 75 (1995), 235–53

MacLURE, M., *A Register of Sermons Preached at Paul's Cross 1534–1642* (Ottawa, 1989)

MADAN, F. (ed.), 'The Day Book of John Dorne', *Oxford Historical Society, Collectanea*, vol. i (Oxford, 1885), 71–177

The Manuscripts of . . . the Duke of Rutland . . . Preserved at Belvoir Castle (1888), vol. i (HMC 14)

The Manuscripts of Wells Cathedral (London, 1907–14) (HMC 12)

MELANCHTHON, P., *The confession of the fayth of the Germaynes . . . translated by Rycharde Taverner* (London, 1536; STC 908)

—— *Loci Communes, 1543*, trans. J. A. O. Preus (St Louis, 1992)

Melanchthons Briefwechsel, ed. H. Scheible (Stuttgart, 1977–)

MITCHELL, W. T. (ed.), *Epistolae academiae 1508–1596*, Oxford Historical Society, new ser. 26 (Oxford, 1980)

MORE, T., *Utopia*, ed. G. M. Logan and R. M. Adams (Cambridge, 1999)

MORISON, R., *A Lamentation in which is shewed what ruyne cometh of seditious rebellyon* (London, 1536; STC 18113.3, 18113.7)

—— *A Remedy for Sedition* (London, 1536; STC 18113.5)

—— *A comfortable consolation wherin the people may se, howe far greater cause they have to be glad for the ioyful byrth of prince Edwarde, than sory for the dethe of queen Iane* (London, 1537; STC 18109.5)

—— *Apomaxis Calumniarum, convitiorumque, quibus Ioannes Cocleus . . . Henrii octavi, famam impetere . . . studuit* (London, 1537; STC 18109)

—— *An invective against the great and detestable vice, treason* (London, 1539; STC 18111–3)

—— *An exhortation to stirre all Englyshe men to the defence of theyr countreye* (London, 1539; STC 18110, 18110.5, 18110.7)

NICHOLS, J. G. (ed.), *Chronicle of the Grey Friars of London*, CS 1st ser. 53 (London, 1852)

NICHOLSON, W. (ed.), *Remains of Edmund Grindal* (Cambridge, 1843)

NORTH, T., *The Lives of the noble Grecians and Romanes* (London, 1579; STC 20065)

Nugae Antiquae, ed. T. Park (London, 1804)

'Nuntiaturen des Pietro Bertano und Pietro Carmeliano 1550–52', in *Nuntiatur Berichte aus Deutschland*, vol. i, ed. G. Kupke (Berlin, 1901)

OCHINO, B., *Des Hochgelehrten und Gottsäligen mans Bernhardini Ochini . . . seiner Apologen* (Augsburg, 1559)

ORIGEN, *The Writings of Origen*, ed. F. Crombie (Edinburgh, 1869–72)

A panegyric of Henry VIII as abolisher of papal abuses (London, 1536–7; STC 13089a)

PARKHURST, J., *Ionnis Parkhursti Ludicra sive Epigrammata iuueniia* (London, 1573; STC 19299)

PARR, C., *Lamentation of a sinner* (London, 1547; STC 4827)

PAYNELL, T., *The Conspiracie of Lucius Catiline* (London, 1557; STC 10752)

PECKHAM, W. D. (ed.), *Acts of the Dean and Chapter of the Cathedral Church of Chichester 1472–1544*, Susssex Record Society, 52 (Lewes, 1951)

PISAN, C. DE, *Here begynneth the table of the rubryshys of the boke of the fayt of armes and of chyvalrye* (London, 1489; STC 7269)

PLINY, *Natural History*, ed. H. Rackham and W. H. S. Jones (London, 1983–95)

—— *Parallel Lives*, ed. B. Perrin (London, 1919–26)

PLUTARCH, *Moralia*, ed. F. C. Babbit (London, 1927–76)

POLE, R., *Defence of the Unity of the Church*, ed. and trans. J. G. Dwyer (Westminster, 1965)

POWELL, E. (ed.), 'The Travels and Life of Sir Thomas Hoby, Kt, of Bisham Abbey', *Camden Miscellany X*, CS 3rd ser. 4 (London, 1902)

A protestation made for the most mighty and moste redoubted kynge of Englande. and his hole counsell and clergie wherin is declared, that neyther his hyghenes, nor his prelates, neyther any other prynce, or prelate, is bounde to come or sende, to the pretended councell, that Paule byshoppe of Rome, first by a bul indicted at Mantua, a citie in Italy, [and] nowe a late by an other bull, hath proroged to a place, no man can telle where (London, 1537; STC 13090)

PUBLIC RECORD OFFICE, *Deputy Keeper's Reports*, x (London, 1850)

QUINTILIAN, *The Orator's Education*, ed. D. A. Russell (Cambridge, 2001)

'The Registers of Cuthbert Tunstall . . . and James Pilkington', ed. G. Hynde, *Surtees Society*, 161 (1952)

Report on the Manuscripts of the Earl of Ancaster preserved at Grimsthorpe, ed. S. C. Lomas (Dublin, 1907)

ROBINSON, H., *Original Letters Relative to the English Reformation* (Cambridge, 1846–7)

—— *The Zurich Letters* (Cambridge, 1842), vol. i

RYMER, T., *Syllabus of the Documents Relating to England and other Countries: contained in the collection known as 'Rymer's Foedera'* (London, 1869–85)

SABELLICUS, M. A., *M. Antonii coccii opera* (Basel, 1560)

[ST GERMAN, C.], *A treatise concernynge generall councilles, the byshoppes of Rome and the clergy* (London, 1538; STC 24237)

SHAW, W. A. (ed.), *Three Inventories of the Years 1542, 1547 and 1549–50 of Pictures in the Collections of Henry VIII and Edward VI* (London, 1937)

SLEIDAN, J., *Histoire de la Reformation* (Le Havre, 1767)

[SMITH, T.], *A Discourse of the Common Weal of this Realm of England*, ed. M. Dewar (Charlottesville, MA, 1969)

SOMERS, F. (ed.), *Halesowen Churchwardens' Accounts, 1487–1582* (London, 1952–7)

STAFFORD, H., *The true differens between the regall power and the Ecclesiasticall power* (London, 1548; STC 11220)

STARKEY, T., *Dialogue between Pole and Lupset*, ed. T. Mayer, CS 4th ser. 37 (London, 1989)

State Papers Published under the Authority of his Majesty's Commission. King Henry the Eighth (London, 1830)

STERRY, W., *The Eton College Register, 1441–1698* (Eton, 1943)

STIGEL, J., *Ad Henricum Octavum Angliae et Franciae regem, carmen elegiacon* (1540)

—— *Historical Collections of the life and acts of . . . John Aylmer, Lord Bp of London* (Oxford, 1821)

STRYPE, J., *Life of John Cheke* (Oxford, 1821)

—— *Life of Matthew Parker* (London, 1821)

—— *Ecclesiastical Memorials* (Oxford, 1822)

—— *Memorials of . . . Thomas Cranmer* (Oxford, 1840)

STURMIUS, J., *De eadem re, ad Cardinalis caeterosquae viros ad eam consultationem delectos* (Strasbourg, 1537)

—— *The epistle that Johan Sturmius . . . sent to the cardynalles and prelates* (London, 1538; STC 23407)

Supplication to the Quenes Majestie (Strasbourg, 1555; STC 17563)

SWINNERTON, T., [alias Robertes], *Tropes and Figures of Scripture*, ed. R. Rex (Cambridge, 1999)

—— *A muster of schismatic bishoppes* (London, 1534; STC 23552)

[SWINNERTON, T.], *The mutterynge of some papists in corners* (London, 1534; STC 23551.5)

TAVERNER, R., *A catechisme or institution of the christen religion* (London, 1539; STC 23079)

THYNNE, F., *The perfect ambassadour treating of the antiquitie, priveledges, and behaviour of men belonging to that function* (London, 1652)

TOWNSEND, G. and CATTLEY, S. R., *The Acts and Monuments of John Foxe* (London, 1837–41)

TOXITES, M. SCHUTZ, *Commentarius Michael Toxites . . . in orationem . . . Ciceronis pro C. Plancio* (Strasbourg, 1551)

—— *Commentarius Michael Toxites . . . in orationem . . . Ciceronis pro P. Quintio* (Strasbourg, 1551)

A treatise prouyng by the kynges laws, that the bishops of rome, had neuer right to any supremitie within this realm (London, 1538; STC 24248)

Two Tudor Subsidy Assessment Rolls for the City of London: 1541 and 1582, ed. R. G. Lang, London Record Society, 29 (London, 1993)

TUNSTALL, C., *A sermon preached before the kinge upon Palm Sunday* (London, 1539; STC 24322)

TWYNNE, T., *Dionysius Periegetus, The surveye of the world* (London, 1572; STC 6901)

TYNDALE, W., *New Testament*, ed. D. Daniel (Yale, 1989)

UDALL, N., *The first tome or volume of the Paraphrase of Erasmus upon the newe testamente* (London, 1548; STC 2854.5)

Ursachen so die Chür und fürsten auch stende und Stedte . . . darumb sie Babst Pauli des namens des dritten/ ausgeschrieben Concilium (Schmalkalden, 1537)

Valor Ecclesiasticus temp. Henr. VIII: Auctoritate Regis institutus, ed. J. Caley and J. Hunter (London, 1810–34)

VERGERIO, P. P., *Risposta del vescovo vergerio/ad libro del nausea vescovo di Vienna scritto in laude del concilio tridentino vicosoprano* (Poschavio, 1552)

VERMIGLI, P. M., *Life, Letters and Sermons*, ed. J. P. Donnelly (Kirksville, 1999)

—— *The Oxford Treatise and Disputation on the Eucharist*, ed. J. C. McClelland (Kirksville, MO, 2000)

VIVES, J. L., *An introduction to wysedom . . . tr. R. Morysine* (London, 1540; STC 24847)

WAGNER, J. A. (ed.), *A Devon Gentleman: The Life of Sir Peter Carew* (Hull, 1998)

WHATMORE, L. E., 'A Sermon against the Holy Maid of Kent', *EHR*, 58 (1943), 463–75

WHETSTONE, G., *The English Mirror* (London, 1586; STC 25336)

The Whole Works of Roger Ascham, ed. J. A. Giles (London, 1865)

WILKINS, D. (ed.), *Concilia Magnae Britanniae et Hiberniae* (London, 1737)

WOOD, A., *History and Antiquities of the Colleges and Halls in the University of Oxford* (Oxford, 1786, 1790)

WOOD, T. and ARBER, E., *A Brief Discourse of the Troubles at Frankfort, 1554–1558* (London, 1907)

WOOLTON, J., *A treatise of the immortalitie of the soul* (London, 1576; STC 25979)

The Works of Sir Thomas Wyatt the Elder, ed. G. F. Nott (London, 1815)

WRIGHT, W. A. (ed.), *The English Works of Roger Ascham* (Cambridge, 1904)

WRIOTHESLEY, C., *A Chronicle of England during the Reigns of the Tudors*, CS 2nd ser. 11, 20 (1875–7), 2 vols.

WYATT, T., *Of the quyet of mynde* (London, 1528; STC 20058.5)

REFERENCE WORKS

Additional MS Catalogue, 1921–25 (London, 1950)

BERKENHOUT, J., *Biographia literaria* (London, 1777), vol. i

272 *Bibliography*

BINDOFF, S. T., *The House of Commons 1509–1558* (London, 1982)
COCKAYNE, G. E. (ed.), *The Complete Peerage of England* (London, 1910–59)
EMDEN, A. B., *A Biographical Register of the University of Oxford, A.D. 1501–1540* (Oxford, 1974)
Fasti Ecclesiae Anglicanae III, Salisbury Diocese, ed. J. le Neve (London, 1962)
HARWOOD, T., *Alumni Etonienses* (Birmingham, 1797)
HASLER, P. W., *The House of Commons 1558–1603* (London, 1981)
HEAWOOD, E., *Monumenta Chartae Papyraceae Historiam Illustratia* (Hilversum, 1950), vol. i
Oxford Dictionary of National Biography (Oxford, 2004)
POLLARD, A. W. and REDGRAVE, G. R., *A Short-title Catalogue of Books printed in England, Scotland and Ireland and of English Books Printed Abroad, 1475–1640*, rev. K. F. Pantzer (London, 1976–91)
Private Libraries in Renaissance England, ed. R. J. Fehrenbach and E. S. Leedham-Green (Marlborough, 1992–)
VENN, J. A., *Alumni Cantabrigienses* (Cambridge, 1924)
WACKERNAGEL, H. G., *Die Matrikel der Universität Basel* (Basel, 1951), vol. ii
WOOD, A., *Athenae Oxonienses, 1500–1714* (Oxford, 1813–20)

PRINTED BOOKS AND ARTICLES

ABRAY, L. J., *The People's Reformation: Magistrates, Clergy and Commons in Strasbourg 1500–98* (Ithaca, 1985)
ALFORD, S., *Kingship and Politics in the Reign of Edward VI* (Cambridge, 2002)
ALLMAND, C., *The Hundred Years War: England and France at War c. 1300–1450* (Cambridge, 1988)
ALSOP, J., 'Nicholas Brigham (d. 1558), Scholar, Antiquary and Crown Servant', *SCJ*, 12 (1981), 49–67
AMOS, N. S., PETTEGREE, A., and VON NIEROP, H. (eds.), *The Education of a Christian Society: Humanism and the Reformation in Britain and the Netherlands* (Aldershot, 1999)
ARMSTRONG, C. D. C. and REX, R., 'Henry VIII's Ecclesiastical and Collegiate Foundations', *HR*, 125 (2002), 390–407
ASTON, M., *England's Iconoclasts* (Oxford, 1988)
BAINTON, R. H., *Bernardine Ochino* (Florence, 1941)
BAKER, J. H., *The Common Law Tradition: Lawyers, Books and the Law* (London, 2000)
—— *The Oxford History of the Laws of England*, iv: *1483–1558* (Oxford, 2003)
BARRINGTON, R., 'Two houses both alike in Dignity: Reginald Pole and Edmund Harvel', *HJ*, 39 (1996), 895–913
BARTLETT, K. R., 'The Household of Francis Russell, Second Earl of Bedford in Venice 1555', *Medieval Prosopography*, 2 (1981), 63–85
BASKERVILLE, C. J., 'Sir Richard Morison as the Author of Two Anonymous Tracts on Sedition', *Library*, 4th ser. 17 (1937), 83–7

BASKERVILLE, E. J., 'John Ponet in Exile: A Ponet Letter to John Bale', *JEH*, 37 (1986), 442–6

BATAILLON, M., *Études sur le Portugal au temps de l'humanisme* (Coimbra, 1952)

BAUMER, F. L. VAN, *The Early Tudor Theory of Kingship* (London, 1940)

BECKER, H.-J., *Appellation vom Papst an ein allgemeines Konzil* (Cologne, 1988)

BEER, B. L., *Northumberland: The Political Career of John Dudley* (Kent, Ohio, 1973)

BELL, G. M., 'John Man, the Last Elizabethan Resident Ambassador in Spain', *SCJ*, 7 (1976), 81–6

—— 'Elizabethan Diplomatic Compensation: Its Nature and Variety', *JBS*, 20 (1981), 1–25

—— 'Elizabethan Diplomacy: The Subtle Revolution', in M. R. Thorp and A. J. Slavin (eds.), *Politics, Religion and Diplomacy in Early Modern Europe* (Kirksville, MO, 1994), 267–89

—— 'Tudor-Stuart Diplomatic History and the Henrician Experience', in C. Carlton et al. (eds.), *State Sovereigns and Society in Early Modern England* (Stroud, 1998), 24–45

BENRATH, K., *Bernardine Ochino of Siena* (London, 1876)

BERKOWITZ, D. S., *Humanist Scholarship and the Public Order: Two Tracts against the Pilgrimage of Grace* (London, 1984)

BERNARD, G. W., 'The Making of Religious Policy, 1533–1546: Henry VIII and the Search for the Middle Way', *HJ*, 41 (1998), 321–49

—— 'The Piety of Henry VIII', in Amos, Pettegree and Nierop (eds.), *Education of a Christian Society*, 62–88

—— 'The Tyranny of Henry VIII', in Bernard and Gunn (eds.), *Authority and Consent*, 113–29

—— *The King's Reformation* (New Haven, 2005)

—— and GUNN, S. J. (eds.), *Authority and Consent in Tudor England: Essays Presented to C. S. L. Davies* (Aldershot, 2002)

BETTERIDGE, T., *Literature and Politics in the English Reformation* (Manchester, 2004)

BINNS, J. W., *Intellectual Culture in Elizabethan and Jacobean England: The Latin Writings of the Age* (Leeds, 1990)

—— 'The Humanist Latin Tradition Reassessed', in Woolfson (ed.), *Reassessing Tudor Humanism*, 186–96

BJORKLUND, N., ' "A Godly Wyfe Is an Helper": Matthew Parker and the Defence of Clerical Marriage', *SCJ*, 34 (2003), 347–65

BLOCK, J. S., 'Thomas Cromwell's Patronage of Preaching', *SCJ*, 8 (1977), 37–50

—— *Factional Politics and the English Reformation, 1520–1540* (Woodbridge, 1993)

BOND, M. F., *The Inventories of St George's Chapel, Windsor Castle* (Windsor, 1947)

BONINI, C. R., 'Lutheran Influences in the English Reformation: Richard Morison Re-examined', *ARG*, 64 (1973), 206–23

BONJOUR, E., *Die Universität Basel, von dem Anfängen bis zur Gegenwart 1460–1960* (Basel, 1960)

BRADDICK, M. J. and WALTER, J. (eds.), *Negotiating Power in Early Modern Society* (Cambridge, 2001)

BRADSHAW, B., 'Transalpine Humanism', in J. H. Burns and M. Goldie (eds.), *Cambridge History of Political Thought 1450–1700* (Cambridge, 1994), 95–131

BRADSHAW, C. J., 'The Exile Literature of the Early Reformation: "Obedience to God and the King" ', in Amos, Pettegree and Nierop, *Education of a Christian Society*, 112–30

BRIGDEN, S., ' "The shadow that you know": Sir Thomas Wyatt and Sir Francis Bryan at Court and in Embassy', *HJ*, 39 (1996), 1–31

BRITNELL, J., 'Anti-Papal Writing in the Reign of Louis XII', in J. and R. Britnell (eds.), *Vernacular Literature and Current Affairs in the Early Sixteenth Century* (Aldershot, 2000), 41–61

BROCKMANN, T., *Die Konzilsfrage in den Flug- und Streitschriften des deutschen Sprachraumes 1518–1563* (Göttingen, 1998)

BROOKS, P. N. (ed.), *Seven Headed Luther* (Oxford, 1983)

BRUGI, B., *L'Universita dei Giuristi in Padova nel cinquecento* (Venice, 1922)

BURKE, P., 'A Survey of the Popularity of Ancient Historians, 1450–1700', *History and Theory*, 5 (1966), 135–52

—— *Languages and Communities in Early Modern Europe* (Cambridge, 2004)

CALDWELL, J., 'Appendix: Music in the Faculty of Arts', in McConica (ed.), *Collegiate University*, 201–12

CARLEY, J. P. (ed.), *The Libraries of Henry VIII* (London, 2000)

—— and PETITMENGIN, P., 'Malmesbury-Sélestat-Malines: The Tribulations of a Manuscript of Tertullian in the Middle of the 16th Century', posted on-line: http://www.tertullian.org/articles/petitmengin_ malmesbury_eng.htm

CASPARI, F., *Humanism and the Social Order in Tudor England* (New York, 1968)

CATTO, J., *The History of the University of Oxford*, ii: *Late Medieval Oxford* (Oxford, 1992)

CHAUNCY, H., *Historical Antiquities of Hertfordshire* (Dorking, 1976), vol. ii

CHAVASSE, R. A., 'Humanism in Exile: Celio Secondo Curione's Learned Women Friends and Exempla for Elizabeth I', *Parergon*, 14 (1986), 165–86

—— 'The Reception of Humanist Historiography in Northern Europe: M. A. Sabellico and John Jewel', *Renaissance Studies*, 2 (1988), 327–38

CHESTER, A. G., *Hugh Latimer Apostle to the English* (New York, 1978)

CHIBI, A. A., *Henry VIII's Conservative Scholar, Bishop John Stokesley, the Divorce, the Supremacy and Doctrinal Reform* (Frankfurt am Main, 1997)

—— 'Richard Sampson, his "Oratio" and Henry VIII's Royal Supremacy', *Journal of Church and State*, 39 (1997), 543–60

CHRISMAN, M. U., *Lay Culture, Learned Culture: Books and Social Change in Strasbourg, 1480–1599* (New Haven, 1982)

CLARKE, W. K. L., *Liturgy and Worship* (London, 1932)

CLEBSCH, W. A., *England's Earliest Protestants 1520–1535* (New Haven, 1980)

COBB, H. S. (ed.), *The Overseas Trade of London Exchequer Accounts, 1480–1* (London, 1990)

COCKLE, H. D., *A Bibliography of English Military Books up to 1642 and of Contemporary Foreign Works* (London, 1900)

COOPER J. P. D., *Propaganda and the Tudor State: Political Culture in the West Country* (Oxford, 2003)

CORDA, S., *Veritas Sacramenti: A Study of Vermigli's Doctrine of the Lord's Supper* (Zurich, 1975)

CROSS, C., 'Oxford and the Tudor State from the Accession of Henry VIII to the Death of Mary', in McConica (ed.), *Collegiate University*, 117–49

CURTIS, C., 'Richard Pace's *De Fructu* and Early Tudor Pedagogy', in Woolfson (ed.), *Reassessing Tudor Humanism*, 43–77

D'ALTON, C., 'The Suppression of Lutheran Heretics in England, 1526–1529', *JEH*, 54 (2003), 228–53

DAVIES, C., *A Religion of the Word: The Defence of the Edwardian Reformation* (Manchester, 2002)

DAVIES, C. S. L., 'Slavery and Protector Somerset: The Vagrancy Act of 1547', *EcHR*, 19 (1966), 533–49

DODDS, M. H., and DODDS, R., *The Pilgrimage of Grace 1536–7 and the Exeter Conspiracy 1538*, 2 vols. (London, 1971)

DONALDSON, P. S. (ed.), *A Machiavellian Treatise by Stephen Gardiner* (Cambridge, 1975)

DORAN, S. and FREEMAN, T. F. (eds.), *The Myth of Elizabeth* (Basingstoke, 2003)

—— and RICHARDSON, G. (eds.), *Tudor England and its Neighbours* (Basingstoke, 2005)

DORMER, E. W., *Gray of Reading* (Reading, 1923)

DOWLING, M., *Humanism in the Age of Henry VIII* (London, 1986)

DUNCAN, G. D., 'The Heads of Houses and Religious Change in Tudor Oxford 1547–1558', *Oxoniensa*, 45 (1980), 226–34

—— 'Public Lectures and Professorial Chairs', in McConica (ed.), *Collegiate University*, 335–61

DUNN, T. F., 'The Development of the Text of Pole's *De unitate ecclesiae*', *Papers of the Bibliographical Society of America*, 70 (1976), 455–68

EDGERTON, W. L., *Nicholas Udall* (New York, 1965)

ELTON, G. R., *Policy and Police: The Enforcement of the Reformation in the Age of Thomas Cromwell* (Cambridge, 1972)
—— *Reform and Renewal: Thomas Cromwell and the Commonweal* (Cambridge, 1973)
—— *Studies in Tudor and Stuart Politics and Government* (London, 1974–92), vols. i–iii
FENLON, D., *Heresy and Obedience in Tridentine Italy: Cardinal Pole and the Counter Reformation* (Cambridge, 1972)
FISHER, R. M., 'Thomas Cromwell, Humanism and Educational Reform', *BIHR*, 50 (1977), 151–63
FLETCHER, J. M., 'The Faculty of Arts', in McConica (ed.), *Collegiate University*, 157–99
—— 'Developments in the Faculty of Arts, 1370–1520', in Catto (ed.), *Late Medieval Oxford*, 315–45
—— and UPTON, C. A., 'Destruction, Repair and Removal: An Oxford College Chapel During the Reformation', *Oxoniensa*, 48 (1983), 119–30
—— 'Humanism and Art in the Early Tudor Period: John Leland's Poetic Praise of Painting', in Woolfson (ed.), *Reassessing Tudor Humanism*, 129–50
FOISTER, S., *Holbein and England* (London, 2004)
—— 'Elyot and the Humanist Dilemma', in Fox and Guy (eds.), *Reassessing the Henrician Age*, 52–73
—— 'Facts and Fallacies: Interpreting English Humanism', in Fox and Guy (eds.), *Reassessing the Henrician Age*, 9–34
FOX, A., 'Rumour, News and Popular Political Opinion in Elizabethan and Early Stuart England', *HJ*, 40 (1997), 597–620
—— *Oral and Literate Culture in England 1500–1700* (Oxford, 2000)
FOOT, M. M., 'Bookbinding in England, 1400–1557', in Hellinga and Trapp (eds.), *Cambridge History of the Book in Britain*, iii. 116–24
—— and GUY, J., *Reassessing the Henrician Age* (Oxford, 1986)
FRANKLIN-HARKRIDER, M., *Women, Reform and Community in Early Modern England: Katherine Willoughby, Duchess of Suffolk and Lincolnshire's Godly Aristocracy, 1519–1580* (Woodbridge, 2008)
FREEMAN, T. S., 'Providence and Prescription: The Account of Elizabeth in Foxe's "Book of Martyrs" ', in Doran and Freeman (eds.), *Myth of Elizabeth*, 27–55
FUDGE, T., *The Magnificent Ride* (Basingstoke, 1998)
FULLER, T., *History of the Worthies of England* (London, 1662)
GARRETT, C., *The Marian Exiles: A Study in the Origins of Elizabethan Puritanism* (Cambridge, 1938)
—— 'The Resurrection of the Masse by Hugh Hilarie or John Bale?' *Library*, 4th ser. 21 (1940), 143–59
GRAY, M., *Images of Piety* (Oxford, 2000)
GREEN, V. H. H., *The Commonwealth of Lincoln College 1427–1977* (Oxford, 1997)

GREENSLADE, S. L., 'The Faculty of Theology', in McConica (ed.), *Collegiate University*, 295–334

GRENDLER, P. F., *Universities of the Italian Renaissance* (London, 2002)

GUGGISBERG, H. R., *Basel in the Sixteenth Century: Aspects of the City Republic before, after and during the Reformation* (St Louis, MO, 1982)

—— *Sebastian Castellio, 1515–1563: Humanist and Defender of Religious Toleration in a Confessional Age* (Aldershot, 2003)

GUNN, S. J., 'War, Dynasty and Public Opinion in Tudor England', in Bernard and Gunn (eds.), *Authority and Consent*, 131–49

GUY, J., 'Thomas Cromwell and the Intellectual Origins of the Henrician Revolution', in Fox and Guy (eds.), *Reassessing the Henrician Age*, 151–78

—— 'The Rhetoric of Counsel in Early Modern England', in *idem, Politics, Law and Counsel in Tudor and Early Stuart England* (Aldershot, 2000)

GWYN, P., *The King's Cardinal: The Rise and Fall of Thomas Wolsey* (London, 1990)

HAIGH, C., *English Reformations* (Oxford, 1993)

HARBISON, E. J., *Rival Ambassadors at the Court of Queen Mary* (Princeton, 1940)

HARRIS, T. (ed.), *The Politics of the Excluded* (Basingstoke, 2001)

HAUGAARD, W. P., 'Renaissance Patristic Scholarship and Theology in Sixteenth Century England', *SCJ*, 1 (1979), 36–70

HEAL, F., *Of Prelates and Princes* (Cambridge, 1980)

HEARN, K., *Dynasties: Painting in Tudor and Jacobean England 1530–1630* (London, 1995)

HEINZE, R. W., *Proclamations of the Tudor Kings* (Cambridge, 1976)

HELGERSON, R., *Forms of Nationhood: The Elizabethan Writing of England* (Chicago, 1992)

HELLINGA, L. and TRAPP, J. B. (eds.), *Cambridge History of the Book*, iii: *1400–1557* (Cambridge, 2000)

—— *Roman Canon Law in Reformation England* (Cambridge, 1990)

HELMHOLZ, R. H., 'The Canon Law', in Hellinga and Trapp (eds.), *Cambridge History of the Book*, iii. 387–98

—— 'Christopher St. German and the Law of Custom', *University of Chicago Law Review*, 70 (2003), 129–39

HERENDEEN, W. H. and BARTLETT, K., 'The Library of Cuthbert Tunstall, Bishop of Durham', *Papers of the Bibliographical Society of America*, 85 (1991), 235–96

HILDEBRANDT, E., 'Christopher Mont, Anglo-German Diplomat', *SCJ*, 15 (1984), 281–92

HOAK, D., *The King's Council in the Reign of Edward VI* (Cambridge, 1976)

HOAK, D., (ed.), *Tudor Political Culture* (Cambridge, 1995)

HOBSON, G. D., 'Et amicorum', *Library*, 5th ser. 4 (1949), 87–99

HOYLE, R. W., *The Pilgrimage of Grace and the Politics of the 1530s* (Oxford, 2000)

Hubert, F., *Vergerios Publizistische Thätigkeit* (Göttingen, 1893)

Hudson, W., *John Ponet (?1516–1556), Advocate of Limited Monarchy* (Chicago, 1942)

—— *The Cambridge Connection and the Elizabethan Settlement of 1559* (Durham, NC, 1980)

Ingram, W., *The Business of Playing: The Beginnings of the Professional Theatre in Elizabethan London* (London, 1992)

Ives, E. W., *Anne Boleyn* (Oxford, 1986)

—— *The Common Lawyers of Pre-Reformation England. Thomas Kebell: A Case Study* (London, 1983)

James, S. E., *Kateryn Parr* (Aldershot, 1999)

Jansen, S. L., *Political Protest and Prophecy Under Henry VIII* (Woodbridge, 1991)

Jardine, L., 'The Place of Dialectic Teaching at Cambridge', *Studies in the Renaissance*, 21 (1974), 31–62

—— 'Ficino and the Platonism of the English Renaissance', *Comparative History*, 4 (1952), 214–38

Jayne, S., *Library Catalogues of the English Renaissance* (Berkeley, 1956)

Jeanes, G., 'A Reformation Treatise on the Sacraments', *Journal of Theological Studies*, 46 (1995), 149–90

Jedin, H., *History of the Council of Trent* (London, 1957)

Jones, J., *Balliol College: A History* (Oxford, 1997)

Jones, P. M., 'Science and Medicine', in Hellinga and Trapp (eds.), *Cambridge History of the Book*, iii. 433–48

Katterfeld, A., *Roger Ascham: sein Leben und sein Werke* (Strasbourg, 1879)

Kelley, D. R., *Foundations of Modern Historical Scholarship* (London, 1970)

Kennedy, W. J., *Authorizing Petrarch* (London, 1994)

Ker, N. R., *Books, Collectors and Libraries* (London, 1985)

Kermode, L. and Scott-Warren, J. (eds.), *Tudor Drama before Shakespeare* (Basingstoke, 2004)

Kesselring, K. J., *Mercy and Authority in the Tudor State* (Cambridge, 2003)

Kidwell, C., *Pontano: Poet and Prime Minister (1426–1503)* (London, 1991)

King, J. N., *English Reformation Literature* (Princeton, 1982)

—— *Tudor Royal Iconography* (Princeton, 1989)

Kirby, T., 'Vermilius absconditus? The Iconography of Peter Martyr Vermigli', in E. Campi, F. A. James and P. Opitz (eds.), *Peter Martyr Vermigli: Humanism, Republicanism, Reformation* (Geneva, 2002), 295–303

Kisby, F., ' "When the King goeth a procession": Chapel Ceremonies and Services, the Ritual Year, and Religious Reforms at the Early Tudor Court, 1485–1547', *JBS*, 40 (2001), 44–75

Knecht, R. J., *Francis I* (Cambridge, 1982)

Kreider, A., *English Chantries: The Road to Dissolution* (Cambridge, MA, 1979)

KRISTELLER, O., 'Humanism', in Schmitt and Skinner (eds.), *Cambridge History of Renaissance Philosophy*, 113–38

KÜNAST, H.-J., 'Entwicklunglinien des Augsburger Buchdrucks von 1468 bis zum Augsburger Religionsfrieden von 1555', in J. Brüning and F. Niewöhner (eds.), *Augsburg in der frühen Neuzeit* (Berlin, 1995), 227–39

LEHMBERG, S. E., *Sir Thomas Elyot, Tudor Humanist* (Austin, 1960)

—— *The Reformation Parliament 1529–1536* (Cambridge, 1970)

—— 'Parliamentary Attainder in the Reign of Henry VIII', *HJ*, 18 (1975), 675–702

—— *The Later Parliaments of Henry VIII, 1536–1547* (Cambridge, 1977)

LEWIS, G., 'Faculty of Medicine', in McConica (ed.), *Collegiate University*, 213–56

LOACH, J., 'Pamphlets and Politics', *BIHR*, 48 (1975), 31–44

—— *Parliament and the Crown in the Reign of Mary Tudor* (Oxford, 1986)

—— 'Reformation Controversies', in McConica (ed.), *Collegiate University*, 363–96

—— *Edward VI* (London, 1999)

LOADES, D., *Two Tudor Conspiracies* (Cambridge, 1965)

—— *The Reign of Mary Tudor* (London, 1979)

McCLAREN, A., *Political Culture in the Reign of Elizabeth I* (Cambridge, 1999)

McCLELLAND, J. C., *The Visible Words of God* (London, 1957)

McCONICA, J. K., *English Humanists and Reformation Politics under Henry VIII and Edward VI* (Oxford, 1965)

—— 'The Rise of the Undergraduate College', in McConica (ed.), *Collegiate University*, 1–68

—— (ed.), *The History of the University of Oxford*, iii: *The Collegiate University* (Oxford, 1986)

MacCULLOCH, D., *Thomas Cranmer: A Life* (London, 1996)

—— *The Tudor Church Militant: Edward VI and the Protestant Reformation* (London, 1999)

—— (ed.), *The Reign of Henry VIII: Politics, Policy and Piety* (London, 1995)

McDIARMID, J. F., 'Humanism, Protestantism, and English Scripture, 1533–1540', *JMRS*, 14 (1984), 121–38

—— 'John Cheke's Translation of Plutarch's *de superstitione*', *JEH*, 48 (1997), 100–20

McENTEGART, R., *Henry VIII, the League of Schmalkalden and the English Reformation* (Chippenham, 2002)

McGRATH, P., 'Winchester College and the Old Religion', in R. Custance (ed.), *Winchester College: Sixth-Centenary Essays* (Oxford, 1982)

McKENNA, J. W., 'How God became an Englishman', in D. J. Guth and J. W. McKenna (eds.), *Tudor Rule and Revolution* (Cambridge, 1982), 25–43

McKitterick, D., 'Libraries and the Organization of Knowledge', in E. Leedham-Green and T. Webber (eds.), *Cambridge History of Libraries in Britain and Ireland*, i: *To 1640* (Cambridge, 2006), 592–615

Mack, P., 'Elizabethan Parliamentary Oratory', *HLQ*, 64 (2001), 23–61

Major, J. M., *Sir Thomas Elyot and Renaissance Humanism* (Lincoln, 1964)

Marshall, P., *Religious Identities in Henry VIII's England* (Aldershot, 2006)

—— and Ryrie, A. (eds.), *Beginnings of English Protestantism* (Cambridge, 2002)

Martin, J. W., 'The Marian Regime's Failure to Understand the Importance of Printing', *HLQ*, 45 (1981), 231–47

Mattingly, G., *Renaissance Diplomacy* (London, 1955)

Mayer, T. F., 'Thomas Starkey: An Unknown Conciliarist at the Court of Henry VIII', *JHI*, 49 (1988), 207–27

—— *Thomas Starkey and the Common Weal* (Cambridge, 1989)

—— 'When Maecenas was Broke: Cardinal Pole's "Spiritual" Patronage', *SCJ*, 27 (1996), 419–35

—— *A Reluctant Author: Cardinal Pole and his Manuscripts* (Philadelphia, 1999)

—— *Cardinal Pole in European Context: A via media in the Reformation* (Aldershot, 2000)

—— *Reginald Pole: Prince and Prophet* (Cambridge, 2000)

Millar, G. J., *Tudor Mercenaries and Auxiliaries 1485–1547* (Charlottesville, VA, 1980)

Mohl, R., *Studies in Spenser, Milton and the Theory of Monarchy* (New York, 1949)

Moran, J. A. H., *The Growth of English Schooling 1340–1548* (Guildford, 1985)

Morris, C., 'Machiavelli's Reputation in Tudor England', *Il Pensiero Politico*, 2 (1969), 416–33

Mottram, S., *Empire and Nation in Early English Renaissance Literature* (Cambridge, 2008)

Mullinger, J. B., *The University of Cambridge* (Cambridge, 1911)

Murphy, V., 'The Literature and Propaganda of Henry VIII's First Divorce', in D. MacCulloch (ed.), *The Reign of Henry VIII* (Basingstoke, 1995), 135–58

Nauert, C. G., *Agrippa and the Crisis of Renaissance Thought* (Urbana, 1965)

Neame, A., *The Holy Maid of Kent: The Life of Elizabeth Barton, 1506–1534* (London, 1971)

Newman, C. M., *Late Medieval Northallerton* (Stamford, 1999)

North, J. D., *The Ambassadors' Secret: Holbein and the World of the Renaissance* (London, 2002)

Orme, N., 'School and Schoolbooks', in Hellinga and Trapp (eds.), *Cambridge History of the Book*, iii. 449–69

Overell, M. A., 'Vergerio's Anti-Nicodemite Propaganda and England', *JEH*, 51 (2000), 296–313

—— 'Edwardian Court Humanism and Il Beneficio de Christi', in Woolfson (ed.), *Reassessing Tudor Humanism*, 151–73

—— 'Bernardine Ochino's Books and English Religious Opinion, 1547–1580', *Studies in Church History*, 38 (2004), 201–11

—— 'Italian Friendship and English Reform: Richard Morison and Michael Throckmorton', *JEH*, 57 (2006), 478–93

—— *Italian Reform and English Reformations, c.1535–c.1585* (Aldershot, 2008)

PAGE, W., *Victoria History of the Counties of England: Oxfordshire* (Folkestone, 1970–)

PARKS, G., 'The Genesis of Tudor Interest in Italian', *PMLAA*, 77 (1962), 529–35

—— 'The Pier Luigi Farnese Scandal: An English Report', *Renaissance News*, 15 (1962), 193–200

PAYNE, J. B., *Erasmus: His Theology of the Sacraments* (Richmond, VA, 1970)

PETTEGREE, A., *Marian Protestantism: Six Studies* (Aldershot, 1996)

PFLANZ, H.-H., *Johannes Stigel als Theologe (1515–1562)* (Breslau, 1936)

PIEPHO, L., *Holofernes' Mantuan: Italian Humanism in Early Modern England* (Oxford, 2001)

PIERCE, H., *Margaret Pole, Countess of Salisbury 1473–1541* (Cardiff, 2003)

PIERCE, R. A., *Pier Paulo Vergerio the Propagandist* (Rome, 2003)

PINEAS, R., 'Some Polemical Techniques in the Nondramatic Works of John Bale', *Bibliothèque d'humanisme et Renaissance*, 24 (1962), 583–8

POTTER, D., 'The International Mercenary Market in the Sixteenth Century: Anglo-French Competition in Germany, 1543–50', *EHR*, 111 (1996), 24–58

POTTER, U., 'Performing Arts in the Tudor Classroom', in Kermode and Scott-Warren (eds.), *Tudor Drama Before Shakespeare*, 145–50

PROCTER, F. and FRERE, W. H., *A New History of the Book of Common Prayer* (London, 1902)

RAAB, F., *The English Face of Machiavelli* (London, 1964)

REDWORTH, G., 'A Study in the Formulation of Religious Policy: The Genesis and Evolution of the Act of Six Articles', *JEH*, 36 (1986), 42–67

—— *In Defence of the Church Catholic: The Life of Stephen Gardiner* (Oxford, 1990)

REED, A. W., 'The Regulation of the Book Trade before the Proclamation of 1538', *Transactions of the Bibliographical Society*, 15 (1919), 157–84

—— *Early Tudor Drama: Medwall, the Rastells, Heywood and the More Circle* (London, 1926)

—— 'The English Campaign against Luther in the 1520s', *TRHS*, 5th ser. 38 (1989), 85–106

REX, R., 'The Execution of the Holy Maid of Kent', *HR*, 114 (1991), 216–20

—— *Henry VIII and the English Reformation* (London, 1993)

—— 'The Crisis of Obedience: God's Word and Henry's Reformation', *HJ*, 39 (1996), 863–94

REX, R., 'The Role of English Humanists in the Reformation up to 1559', in Amos, Pettegree and van Nierop (eds.), *Education of a Christian Society*, 28–40

RICE, E. F., 'The Humanist Idea of Christian Antiquity: Lefevre d'Etaples and his Circle', in W. L. Gundersheimer (ed.), *French Humanism, 1470–1600* (London, 1969), 163–80

RICHARDS, J., *Rhetoric and Courtliness in Early Modern Literature* (Cambridge, 2003)

RIORDAN, M. and RYRIE A., 'Stephen Gardiner and the Making of a Protestant Villain', *SCJ*, 34 (2003), 1039–63

ROBERTS, J., 'Extending the Frontiers: Scholar Collectors', in E. Leedham-Green and T. Webber (eds.), *Cambridge History of the Library in Britain and Ireland*, i: *To 1640* (Cambridge, 2006), 292–321

ROBERTSON, C. G., *All Souls College* (London, 1898)

ROBIN, D., *Filelfo in Milan* (Oxford, 1991)

ROBISON, W. B., 'The National and Local Significance of Wyatt's Rebellion in Surrey', *HJ*, 30 (1987), 769–90

RODRIGUEZ-SALGADO, M. J., *The Changing Face of Empire* (Cambridge, 1988)

ROSS, J. B., 'Venetian Schools and Teachers, 14th to Early 16th Centuries: A Survey and Study of Giovanni Battista Egnazio', *RQ*, 29 (1976), 521–66

ROTT, J., and FAERBER, R. 'Un anglais à Strasbourg au milieu du XVIe siecle: John Hales, Roger Ascham et Jean Sturm', *Études anglaise*, 21 (1968), 381–94.

ROWLANDS, J., *Paintings of Hans Holbein* (Oxford, 1985)

RUSSELL, J., *Peacemaking in the Renaissance* (London, 1986)

—— *Diplomats at Work: Three Renaissance Studies* (Stroud, 1992)

RYAN, L.V., *Roger Ascham* (Stanford, CA, 1963)

RYRIE, A., *The Gospel and Henry VIII: Evangelicals in the Early English Reformation* (Cambridge, 2003)

SAUNDERS, W. R., *History of Watford* (Watford, 1931)

SAWADA, P. A., 'Two Anonymous Tudor Treatises on the General Council', *JEH*, 12 (1961), 197–214

—— 'Das Imperium Heinrichs VIII und die erste Phase seiner Konzilspolitik', *Reformata Reformanda*, 1 (1965), 476–507

SCARISBRICK, J. J., *Henry VIII* (London, 1968)

SCHMITT, C. B. and SKINNER, Q. (eds.), *The Cambridge History of Renaissance Philosophy* (Cambridge, 1988)

SCHUTTE, A. J., *Pier Paul Vergerio* (Geneva, 1977)

SELWYN, D., *The Library of Thomas Cranmer* (Oxford, 1996)

SHAGAN, E. H., 'Print, Orality and Communications in the Maid of Kent Affair', *JEH*, 52 (2001), 21–33

—— 'Rumours and Popular Politics in the Reign of Henry VIII', in T. Harris (ed.), *The Politics of the Excluded* (York, 2001), 30–66

—— *Popular Politics and the English Reformation* (Cambridge, 2003)

—— and GUNTHER, K., 'Protestant Radicalism and Political Thought in the Reign of Henry VIII', *PP*, 194 (2007), 35–74

SHAKESPEARE, J., 'Plague and Punishment', in P. Lake and M. Dowling (eds.), *Protestantism and the National Church* (London, 1987), 103–23

SHARPE, K. M., *Reading Revolutions: The Politics of Reading in Early Modern England* (London, 2000)

—— and ZWICKER, S., *Writing Lives: Biography and Textuality, Identity and Representation in Early Modern England* (Oxford, 2008)

SHAW, J. E., *The Justice of Venice* (Oxford, 2006)

SHRANK, C., *Writing the Nation in Reformation England 1530–1580* (Oxford, 2004)

SIMONCELLI, P., *Il caso Reginald Pole* (Rome, 1977)

SKINNER, Q., *The Foundations of Modern Political Thought* (Cambridge, 1978), vol. ii

SMITH, L. B., 'English Treason Trials and Confessions in the Sixteenth Century', *JHI*, 15 (1954), 417–98

SMITH, M. H., 'Some Humanist Libraries in Early Tudor Cambridge', *SCJ*, 5 (1974), 15–34

SOUTHGATE, W. M., *John Jewel and the Problem of Doctrinal Authority* (Cambridge, MA, 1962)

SOWERBY, T. A., ' "All *our* books do be sent into other countreys and translated": Henrician Polemic in its International Context', *EHR*, 121 (2006), 1271–99

STARKEY, D. R., *The Reign of Henry VIII: Personalitites and Politics* (London, 1985)

—— (ed.), *The English Court from the Wars of the Roses to the Civil War* (Harlow, 1996)

STEIN, P., *Roman Law in European History* (Cambridge, 1999)

STEWART, A., 'The Trouble with English Humanism: Tyndale, More and Darling Erasmus', in Woolfson (ed.), *Reassessing Tudor Humanism*, 78–88

STRAUSS, G., *Law, Resistance and the State* (Princeton, 1986)

STREITBERGER, W. R., *Court Revels, 1485–1559* (Toronto, 1994)

STRONG, R., *Holbein and Henry VIII* (London, 1967)

STURGE, C. T., *Cuthbert Tunstal: Churchman, Scholar, Statesman* (London, 1938)

SWENSON, P. C., 'Patronage from the Privy Chamber: Sir Anthony Denny and Religious Reform', *JBS*, 27 (1988), 34–42

TANNER, T., *Biblioteca Britannica-Hibernica* (London, 1748)

TILLEY, A., 'Greek Studies in the English Renaissance', *EHR*, 53 (1938), 221–39

TITTLER, R., *Nicholas Bacon, the Making of a Tudor Statesman* (London, 1976)

TRAPP, J. B., 'The Humanist Book', in Hellinga and Trapp (eds.), *Cambridge History of the Book*, iii. 285–315

TUDOR-CRAIG, P., 'Henry VIII and King David', in *Proceedings of the 1987 Harlaxton Symposium* (Woodbridge, 1989), 183–206

UNDERWOOD, W., 'Thomas Cromwell and William Marshall's Protestant Books', *Historical Journal*, 47 (2004), 517–36

UNGERER, G., *Anglo-Spanish Relations in Tudor Literature* (Bern, 1956)

VETTER, T., *Relations between England and Zürich during the Reformation* (London, 1904)

WALKER, G., *Writing Under Tyranny* (Oxford, 2005)

WALSHAM, A., ' "A Very Deborah?" The Myth of Elizabeth I as a Providential Monarch', in Doran and Freeman (eds.), *Myth of Elizabeth*, 143–68

WARD, P., 'The Politics of Religion: Thomas Cromwell and the Reformation in Calais, 1534–40', *JRH*, 17 (1992), 152–71

WATT, T., *Cheap Print and Popular Piety 1550–1640* (Cambridge, 1991)

WELTI, M. E., *Der Basler Buchdruck und Britannien* (Basel, 1964)

WHITE, P. W., 'Holy Robin Hood! Carnival, Parish Guilds and the Outlaw Tradition', in Kermode and Scott-Warren (eds.), *Tudor Drama before Shakespeare*, 67–89

WIEDERMAN, G., 'Cochlaeus as Polemicist', in P. N. Brooks (ed.), *Seven Headed Luther* (Oxford, 1983), 195–206

WIJFFELS, A. 'The Civil Law', in Hellinga and Trapp (eds.), *Cambridge History of the Book*, iii. 399–410

WILLIAMS, G., *The Edwardian Reformation in Wales* (Bangor, 1991)

WILLIS BUND, J. W., *Victoria History of the County of Worcestershire* (Folkestone, 1971)

WILSON, H. A., *Magdalen College* (London, 1998), 2nd edition

WOODING, L., *Rethinking Catholicism in Reformation England* (Oxford, 2000)

—— *Henry VIII* (Abingdon, 2008)

WOOLFSON, J., *Padua and the Tudors* (Cambridge, 1998)

—— (ed.), *Reassessing Tudor Humanism* (Basingstoke, 2002)

WRIGHT, J. 'Marian Exiles and the Legitimacy of Flight from Persecution', *JEH*, 52 (2001), 220–43

WYATT, M., *The Italian Encounter with Tudor England: A Cultural Politics of Translation* (Cambridge, 2005)

YOST, J. K., 'German Protestant Humanism and the Early English Reformation', *Bibliothèque d'humanisme et Renaissance*, 32 (1970), 613–25

—— 'Taverner's use of Erasmus and the Protestantization of English Humanism', *Renaissance Quarterly*, 23 (1970), 266–76

YOUINGS, J., *The Dissolution of the Monasteries* (London, 1971)

ZEEVELD, W. G., 'Richard Morison, Official Apologist for Henry VIII', *PMLAA*, 60 (1940), 406–25

—— *Foundations of Tudor Policy* (London, 1948)

THESES AND UNPUBLISHED PAPERS

BONINI, C. R., 'Richard Morison, Humanist and Reformer under Henry VIII', Ph.D. thesis (Stanford, 1974)

CHRISTIE, S. K., 'Richard Morison: An Analysis of his Life and Work', Ph.D. thesis (West Virginia, 1978)

CURTIS, C., 'Richard Pace on Pedagogy, Counsel and Satire', Ph.D. thesis (Cambridge, 1997)

GRUMMITT, D., ' "For Divers and Great Charges": Justifying Taxation in Late Medieval and Early Modern England', unpublished paper

HARRIS, J., 'Parliamentary Attainder in the Reign of Henry VIII', undergraduate thesis (Oxford, 2008)

HÖLLGER, C., 'Reginald Pole and the Legations of 1537 and 1539; Diplomatic and Polemical Responses to the Break with Rome', D.Phil. thesis (Oxford, 1989)

JOHNSTON, A., 'William Paget and the Late Henrician Polity', Ph.D. thesis (St Andrews, 2004)

MacMAHON, L., 'The Ambassadors of Henry VIII, the Personnel of English Diplomacy, 1500–1550', Ph.D. thesis (Kent, 2000)

NEEDHAM, P. S., 'Sir John Cheke at Cambridge and Court', Ph.D. thesis (Harvard, 1971)

NICOD, L. P. M., 'The Political Thought of Richard Morison: A Study in the Use of Ancient and Medieval Sources in Renaissance England', Ph.D. thesis (London School of Economics, 1998)

ROBERTSON, M. L., 'Thomas Cromwell's Servants: The Ministerial Household in Early Tudor Government and Society', Ph.D. thesis (University of California, Los Angeles, 1975)

SOWERBY, T. A., ' "A brave knight and learned gentleman": The Careers of Sir Richard Morison c. 1513–1556', D.Phil. thesis (Oxford, 2006)

STARKEY, D. R., 'The King's Privy Chamber 1485–1547', Ph.D. thesis (Cambridge, 1974)

ONLINE RESOURCES

Ian Archer's website: http://weblearn.ox.ac.uk/site/human/modhist/personnel/785598/research/

J. Leland, *Epigrammata*, ed. D. F. Sutton (2007): http://www.philological.bham.ac.uk/lelandpoems/contents.html

Index